Winnicott and Religion

Winnicott and Religion

Stephen E. Parker

JASON ARONSON
Lanham • Boulder • New York • Toronto • Plymouth, UK

Published by Jason Aronson
A wholly owned subsidiary of The Rowman & Littlefield Publishing Group, Inc.
4501 Forbes Boulevard, Suite 200, Lanham, Maryland 20706
www.rowman.com

10 Thornbury Road, Plymouth PL6 7PP, United Kingdom

British Library Cataloguing in Publication Information Available

Library of Congress Cataloging-in-Publication Data

Library of Congress Cataloging-in-Publication Data Available
ISBN 978-0-7657-0906-6 (cloth : alk. paper)

♾️™ The paper used in this publication meets the minimum requirements of American
National Standard for Information Sciences-Permanence of Paper for Printed Library
Materials, ANSI/NISO Z39.48-1992.

Printed in the United States of America

Contents

Acknowledgments

Many people have assisted with the completion of this book and I take this opportunity to thank them for their various contributions.

First, I wish to thank a host of people at Regent University. I am grateful to the administration of the university and former dean of the School of Psychology and Counseling, Rosemarie Hughes for a sabbatical in the spring of 2008 which allowed me to begin work on this book. I also would like to thank Randall Pannell, former Vice President for Academic Affairs and the University Faculty Grants committee for a research grant that allowed me to travel to London and New York to research the Winnicott archives in the spring of 2009. Amanda Mogle was the first of several capable graduate assistants that helped with sorting through the numerous Winnicott quotations and citations; my thanks also to Lisa-Marie Doherty, Enoch Charles, and Elizabeth Wine. The Regent University Library staff was most helpful in securing a variety of items. William Hathaway, Dean of the School of Psychology and Counseling has been encouraging of the work on this book. Thanks also go to my colleagues and students for their support and good grace in enduring my many references to Winnicott (regardless of context)!

I would like to thank Jan Abram, former Honorary Archivist of the Winnicott Trust for permission to read the unpublished papers and letters in the Winnicott Archives. I would like to thank Jennifer Haynes and the staff at the Wellcome Library, London, for their assistance in accessing the materials archived there. I especially appreciate the extra help needed to view the many framed squiggle drawings. I also wish to thank Diane Richardson of the Oskar Diethelm Library at Cornell Medical Center, New York, for the ease of use of the Winnicott materials there.

John Harding, Historian for The Leys School was an excellent host for my trip to Cambridge. He provided access to *The Leys Fortnightly* issues from the years of Winnicott's attendance and reviewed several important items with me. I especially thank him for the tour of the grounds, including the archives room where to my surprise there was an enlarged photograph of The Leys rugby team from years past that included the young Winnicott. Kelly O'Reilly and Fiona Slot, secretaries at The Leys were delightful lunch companions in the building where Winnicott would have given his award-winning speech his last year there.

I would like to thank The Marsh Agency and the Winnicott Trust for permission to quote from the unpublished resources of the Winnicott archives. I am especially grateful to the Winnicott Trust for permission to reproduce the incomplete and unpublished manuscript included as Appendix A.

In addition to permission to quote from the published works of D.W. Winnicott, I wish to thank the Marsh Agency, London for permission to quote from several miscellaneous items by Winnicott that have appeared in other publications. These include the interview published in the *St. Mary's Hospital Gazette* at the time of Winnicott's retirement from Paddington Green Hospital, the interview of Clare Winnicott by Michael Neve subsequently published as Appendix B in Rudnytsky (1991, pp. 180–193), and a letter Winnicott wrote to his mother from Cambridge published in Rodman (2003, p. 34). I also wish to thank the Marsh Agency for permission to reproduce the poem "The Tree" in chapter 6 (portions also appear in chapter 2). The poem is also published in Rodman (2003, pp. 289–291). The Scriptural emendations to the poem are reprinted from *Psychoanalytic Dialogues 14*, pp. 777–779. Portions of chapter 6 appeared in an earlier version in *The Psychoanalytic Review, 96*, pp. 597–612.

I would like to thank Regina, my wife and friend for her love and support throughout this project. Her comments on an earlier draft have contributed to the readability of this project.

The following acknowledgments constitute an extension of the copyrights page. I would like to thank the following for permission to quote from the identified copyrighted materials:

Grove/Atlantic, Inc. Excerpt from *Holding and Interpretation* by D.W. Winnicott, Introduction copyright © 1986 by Prince Masud Khan. Used by permission of Grove/Atlantic, Inc.

Harvard University Press. Reprinted by permission of the publisher from *Psycho-Analytic Explorations* by D. W. Winnicott, edited by Clare Winnicott, Ray Shepherd, and Madeleine Davis, pp. 58, 155, 205, 237, 242, 276, 549, 560, 573, 574, 580, Cambridge, Mass.: Harvard University Press, Copyright © 1989 by the Winnicott Trust.

Houghton Mifflin Harcourt Publishing Company. Excerpt from *The Letters of Sigmund Freud & Arnold Zweig*, Edited by Ernst L. Freud, copyright © 1970 by Sigmund Freud Copyrights Ltd and the Executors of the Estate of Arnold Zweig, Translated by Elaine and William Robson-Scott, reproduced by permission of Houghton Mifflin Harcourt Publishing Company.

Karnac Books for permission to quote from Brett Kahr, *D.W. Winnicott: A Biographical Portrait*. http://www.karnacbooks.com/isbn/9781855751361 published by Karnac Books in 1996.

Marsh Agency Ltd., London. Excerpt from *The Letters of Sigmund Freud & Arnold Zweig*, Edited by Ernst L. Freud by permission of The Marsh Agency Ltd on behalf of Sigmund Freud Copyrights. Excerpts from *Babies and Their Mothers*; excerpts from *Child and Family*; excerpts from *Clinical Notes on Disorders of Childhood*; excerpts from *Collected Papers: Through Paediatrics to Psychoanalysis*; excerpts from *Home is Where We Start*

From: Essays by a Psychoanalyst; excerpts from *Human Nature;* excerpts from *The Maturational Processes and the Facilitating Environment: Studies in the Theory of Emotional Development;* excerpts from *Psychoanalytic Explorations;* excerpts from *Spontaneous Gesture: Selected Letters of D. W. Winnicott;* excerpts from *Talking to Parents;* excerpts from *Thinking about Children;* and excerpts from *Therapeutic Consultations in Child Psychiatry* by permission of The Marsh Agency Ltd on behalf of the Winnicott Trust. Excerpts from the Michael Neve interview with Clare Winnicott (1983); excerpts from a letter by D. W. Winnicott (1916) written from Jesus College; excerpts from *St. Mary's Hospital Gazette;* and the poem "The Tree" by permission of The Marsh Agency Ltd on behalf of the Winnicott Trust. Excerpts from unpublished archive material at the Wellcome Library (Donald Woods Winnicott Papers) and the Oskar Diethelm Library (Donald W. Winnicott Personal Papers) are reproduced by permission of The Marsh Agency Ltd on behalf of the Winnicott Trust.

W. W. Norton & Company, Inc. From *Home is Where We Start From: Essays by a Psychoanalyst by D. W. Winnicott.* Copyright © 1986 by the Estate of D. W. Winnicott. Used by permission of W. W. Norton & Company, Inc.

Zondervan. Excerpts taken from *The Works of John Wesley,* 14 Vols., 3rd Edition, Thomas Jackson (Ed.). Copyright 1872 by the Wesleyan Methodist Book Room. Use by permission of Zondervan. www.zondervan.com

Chapter 1
Introduction

"Brought up as a Wesleyan Methodist"

About two years before he died, D. W. Winnicott, the noted British pediatrician and psychoanalyst, gave an address to a conference on family evangelism in which he commented briefly on his own religious upbringing. To his audience Winnicott (1968b) noted that although he had been "brought up as a Wesleyan Methodist, I suppose I just grew up out of church religious practice, and I am always glad that my religious upbringing was of a kind that allowed for growing up out of" (pp. 142–143). And yet, the topic of his presentation was on the capacity to "believe in" and how the development of such a capacity owes its origins to the quality of care in the infant's early environment. How does Winnicott's insistence on the importance of "believing in" (a concept closely associated with religion) fit with his admission about growing up out of his own "church religious practice"? And what exactly does he mean by this last phrase? These are some of the questions that provide impetus for this book about the role of religion in the life and work of D.W. Winnicott.

Beginning with his own religious upbringing, this book inquires about the influence of this aspect of Winnicott's own background upon his theory of emotional development. It also inquires about the nature of his religious behavior and practice as an adult. It explores not only how religion shaped and influenced his life and work, but also how his career in psychoanalysis influenced and changed Winnicott's view of religion.

All Winnicott's biographers mention the importance of his religious background and various ways that it influenced him (Goldman, 1993; Jacobs, 1995; Kahr, 1996; Phillips, 1988; Rodman, 2003), but no one has done an extended treatment of this topic. Adam Phillips observed that "Winnicott's work can be seen as both continuing and reacting against different strands" of his religious tradition (p. 23). In one sense this book seeks to flesh out the particulars of the various strands of continuity and discontinuity of Winnicott's thought with his religious background. It tries to come to terms with the seeming contradiction between Goldman's claim to a "lingering religiosity" (p. 122) in Winnicott and

1

Hopkins' (1997) claim that "religiously, Winnicott remained a skeptic" (p. 492). However, before embarking on this task, a few comments to place Winnicott into a larger context will be helpful.

D.W. Winnicott was a pre-eminent British psychoanalytic theorist and practitioner who has contributed enormously to the understanding of the emotional development of children. He is probably best known for his concept of the "transitional object," a concept that Anna Freud once commented had "conquered the analytic world" (cited in Rodman, 1987, p. xix). Today, the influence of his psychological theory regarding such objects extends far beyond the world of psychoanalysis into everyday life. Rare is the person who is not familiar with the concept of the "security blanket" or the special attachment that children can have to their teddy bears, even if they have never heard of D.W. Winnicott. Although much of Winnicott's subtlety in writing of such objects is lost in their popularization, his work on the uses that the young child makes of these "first not-me possessions" (Winnicott, 1951b, p. 229) continues to illumine the understanding of the psychic world of the young child. Not only does his theory provide insight into the mind of the young infant, it offers guidance into the psychological workings of the adult mind and the significance of cultural phenomena such as art and religion as well.

Winnicott was a London pediatrician who became interested in the work of Sigmund Freud during his medical training (Rodman, 2003). As a pediatrician Winnicott became interested in how his observations of children's development matched with Freud's theory of a child's development. Following his own analysis and supervision of his analytic work with children, Winnicott became the first analytically certified pediatrician. In later years he would describe himself as a "child psychiatrist" (Winnicott, 1963j, p. 95). His skills in this area were honed during World War II through his work with children who had been evacuated from London during the German bombings.

As a member of the British Psychoanalytic Society, Winnicott came to be identified with what was called the "middle" (later "independent") group and with the general approach known as "object relations" theory (Phillips, 1988). Broadly speaking, the object relations theorists were those who modified Freud's original focus on the formative influence of the biological drives to articulate the formative influence of interactions with one's early caregivers on personality development. Object relations theory, in its various articulations, continues to guide much of contemporary psychoanalytic theory and practice.

In accord with his own psychological theory, one would note that long before he became interested in psychoanalysis and its various articulations, Winnicott was being shaped by early interactions with his own caregivers. Part of the context in which Winnicott was reared was that of religiously devout parents and siblings. This monograph attempts to trace the influence of this early, religiously tinged care-giving environment on the development of Winnicott's life and work.

Significant in this regard is his comment about the religious tradition to which he was exposed as a child; that of "Wesleyan Methodism." Hoffman (2004) has called special attention to the significance of this tradition for understanding Winnicott. Others have written on the influence of Wesleyan Methodism on English history and cultural development (Heitzenrater, 1995; Rack, 1983; Semmel, 1973; Turner, 1983). This treatise seeks to explain not only how growing up in a religiously devout home seems to have influenced Winnicott, but how this particular way of being religious contributed to Winnicott's life and thought.

However, a look at how Winnicott's religious background influenced his life and work also raises questions as to how his life and work as a psychoanalyst influenced his religious life. From Freud's first essay on the topic in 1907, psychoanalysis had taken a dim view of religious practice and sentiments. How Winnicott's exposure to such censorious attitudes toward religion impacted his own religious life and view of religion is another question taken up in this book.

Why This Book?

As interesting as some readers may find these questions, others may be asking what is significant about a book on the role of religion in the life and work of D.W. Winnicott? There are, of course, several reasons why such a topic might be of interest.

One reason is the recent surge of interest in the relationship between religion (and spirituality) and psychology, especially in clinical practice (e.g., Aten, O'Grady & Worthington, 2011; Frame, 2002; Miller, 2002; Pargament, 2007; Richards and Bergin, 2005; Sperry & Shafranske, 2004). Such an interest has encompassed psychoanalytic work as well, despite a historical animosity toward religion and spirituality dating back to Freud. Those who are interested in this broader social shift may be interested to read about the contributions of a significant person in analytic psychology who has helped shape the current dialogue about the role of religion in therapeutic work.

Winnicott's work has been especially influential among those who have sought some sort of rapprochement between religion and psychoanalysis (e.g., Jones, 1991; Meissner, 1984; Rizzuto, 1979, 2005). Winnicott brings a new theoretical lens for reflecting on the relationship between religion and psychoanalysis. He offers a creative, yet analytic way to reflect on the positive, vitalizing qualities of religion and not just the obsessional or neurotic qualities that Freud was wont to describe. Though very much aware of traditional psychoanalytic positions about religion and remaining very analytical in his own analysis, Winnicott nevertheless reframed the analytic questions regarding the role of religion in life and culture in ways that offered new insights into the positive role of religion.

For instance, Winnicott (1951a) pointed out the "transitional" quality of religion. His concept of transitional phenomena helps one understand the role of religion as contributing to and emerging from an "intermediate" area in life that vitalizes all human interactions. This psychoanalytic view of religion reversed Freud's position that religion is primarily pathological and opened up a way to see and appreciate the positive, adaptive, and creative aspects of religion. Furthermore, viewing religion as transitional phenomena opened a window on how emotional, intrapsychic images or representations of God are formed and how these influence one in various ways. This insight, as elaborated by people such as Ana-Marie Rizzuto (1979) and William Meissner (1984) has spawned numerous articles on the formation and the role of God images, both in health and in pathology (cf. Brokaw & Edwards, 1994; Lawrence, 1997; Moriarty and Hoffman, 2007).

This work on the transitional quality of religion as seen in God representations also offers ways to think about religious development. According to analytic theory, people transfer to God the qualities of relationships that they have learned in other arenas of life (Meissner, 1984; Rizzuto, 1979). (Freud (1927) had argued this as well but he also had argued that such relationships by their nature were infantile not only in origin but expression.) However, Winnicott's work, and those who build from it, helps one understand "God" as someone that can be related to in ways similar to those employed in relating to others. Thus, one has the potential for more mature relating to God (versus a relationship that reflects only infantile ways of relating) just as one has the possibility of mature relations in other contexts. Further implications of Winnicott's thought for understanding religious development are explored later.

Of course, Winnicott's approach does not solve all the problems connected to the integration of religion and analytic thought, especially about the psychological origins of God. He is quite aware of the negative psychological uses to which religion and religious practice can be put and he left open the question of the "reality" of God (Winnicott, 1968g). These and other topics are taken up throughout the course of this book as Winnicott's own religious expression, how it influenced his work, and how it changed over the course of his life are explored.

However, Winnicott's influence lies beyond his contributions to a new analytic way of viewing religion. He also has been an influential figure in shaping current psychoanalytic theory, especially its turn toward the relational (cf. Aron & Mitchell, 1999; Clarke, Hoggett & Hahn, 2008; Mitchell, 1988). He has bequeathed to psychoanalysis concepts of transitional objects, primary maternal preoccupation, good enough mothering, anti-social tendency, true self/false self, play, hate in counter-transference, regression to dependence, and use of an object to name a few (cf. Abram, 2007b; Newman, 1995). He has especially illumined the understanding of the power of developmental forces at work in what he termed the inner life, the outer life and the intermediate area. Analysts will find it of interest to see how Winnicott's religious background influenced and contributed to his analytic theory (perhaps unconsciously at times). Those interested in general developmental psychology will have a similar interest in looking at the influence of his religious background on Winnicott's theory of child development.

Although this book should be of interest to psychoanalytic specialists, it is not, strictly speaking a psychoanalytic biography or psychoanalytic monograph. Although not a psychoanalytic book as such, it is influenced by psychoanalytic perspectives, especially Winnicott's own. This influence shows up in certain questions entertained along the way such as how Winnicott's own concepts and images of God reflect his early care-giving environment.

In noting that those interested in the current rapprochement between religion and psychology might be interested in this book as might those of analytic background who would be interested in the influences that shaped Winnicott the psychoanalyst, I have had the clinician in mind. However, there is an intriguing parallel interest in the rapprochement between religion and psychology among theologians, several of whom also have found Winnicott and the object relations theorists helpful (cf. Burns-Smith, 1999; Jones, 1991; Price, 2002). Those with similar theological concerns should find this book engaging, especially those interested in the interface of John Wesley's theology and psychology (e.g. Grentz, 2001; Maddox, 2004; Malony, 1999; Strawn & Leffel, 2001).

There is yet another audience that I had in mind as I wrote this book and that is my students and the type of person they represent. I teach counseling theory and practice in a master's program in counseling and personality theories in a doctoral program in clinical psychology. The kind of person that is drawn to a major in counseling and clinical psychology tends to share an interest in the inner workings of the person. Often such people also are deeply interested in learning more about themselves and in most clinical programs such self-exploration is encouraged. Thus, people interested in the importance of psychological factors in human growth also might be interested to learn more about the developmental influences on a figure who has helped shape important understandings of these processes. Often, in coming to understand someone else people come to know themselves better. Thus, in exploring the formative influences on Winnicott's development, as well as his insights into emotional growth, there is the hope that one comes to learn something of the forces that shaped one's own life.

This last answer as to why this book acknowledges that there are always personal reasons behind the writing of a book. It is sometimes said that an author reveals as much about him/herself as about the subject, especially in biographical works. This danger of projecting one's own ideas and calling them another's would seem especially problematic from a psychoanalytic perspective. Furthermore, Freud once said to a would-be biographer "anyone who writes a biography is committed to lies, concealments, hypocrisy, flattery and even to hiding his own lack of understanding, for biographical truth does not exist, and if it did we could not use it" (Freud, E.L., 1970, p. 127; cited in Abram 2007a). The reader will have to judge the extent to which this proves true in this endeavor. I have tried to be aware of this twin set of dangers, but so that the reader might also be alert to these tendencies I offer some of the more important personal reasons for writing this book. That being said, although offered as personal reasons I also anticipate that readers may share some of these same interests.

I certainly did not envision writing a book on Winnicott when I first became acquainted with his work. However, the more I studied his thought, the more intrigued I became with Winnicott's own developmental journey. I came to see pieces of my own journey in Winnicott's journey and thus coming to understand him better I was able to understand better my own journey. Perhaps some motivation of this sort lies behind all books about others. At some point I became convinced that there was a story here worth telling. Having profited by learning about Winnicott and his journey I am hoping others might profit from hearing it.

I have long been interested in the intersection of psychology (including psychoanalysis) and religion. How do these two disciplines mutually inform one another? In what ways are they compatible? In what ways do they seem at odds? These questions not only intrigued me, I discovered that they intrigued Winnicott and were ones on which he sought to speak and to enlighten. So, one attraction to Winnicott was an affinity with his interest in psychoanalysis and religion. In addition, I share a religious background that had strong Wesleyan Methodist influences. Since this was Winnicott's religious background, I was intrigued about how it might have influenced him since I have long pondered its influence on me and have offered reflections on how it influences my clinical work (Kilian and Parker, 2001).

I first became acquainted with Winnicott's work while reading *The Living Human Document* by Charles Gerkin (1984). Gerkin spoke of Winnicott's developmental psychology as giving insight into the importance of growing up in a world that does not cater to one's every wish. The formation of healthy self and other relationships occurred in "a crucible of a degree of suffering and sacrifice on the part of both mother and infant" (p. 88). I was intrigued by this thought, especially in a culture that often suggested that suffering and sacrifice belonged to ill health (cf. Tatelbaum, 1989). Furthermore, Gerkin placed Winnicott's work in the context of religious and spiritual growth (what he called the "journey of the soul"). It was Gerkin's summary of Winnicott's work and his acquainting me with the work of Ana-Marie Rizzuto (1979) that first helped me to understand Winnicott's position about the positive role of religion in life and culture. I became intrigued with the question of the sources of such a positive attitude, an attitude that seemed so at odds with his intellectual mentor Freud. I wondered if the sources for such a positive attitude toward religion might lie in Winnicott's own experience with things religious while growing up.[1]

I discovered more about the influence of religion on Winnicott by reading works by Goldman (1993) and Hoffman (2004, 2007). Goldman argued that there was a "lingering religiosity" in Winnicott. I wanted to know more about the nature of this lingering religiosity, particularly its Wesleyan Methodist character. What are the contours of a Wesleyan Methodist piety and how does it compare and contrast with Winnicott's thought? In what ways does this type of religion show up in his work and in what ways did Winnicott diverge from his religious background? These are some of the questions I try to answer in this study.

In addition to the shared affinities with Winnicott, there are other personal reasons in wanting to write about Winnicott as well. Winnicott (1945d) spoke at one point of the difference between "verbalizers" (or "word" people) and "intuitive" people. He clearly located himself among the latter. "Intuitive people are liable to be hopeless at talking about the things they 'know' so easily. I think we would always rather hear the thinkers talking about what they are thinking out than hear the intuitive people talking about what they know. But when it comes to having our lives planned for us, heaven help us if the thinkers take over" (1945d, p. 170). At another time he wrote: "Somehow the word people tend to claim sanity, and those who see visions do not know how to defend their position when accused of insanity. Logical argument really belongs to the verbalizers. Feeling or a feeling of certainty or truth or 'real' belongs to the others" (Winnicott, 1965c, p. 155). And despite his deep appreciation for the scientific approach to human problems that Freud introduced, Winnicott even found in Freud a comrade willing to defer to the intuitive side over against the more scientific approach, noting on one occasion that Freud was always ready to permit a "poet or philosopher or his own intuition [to] open up the way for phenomena that had not been covered by the metapsychology of the time" (Winnicott, 1969l, p. 241).

One can see some of the differences between intuitive types and verbalizers working its way out in the way Winnicott put together his papers. As he once remarked, "I gather this and that, here and there, settle down to clinical experience, form my own theories and then, last of all, interest myself in looking to see where I stole what" (Winnicott, 1945c, p. 145). My first impression on reading Winnicott was the lack of linear progress in his thought processes. One wanders in and out of intuitive snatches of insight; presentations of *gestalten* without a structured, linear unfolding. At one point he stated how difficult it was for him to trace the history of ideas in his papers (Winnicott, n.d. 2). Thus, one comes to understand his well-known problems with being able to cite his sources when he writes (Rodman, 1987, 2003). I, on the other hand, would locate myself among the word people, those who take delight in tracing the history of ideas. Thus, one could say that I find a complement in a person like Winnicott. I think part of my attraction to Winnicott was in trying to understand someone so different than me in some regards. That is, in coming to understand him better I hope to understand a neglected dimension of myself.

Finally, in terms of personal motivation for this book, I should simply say that I have found Winnicott an interesting person and I think others will as well. Several qualities contribute to this interest including his openness to new things, his efforts at continued growth, and his humor.

Winnicott's openness to try new things manifested itself in several ways. It included his willingness to take risks such as those he took early in his career as a pediatrician with rheumatic children. He was willing to go against the standard protocols that called for lots of bed rest for these children and instead encouraged them to play because he thought that there might be psychological factors as well as physical ones that contributed to this disease (Winnicott, 1931a). This willingness to take some risks seems motivated in part by the death of a patient during his early training. Winnicott thought this death was due in part to his following of protocols for illness without taking individual differences adequately into account (Winnicott, 1970d). This event made him want to be more attentive to his own inner voice regarding the care of his patients.

His openness to try new things also is seen in his willingness to adapt the analytic perspective to varying modes of therapy. One of the innovations he introduced was the single-session consultation. He used this when he knew that it would not be possible to do analysis with a child beyond the initial consultation. In his book *Therapeutic Consultations in Child Psychiatry* he offered insight into adapting the analytic framing so as to creatively engage the child's premeeting projections about the magical qualities of doctors and in this way move the child toward greater emotional healing that could then be carried on by the parents at home. Other creative adaptations of analytic framing involved Winnicott's use of the spatula and squiggle techniques (Winnicott, 1941a, 1964–1968, 1968a). The spatula technique involved Winnicott's ability to draw conclusions about the emotional health of a baby by watching the various dynamics displayed when an infant was allowed to play with a shiny metal tongue depressor (e.g., watching how the infant sought the mother's permission, how joyful or restrained the play was, the infant's ability to be done with the spatula and shift attention elsewhere). The squiggle technique involved Winnicott's ability to be attuned to unconscious processes that would manifest themselves in children's conversions of squiggly lines into drawings.[2]

Pertinent to the interests of this book, Winnicott's openness to new things is seen in his exploration of the creative and adaptive qualities of religion over against the traditional pre-occupation with its pathological qualities in psychoanalysis. Here, in an often maligned area, Winnicott offered fresh, positive ways to conceive the contributions of religion to life and culture.

A second quality that made Winnicott interesting was his efforts to be continually growing. This included a willingness to learn from his mistakes as one saw in his decision to be more attentive to his own inner voice in the care of his patients. He also learned from his mistakes in doing analytic practice. He noted late in life that he had learned that interpretations are not as needful or as useful as he had once thought (Winnicott, 1971k; cf. also Winnicott, 1959a, p. 122 with Winnicott, 1969d, p. 508). Through years of practice Winnicott concluded it is much more effective to let the client discover on his or her own noting in one place that he interpreted primarily to let the patient know he was human (Winnicott, 1963a).

One also sees his efforts at continuing to grow in other ways. Rodman (2003) noted that his evolving theoretical work was one way Winnicott carried on the insights from his analysis. That is, in continuing to evolve his theory Winnicott was engaging in a kind of self-analysis. For instance, Rodman noted that Winnicott continued to engage throughout his life his struggles over his own aggression and how to express this. Certainly his theoretical work on "hate in the counter-transference" was one way Winnicott (1947c) continued to learn about his own aggression. He also sought to find the most helpful ways to express his aggression whether with a temporary foster child or through the numerous letters he wrote, often to friends and colleagues at the British Psychoanalytic Society with which he disagreed (Rodman, 1987, 2003). Another aspect of Winnicott's continued growth through self-analysis was his interpretation of his own dreams. For instance, a dream he had prior to reviewing a book by Carl Jung gave him insight about his own destructiveness that eventually found its way into his paper on object usage (Winnicott, 1963d).

A poignant aspect of Winnicott's efforts to be continually growing is seen in his ongoing journey to find and express his true self, an incommunicado core that he thought was never fully revealed (Winnicott, 1963a; cf. Rodman, 2003). Certainly his theoretical work in this area was an attempt to nurture his own true self, but one sees something of the difficulty of his personal struggle when this quest for the true self is connected to Winnicott's ongoing need to feel real and alive. A chief way this need to feel alive and real manifested itself in his own life was his need to cast everyone else's ideas into his own words. This often raised the ire of his colleagues because they thought he did not give them sufficient credit in his writings for ideas he had borrowed from them (Rodman, 1987). Yet he confessed on more than one occasion that to try to engage another's ideas other than re-casting them made him lose interest (Khan, 1975). Near the end of his life he confessed that this was a great fault in him and he made at least one attempt to remedy this by inviting his colleagues to help him make some of these connections (Winnicott, 1967h). Thus, though he did not seem to make much progress in this regards, given that it was a deep part of his nature (perhaps his true self), he acknowledged his need to grow in this area.

It is in his religious life that one encounters one of the ironies of Winnicott's efforts to be continuously growing. His efforts and failures along these lines are explored later.

However, Winnicott's openness to new things and willingness to grow was not without its downside. His riskiness for instance, revealed a narcissistic streak that also manifested in other ways, not always balanced and healthy. For instance, Katherine Rees (see Goldman, 1993, p.10) reported that Winnicott seems to have felt that a little Winnicott therapy was worth more than a lot of therapy from others and he often agreed to see patients for periodic visits who might have profited more from a conventional analysis with someone else, even though they may not have been of Winnicott's stature. At other times, Winnicott (1960e) offered cautions that indicate some insight into the need to keep one's narcissism in check as when he advised that one take only one patient at a time in need of an analysis that included severe regression to dependence. However, it appears that he did not always take his own advice in this area.

A third quality that made Winnicott interesting was his humor. This also manifested itself in several ways: from his tendency to play the clown, even during presentations at the British Psychoanalytic Society to stunts with his car and bicycle, to remarks in his letters and writings. Both Clare Winnicott (his second wife) and Masud Khan (a former analysand who helped edit several of his books) gave examples of his clowning around (Winnicott, 1978; Willoughby, 2005). Sometimes this had unintended consequences such as the time when he spilled Princess Marie Bonaparte's plate in her lap at a formal dinner (Willoughby). The humor in his letters can be seen in the case of a friend who wrote that he and his wife were reading a letter from Winnicott on the way home from the post and found themselves laughing so hard that people in the street began to stare (Ede, 1940). Although part of the impetus for his humor may have derived from trying to cheer up a depressed mother (Rodman, 2003), one cannot help but smile when reading some of his remarks. For example, one sees something of Winnicott's (1969a) humor in his comment about behavior therapy: "What is left out is this, that human beings, even those with intelligence of quite low grades, are not just animals. They have a great deal that animals do not have at all. I personally would think of behavior therapy as an insult even to the higher apes, and I would include cats" (p. 560). His comment that it is impossible to work with certain kinds of difficult clients "when the analyst knows that the patient carries a revolver" also captures his wit (Winnicott, 1971k, p. 92).

Although Winnicott's use of humor, like all personal characteristics, was multiply determined I think his humor also needs to be seen in the context of his remarks on play and playing. Winnicott's (1971i, 1971j) thoughts on playing form one of his chief contributions to analytic theory. Play and playing for Winnicott is not to be restricted to the carefree activities of childhood (though these can certainly be play). Playing is a multivalent concept that takes in a person's ability to creatively engage the demands and limits of life. Playing evokes the creative capacities of the "intermediate area"; playing helps one tolerate the vicissitudes of life and bridge the chasm between overwhelming feelings and numbing reactions. Thus, playing is appropriate not only to children but to adults. Playing makes one alive; feeling real is an aspect of play. Playing belongs to the whole of life for Winnicott. Therapy then becomes a place to help people recover the ability to play (for both client and therapist).

As one who knew the power of playing, Winnicott strove for playfulness in his own life (Winnicott, 1978). His humor was a way he sought to stay alive and real to himself. It is no surprise then that both his humor and playfulness emerged in his treatment of religion. Theoretically, religion at its best also participates in the creative power of play for Winnicott; there also is playfulness in the way he engages this potential.

In identifying these interesting qualities in Winnicott, I also note that one is drawn not only to the strengths and heroics of a person, but to their failings and quirks. Both of these dimensions make others attractive. Perhaps one sees in another ways to be like them; to live up to the ideals they espoused or embodied. Or perhaps one sees in their lives things to avoid. Conversely, their failures remind one that all are human and one does not have to live a life of perfection. All of these things are found in Winnicott—heroics, failings, quirks. He is, by turns, creative, narcissistic, a risk taker, a maker of mistakes (who admits to such), and he does all of this with good humor. These are some of the things that made learning about the formative influences on him interesting. Of course in looking at such influences I had a more specific interest in mind as well. How were such a temperament and practices shaped by, as well as reflective of, a Wesleyan Methodist background?

What the Book Is About

The broad theme of this book is the role of religion in the life and work of D.W. Winnicott. This topic involves several interconnected questions and various theses that previous Winnicott scholars have proposed. This book takes up several of these theses, at turns defending, challenging, expanding and refining them. At one level it may be seen as giving particulars to Phillips's (1988) comments that Winnicott's work can be understood as a reflection of his religious background, either in its continuity with or reaction against.

At another level this book takes up Goldman's (1993) thesis of a "lingering religiosity" in Winnicott. It explores Goldman's claim that both the "form and content" of Winnicott's work was influenced by his religious background. It illustrates and elaborates these claims but also identifies their limitations. Goldman further argued that Winnicott remained religious in the sense that he retained a sense of wonder about the world. Although a sense of wonder is certainly part of what is gathered up by religiosity, the general sense of this term implies more. Thus, this book also takes up the question of the nature of Winnicott's lingering religiosity. Can it be described with more detail than his sense of wonder? For instance, does Winnicott retain a belief in God consistent with his early religious background? How do his beliefs about God change over the course of his life? How did Winnicott live out or practice his religiosity? For instance, did he maintain an active connection with organized religion?

In line with Goldman's thesis of a lingering religiosity that influenced both the form and content of Winnicott's thought is Marie Hoffman's (2004, 2007) work demonstrating the particularly Wesleyan Methodist influence of Winnicott's religious background on his work. Although Winnicott converts to Anglicanism as a young adult, Hoffman shows how the Wesleyan Methodist emphasis on the immanence of God and the goodness of people is more characteristic of Winnicott's work in contrast to a Reformed (Calvinistic) piety that influenced Winnicott's contemporary, Ronald Fairbairn. This book seeks to outline the particular aspects of a Wesleyan Methodist piety and how this way of being religious in his formative years continued to influence Winnicott's life and work.

Winnicott's remark that he had grown up out of the "church religious practice" associated with his Wesleyan Methodist background has been noted. This is an interesting reflection from someone who said elsewhere of "religious practice" that it contributed to the "unification and general integration of the personality" (Winnicott, 1942, p. 151). Furthermore, lest this be thought an early sentiment that he gave up in later life, Winnicott (1971l) continued to argue in his last published book before his death for the "transitional quality" of religion—that is, that religion participates in an "intermediate" area of experience that is essential to mental health and which is never outgrown (pp. 2-3). What then is one to make of this apparent contradiction? Is there something about Wesleyan Methodism that makes it a particularly easy type of religion to grow up out of? Or is Winnicott's choice of words misleading when it comes to his religious growth? If there is a lingering religiosity in Winnicott, what is its nature? If, on the other hand, Winnicott did indeed "grow up out of" religious practice, how and in what ways did this occur?

Peter Rudnytsky (1991) has labeled Winnicott a "believing skeptic." He placed the emphasis on the adjective and noted that Winnicott continued to believe in ways reflective of a "liberal Protestant tradition" (p. 96). Others, such as Brooke Hopkins (1997) and Michael Jacobs (1995) omitted the adjective and emphasized the noun suggesting that Winnicott was not religious as an adult. Such divergent opinions owe their origin to various statements about religion made by Winnicott over the years. This book looks at the context in which Winnicott's attitudes toward religion developed and how these attitudes changed over the course of his life. It explores apparent contradictions in Winnicott's theoretical statements about the positive, creative role of religion in life and culture and his attitude about his personal religious practice.

It will become obvious that Winnicott's religiosity had its own bent and that although it is correct to speak of a lingering religiosity the nature of this religiosity is sometimes at variance with what might commonly be meant by religiosity. Winnicott wrestled with his religious background and moved beyond it in some important ways; his religiosity contained elements of skepticism and doubt. Although there are many ways that Winnicott affirmed the positive aspects of religion and although one can see the origins of such positive attitudes in his religious upbringing, one also encounters in Winnicott an apparent inconsistency to live out his own highest ideas about the nature of religion. He was a man who struggled with bringing together his theoretical ideas about the positive role of religion with the role he was to allow to religion in his later adult life. Nevertheless, the nature of the Wesleyan Methodist influence on Winnicott runs very deep; sometimes more deeply than he himself seems to have been aware. His supposed divergence from religion in his own mind was not as far from his Wesleyan Methodist heritage as he seems to have thought. This book tries to understand these aspects of Winnicott's religiosity.

It seems important to say a word or two about what this book is not. First, although it looks at various religious ideas in Winnicott such as his view of the nature of the soul and original goodness in humans, it does not formally evaluate the theological adequacy of these positions. Although his vision of human nature is assessed in a general way, the book is more descriptive than prescriptive along these lines. It does look at how certain religious views (and their modifications) influenced his way of thinking about and working with his patients.

Second, the book it is not a comprehensive introduction to Winnicott nor is it a primer on Winnicottian theory or its practice in therapy. Although it will introduce certain of Winnicott's central concepts it will mostly cover those germane to the larger project of exploring the influence of Winnicott's religious background on his theory. Thus, there are areas of Winnicott's theory that receive little attention. Similarly, the kinds of refined distinctions between concepts like potential space and the intermediate area that Winnicott scholars make are not as relevant to this project and its anticipated audience.

Finally, I should note that this book is not a primer in Wesleyan theology either. Though it touches upon many aspects of Wesleyan thought, the purpose is to understand how Winnicott's thought has been influenced by Wesleyan piety. To this end, certain characteristics of a Wesleyan piety will be explored and the central ideas of this way of being religious will be tied to various themes and practices in Winnicott's life and work. However, this falls far short of being a specialty work on Wesleyan Methodism or theology.

Outline of the Chapters

Chapter 2 describes Winnicott's early home environment with a focus on religious dimensions of the household. It summarizes how this environment influenced Winnicott's later life. It looks especially at the religious life of Winnicott's parents and how the Wesleyan Methodist influence is obvious in their lives. It also looks at the nature of Winnicott's interactions with his parents and how this seems to have influenced his own religious life and his thoughts about religious things.

Chapter 3 looks at the wider influence of the Wesleyan Methodist tradition upon Winnicott as it was manifest in the boarding school he attended. It characterizes the nature of the adolescent Winnicott's spiritual activities. It summarizes the nature of the influences of this period upon Winnicott's personal religiousness and describes aspects of this influence that carry over into his later life.

Chapter 4 continues this chronological approach to Winnicott's religious life and journey by looking at the role of religion during his young adult years. It looks at his religious activities during this period and charts continuities and discontinuities between his religious upbringing and the type of religiosity he developed as a young adult. It looks at major events during this time of his life and how they seem to have influenced his view of religion, especially his encounter with psychoanalysis. It looks at how his ideas about religion began to change during this period as well.

Chapter 5 breaks from the chronological approach to look at how Winnicott's religious upbringing seems to have influenced his practice of psychoanalysis. In some ways, chapter 5 begins a series of chapters that seek to add particularity to Goldman's (1993) thesis of a lingering religiosity in Winnicott by indentifying some of the many ways this lingering influence can be seen. Chapter 5 focuses on certain lingering influences of his religious background as they manifest in his psychoanalytic work. It might be thought of as illustrating Goldman's claim that the "form" of Winnicott's thought is influenced by his religious background. For instance, it looks at various themes from Wesleyan Methodist piety that are reflected in Winnicott's general temperament and his attitudes toward psychoanalysis. The influence of his religious background on the form of his thought can also be seem by comparing the similarities and differences in the goals of religion and psychoanalysis as conceived by Winnicott. Finally, Kirschner's (1996) thesis that the developmental theory behind psychoanalysis was a secular version of the concept of "salvation" also is explored as a way in which religion influenced the form of Winnicott's thought.

Chapter 6 continues the look at Winnicott's lingering religiosity by identifying Winnicott's frequent scriptural and religious allusions. It notes the various ways that Winnicott alluded to Scripture and religious concepts throughout his writings. It looks at how he used such allusions and the significance that can be attached to his use of Scripture and reference to religious themes.

Chapter 7 shifts the focus to explore Goldman's (1993) thesis that not only the form of Winnicott's work was influenced by his religious background, but the content as well. This aspect of Winnicott's thought is explored by looking at the similarity between some of the seminal ideas in Winnicott's theory and certain theological ideas prevalent in Winnicott's religious background. One way this is observed is a consideration of the theological nature of key questions in which Winnicott is interested. Another way this is observed is through an exploration of the similarity between several central concepts in Winnicott and various religious ideas.

Chapter 8 can be seen as a counter-point to the influence of Winnicott's religious background on his psychoanalytic thought in that it takes up the question of how psychoanalysis influenced Winnicott's view of religion. It looks at arguably his most significant contribution to psychoanalytic theory—the concept of transitional phenomena—and the implications of this theoretical concept for understanding religion. It looks especially at the creative, adaptive roles of religion in life and culture.

Chapter 9 returns to the role of religion in Winnicott's personal life. It looks at his way of being religious as an adult and as a psychoanalyst. It charts the changes in his religious life as an adult both in terms of its continuities with his early religious background and its divergence from this early upbringing. It takes up the question of Winnicott's apparent inconsistency in the way he argued for the creative, adaptive quality of religion in the abstract and his own personal attitude and practice of religion.

Chapter 10 can be thought of as an exercise in reflexive application of Winnicott's theory. More specifically, this chapter asks whether Winnicott's theoretical contributions to developmental psychology and to religious behavior help one understand Winnicott's own God images and their sources. What specifically does Winnicott have to say about God and can these comments be traced to sources in his early childhood? This chapter explores these questions by looking at the contributions of his parents and his wider religious tradition to the images of God found in his writings.

Chapter 11 steps back to reflect upon the various things enumerated in the previous chapters as a means of constructing what might be called Winnicott's "implicit theology." Theology is the discipline traditionally associated with providing a vision of what humans are meant to be and do; a vision of the "good life." Given Winnicott's interest in human development, the human condition and how one navigates this for successful living, one can discern in Winnicott a similar vision. This chapter seeks to make plain Winnicott's answers to more traditional theological questions. From his various comments on human nature and the environment, this chapter offers thoughts on Winnicott's epistemology (how one knows), anthropology (nature of the human), and soteriology (what humans yearn for) and how these compare and contrast with Wesleyan perspectives. The book concludes with brief reflections on what one can learn from Winnicott's religious journey.

Notes

1.   Encountering Winnicott's work in the writings of Gerkin (1984) and Rizzuto (1979) made me aware that he took a position about the role of religion in life and culture that seemed 180 degrees different than Freud's position. I became intrigued how a psychoanalyst, especially one as influential as Winnicott, could take a position at such variance from one of his intellectual mentors (Freud). Thus, part of the impetus for this book was to discover the sources for Winnicott's position. From an analytic perspective, one would argue that all decisions have multiple determinations, some conscious, others unconscious. Thus, Winnicott's reversal of Freud's position on religion also has multiple sources. These sources include his own positive experiences of religion in his childhood. It also includes Winnicott's opposition to anything that smacked of dogma (see chapter 5). By Winnicott's time, Freud's position on religion as pathological defense had taken on the air of dogma for psychoanalysis and Winnicott fought against dogmatism wherever it might be found, in religion or in psychoanalysis. A third possibility is to see Winnicott's modifications of Freud's theory of religion as a sort of oedipal victory over the father; a way of subverting the father's authority—a very intriguing possibility from an analytic perspective (cf. Greenberg & Mitchell's [1983] claim that Winnicott intentionally subverted Freud's ideas), but one that is not taken up in this monograph.
2.   The Donald Woods Winnicott Papers at the Wellcome Library, London has a collection of over two hundred squiggles done by Winnicott over his life time. Not only did Winnicott use this technique with his young patients, he continued to draw squiggles for his own enjoyment (Rodman, 2003). Some of these are painted; others have been colored and several of them have been framed. It is interesting in terms of the subject of this book that only four of the squiggles at the Wellcome Library have overtly religious themes. The possible significance of this is taken up in a later chapter.

Chapter 2
Religion in the Winnicott Household

"My father had a simple (religious) faith"

As a young boy in Plymouth, England, Donald Winnicott would walk the ten minutes from church to his home in the company of his father after the family's weekly attendance at the Wesleyan Methodist congregation. As the youngest child, and only son, this walk was his "privilege"; a special time with a very busy father, who left his son mostly to the care of the many females in the house (Winnicott, 1983). These walks provided the occasion for the young Winnicott to observe and engage his father about his religious faith. One can easily imagine the young Winnicott asking the question one of his younger patients would later ask: "if God is the Father, then who is God's father and who is the father of God's father?" (Winnicott, 1970b, p. 209). Developmental research indicates that children of a certain age are absorbed with the apparent logical inconsistencies in such problems due to the limits of their "concrete" mental operations (Piaget, 1970; cf. Fowler, 1981). The actual questions the young Winnicott asked his father about his religion are lost to history; all that is known is that one conversation involved a question that could have led to a "long argument." It was the father's answer that is most memorable to Winnicott. His father said "read the Bible and what you find there will be the true answer for you" (Winnicott, 1978, p. 23). This memory of talking with his father about religion is framed as a time in which the young Winnicott is granted a freedom to find his own way toward faith without having to believe in the way his father does. Rudnytsky (1991) concluded that Winnicott took from these early times a positive attitude about both his father and religion.

Although not the only quality that defined the household, clearly their religion was a key factor that characterized the Winnicotts (Kahr, 1996; Phillips, 1988; Rodman, 2003; Winnicott, 1983). Winnicott referred to his family's religion as being "Wesleyan Methodist," which was one of several "nonconformist" Christian groups that thrived in the Western coasts of Britain. The purpose of this chapter is to explore the nature of the deep Wesleyan Methodist piety that characterized the Winnicott household and to describe the impression that this type of religious upbringing left on the young Winnicott.

17

The Family's Religious Practice

There are several sources of information about the religious practices of the Winnicott family. Winnicott's second wife, Clare (Winnicott, 1983), described the Winnicott family as "profoundly" religious people who attended church every Sunday (p. 180). Winnicott's biographers attest to the active role of religion in the Winnicott household (Goldman, 1993; Kahr, 1996; Phillips, 1988; Rodman, 1987, 2003), and Winnicott himself spoke occasionally of his religious upbringing in his published essays (1968b; 1969d) and letters (1967f). Unpublished letters from Winnicott and members of his family also affirm a lifelong religious influence on Winnicott's family (e.g., J.F. Winnicott, 1934, 1940, 1942a, 1942b; V. Winnicott, 1942). In looking for the outworking of this Wesleyan Methodist heritage in the Winnicott household, one finds more information about Winnicott's father and his activities in the church than about his mother, although Clare (Winnicott, 1983) speaks of both as "leading lights" in the church.

The Nature of His Father's Piety

Winnicott's father, J. Frederick Winnicott, was a descendent of Methodist ancestors who had occupied the area of Plymouth in Devon, England for several generations. This area of England had been a center for several variants of "non-conformist" (non-Anglican) Christianity including the Methodists and Plymouth Brethren (Rodman, 2003).

The non-conformist or "dissenting" tradition in Britain included people such as John Wycliffe, an early translator of the Bible into English, and the Lollard sect, a fourteenth-century group associated with Wycliffe and his belief that the Bible was more authoritative than the Pope (Goldman, 1993; Heitzenrater, 1995). (Winnicott would become interested in the Lollards during the last few years of his life, a point developed later). Plymouth, England, one might recall was also the site from which the Pilgrims sailed for the New World. The Pilgrims were part of another non-conformist group, known as Puritans, whose original purpose had been to "purify" the Church of England of some of its more "non-scriptural" (i.e., Roman Catholic) practices (Heitzenrater, 1995).

The specific form of non-conformity known as Methodism had its roots in John and Charles Wesley's attempts to bring a more heartfelt, personal religious experience to their Anglican heritage (cf. Clapper, 1989). After John Wesley's death, the "Methodists" (those who had adopted Wesley's "methods" for the religious life, and who had an allegiance to him) separated from the Anglican church to become their own religious organization. This separation occurred for a variety of personal and political reasons (on both sides), and produced an interesting blend of Wesley's Anglican heritage with a more obvious dissenting tradition (Heitzenrater, 1995).

By the nineteenth century, the Wesleyan Methodist heritage in Western England to which Frederick Winnicott would have found himself heir would have been characterized by a piety that emphasized several themes from Wesley's attempts to revive religious fervor in England. Some of these themes included Wesley's emphasis on a gracious, loving God, the personal nature of religious experience, a concern for the poor and underprivileged, the notion that the laity and formal clergy should cooperate more closely, and that there should be tolerance for differences in religious opinions (Chilcote, 2004; Clapper, 1989; Semmel, 1973). This latter emphasis on tolerance especially grew out of Wesley's (e.g., 1746c, 1763b) own attempts to find a "middle way" between the more Protestant emphases of some dissenters, and the more Roman Catholic emphases of high church Anglicanism. Chilcote (2004) described what he called Wesley's "both/and" theology. Proper Christian piety is to be found in both frequent observance of the Lord's Table (i.e., scared rituals) and preaching from the pulpit; in belief that faith both comes by grace and produces good works; in union of both "head" and "heart" in Christian service to both "church" and "world."

Frederick Winnicott seems to have taken a deep pride in his family and community roots, and to have drunk deeply from the wells of its spiritual heritage. One sees a great civic pride from the enormous amount of time and energy devoted to civic and commercial activities. Frederick Winnicott, in addition to being a successful merchant, was Chairman of the Mercantile Association and later the Chamber of Commerce; he was trustee of a local bank, a Justice of the Peace, and twice elected mayor of Plymouth. He was knighted in 1924 for his services to the public welfare (Kahr, 1996). Winnicott would later describe his father as "extremely preoccupied in my younger years with town as well as business matters" (Winnicott, 1978, p. 23).

Sir Frederick seems also to have taken great pride in the religious heritage of Plymouth as well. He sponsored a memorial to the Pilgrim's egress and as one of the leading citizens of Plymouth dedicated the marker (Rodman, 2003). It may be that part of what Sir Frederick was memorializing was a tribute to the non-conformist tradition so associated with Plymouth, and which he knew so well in its Methodist variation (Winnicott, 1983).

Winnicott's father also seems to have deeply valued his Wesleyan Methodist heritage at a personal level if his activities in his church are any indication. His father's deep involvement in religious activities pre-dates Winnicott's birth and continued throughout not only Winnicott's childhood but the remainder of Sir Frederick's life. In several letters to his son, at least one written in his nineties, Frederick Winnicott mentioned his activities in the local congregation at Mutley Plain (J.F. Winnicott, 1947).

Before his son's birth, and apparently before his own marriage, Frederick Winnicott was a Sunday School teacher at the King Street Wesleyan Church where he also would later serve as Honorary Secretary to the class in Bible Instruction. In his mid-twenties, and not long after his marriage, he helped to build the Wesleyan Church on Mutley Plain, not only by contributing his own funds, but by soliciting funds from his neighbors. His involvement in this church included not only weekly participation in the worship services, but singing in the choir and holding various church offices. He would be involved in this church for the remainder of his life, serving at various times as church Treasurer and as Steward until his death (Kahr, 1996; Rodman, 2003). A Steward in the Methodist church was the person in charge of funds collected for non-member care, such as for the poor and underprivileged of the community (Runyon, 1998).

His father's involvement in church activities extended beyond his local church and included being Honorary Treasurer for the local Theological Colleges and a member of the Wesleyan Synod. All of these activities would involve time and energy, often away from his family, to carry out effectively, and Frederick Winnicott seems to be the kind of conscientious person who would not have taken such responsibilities lightly (Rodman, 2003).

One also gets some sense of Frederick Winnicott's appreciation for his Wesleyan Methodist heritage in his choice of a boarding school for his son to attend. He sends his son to The Leys, which was established as the "first Methodist public school" (Rodman, pg. 24). Kahr (1996) noted that "Frederick Winnicott would have held The Leys School in very high regard, because of its staunch and long-standing tradition of English Methodism and its status as a very respectable school for the middle classes" (pg. 14).

When one imagines the hours necessary to engage in all the activities noted above, one senses the importance of his religion to Frederick Winnicott. One concludes that his father's faith, though a "simple" one according to Winnicott (1978, p. 23), was not one restricted to Sunday worship. His many activities for the betterment of his community can be seen as a particularly Wesleyan expression of faith (Chilcote, 2004; Semmel, 1973).[1]

Frederick Winnicott's faith seems typical of his tradition, in that it included some sense that religion was personal, a matter of the heart. In letters to his son, he noted that he prayed for God's guidance for his son; he offered praise to God for blessing the family; and he remarked on God's comfort when a relative died (J. F. Winnicott, 1934, 1942b, 1943). One senses that such remarks were part of the fabric of his character and not contrived for effect. Frederick Winnicott shared his faith with the family in that the whole family attended weekly Sunday services. According to Rodman (2003), at a later time when only Sir Frederick and his daughters were living at home, a servant remembered that the family's main reading was "the Bible" and that there were "prayers each day" (pg. 17). Given the nature of his father's religious involvement, it is not unreasonable to assume that such practices may have been observed in the household for years, including those in which Winnicott was young.

Clare Winnicott (1983) further described the nature of religion in the Winnicott household as being a religion "based on love, based on helping people" (p. 181). To base religion on love, first God's love toward humans, then their love toward one another, is very Wesleyan (Chilcote, 2003; Maddox, 1994). As

Wesley (1745) himself once advised: "Condemn no man for not thinking as you think. Let everyone enjoy the full and free liberty of thinking for himself. . . . If you cannot reason or persuade a man into the truth, never attempt to force him into it. If love will not compel him to come in, leave him to God" (p. 130).[2]

Of Frederick Winnicott's "simple faith" Rodman (2003) noted that he did not seem to experience the crisis of faith that characterized some who were not able to "manage a transition from traditional religious teachings about man's origins to the new ideas promulgated by Darwin" (p. 12). Whether the absence of spiritual crises was because of more tolerance toward Darwin or more certainty about his religious teachings is not knowable at this distance. Both options are possible.

Clare Winnicott (1983) stressed that Frederick Winnicott's way of being religious was one that was not hard or strict. She saw the non-conformist tradition to which he belonged as being embodied in a lack of dogmatism toward his religious beliefs. According to her, although the family was deeply religious their religion was not oppressive in any way. Rodman (2003) suggested that it was his father's encouragement to pursue his own way of being religious that may have given the younger Winnicott the freedom to pursue his later studies of Darwin at boarding school without creating a significant rupture in the relationship with his father. However, one might put over against this reading of Frederick Winnicott's simple faith, Winnicott's (1961d) own criticism of the "certainty" that belonged to religion. Furthermore, the context in which he described his father's as a "simple faith" lends itself to varied interpretations as will be noted later.

The Nature of His Mother's Piety

Less is known about Winnicott's mother and her activities, including religious ones, than about his father. This is a bit surprising given that one of the major thrusts of Winnicott's work is to illumine the role of the mother in the infant's development.

Winnicott's mother was Anglican prior to her marriage but she converted to her husband's church afterwards, although the wedding was in the Anglican parish church, St. Andrews, Plymouth (Rodman, 2003). It is not known how active Elizabeth Winnicott was in her Anglican church but Clare stated she became a "leading light" in her husband's Wesleyan Methodist church (Winnicott, 1983). In addition to her weekly attendance at the Sunday services she hosted several gatherings at her home, in her role as the wife of a civic leader. Whether she also hosted events as the wife of a leading churchman is not known, although like many women of her day, she kept a register of guests at her home (Rodman, 2003).

Clare Winnicott (1983) stated that religion was a "binding force within the family." She elaborated "I think that nonconformism meant a lot to them all, and bound them in a way" (p. 181). One might infer from this description, and her further indication that Elizabeth Winnicott was a leading light in the church that Winnicott's mother was supportive of the family involvement in the Wesleyan Methodist tradition. What specific activities she might have engaged in is not known, nor is how she might have incorporated her faith into other activities. Unlike his father, Winnicott does not characterize the nature of his mother's faith.

Winnicott's Early Participation in This Religious Tradition

The piety of Winnicott's parents conveys something of the religious environment into which he was born, April 7, 1896, the last of three children. According to records from the Mutley Plain Wesleyan church he was baptized as an infant in this congregation on May 16, a further affirmation of the importance of the Winnicotts' non-conformist religion. However, little is known about the participation of the Winnicott children in the Wesleyan Methodist church. Winnicott (1968b) said that he was "brought up as a Wesleyan Methodist" (p. 142) but did not offer many specifics about this upbringing. Clare Winnicott (1983) recorded that the family routine was to attend Sunday morning services each week. Later, after Elizabeth Winnicott had died and Winnicott's two sisters lived with their father, Rodman (2003) quoted a servant in the household stating that Bible reading and daily prayers were very much a part of the household. She also noted that Christian literature was prevalent in the house in the form of *The Christian Herald* magazine and the *Weekly Methodist Recorder*. In later years, Winnicott's sister Violet shared in several letters her spiritual struggles and inquired of Winnicott his thoughts and feelings about religious issues (V. Winnicott, ca. 1941-44; V. Winnicott, n.d.). One might easily suppose that these reflect long-standing patterns in the family involvement in religion.

Winnicott's participation in the religion of his childhood included his attendance at the weekly Sunday services with the family. More specifically, his participation included his walking home from church each week in the company of his father, a ritual that seemed to have been one of the few occasions when the young Winnicott had his father's presence and attention (Phillips, 1988). These walks were remembered with fondness by Winnicott (Rudnytsky, 1991; Winnicott, 1978).

Winnicott's Broader Interaction with His Family

Winnicott taught us that the influence of a family's faith comes through more than formal church practices; it involves the wider interaction of the child with his or her parents, the extended household, and later the whole of culture. To understand how his religious upbringing might have influenced Winnicott, this section explores several stories told by Winnicott and his biographers that give insight into Winnicott's broader interaction with his family.

Interaction with His Father

Winnicott (1978) once said of his father that he was there "to kill and be killed" (p. 24). In this language lifted from Winnicott's developmental theory he implied (among other things) that his father was one who was able to set boundaries for his son and able to survive the son's aggression (both inwardly and outwardly) against those boundaries. Not long before he died, Winnicott began a series of notes for an autobiography (Winnicott, 1978). From those notes one gets a picture of the young Winnicott and his relationship with his father. In his autobiographical notes Winnicott told a story that showed something of his push against his father and his father's survival.

Winnicott noted that when he was three his father teased him about his affection for one of his sister's dolls named "Rosie." Winnicott stated, "I knew the doll had to be altered for the worse" and so Winnicott took his croquet mallet and flattened the nose of the doll. He seems to have been both relieved temporarily from the source of his torment but also distressed at his destructiveness. He wrote:

> I was perhaps somewhat relieved when my father took a series of matches and, warming up the wax nose enough, remolded it so that the face once more became a face. This early demonstration of the restitutive and reparative act certainly made an impression on me, and perhaps made me able to accept the fact that I myself, dear innocent child, had actually become violent directly with a doll, but indirectly with my good-tempered father who was just then entering my conscious life. (Winnicott, 1978, p. 23)

Winnicott is writing of course from the perspective of a theorist who has much to say about the emergence of guilt feelings in children, and about the reparative gesture that can be made after a child reaches the "stage of concern" (Winnicott, 1950a). Despite Winnicott's positive gloss on his father's behavior and his interpolation of later theory onto this early event, one gleans something of the quality of interaction between Winnicott and his father. He remembers his father as "good-tempered" and yet one sees some insensitivity to his son's distress in the teasing. Phillips (1988) suggested that describing his father as a "good-tempered" "teaser" expressed the ambivalence that so characterized the oedipal struggle to which Winnicott alluded.

In the autobiographical notes, Winnicott told another story that illustrated his father's ability to set limits on his son's behavior. He noted that when he was twelve, he sat down to midday dinner one day and said the word "drat." His father "looked pained as only he could look, blamed my mother for not seeing to it that I had decent friends, and from that moment he prepared himself to send me away to boarding school" (Winnicott, 1978, p. 23). While the father's decision to send his son to boarding school was multiply determined as noted later, one gets again a glimpse into the relationship of the father with the son. Here again, Winnicott tells this story with a favorable gloss on his father's actions that also is perhaps indicative of ambivalence. "'Drat' sounds very small as a swear word, but he was right; the boy who was my new friend was no good, and he and I could have got into trouble if left to our own devices" (p. 23). And yet, from his description of his father's "pained" look and his subsequent actions, one also gets a sense of a son familiar with a father who conveyed in his expressions a certain strictness about what was allowed to his son.

Though mild, "drat" seems a way of pushing against the father's strictness, a movement common to the teen years (Erikson, 1968), and perhaps a venture in expressing aggression. There seems to have been other pushes against a house perhaps restrictive because of its moral and religious background (Kahr, 1996; Phillips, 1988; Rodman, 2003). For instance, at the age of nine, Winnicott remembered looking in the mirror and thinking himself "too nice" and purposing to be less so. He acted this decision out by messing his notebooks and letting his grades fall (Khan, 1975; Winnicott, 1983).

The extent to which one should attribute a whole relational ethos to such singular incidents is debatable. Nevertheless, Rodman (2003) commented that Winnicott's "subsequent career, featuring the absence of the father in his extensive theorizing about childhood, leads us to believe that whatever comes down to us anecdotally in the form of 'drat' constituted a deeper and more enduring issue than the passing phase of adolescence" (p. 24). What is clear is that while Winnicott's relationship with his father clearly has some positive tones, especially in his remembrance of his interaction with his father around religious questions, there are also indications that Winnicott found his father somewhat insensitive to and unreceptive of his feelings. In further remarks about his father, one discerns a disappointment, particularly regarding his father's absence. Although his father is "there to kill and be killed" in some ways, in other ways he is "not there" for his son. As Winnicott noted "in the early years he left me too much to all my mothers" and "things never quite righted themselves" (Winnicott, 1978, p. 24). Perhaps one also detects in the father's blaming of the mother for Winnicott's absence of decent friends a lack of the father's involvement in the son's social interactions; this seems a task left primarily to the mother.

Interactions with His Mother

As with her religious activities, less is known of Elizabeth Winnicott's general nature than of Frederick Winnicott. From his autobiographical notes, Winnicott has left several stories of his interaction with his father. He left no similar reminiscences of his interaction with his mother. Although a handful of letters written home from boarding school survive that give some indication of how the young Winnicott interacted with his mother (Rodman, 2003), as an adult Winnicott says almost nothing of his own mother in the hundreds of pages he devoted to the role of mothers. At one point, he expressed a "fully informed and fully felt acknowledgment for his mother and her bountifulness" (Winnicott, 1957d, p. 143), but gave no specific details as to his own mothering.

There are two images of Winnicott's mother that one encounters in the biographical material. One image comes primarily from the memoir by Clare (Winnicott, 1978) and casts Elizabeth Winnicott as a woman of "vitality" and "sense of humor" (p. 21). The other image is of a woman who suffered (at least intermittent) bouts of depression. This image comes from several sources including a poem by Winnicott himself.

Clare Winnicott described Winnicott's mother as "vivacious" and "outgoing" (Winnicott, 1978, p. 21). One must assume these descriptions come from conversations with her husband and his family, since Clare Winnicott would not have known Elizabeth Winnicott personally, the later having died in 1925, long before Clare met her husband in 1941. That Elizabeth Winnicott could be a pleasant woman is substantiated by Rodman's (2003) interviews with one of Winnicott's childhood friends who described Mrs. Winnicott as a "loving woman" "extremely kind" who "tolerated the boys' habit of moving the furniture, including a grand piano, around in the drawing room." He further remembered Mrs. Winnicott "coming down the large staircase in the morning clapping her hands, as if to strike a pleasant note for the day" (p. 13).

That Elizabeth Winnicott also suffered from depression is most poignantly noted in a poem written by Winnicott late in his life. He sent the poem to his brother-in-law with a note that said, "Do you mind seeing this that hurt coming out of me. I think it had some thorns sticking out somehow. It's not happened to me before & I hope it doesn't again" (quoted in Phillips, p. 29). The poem was called "The Tree" and included these lines (also quoted in Phillips):

Mother below is weeping
   weeping
   weeping

Thus I knew her

Once, stretched out on her lap
 as now on dead tree
I learned to make her smile
  to stem her tears
  to undo her guilt
  to cure her inward death

To enliven her was my living.
(By permission of The Marsh Agency Ltd on behalf of The Winnicott Trust)

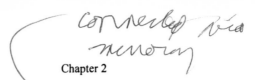

This poem has multiple roles in understanding the role of religion in Winnicott's life, and more will be said about it later. In the larger context of the poem, the tree referred to is the Cross and Winnicott clearly identifies with the Christ in certain ways (Rodman, 2003). Here, however, it is sufficient to note that the poem refers to a type of interaction between Winnicott and his mother in which she does not seem to note the child stretched out upon her lap. Rather, it is the child who must attend to the mother's feelings.

Other evidence that Elizabeth Winnicott was depressed comes from Marion Milner, a former colleague of Winnicott, who commented to Linda Hopkins that both she and Winnicott had depressed mothers (Hopkins, 2004). Rodman (2003) described several letters of the young Winnicott written to his mother from boarding school in which he tried to cheer his mother through humorous accountings of school activities. Rodman especially noted a letter that gave his mother directions for finding a Mother's Day present left for her while Winnicott was home on break as indicating a boy trying to "enliven" his mother's day. Rodman wondered if Winnicott's well-known penchant to play the "clown" as an adult found its origins in learning to enliven a depressed mother.

Winnicott would write of the impact of a depressed mother on the child in two of his essays. In one article he observed that children with depressed mothers have not only to contend with the mother's mood but that the "delightful" child was often a response to the mother's inner "deadness" (Winnicott, 1948b). In another essay, he wrote that the child of a depressed mother can feel "infinitely dropped" (1960d, p. 75). To what extent he is describing his own experience is not known. That he carried some deficit from his mother's depression might be seen in his lifelong struggle to feel "alive" and "real" and to "enliven" for himself the ideas he encountered (Goldman, 1993). How these interactions with his mother may have influenced Winnicott's religious sensibilities is a topic taken up later.

Interactions with the Rest of the Household

In his autobiographical notes, Winnicott once remarked that in his early years his father had left him "too much to all my mothers" (Winnicott, 1978, p. 24). This is a reference to all the women of the Winnicott household who seem to have doted on the young Winnicott, the last child and only boy in the family (Winnicott, 1978, 1983). Winnicott's sister Kathleen once wrote to Winnicott of these years that "you were so much loved and you were such a darling little boy" (K. Winnicott, 1966). There seems to have been little male influence in his life up until about seven, when two male cousins may have lived for a time in the same house (Rodman, 2003).

In addition to his mother, the Winnicott household consisted of two sisters, who had some care of the brother five and six years younger; a nanny hired specifically for Winnicott's care; a governess for his sisters; an aunt who lived in the home for a period during his younger years; the cook, with whom he seemed to have spent a good deal of time as well; and several parlourmaids (Rodman, 2003; Winnicott, 1983). Clare noted that even as an adult, Winnicott often made his way to the kitchen when in a new place (Winnicott, 1983).

With the exceptions of the walks home from church with his father, he seems to have passed most of his time in the presence of all these "mothers." Even so, Winnicott does not give any specifics about his "mothering." From his interactions with all these women, Winnicott received a kind of mothering that led to a life that interestingly enough was devoted to understanding the mother and her role in early childhood development.

Influence of Religion on the Household

Having looked at the nature of the piety of Winnicott's parents the question of how this piety seems to have influenced the household and how it was run demands attention. How did the family's religion function within this household?

Unites the Family

In her recollections of conversations with her husband about his family's religious practice, Clare Winnicott (1983) spoke of the role of religion in uniting the family. "It was sort of a binding force within the family, their religion" (p. 181). Participation in the weekly Sunday services was a shared activity of the entire family. One can easily imagine that the various civic and church activities that the father and family were involved in contributed to the content of family conversations. These activities inform the content of letters exchanged by Winnicott and his family for years; it is no stretch to see them as a focal point of the family during Winnicott's early years. Winnicott (1969d) once remarked that his exposure to the "cultural life" prior to his attendance at public school came only in the form of his "evangelical" religion. One might readily conclude with Goldman (1993) that "religion was the core of the family's cultural life" (p. 116).

Shapes the Moral Character of the Home

From Clare Winnicott's (1983) remark about religion binding the family together, one assumes that religion not only bound the family together in shared activities but shared values as well. Thus, one might think of the family religion as shaping the moral character of the household. This shows up in several ways. Frederick Winnicott's decision to send his son to boarding school is motivated in part by his concern for his son's moral character, as evidenced by his saying "drat" and his choice of friends. His choice of boarding school also seems motivated in part because of the school's reputation as a "staunch" Methodist school in which "religion featured prominently" (Kahr, 1996, p.20). Frederick Winnicott's involvement with the theological schools would have made him familiar with their regimens.   .

One also can see the influence of a Wesleyan Methodist sense of moral duty in Frederick Winnicott's involvement in civic obligations. From Wesley's time, the Methodists had placed a strong emphasis on the importance of ministering to and making better the community to which one belonged. Several of Frederick Winnicott's civic activities such as his interests in libraries (Rodman, 2003) can be seen as similar to the Methodist focus on building clinics and schools in their communities (Heitzenrater, 1995; Runyon, 1998).

Frederick Winnicott's involvement as Steward in his local church is also indicative of the Wesleyan influence on care of the community. "Many Societies organized what they called a Strangers' Friend Society which, according to Wesley's instructions, had the express purpose to be 'wholly for the relief not of our society but for poor, sick, friendless strangers'" (Runyon, 1998, p. 124 quoting Wesley, 1790a, p. 49). One recalls that the Steward was appointed to manage these funds for reaching out to those who were not members of the Methodist Societies.

Another way that religion may have influenced the moral tone of the Winnicott household is in the restrictive manner in which swearing, anger, and sexuality were addressed, or rather, not addressed. Frederick Winnicott's reaction to his son saying "drat" has been noted. This reaction suggests household restrictions around the use of "swear words." Goldman (1993) further suggested "that within the Winnicott household there was not much room for the direct expression of anger" (p. 40). This restriction may have received reinforcement from Wesley's (1777) view that anger was sinful. Rodman (2003) illustrated the restrictive way in which sexuality was acknowledged in the Winnicott household by telling a story about Winnicott being weaned early because it caused his mother too much excitement. He further pointed to a "blank spot" in Winnicott's theory in terms of his omission of the sexuality of the mother in his elaboration of her role as nurturer (p. 22). The sexually restrictive nature of the Winnicott household may not be due entirely to their religious background, and one must not make too much of this point. However, the description of the two Winnicott daughters by friends as "saintly" hints that their decision not to marry, and perhaps remain virginal throughout their life, while multiply determined, may have included a religious dimension (p. 17).

Winnicott commented in later years about the role of religion as a chief conveyor of moral values (1963j). He further commented on the need to appreciate the appropriate developmental timing for the introduction of moral values and the importance of not imposing moral values in such a way that the child's own natural moral gestures were undercut. Whether he spoke from personal experience in his own home about the influence of religion on morals is speculative. His father was rather strict in the behavior allowed to the son; whether religion was the prime impetus for this strictness is uncertain, although it is not unreasonable to assume it played a role.

Contributes to the Equanimity of the Home

In her memoir, Clare Winnicott (1978) said of the Winnicott home that "there were no 'tragedies' . . . only amusing episodes" (p. 22). To illustrate this she told how the water tank once burst, flooding the house. Instead of becoming distressed at this incident, the occasion was treated as an adventure. While she was aware that the picture she painted of the Winnicott household might seem to the reader too good to be true, she nevertheless affirmed "but the truth is that it was good, and try as I will I cannot present it in any other light" (1978, p. 25). Goldman (1993) summarized, "The extended Winnicott household was blessed with what appears to have been a generally cheerful disposition. They were all endowed with an irrepressible sense of humor" (pp. 35–36). Kahr (1996) also noted that the Winnicott household was characterized by a calm reliability: "on the whole, Winnicott seems to have enjoyed a fairly solid and predictable childhood. He suffered no bereavements or physical losses, he had no younger siblings to displace him, and he experienced tremendous continuity and consistency" (p. 7).

It is fair to ask the sources of this equanimity. Although Goldman (1993) suggested it may be partly attributable to the family's supposed inability to express anger (cf. the father's reaction to the word "drat"), one must conclude that it flowed from other sources as well.[3]

The Winnicott household was one characterized by a high degree of financial and physical security. Their house was quite large, and the father's mercantile store very successful. They were leading citizens of town and church. They were "so much an integral part of the land and community that a village was eventually named for them" (Goldman, 1993, p. 37). This connection to people and place gave them a deep confidence that characterized their approach to life.

Goldman (1993) observed that one should not underestimate the social order of Plymouth in the late nineteenth and early twentieth century as a kind of "holding environment" for the Winnicott family. "The continuity of the family's existence . . . was ensured by . . . a social setting that the Winnicotts perceived as a natural extension of themselves. . . . The wider social circle enabled the Winnicott family to feel safe" (p. 37–38).

As a holding environment, one should not forget that the heritage of Plymouth to which the Winnicotts belonged and participated in included a deep religious dimension that was memorialized to some extent by Sir Frederick's monument to the Pilgrim's egress. Given the religiousness of the household, one might reasonably ask to what extent the religious atmosphere could have contributed to this sense of equanimity. There are several indications that it played a role.

One indicator of religion as a contributor to the equanimity of the family is Rodman's (2003) observation that Frederick Winnicott did not undergo a crisis of faith that many of his time did after the introduction of Darwin's ideas. While the reason for the lack of crisis may be multiple (he may not allow questions, or he may not have held his faith in a dogmatic way), the lack of crisis likely made his religion a stabilizing force for him and perhaps by extension for his family.

In turning to Winnicott's mother, one wonders about the contributions to Elizabeth Winnicott's sense of vivacity? How does a woman who struggled with depression find this kind of equanimity? Might religion have played a role in this? We do not know for certain, but the Wesleyan Methodist faith has core beliefs that would certainly contribute to a sense of equanimity in the world. One of Wesley's (1738c) core teachings concerned the abundance of God's grace ("grace upon grace," p. 118). God's grace not only pardoned, it empowered. "As soon as ever the grace of God (in the former sense, his pardoning love) is manifested to our soul, the grace of God (in the later sense, the power of his Spirit) takes place therein. And now we can perform, through God, what to man was impossible" (Wesley, 1746e, p.309). One wonders whether Winnicott might have had his mother in mind when he commented on the ability of the Christian religion to help people recognize "sadness, despair, hopelessness" and to cope with these through the "ascensive" experiences of religion (Winnicott, 1935, p. 135)?

There was a piano in the home, and Rodman (2003) noted that Winnicott had learned to play the piano as a child. His sisters also were musically talented and one might assume an encouragement toward music in the home (Kahr, 1996). While in his adult years Winnicott enjoyed a variety of music and activities (Rodman, 2003), Kahr asserted that "of his many hobbies, Winnicott derived most pleasure from music, especially singing and playing the piano" (p. 104). Kahr recorded that a close friend of Winnicott told him "Winnicott loved to sing to himself whenever he walked up or down the stairs, preferring the church hymns of his Wesleyan Methodist childhood" (p. 105). (The stairs were those in his house where he had his office for seeing patients.) Might this love of Wesleyan Methodist hymns come from early exposure to such, not only in the church where his father sang in the choir, but to the singing of hymns at home? There is no concrete evidence of this, but it is a distinct possibility. After all, Wesley's theology found its way into the hearts of the Methodist people because it was sung as much as it was preached, thanks to the six thousand hymns of his brother Charles (Chilcote, 2004). If clapping her hands was a way that Elizabeth Winnicott warded off tendencies toward depression (Rodman, 2003), might religion have been employed in a similar way? It is interesting to speculate whether a hymn such as Charles Wesley's "Wrestling Jacob" might have helped Elizabeth Winnicott to face the day in much the same way as clapping her hands:

'Tis Love! 'Tis Love! Thou diedst for me;
    I hear thy whisper in my heart.
The morning breaks, the shadows flee,

Pure Universal Love thou art;
To me, to all, thy mercies move—
Thy nature, and thy name is LOVE (Wesley, 1780, p. 251).

Allows Freedom of Thought

Another way that religion shaped the character of the Winnicott household is through its allowance for a certain freedom of thought where religious matters were concerned. In an interview with Michael Neve, Clare Winnicott (1983) described the Winnicotts' religion as very freeing and non-oppressive. "I think nonconformism meant a lot to them all . . . but it wasn't a hard, strict religion. They were very . . . very free" (p. 181). She further stated that the nature of religion in the Winnicott household permitted questions. "I mean, this is the point about nonconformists anyway. He was allowed to question and he did" (pp. 181).

To illustrate her point that the Winnicotts were not dogmatic in their way of being religious, Clare Winnicott told the story of Winnicott walking home from church with his father and of a particular conversation they had. "Walking home one day with his father from church, Donald started to get him to talk about religion—asked him about something—his father replied, 'Listen, my boy. You read the Bible—what you find there. And you decide for yourself what you want, you know. It's free. You don't have to believe what I think. Make up your own mind about it. Just read the Bible'" (Winnicott, 1983, p. 181). This story followed her comment about the family not being "strict" with their religion, but rather "very free" and is clearly designed to illustrate this point.

Several of Winnicott's biographers appropriate Clare's description of the family's way of being religious as one that allowed a freedom to think about religious matters (Goldman, 1993; Jacobs, 1995; Kahr, 1996; Phillips, 1988, Rodman, 2003). Usually the point drawn is that there was a lack of dogmatism in the way the Winnicotts expressed their religion and that this non-dogmatic way of being religious influenced a later aversion to dogmatism in Winnicott, whether it occurred in religion or psychoanalysis. For instance, Winnicott's (1954d) own admission that he is one who can "no more stand the falsity of a rigid system in psychology than [he] can tolerate it in religion" (p. 72) is traced back to the non-dogmatic way in which the Winnicotts expressed their religion (cf. Goldman, Kahr, Rodman).

Often central to this description of the Winnicotts' religion as non-dogmatic is the story of Winnicott's walks home with his father and the conversation in which he is told to read the Bible for himself and to find his own answers. This story has taken on "mythic" proportions in Winnicott biography. All the major biographers tell this story and Rudnytsky (1991) went so far as to call the story a "parable" which he used to illustrate the differences in Winnicott's walk with his father and a similar walk that Freud had with his father. The story perhaps illustrates Michael Jacobs' (1995) point that the sources for Winnicott's early life are "disappointingly repetitious" because they turn out to be "based for the most part on the reminiscences of his second wife, Clare Winnicott" (p. 2). While Rodman's (2003) more substantial biography has helped address the larger issue of a paucity of childhood stories about Winnicott, it does not do more than repeat this particular story.

Since the story is repeated so often and quite obviously to illustrate and justify a later personal quality in Winnicott, the story requires a more critical assessment than has currently appeared. What is one to make of this "parable" of Winnicott's early religious upbringing? What is known of its origins and what people have made of it?

The story as recounted above comes from an interview of Clare Winnicott by Michael Neve in 1983 which was transcribed and later published by Rudnytsky (1991). In Clare's telling of the story the point about the walks home from church is to illustrate that young Winnicott was accorded a special privilege and sense of favor from his father. The inclusion of the conversation that occurs on one of these walks is clearly intended to illustrate the point that Frederick Winnicott gave his son freedom to find his own way toward religious truth. It is from Clare Winnicott that one gets the sense that this conversation happened when Winnicott was young ("my boy") and that it occurred on one of the walks home from church.

Clare stated she got the information about the walks home from church in conversations with her husband. "I remember him saying one day, he always walked home from church with his father. That was his privilege, because he was very much the youngest in the family. This was the important thing about him" (Winnicott, 1983, p. 180). One assumes from her remarks that the characterization of the walks as a time of privilege was one disclosed by her husband. Her further noting that his being given the privilege because he was the youngest and that this revealed something important about his place in the family may have come from his assessment although this may be her own interpretation. Phyllis Grosskurth (1986) reported that Clare used to tell her husband "that he knew from the moment he opened his eyes on the world that he was loved, and that she teased him that he suffered from 'benignity'" (p. 399).

Does Clare also get the idea that the conversation with his father about religion occurred on one of the walks home from church from talking with her husband or is this idea an interpolation and elaboration of a brief story told by Winnicott himself in the autobiographical notes he had prepared shortly before his death? These notes are the source of the brief remarks about Winnicott's interactions with his father described earlier and are shared by Clare in a memoir about her husband (Winnicott, 1978). In these notes Winnicott disclosed that "my father had a simple (religious) faith and once when I asked him a question that could have involved us in a long argument he just said: read the Bible and what you find there will be the true answer for you. So I was left, thank God, to get on with it myself" (Winnicott, 1978, p. 23). In her sharing of the notes in this earlier reflection Clare made no elaboration of this brief story that offered no indication of the location or the age at which the conversation occurred. Are there two incidents with similar conversations or is this simply a shorter version of the same memory?

It appears that the autobiographical note is the source for Clare's later interview remarks about his father's comment to his son. This creates a problem when one notes that Clare said in this earlier memoir that she did not discover the autobiographical notes until after Winnicott died (Winnicott, 1978). To what extent Clare's reminiscences in 1983 are interpolations on the autobiographical notes or veridical memories from additional conversations with her husband cannot be known at this point, but the former seems the most likely.[4]

Rudnytsky's (1991) characterization of the story as "parable" suggests that one finds the "truth" of the story in its function.[5] The differences in the two constructions are of interest. Besides the absence of location and age in Winnicott's version (both of which appear in Clare's version), what is of more import is the difference in context and purpose when compared to Clare's. Gone is the sense of privilege because the context of the walk home from church is missing. Even more telling, is that Winnicott used the story to illustrate his father's "simple religious faith." Winnicott's version may also illustrate a lack of dogmatism, but that is less certain.

However, as with all the stories that come from Winnicott's autobiographical notes there is a certain ambiguity that attends to this story. That the positively framed remembrance of his bashing the face of the doll Rosie contained intimations of his father insensitively "teasing" his son has been noted. Similarly, his positive remembrance of his father's reaction to his saying "drat" ("he was right") also indicated a severity in the father that did not match the "mild" offense of the son. Here too, one notes the positive affirmation of the father's granting his son the freedom to pursue the reading of the Bible for his own answers. Yet one is also left wondering whether this is a story of dismissal of the son's questions by a pre-occupied and emotionally insensitive or distant father who does not have the time to engage his son in religious discussion, and not simply a story of freedom to think for himself. This conclusion would accord with the observations of Rodman (2003) and Phillips (1988) that Sir Frederick seems to have had little time to spend with his son (other than these walks), given his many civic and church obligations. If the context for the religious discussion was a walk home from church, one would understand the "long discussion" to be one that might exceed the ten minutes of the walk and thus not a topic the busy father was prepared to engage past the time allotted to the walk.

Even more problematic is the question of whether the story is to be read as a negative illustration of his father's simple faith as one that does not tolerate questions well. If so, instead of illustrating a non-dogmatic way of being religious, it might well illustrate the opposite. When Winnicott (1961d) later spoke disparagingly of the "certainty" that belonged to religion versus the scientist's willingness to tolerate gaps in knowing, was he thinking of his father's simple faith (with the further implication that he no longer held to such a simple faith)? There is no way to know for certain, but it is a possibility that must be kept in mind.

Nevertheless, one notes that what both versions share in common is a sense that Winnicott experienced the conversation as granting a certain freedom to pursue his own road toward religious truth. This framing of the story gives a positive atmosphere to both versions and suggests a theme regarding Winnicott's religion that is taken up in a later chapter.

When one turns to the appropriations of this story by Winnicott's biographers, one also gets primarily a positive assessment of this story. It is generally used to illustrate Clare's point about the family's non-dogmatic way of being religious. Kahr (1996) told her version to illustrate how Winnicott "acquired the permission to be free-spirited and unshackled by dogma" (p. 9). Rodman (2003) referred to Clare's version and surmised that this encouragement to "read the Bible and find in it whatever he could as a personal guide" would have "led easily to the freedom that he would one day celebrate in his own brand of thought" (p. 12). Although Goldman told the version from Winnicott's autobiographical notes he connected this primarily to the non-dogmatic, but intensely personal way that the Winnicotts were religious. Jacobs (1995) simply repeated Clare's version and connects it to the non-dogmatic way that the Winnicotts were religious. Phillips (1988) was more balanced in framing the autobiographical account in the context of both Winnicott's strong "inner conviction" and "fierce" protection of his own way of thinking, and his father's tendency to be "severe and belittling in his attitude to his son" (p. 25). Rudnytsky (1991) also shared Clare's version and used the story to illustrate the very positive feelings toward both his father and religion that Winnicott would have associated with this.

So, what is one to make of this "parable?" Clearly Winnicott's own interpretation contained a positive remembrance, but as noted he was apt to gloss over the negative aspects of these remembrances. There is the clear possibility that Frederick Winnicott may not have been as non-dogmatic in his religion as one is led to believe by Clare's interview. Certainly, one sees that he could be restrictive in terms of behavior allowed to his son. Nevertheless, was this lack of freedom in *action* accompanied by a freedom of *thought* allowed around religious matters? This is quite possible; it is clearly a part of the Wesleyan Methodist religion. Although Wesley wrote restrictively about certain behaviors and attitudes (e.g. anger; see Wesley, 1745, 1777), Wesley (1772) also wrote passionately about "the liberty to choose our own religion, to worship God according to our own conscience, according to the best light we have. Every man living . . . has a right to this. . . . And every man must judge for himself, because every man must give account of himself to God" (p. 37). Frederick Winnicott's words to his son seem clearly to capture this personal choice dimension to one's spirituality. One is left to conclude that while his father could be very restrictive in terms of behavior, he granted to his son some measure of freedom regarding religious ideas. Thus, religion as embodied in the Winnicott household seemed to allow a freedom of thought even if curtailing other freedoms.

Influence of His Childhood Religion on Winnicott

The nature of the Wesleyan Methodist piety that characterized the Winnicott household has been explored and this chapter has tried to place this within the larger context of Winnicott's broader interactions with his family. This section now offers some thoughts on what the young Winnicott seems to have taken away from the religious atmosphere of the home in which he grew up.

Religion as Something Personal

Winnicott appears to take from his upbringing the notion that religion is deeply personal. One reads the Bible for one's own answers; the truth of religion is not to be found in someone else's explanations. This idea seems to translate into the adult Winnicott's notion that he must make ideas come alive for himself; it is not sufficient to simply parrot the words of his teachers and mentors (cf. Khan, 1975). Winnicott did not feel real when he did this. His confession that he felt compelled to find his own way of expressing ideas may owe part of its origin to the Wesleyan Methodist encouragement toward personal experience (Winnicott, 1953a). Religion is not defined by prescribed beliefs and practices, but by the more personal living out of its ideals.

Religion as Something Basically Positive

The next thing to note is that Winnicott takes away from this upbringing a notion of religion as something basically positive, an attitude that remained throughout Winnicott's life. The sources of this positive attitude were multiple and mutually reinforcing.

As noted above, Winnicott made very positive associations to religion in that it was connected to one of the few times he had his father to himself. Religion, for the young Winnicott is associated with positive times and a sense of special favor. It was his privilege to walk home from church with his father, and the one remembrance of engaging his father around a religious question left him with a feeling of freedom to pursue his own path toward religious truth (even if it also contained hints of dismissal). These walks were clearly opportunities for the young Winnicott to observe his father's way of being religious. Despite the implied criticism that his father's faith is not more complex, his statement about his father's simple faith seems to confirm that Winnicott viewed his father's faith as genuine and sincere. He does not describe it as a faith contrived for social advantage or convenience. In his comparisons of Winnicott's walk home with his father with a similar walk by Freud with his father, Rudnytsky (1991) pointed out that the young Winnicott took from this both positive feelings about his father and about religion.[6]

Another source of Winnicott's positive attitude toward religion and its role in life and culture is his observation of its contributions to the cohesiveness and equanimity in his family. From his family example, he likely came to understand, both at the conscious and unconscious level, the ability of religion to provide a stable "holding" environment. He also may have experienced religion as contributing to a joie de vivre that helps one turn "tragedies" to "adventures." It is possible that he observed the singing of hymns as one way religion contributed to the positive atmosphere in the home. He certainly knew from his father's example something of the ability of religion to motivate the betterment of the community. When Winnicott (1951b) wrote in his pivotal essay on transitional phenomena about the creative and adaptive aspects of religion (even though as a psychoanalyst he also was aware of the ways in which religion could be abused), it is reasonable to assume that he drew upon memories of early experiences of religion in his own household.

In his later years, Winnicott (1971a) argued that psychology needed to explore the question of "what life itself is about," a rather religious sounding question (p. 98). His answer centered in a capacity to "be," a sense of being "alive" or "real" which evolved out of the ability to "play." All these terms get elaborated in Winnicott's theory and are explored more fully later. What is important to note here is that the ability to play as an adult leads to cultural expressions, including that of religion. Thus, religion has the potential to be life-giving and freeing. Winnicott certainly experienced in some measure the non-coercive, freeing capacity of religion in his father's encouragement to read the Bible for himself.

But Not Always Positive

Although Winnicott's overall assessment of religion pointed to its creative and adaptive functions, this is not the total picture. He was well aware that religion could be used in defensive and obsessional ways (e.g., as a defense against the fear of dying, or as rituals to ward off other anxieties. See Winnicott 1963e, 1968i). In his own home he quite possibly encountered religion's role in restricting certain behaviors (e.g., saying "drat" and expressing sexual feelings or anger). Although less certain, he may also have met some rigidity of belief in his father's "simple faith." If Winnicott did not meet religion in its more dogmatic forms in his own home, he certainly became acquainted with and aversive to such expressions later in his life.

The Question of "God Images"

Before concluding this chapter on Winnicott's early years at home, the question of "God images" deserves attention. Winnicott's pioneering work on transitional objects led him to speculate about the formation of "God concepts" in the young child (Winnicott 1951b, 1963j). He argued that ideas or images about God have their beginnings in one's interactions with one's primary caregivers, and later expand to include ideas from one's interactions with the larger household and society. It therefore becomes intriguing to ask what "God concepts" Winnicott may have taken away from his religious upbringing and his interactions within his home. What images of God emerged from his interactions with a sometimes depressed mother, or from a father who was alternately teasing and good-natured? How did the care of his many "mothers" contribute to concepts about God? Given Winnicott's own work in this area it is natural to wonder. A later chapter takes up these most intriguing questions.

Notes

1.   In reflecting on the extent that Sir Frederick Winnicott's religion influenced his life, one might note that according to former employees he was very conservative in terms of the wages offered. As one former employee remarked, one "had to ask Sir Frederick individually, Oliver Twist style, for any increase" (Rodman, 2003, p. 384). Whether this conservatism with wages was influenced (or not) by his religious beliefs is hard to know at this point. For instance, does one see this behavior as displaying a lack of consideration or did he see learning to ask for oneself an expression of the strong character valued by the dissenting tradition?

2.   All citations to Wesley's works are to *The Bicentennial Edition of the Works of John Wesley* (Nashville, TN: Abingdon Press and NY: Oxford University Press) where available. Citations to sources not yet available in the *Bicentennial Edition* are noted in the references.

3.   Whether the reluctance to express anger was more temperamentally derived or also influenced by Sir Frederick's religion is not easily answered. Although in his treatise on "Christian Perfection" Wesley (1777) conceded that there might be a righteous anger "at sin," he generally treated anger and its expression as something sinful and from which one should refrain (cf. "A person may be sincere who has all his natural tempers, pride, anger, lust, self-will. But he is not perfect till his heart is cleansed from these, and all its other corruptions" (p. 418). Furthermore, love "expels all anger from the heart," p. 416). Thus, there is a strong sentiment in the Methodist tradition to regard most anger as sin. However, people also are drawn to religious expressions that match their temperament (James, 1902) so that Sir Frederick's great attraction for Wesleyan Methodism may have temperamental motivations in part. Whatever the source for the reluctance to express anger what is clear is that Winnicott's household bequeathed to him a lifelong struggle in terms of how to express his aggression, or what he sometimes called his "hate" (Rodman, 1987, 2003).

4.   When one compares comments from the interview with points made in the earlier memoir, one clearly get the sense that Clare draws upon the autobiographical notes in addressing some of Neve's questions. For instance, both the memoir and the interview share several stories in common. There is the story about the father's advice to "read the Bible" as well as the "drat" story, and comments of the headmaster that Winnicott was "not brilliant." Both include the story of Winnicott's earlier plans to be a GP before going into pediatrics, a friend's comment that the Winnicotts "play," and remarks about his love

of Bach among several others. What is noticeable is that the interview often elaborates on (and moderately changes) something said in the memoir. For instance, in the memoir, Winnicott's decision not to be a GP is said to evolve from his discovery of psychoanalysis and his recognition that he would need to stay in London in order to be analyzed. In the interview one is given the further information that not becoming a GP broke a promise to his first wife (perhaps to live in the country—see Rodman [2003]), and that being a pediatrician in London was more attractive to him than being a GP in the country.

By the time Clare does the interview, she has known the stories from the autobiographical notes for five years. Furthermore, the earlier memoir makes it plain that some material from these notes was clearly new to her; i.e., not known before Winnicott's death (Winnicott, 1978). She also remarked that there were times when Winnicott "related with amusement" stories of his earlier life. Whether she may have known earlier versions of the "read the Bible" story from such conversations is unknown. From comparing the information in the autobiographical notes with that shared by Clare in the interview with Neve, I am inclined to think she did not and that she has interpolated this information from the autobiographical notes back into conversations about Winnicott's childhood walks home with his father.

5.   In terms of function one also notes that this "parable" is reminiscent of the stories in the Hebrew Bible where the father "blesses" the son (cf. Genesis 49).

6.   The story of Freud's walk with his father is told in his *Interpretation of Dreams* (1900). There Freud recounted that on a walk with his father his father shared a story of being set upon by some anti-Semitic youths who tossed his new hat into the gutter. When Freud heard that his father (rather un-heroically in Freud's mind) simply picked up the hat without confronting the youths, his disappointment is palpable.

Rudnytsky (1991) pointed out how different the outcome in terms of the respective boys' attitudes toward their fathers and how these differences seem to have influenced each in their view of religion. Freud is deeply disappointed with his father's weakness, and gravitated toward a position that found religion weak (especially a religion of the father—see Freud's (1939) *Moses and Monotheism*). Winnicott found the experience with his father deeply freeing, and went on to argue that religion is one of the more freeing, creative activities in which humans engage.

Chapter 3
Winnicott's Religious Development as an Adolescent

"So I was left, thank God, to get on with it myself"

Winnicott related in some unpublished autobiographical notes that when he was twelve he once came home to midday dinner and uttered the word "drat" in front of his father. His father expressed concern as to whether a friend Winnicott had begun to keep company with was contributing to moral laxity in his son and according to Winnicott purposed "from that moment . . . to send me away to boarding school" (Winnicott, 1978, p. 23). The boarding school he referred to was The Leys, a well-respected school established by the Methodists to educate "sons of the middle class" in ways that would not alienate them from "the Church of their fathers" (Rodman, 2003, p.23). Thus, Winnicott's religious upbringing occurred not only in the religion of his immediate home and the Plymouth community, but included exposure to the wider tradition of Wesleyan Methodism embodied in the studies and activities at his boarding school.

Despite Winnicott's remark about the singular determinant of his father's decision to send him away, other factors besides his uttering a "small swear word" contributed to Winnicott being sent to boarding school. Like all decisions this one was multiply determined and it would be nearly two years before Winnicott actually went away. While his father's concern for his son's moral guidance was certainly a factor in this decision, one wonders whether his father also may have recognized something in his son's behavior that needed a different environment to thrive. Winnicott once remarked of his early childhood that his father had "left me too much to all my mothers" and "things never quite righted themselves" (Winnicott, 1978, p. 24). The father's decision may have taken into account his son's growing need to differentiate from all his "mothers" and to find alternative male companionships (Rodman, 2003). Winnicott (1960f) wrote that a family contributed to the emotional maturity of the individual in two ways: (1) by providing continuing opportunities for dependence, and (2) by providing opportunities for the individual to differentiate first from parents and then from the family to identify with larger social units. In her memoir and interview, Clare Winnicott (1978, 1983), pointed to his going off to boarding school as one of the means by which Winnicott learned to differentiate himself from his tight-knit family.

This chapter will trace the influence of Winnicott's Wesleyan Methodist heritage as seen in his exposure to and participation in various religious activities as an adolescent. It is clear that his time at boarding school deepened the influences of his Wesleyan Methodist upbringing in some ways while also providing a means for him to "get on with" thinking for himself, both about religion and other issues of life.

Winnicott's Religious Participation at The Leys

Sir Frederick's choice of boarding school to help shape the moral character of his son was The Leys School, founded in 1867 with W. F. Moulton as its first headmaster. Moulton was a famous biblical scholar, descended from a long line of Methodist ministers, whose *Concordance on the Greek language* is still used by scholars. Rodman (2003) helps one get a sense of this school during Winnicott's time there:

> The Leys was the first Methodist public school. It is the school described in James Hilton's novel, *Goodbye Mr. Chips*. The master on whom Mr. Chips was based, W.H. Balgarnie (an expert on "Fives"), was teaching at the school in those days. Balgarnie represented a whole side of the Leys that was encouraging to its students. It was not a place characterized by the same sort of bullying that typified other public schools. (p. 24)

As noted above, The Leys was a school founded to promote Methodist piety while providing a sound educational foundation for university (Pritchard, 1983; Rodman, 2003). Kahr (1996) noted that "Frederick Winnicott would have held The Leys School in very high regard, because of its staunch and long-standing tradition of English Methodism and its status as a very respectable school for the middle classes" (p.14).

A Holistic Curriculum

The curriculum at The Leys was one in which religion, academics, and athletics came together. This holistic focus embodied Wesley's concerns not only for the salvation of "souls" but for the physical and mental well-being of people (e.g., his founding of clinics and schools in addition to conducting his preaching tours). Runyon (1998) stated that Wesley's was "an evangelism based not on the hard sell but the inherent attractiveness of a holistic concern for persons at the point of their need" (p. 125). Kahr (1996) described life at The Leys during Winnicott's days there:

Dr. Moulton had created an environment in which scholarship, religion, and athletics could be pursued simultaneously. At the time of Donald Winnicott's stay there, the boys would have been awakened early in their dormitory rooms by the clanging of a bell. Breakfast and morning chapel would be followed by an hour of academic lessons. After a period of gymnastic activities, they would then proceed to luncheon. After the midday meal, the students would have a further hour of academic work, with additional playtime afterwards. Between 4:30 p.m. and 6:30 p.m., the boys attended two further periods of lessons, and then, following dinner in the Hall, there would be evening preparation from 7:05 p.m. until 7:35 p.m., and evening prayers. On Wednesdays and Saturdays, the boys enjoyed special half-days. (p. 14; from Baker, 1975)

Winnicott participated very fully in the activities offered at The Leys including academic courses, sporting events, and spiritual activities. The Leys was a place for him to experience firsthand the holistic attention to body, mind and spirit, all of which are God's gift according to Wesley. In a holistic curriculum such divisions are artificial in that all these processes are interrelated and contribute to the maturation of the whole person. Nevertheless, they provide a rubric for reviewing Winnicott's various involvements while at The Leys.

Academic Achievements

Winnicott was involved in a variety of academic pursuits. These included not only his course work, but participation in several academic clubs. He was a member of the Debate club, the Biology club and the choir. He participated in the Speech awards day and won the top speech award in his last year. He also wrote two award-winning essays for the school newspaper, *The Leys Fortnightly*, under the editorship of Balgarnie. Kahr (1996) noted that beginning with his second year he nightly read a story to the other boys in the dormitory. In his last year Winnicott won special recognition for his musical abilities on the piano.

The overlap between areas such as the academic and spiritual is seen in the emphasis on moral reasoning and development that was encouraged at The Leys. This aspect of the religious heritage in the curriculum is illustrated by essays that Winnicott wrote for the *Fortnightly*. Rodman (2003) summarized a couple of essays written by Winnicott for the school paper and concluded: "By this time Donald had given a good deal of thought to the relationship between the individual, society, and culture, and in particular to how morality enters into the structure of society and therefore the shaping of individuals within that society" (p. 26). In one prize-winning essay Winnicott wrote of the differences between the English and German temperament and how this impacted the way each country planned and provided for its towns and villages. Although extolling the controlled way town plots were given permits for buildings or parks by the town councilors in Germany, and how this planning contributed to healthier living in some towns, Winnicott remarked that "in England, private feuds would take the place of beautiful buildings, and civil war would be fought in the vast parks." England, he concluded, "must find other methods—though they will not be so direct—for lowering the death-rate and improving the towns" (Winnicott,

1913, p. 28). In another award-winning essay he wrote with humor and clarity on practical ways to help people comprehend the good to which their taxes went (Winnicott, 1914).

Sports Participation

Winnicott also engaged in a variety of sports activities. These activities included playing and being captain of a rugby team, running track, swimming, and playing on the cricket team. He also was Captain of Fives (a game of hitting a ball with one's hands on a court) (*The Leys Fortnightly* V. 38, # 664, Oct 3, 1913). The *Fortnightly* recorded his participation in a couple of rugby games. In one game it was noted that "Winnicott at 7/8 nearly always gained a lot of ground when he got the ball, but failed to pass back inside" (V. 38 # 666 Oct 31, 1913) and of his participation in another game there was this notation: "small, and not clever, but runs hard and defends well" (V. 38, #669 18th Dec 1913). When I visited the archives room at The Leys there was a picture of Winnicott and his rugby team on prominent display.

Winnicott also was an avid runner who at one point had hoped to participate in the Olympics for 1916 until an injury sidetracked this ambition. While at The Leys he ran the half mile and mile race. His last year there he was winner of both races, breaking his own record from the previous year (V. 37 #657 Apr 1, 1913). This attention to the physical body, its growth and care reflects the holistic concern in Wesleyan thought for body and soul as both belonging to the God who gave them. According to a later reflection by Winnicott (1961c) it was a sports injury while at The Leys that helped motivate him for a career in medicine. As we shall see, an aspect of this motivation may have included an appreciation for the holistic nature of humans.

Spiritual Activities

Various religious activities filled the days at The Leys as well. These included chapel attendance, Bible readings and prayers. A new chapel had been constructed five years before Winnicott enrolled and would have been a centerpiece of the campus (Harding, 2006). Named after the first headmaster, Moulton Chapel became a focal point for the spiritual life of The Leys. Kahr (1996) noted, "in addition to academic activities and sporting events, religion featured prominently in the life of this Methodist school. All the pupils were required to attend chapel twice daily for compulsory prayers, once in the morning and once in the evening" (p. 20).

In addition to the general religious life of the college, Winnicott also was active in the Leys Christian Union, a group composed of those boys who were devout (*The Leys Fortnightly*, V. 38 #664, Oct 3, 1913). This same issue contained a note about a debate on warfare and aerial navigation and referred to young Winnicott's enthusiasm and perhaps his devoutness by noting "the best speech was by J. L. Elmslie, while DWW[innicott] allowed himself to be carried away into a detailed description of the Palace of Peace, the point of which was somewhat doubtful." In a letter written to correct the notion that he had been a parson at one time, Winnicott (1954e) remarked of this time in his life: "This is not to deny that I was religious as an adolescent because I certainly was."

On the day that Winnicott gave his award-winning speech, he would have heard a sermon on giving one's best for Christ's service by Harrington Lees, an Old Leysian invited back for this occasion. The summary of the sermon from *The Leys Fortnightly* gives a glimpse into the character of the religion at The Leys to which the young Winnicott would have been exposed.

> After the Anthem "O how plentiful is Thy goodness," Mr. Lees preached from Isaiah LX: 17—"For brass I will bring gold." The chapter, said the preacher, was the anthem of the coming of the king, and the prophecy meant when Christ takes command, all values will go up. The Christian's golden age is always in front of him. Perhaps in these words there is a reminiscence of previous history. In the palace of David and Solomon were hung shields and bucklers cast out of pure gold. But these were taken by Shishak, king of Egypt. So, to cover the vacant spaces, Reheboam made brazen shields. For gold he brought brass. This is very like a temptation that is common in school life, as in the larger world. It is easy to substitute conduct for character, outward purity for inward cleanness. This temptation is overcome when Christ reigns in the heart, and so we might say that the prophecy symbolizes three things: First, it tells of the transformation of the unreal into the real. Here Mr. Lees made a fine appeal for genuine decision for Christ, which would make all character and work genuine to the highest degree. Second, it figures the transformation of the good into the best. The clever boy thinks he is well enough equipped without Christ. But he cannot afford to use debased metal when he can have gold for the asking. Third, it speaks of the transformation of the bad in to the best. There followed a strong appeal to the discouraged and disheartened, supported by a fine confession of what the preacher himself owed to the friendship and Lordship of Jesus Christ. (V. 38 #679 July 14, 1914)

In his second year Winnicott joined the "fine choir" that the school boasted, directed by Arthur Mann, also director of music at King's College, Cambridge (Harding, 2006; Kahr, 1996). Although the musical repertoire of the school is not known,[1] one would assume that the choir would sing, at least on occasion, the hymns of Charles Wesley; certainly these hymns would have been a part of the compulsory chapel services.

The singing of hymns would have touched Winnicott on several levels. One level might involve identification with his father who sang in the choir at his home church in Plymouth. The question of whether the hymns were likely part of the Winnicott's activities at home as well has been noted. The hymns of the Methodist church sank deeply into the fabric of Winnicott's being; as an adult he continued to sing this "catechism set to music" to himself between his visits with patients (Hoffman, 2004, p. 775; Kahr, 1996). The singing of Methodist hymns into adulthood may have transported Winnicott briefly to that "intermediate area" one seeks for relief from the strains of life (1951b, p. 240). Winnicott (1951b) noted that such transitional phenomena may include "songs or tunes"

(p. 232). Perhaps Winnicott's preference for singing Methodist hymns established an unconscious continuity with the pleasant associations of his childhood.

Charles Wesley was certainly aware of the ability of music to foster religious sensibilities. It has often been noted that Methodist theology was learned as much from singing it as hearing it preached (Chilcote, 2004; Hoffman, 2004). There was hardly a theme preached by his brother John that Charles Wesley did not set to music. There are hymns extolling God's abundant love and grace, encouraging one to know God, to serve others, to sit at the Lord's Table, to read the Scriptures, to blend good works with faith, to be transformed inwardly and outwardly (Chilcote, 2004). While one cannot know for certain which hymns Winnicott would have sung (and later preferred), noted below are some Methodist hymns that inculcate aspects of the Methodist piety that belonged to Winnicott's religious upbringing and that would have been reinforced at school.[2]

While at The Leys (and later), Winnicott also participated in the Scouts. One might consider this involvement as part of his religious activities although the full range of scouting activities also demonstrated a holistic view of the person. The Scouts were founded by Robert Baden-Powell in 1907. Baden-Powell was a career military officer in the British Army and the son of a minister. While he focused primarily on teaching boys outdoor skills, the Scouting movement had a religious dimension to its mission (cf. the Scout Promise: On my honor I promise that I will do my best to do my duty to God and the King). As a member of the Scouts while at boarding school, Winnicott was involved in working with the poorer children in Cambridge, and occasionally wrote home to his mother about his work there (Rodman, 2003; Winnicott, 1978). He later remembered his work with the Scouts as one of the few things he accomplished while at Cambridge (Winnicott, 1968e). As noted a concern for the poor was a passionate theme in John Wesley's preaching and work (Runyon, 1998).

This last point reminds one again that spiritual activities are not simply adjunctive but that attention to the spiritual lies at the heart of being a whole person for Wesley. There is a personal dimension to such spirituality and this is seen in things like Winnicott's participation in the Christian Union. Organizations like the Christian Union would have emphasized the personal piety of Methodism while also harking back to Wesley's own use of prayer "bands" where early Methodists met to encourage each other in the life of holiness (Maddox, 1994; Runyon, 1998). Winnicott's work with the Scouts would illustrate the social dimension of Wesleyan piety in its emphasis that service to others is service to God. His reading nightly to the other boys in his dorm would be understood in a similar way.

Encounter with Darwin

Winnicott seems to have occasionally neglected the formal academic curriculum; the culprit: his encounter with the writing of Charles Darwin. He said of his discovery of Darwin's *Origin of Species*, "I couldn't leave off reading it, and this got me into serious trouble because it seemed so much more interesting than prep" (Winnicott, 1945e, p. 129). Winnicott developed a strong attachment to the works of Darwin while at The Leys and set about collecting all his books, often writing home for more money to purchase them (Winnicott, 1983). In a reference to quintessential English behavior, he confessed that Darwin was his "cup of tea" (Winnicott, 1967h, p. 574).

The encounter with Darwin changed him irreversibly according to Clare Winnicott (1983) who said his exposure to Darwin was a "revelation to him. It changed his whole life" (p. 182). What fueled this attraction and what were some of the ways in which it changed Winnicott?

A "Method" of Thought

In a reflection on his attraction to Darwin, Winnicott wrote that he was drawn to Darwin's method and to a certain attitude it fostered. "[T]he main thing was that it showed that living things could be examined scientifically, with the corollary that gaps in knowledge and understanding need not scare me. For me this new idea meant a great lessening of tension and consequently a release of energy for work and play" (Winnicott, 1945e, p. 129). This assessment of Darwin's influence is, of course, the reflection of a more mature man looking back and may attribute to the young Winnicott an appreciation not originally there. He did admit, "At the time I did not quite know why it was so important to me" (p. 129).

Nevertheless, this later reflection may capture something of the young boy's delight in discovering a new way of exploring the wonder of the world. Winnicott (1949h) once wrote that "the teaching of biology can be one of the most pleasant and even the most exciting of tasks for the teacher, chiefly because so many children value this introduction to the study of what life is about" (p. 44). While some people "come at the meaning of life" through religion (or history or the classics), some "come at the soul through the body" (p. 44). Is this a bit of self-disclosure? Is he one of those children who "come at the soul through the body"? While at The Leys, Winnicott was a participant in the Biology section of the Natural History Society Committee (*The Leys Fortnightly*, V. 38 #275, May 18, 1914). It seems that part of the attraction to Darwin is that Darwin and the physical sciences provided him a new way to "come at the meaning of life."

Since adolescence is a time of exploration and thinking about questions like the scientific origins of life and the universe (Fowler, 1981), inconsistencies between science and religious teaching (about creation, for instance) often become a source of intellectual curiosity and emotional conflict. There is both delight and pain in finding one's way toward individually satisfying answers. Fowler (1996), for instance spoke of the phenomenon of the "11-year-old-atheist" to describe the rather common experience of the young adolescent coming to terms with the discovery that one does not live in a "quick payoff universe"; that is, there is a recognition that sometimes bad things happen to good people or that bad people do not always get punished for their misdeeds (p. 172). Winnicott's description of two child patients gives evidence to his personal acquaintance with the kinds of questions that arise during this phase of life. He noted one young patient's recognition that people often invoke God to explain phenomena (such as gravity) for which they have no better answer (Winnicott, n.d. 4). Regarding another young patient's inability to accede to an expected belief in God at his school Winnicott responded by trying to help the young man appreciate the importance of a capacity to "believe in" that preceded specific beliefs (1970b). (This notion of belief in is an important concept in Winnicott that is taken up in a later chapter.) One wonders if Winnicott's sensitivity to the questions of his child patients evoked memories of similar questions in his own development.

Thus, Darwin helped Winnicott discover a "scientific" method for observing the environment, including human participation in the environment. He also took from Darwin a comfort with "not knowing." Furthermore, the physical sciences fostered an appreciation for how the "soul" was illuminated by the body. Jacobs (1995) added that Darwin's theory "gave Winnicott a deep belief in the developmental process and in the drive toward health" (p. 7). All of these things that Winnicott took from Darwin were themes that wove their way through his adult writings, and yet there also were more personal, developmental factors involved in Winnicott's attraction to Darwin.

A Means of Differentiation

Surely one reason that Winnicott found Darwin attractive resides in the opportunity to "get on with" thinking for himself in categories other than those of his family. That is, one might think of Darwin as offering the young Winnicott a way to break away in some degree from his family and to move toward "individuation." Developmentally, adolescence is a time for exploring one's sense of personal identity; this is done in part by differentiating from one's family of origin (Erikson, 1968). Phillips' (1988) comment that "the relatively secure, and perhaps sometimes to his mind overseductive, happiness of his family life made the boarding school . . . an exciting opportunity for Winnicott" is highly suggestive in this regard (p. 30). If "his father posed a threat to the independence" (p. 31) the young Winnicott desired, Darwin provided him a way to "get on with it" that was quite dissimilar to his father's "simple religious faith."

Oddly enough, Winnicott's ability to read Darwin with such abandon may derive from his father's non-dogmatic way of being religious. In his autobiographical note about his father's "simple religious faith" and encouragement to "read the Bible and what you find there will be the true answer for you," Winnicott concluded by saying "So, I was left, thank God, to get on with it myself"(Winnicott, 1978, p. 23). About the impact of his father's remarks, Rodman (2003) concluded, "Donald, under no paternal pressure to adhere to a specific view in the matter, would embrace Darwin's ideas enthusiastically" (p. 12).

However, that Rodman's (2003) use of Clare's version of his father's admonition to "read the Bible" for his own answers must be read with a critical eye has been noted. Does Sir Frederick's encouragement to read the Bible for himself open up a way for Winnicott to read and embrace Darwin without creating a rift in relationship? Or is Sir Frederick's comment a dismissal of a son embracing a view of the world too at variance with the religious views of his father? The complexity associated with interpreting this story has already been noted. Because Winnicott's telling of the story does not give a location or time, one could speculate that it could have occurred after Donald had gone off to The Leys (or college). This would imply an older son (than Clare's version), with more serious questions about his father's faith (maybe a question about Darwin versus the Bible?).

As Winnicott's time at the boarding school drew near its end, he found it difficult to approach his father about his desire to study medicine rather than follow his father into the family business. He engaged an older friend from school to broach the subject with his father first so that he could gauge better his own approach (Rodman, 2003). If his father was hard to approach about vocational desires, was he also hard to approach with a religious question, especially if it challenged his belief?

However, this is speculation and one must not push it too far. Winnicott clearly experienced his father's words as granting a freedom to pursue religious questions in his own way. Winnicott would later express his appreciation for the kind of religious upbringing that one could "grow up out of" (1968b, p. 143). This remark also implies a non-coercive quality to his father's religion, even if one sees the father's above comments as dismissive. However, left to get on with it for himself, the son does not seem to pursue religion in the same kind of way his father embraced it.

Clare Winnicott (1983) noted that Winnicott's encounter with Darwin "really changed his attitude to religion—began to change it" (p. 182). While Darwin may have turned Winnicott toward a "scientific way of working," she was right to modify her observation that this did not occur all at once. Despite his obvious attraction to Darwin (and perhaps away from his father's "simple" faith), Winnicott continued to participate in a variety of religious activities at school (and even into young adulthood).

Influence of the Methodist Piety at The Leys on Winnicott

Although his exposure to Darwin provided some points of divergence from the "faith of his fathers," Winnicott's time at The Leys School provided mostly a continuation and deepening of his religious upbringing. This continuity is seen in several ways.

Holistic View of the Person

From this staunchly Methodist school Winnicott came to value a holistic perspective of the person. Here was a school where mind, body and soul came together in the curriculum. He is able to combine his interest in Darwin and religion; he can belong to both the Biology Club and the Christian Union. This holistic focus was very much a part of Wesleyan tradition (Runyon, 1998). One can well imagine the Leys students of Winnicott's time singing Charles Wesley's hymn about bringing together of mind and soul in vital living:

Unite the pair so long disjoined;
   Knowledge and vital piety;
Learning and holiness combined,
   And truth and love let all men see
In these, when up to thee we give,
   Thine, wholly thine, to die and live. (Wesley, 1780, p. 644)

Although one must be careful not to over-read back into his early life concerns that emerge in his adult work, one can see that this question of a holistic view of persons emerged in some of Winnicott's writings, especially his concern with the "psyche-soma" unity and the "bodily" basis for experience. This interest is discussed in more detail later.

Concern for the Poor and Underprivileged

Winnicott also took from his time at The Leys a reinforcement of the well-known Wesleyan emphasis on concern for the poor and underprivileged and the need to work for the betterment of society (Chilcote, 2004; Heitzenrater, 1995; Maddox, 1994; Runyon, 1998; Semmel, 1973). Serving one's neighbor was a key way in which one served God. His work with the Scouts and the poor children of Cambridge would have deepened this concern of which Methodists were wont to sing:

Help us help each other, Lord
   Each other's cross to bear
Let each his friendly aid afford
   And feel his brother's care. (Wesley, 1780, p. 677)

Furthermore, it was while at The Leys that Winnicott decided to become a doctor. This decision is recounted in a brief article published on the occasion of Winnicott's retirement after forty years as children's physician at Paddington Green Hospital (1961c). As recounted by Winnicott (and repeated by Clare [Winnicott, 1978]) the decision to become a doctor came in part as a result of fracturing his clavicle during sports and realizing that he would always be dependent on doctors when he got sick unless he became one himself. Although these events undoubtedly contributed to his motivations to become a doctor, like all decisions it has multiple determinants and becoming a doctor also may have been a way to "feel his brother's care" and "friendly aid afford."

Freedom to Think for Oneself

Winnicott also would have taken from this period a deepening appreciation for the freedom to think for oneself and to learn to tolerate differences around religion. Pritchard (1983) noted that one of the pillars of Methodist education at this time was "the preservation of individual liberty in matters of faith and worship" (p. 294). His father's blessing to find his own answers would have been strengthened and encouraged by masters like Balgarnie and Barber, the headmaster during Winnicott's time there, who was known for his broad-minded religious tolerance (*The Leys Fortnightly*, V. 38 # 679, July 14, 1914). One concludes that it is such tolerance that would have encouraged the young Winnicott to be active in both the Biology Club and the Christian Union. (However, one also should note that this freedom to think for oneself was something that Winnicott, like any adolescent, also struggled with from time to time despite the continuity of this freedom with his upbringing and the progress he had made in this area. For instance, though he wanted to become a doctor instead of join his father's business he struggled to find the courage to approach his father directly about this career decision.)

A Connection to His Father's Piety

Another way that The Leys may have reinforced Winnicott's connection with his father's values and piety is through the religious worship. The singing of Methodist hymns may be especially apropos to this point. Recall that Winnicott's father was a member of the choir at the church in which Winnicott spent his younger years. And although what was sung in the daily services at The Leys is not known, it is reasonable to assume that hymns that reinforced the Wesleyan piety of his childhood were part of these services. So, although Winnicott may have diverged from his father's religion in some ways, one must also acknowledge a powerful emotional continuity with his father's religion that would be evoked by the religious hymns. This emotional continuity through Methodist hymns also may connect him to aspects of his mother's piety. That Winnicott loved to sing the Methodist hymns of his youth during interludes between patients has been noted (Kahr, 1996).

Thoughts on Teaching Religion and Moral Character

The final continuity noted between Winnicott's religious upbringing and his time at The Leys also provides an entrée into some discontinuity. As a student he would have been exposed to various ways for teaching religion and moral character. He would surely have taken from his time there some thoughts on ways to do and not to do moral education. As to a good way that a headmaster might preside over a boy's growing interest in religion Winnicott once shared a case in which a boy had all kinds of interesting and troubling questions about God. These questions were disturbing his parents but the boy's headmaster had remarked that he hoped the school would not stifle the child's inquisitive mind. Winnicott (n.d. 4) thought the headmaster's attitude commendable.

However, Winnicott (1963j) was much more apt to be critical of moral education because he felt that moral and religious educators were more likely to "steal" the innate morality of the child and then forcefully "inject" it back into the child. For Winnicott, morality was not to be imposed on the child, but allowed to emerge naturally and to be discovered by the child at developmentally appropriate times. To illustrate the absurdity of forcing morality onto children he repeated from a colleague the story of a Professor Keate who threated to beat a child unless the child "believed in the Holy Ghost" by a certain time in the afternoon (Winnicott, 1963j, p. 93). It is likely he also drew from his early experience of moral and religious education at The Leys to understand what is good and bad in terms of ways to do it. In a similar way, although time at The Leys is likely to have exposed him to helpful ways of nurturing the moral development of children, it also is likely that it exposed him to some of the more dogmatic ways of being religious to which he would become quite averse. Winnicott would take from his time at The Leys a question about the developmentally appropriate way to expose children to religion and morals. He will later ask whether religion and morals can be taught without imposing or implanting them.

Thus, one sees in the adolescent Winnicott a young man who struggled with his father's "simple" faith in some ways, who nevertheless was still deeply influenced by the "faith of his fathers" and adopted, both explicitly and implicitly, many of the tenets of his Wesleyan Methodist heritage. Winnicott remembered this period of his life as one in which he was quite religious (1954e) and especially noted his work with the Scouts as one of the most meaningful experiences he took from this time (1968e). However, the questions that began to arise from his attempts to "come at the soul" through biology (and Darwin in particular) are ones that will occupy him for many years to come.

Notes

1.   There appears to be no record from these years of the music that was performed by the choir; neither is there a record of the order of service for the daily worship times (although Harding [2006] noted that the sermons could be quite long!). There does not even

appear to be a record of the hymnal used during the years Winnicott would have attended. From brief notes in the *Fortnightly* for the years that Winnicott attended one observes that the choir performed "Tell me, thou soul of her I love" by Sydenham and "Good night, beloved" by Pinsuti with words from Longfellow (V. 37, # 656 Mar 14, 1913), neither of which are hymns. The notation that the anthem "O how plentiful is Thy goodness" was sung on Speech Day is the only other remark in the *Fortnightly* about music performed during Winnicott's time at The Leys.

2.   The use of Methodist hymns as illustrative of key Wesleyan ideas is suggested by Marie Hoffman (2004). It is interesting to note that the only hymn that Winnicott directly quoted in his published writings was a couple of lines from the Augustus Toplady hymn, "Rock of Ages." In his essay on "Cure" Winnicott (1970d) noted that the lines "Let the water and the blood, Be of sin the double cure" pointed to a movement toward understanding cure as "remedy" rather than "care" (its earlier meaning according to the *Oxford English Dictionary*). Interesting, Toplady was a very vocal contemporary critic of Wesley. His original version of the hymn was slightly changed by Thomas Cotterill (a compiler of hymns) to perhaps make it more acceptable to Methodists (Julian, 1892). Cotterill changed the object of the double cure from Toplady's original (i.e., "cleanse from its guilt and power") to "save from wrath and make me pure" the more widely known lyrics and ones that better reflect the Wesleyan emphasis on a second (or "double") work of grace that not only redeemed one from God's wrath (conversion) but that led one to purity of "Christian perfection" (sanctification—see Wesley, 1777). By the time Winnicott would have been a Wesleyan Methodist, however, this hymn had long appeared in Methodist hymnals (in the Cotterill version), and was a favored song among Methodists despite its earlier origins (Julian). It is doubtful that Winnicott was aware of the theological subtleties behind this particular hymn.

Winnicott may have indirectly referred to another hymn in his comments about the concept of "everlasting arms" that can be communicated to children (1968b, p. 149). A famous hymn by E. Hoffman, "Leaning on the Everlasting Arms" was also sung by the Methodists. However, the concept of everlasting arms also is found in the Scriptures (Deut. 33:27). In addition to providing the basis for the hymn, this Scripture rather than the hymn may have been the source for Winnicott's reference (see chapter 6).

Chapter 4
Winnicott's Religious Development as a Young Adult

"I suppose I grew up out of church religious practice"

During his studies at medical school Winnicott encountered the writings of Freud. Interestingly, his encounter came through reading a book on psychoanalysis by Oskar Pfister (1917), a Swiss Reformed pastor and friend of Freud who became a psychoanalyst. Pfister's book led Winnicott to Freud's *Interpretation of Dreams*. From a letter to his sister Violet one senses how his religious upbringing still shaped his thoughts at this time, but also how his religious landscape was shifting. In this letter he devoted a long section to explaining Freud's theory of the mind. He asked her to tell him if he has not made things "completely simple for anyone to understand" because he hoped one day to introduce psychoanalysis to England so that "who runs may read" (Winnicott, 1919, p. 2).

Flush with the excitement of his discovery of Freud's model, he went on to suggest to his sister that "Christ was a leading psychotherapist." He then observed that extreme religious acts and obsessions could correspond to various mental disorders. He concluded by noting that "by psychotherapy, many fanatics or extremists in religion can be brought (if treated early) to a real understanding of religion with its use in setting high ethical standards" (Winnicott, 1919, p. 3).[1]

There are several interesting points to note in Winnicott's first comments about psychoanalysis. First, one notes that even at this early stage he was sensitive to the deep antipathy that tended to characterize Freudian theory and religion. He stated "I shall probably be accused of blasphemy" for calling Christ a psychotherapist (although he also rightly noted that calling Christ a therapist does not meet the technical criteria for blasphemy) (Winnicott, 1919, p. 3). That he drew this comparison shows his mind at work trying to find connections between his religious upbringing and Freud's thinking, though the comparison lacked critical development. One might also note that Winnicott's religious background was obvious in his desire to speak simply about psychoanalysis. This language not only evokes John Wesley's (1746b) desire to speak in plain language (cf. Phillips, 1988), but his reference to "who runs may read" is an

53

allusion to a scriptural text about making the word of the Lord plain (see chapter 6).

His comparison of certain mental disorders (specifically, the unconscious trauma that may lie behind "shell shock") also indicated an attempt to apply what he has learned from Freud to certain types of religious behavior with which he was familiar. One also observes that he made some distinction between the roles of religion and psychotherapy. One sees the final insight into his thought about religion during this period by noting that he saw the purpose of religion as providing "high ethical standards." The mutual influence of Winnicott's religious background and his study of psychoanalysis is a recurring theme in the chapters that follows.

Significant Events during Winnicott's Young Adult Years

Winnicott's years as a young adult take in several important life events. He began his training to become a medical doctor, only to have this training interrupted by World War I, in which he served on a navy ship. He returned to complete his medical studies after the war, got married and began a ten-year period of analysis. All of these events have a bearing on the unfolding of his religious sensibilities and activities as a young adult.

This chapter follows a similar pattern to the previous one in first describing Winnicott's religious involvement during his young adult years and then commenting on how this seems to have influenced him. It describes continuities with his previous religious background while noting some of the ways he begins to move away from this tradition.

Studies at Jesus College

Winnicott began his studies to become a doctor at Jesus College, Cambridge, in fall 1914 after finishing his studies at The Leys. While a student at Jesus College, Goldman (1993) notes that Winnicott continued to attend the Methodist church regularly. Although studying for a degree in biology in preparation for becoming a doctor, Winnicott wrote home with pride that others liked to look at his library at Cambridge because of its variety. He noted that it included a couple of versions of the Bible and the Greek Testament (Rodman, 2003, p. 36).

Winnicott also continued his work with the Scouts and the poor of Cambridge while a student at Jesus College. This included organizing activities and staging plays for the children. Rodman (2003) quoted from a long letter from this period in which Winnicott (1916) described his efforts in raising money to assist one of the poorer scouts with some medical expenses:

One of the poorest (and also one of the best) scouts has been ill and cannot afford very easily the emulsions the doctor would like him to have. . . . [T]he
chemist is supplying him at a slightly reduced fee since he said it would cost
me a lot if I was doing it myself alone. So I have it sent him every fortnight. . . .
I have paid this week and I propose asking a few . . . relations, and . . . friends
to send me a few pence towards the next. . . . I could tell you a lot about the
wonderful mother of this boy. . . . The woman is the brightest of all the scouts'
mothers and always has a smile on her worn face. She knocked herself up . . .
staying up all night two nights a week . . . to earn money for the children. . . .
On the whole I feel that Mother deserves a little help. And this is a way that I
can help without hurting any feelings. (Winnicott, 1916; used by permission of
Marsh Agency, London; quoted in Rodman, 2003, p. 34)

Although this description of the scout and his family might reflect a certain
idealism of youth, it also shows a warmth and tenderness reminiscent of Wesley's charge that one "not grieve the poor. Give them soft words, if nothing else.
. . . Let them be glad to come, even though they should go empty away. Put
yourself in the place of every poor man, and deal with him as you would God
should deal with you" (Wesley, 1747, pp. 176–177). Thus, one can see in Winnicott's involvement with the Scouts a particularly Wesleyan way for him to
express his religious sentiments. Furthermore, it is a distinct possibility that
working with the poor and underprivileged of Cambridge also may have
strengthened his resolve to become a doctor.

Service in World War I

Winnicott's medical studies were interrupted by World War I. For a time he
cared for those hospitalized in college buildings converted to this purpose; eventually he joined the Royal Navy and served as a Surgeon Probationer aboard a
ship that saw some combat action, although he also had a lot of free time aboard
ship. His lack of both medical as well as naval experience seems to have been
the occasion for some good-natured banter aboard the ship (Winnicott, 1978).
Winnicott (1961c) remarked at a later time that he was only there "to reassure
the sailor's mothers that their boys had a doctor on board" (pp. 137–138).

One does not know fully how the war influenced or changed Winnicott's religious sensibilities but one can see that it left profound questions in his mind as
to why he had survived while others had died. It may have given him some
sense of a greater coherence to all of life, although this sentiment, like his appreciation of Darwin, may not have been fully present at the time. "[S]o many of
my friends and contemporaries died in the first World War, and I have never
been free from the feeling that my being alive is a facet of some one thing of
which their deaths can be seen as other facets: some huge crystal, a body with
integrity and shape intrinsical in it" (Winnicott, 1978, p. 20). Goldman (1993)
pointed to the religious overtones in this passage: "Still, there was, as always for

Winnicott, an element of connection—connection through some higher religious order where life and death are transcended" (p. 33). It is of interest that this comment from his autobiographical notes had been repeated earlier in comments he made at the time of his retirement from Paddington Green (Winnicott, 1961c) and are represented in an unpublished note written near his 70th birthday (Winnicott, 1966b).[2] Clearly, these thoughts bore on his mind for several years.

Medical Studies at St. Bartholomew's Hospital

After his war service, Winnicott returned to medical studies, this time at St. Bartholomew's Hospital (Bart's) in London. During his medical studies he converted from Methodism to the Anglican faith (Rodman, 1987). The reasons for this conversion are unknown. Though he offers no evidence, Rodman speculated that it may have involved some sort of religious crisis having to do with religious expressions that were too demanding of obedience, resulting in his development of an aversion to more dogmatic expressions of religion (and psychoanalysis as well). More likely is that the conversion involved some sort of upward social mobility. This change from Methodism to Church of England would match the change in social status and setting as a lad from merchant parents of the rural, middle class found himself a physician in training in the metropolis of London (Goldman, 1993). Hoffman (2004) observed that such conversions were often a way to join the "establishment," an accepted social convention for upward mobility. Goldman noted a third possible contributing factor. Given his lifelong preoccupation with mothers his conversion may have expressed identification with his mother, who had been Anglican before her marriage.

As noted in the introduction to this chapter, it was during his medical studies at Bart's that Winnicott had his first encounter with the writings of Freud. This exposure to Freud provided Winnicott a new way to reflect upon religious practices and experience. He began to see a more critical way to evaluate certain religious experiences (e.g., they were like obsessional neuroses; they may be a defense against anxieties), but one also sees him trying to preserve some continuity with his religious tradition through his trying to understand how this new way of thinking about religion can connect with his prior religious understanding (e.g., wanting to understand Christ as a psychotherapist). Exploring how psychoanalysis can illuminate religious practice while maintaining a positive role for the helpful things he knows religion can provide will become a lifelong interest for Winnicott.

First Marriage

Following the completion of his medical studies, Winnicott married for the first time at the age of twenty-eight. His bride, Alice Taylor, was the daughter of a "deeply religious Wesleyan Methodist" (who converted to Anglicanism), who was also a very successful businessman with "little time for his children" (Rodman, 2003, p. 52–53). In several ways Winnicott's bride has a similar religious upbringing to his own. As Rodman noted, the description of Alice's father might well describe Winnicott's father. Winnicott weds his Anglican wife in the parish church at Frenshem, Surrey (Rodman) and his marriage seems to have been the occasion for his confirmation in the Anglican faith (to which he had previously converted) (Goldman, 1993). Apart from a church wedding one does not know how Alice may have influenced Winnicott's religious activities. A close family friend described Alice as "very sweet" and "Christ-like" (Rodman, 2003, p. 56). Rodman, who gives the fullest picture of Alice did not comment upon her religious nature, though he did describe her as "emotionally disturbed, neurologically impaired, or some combination of both" (p. 57). Winnicott's marriage to Alice required attention to her emotional problems but also seems to have had times of shared enjoyment, especially with music (Rodman).

Although Winnicott's attraction to Alice as a marriage partner is a complex decision with multiple determinants (Kahr, 1996; Rodman, 2003), one must wonder if part of his attraction to Alice was due to her similar religious background.[3] They seem to have initially attended church regularly according to Clare (Winnicott, 1983), although she also indicated that he fairly soon drifted away from active attendance. However, a letter from his father during World War II suggests that regular attendance at church may have continued longer than Clare indicated. In an undated letter that asked about the Blitz in London Frederick Winnicott wrote "hope you and Alice enjoyed a peaceful Sunday rest following your usual early morning service" (J. F. Winnicott ca. 1941). The reasons for Winnicott's declining church activities are multiple as one shall see.

First Analysis

The final thing to note about this period of Winnicott's life that draws his young adult years to a close and opens up the more obvious adult period of his life is that he began what would become a ten-year psychoanalysis with James Strachey (Rodman, 2003). Already noted is how his exposure to Freud's writing led to reflections upon and connections to his religious upbringing. This section reflects more directly on the connection between undergoing psychoanalysis and his religious sensibilities.

Winnicott does not disclose any information that helps one understand how his analysis may have impacted his religion or vice versa. In his later psychoanalytic writings he would say that a full analysis cannot be accomplished if a patient held back in any area, including the religious (Winnicott, 1961f). One assumes he speaks from personal experience as an analysand and not only as an analyst.

Of interest in this regard are a couple of comments from Winnicott's first formal psychoanalytic paper. This paper was the basis for his admission to full membership in the British Psychoanalytic Society and was delivered about two years after the conclusion of his analysis with Strachey. In that paper he observed:

> [I]n the analysis of the most satisfactory type of religious patient it is helpful to work with the patient as if on an agreed basis of recognition of internal reality, and to let the recognition of the personal origin of the patient's God come automatically as a result of the lessening of anxiety due to the analysis of the depressive position. It is necessarily dangerous for the analyst to have it in his mind that the patient's God is a "fantasy object." (Winnicott, 1935, p. 133)

It is always problematic to try to discern self-disclosures in analytic papers despite the fact that self-disclosure often happened in disguised form in psychoanalytic writing (cf. Grosskurth, 1986; Roazen, 1974). Winnicott may be drawing from his work with patients, but one wonders if he also might be commenting from his own experience of analysis (or maybe a combination of both sources). Was Strachey the kind of analyst who let Winnicott's "recognition of the personal origin" of his God come out at the patient's developmental pace or was he one who thought Winnicott's God a "fantasy object"? Of course, there is no way to know in the absence of clinical material on Winnicott, but the question is intriguing.[4] Winnicott (1935) also commented on those in analysis who "jeer against religion" as demonstrating their own kind of defensiveness (p. 135).

One further comment on the question of the interaction between analysis and the patient's religion needs made. Sorenson (2004) has shown that the analyst's stance toward spirituality directly impacts how the analysand comes to experience his or her own spirituality. At the end of analysis those in analysis are likely to reflect a position toward spirituality similar to their analyst's position. Although Strachey had shown some interest in telepathy and other psychic phenomenon (Meisel & Kendrick, 1985), he did not seem to have been particularly religious according to Winnicott (1961e). One cannot say for certain what influence Strachey's lack of religion may have had on Winnicott, but in the light of Sorenson's work Winnicott's comments in his obituary of Strachey are striking. Winnicott (1969d) noted that at one point Strachey worked for a Quaker organization and that according to his wife, Alix, experienced something like a "conversion" to the value of love from this contact with the Quakers even though Strachey remained detached from "church religion." Winnicott too, according to his wife Clare (Winnicott, 1983), was still religious as an adult, but that it was a religion based on "love" and "helping people" and not church attendance (p. 181). If Winnicott drifted away from regular church attendance shortly after his marriage to Alice, it also would mean he drifted from regular church attendance shortly after beginning his analysis. However, as already noted, Clare may have thought Winnicott's regular church attendance stopped earlier than it did. Thus, there is no way to fairly gauge the extent that being in analysis may have contributed to a drop in his church attendance.[5]

What Winnicott Takes from This Period

From these events one sees several continuities with his religious heritage as well as some ways in which he began to diverge from his upbringing. Winnicott maintained a connection to his religious tradition in several ways during these years. For instance, as a young adult at college one can see continuity with his religious upbringing in his work with the Scouts and the poor of Cambridge, and in his regular attendance at church. One also sees continuity with Winnicott's religious upbringing in his continuing interest in religion and how it might connect with the new things he is learning (e.g., Christ as a psychotherapist).

However, one also can see Winnicott begin to diverge from his religious upbringing in important ways. He began to bring an analytic frame to religious questions, as when he used the lens of psychoanalysis to understand religious practices (e.g., religious obsessions as similar to mental disorders). At some point he stopped attending church regularly and began to think of religion in more functional (e.g., as providing high ethical standards) and principled ("love," "helping people") ways.

Given these events and the changes that were going on in Winnicott, what are some of the lingering influences from this time in his life? How does his religious participation as a young adult continue to influence him in later years?

A Sense of Mystery about Life

From Winnicott's comments about his grief over the loss of friends in World War I one gets the sense that he began to think of life as more complex and shrouded with mystery in a way not previously entertained. These years seem to have been a time in which he realized that the previous answers that his religion gave may not be as satisfactory as they once were. Some of his questions about life would have to be re-framed and perhaps given new answers. Here one thinks of his comment about life having an "intrinsical" pattern that joins things together in previously unanticipated and unfathomed ways.

Service to Others as Service to God

The idea that service to others is service to God shows continuity with his previous religious upbringing. It seems to get strengthened in new ways however. Certainly his work with the Scouts could be seen as a way in which service to neighbor was service to God. However, one begins to get some sense that Winnicott's thoughts about a career in medicine might be seen in a similar way. He certainly begins to see medicine not simply as a way to mitigate his dependence on others, but as a way to serve others. In the religious tradition to which Winnicott was exposed, serving the physical needs of one's neighbor was also a spiritual service, given the holistic view of humans held by Wesley.

New Categories for Old Concepts

This period in Winnicott's life also would have reinforced the ideas from his religious tradition that it was permissible to think for oneself. He took from this period new ways for thinking about older concepts. For instance, psychoanalysis became a new lens by which to reflect upon and understand religious behavior and practices. Furthermore, psychoanalysis became a new way to reflect upon the importance of the interior life, an emphasis long associated with the Wesleyan Methodist focus on personal experience and the religious affections. From his Wesleyan Methodist heritage Winnicott knew that religion attended to one's deep emotions; it was a matter of the heart. It was aware of the depth of negative emotions such as sadness, despair and hopelessness (cf. Winnicott, 1935). Conversely, it emphasized the depth of positive emotions such as love (of God and neighbor) and the need to nurture these positive religious "tempers" or affections (cf. Clapper, 1989). Psychoanalysis helped Winnicott reframe his interest on the importance of personal experience and the interior life.

A Need to "Grow Up Out Of"

Finally, one notes that Winnicott took from this period a need to "grow up out of" certain religious practices. The young adult years are a time especially given to more reflective and individuating activities including religious ones (Fowler, 1981). It is a time of increased questioning of previous assumptions and a distancing from one's previous socializing authorities and groups; one begins to form one's own ideas about religion. Conversely, one also may grieve the loss of previous relationships and ideals (Parker, 2011). What were some of those things that Winnicott saw himself needing to grow up out of?

"Growing Up Out Of"

As noted in the Introduction, Winnicott (1968b) commented to the conference on evangelism that "I suppose I just grew up out of church religious practice, and I am always glad that my religious upbringing was of a kind that allowed for growing up out of" (pp. 142–143). Phillips (1988) has argued that "Winnicott's work can be seen as both continuing and reacting against different strands of the

Dissenting tradition" (p. 23). Although Winnicott's Wesleyan Methodist up-bringing continued to deeply influence his life and work in various ways, in the closing years of Winnicott's young adulthood one sees the beginning of a more complex relationship between his religious upbringing and his emerging career in pediatrics and psychoanalysis. This more complex appreciation and appropri-ation of his religious heritage involved a deepening of certain aspects of Wes-leyan Methodist piety, a revising of others, and a rejection of yet other aspects. The unfolding of the various aspects of this relationship is the task of the next several chapters. Although one will see continuity—how the deep influence of his religious upbringing continued to show up in his work—one also will dis-cover discontinuity and inconsistencies in Winnicott's religious pilgrimage. However, before turning to the story of this "lingering religiosity" (Goldman, 1993, p. 115), it will be helpful to comment on some of those aspects of his background that Winnicott moved away from. These comments are framed with one of Winnicott's "more memorable snatches of prose" (Jacobs, 1995, p. 5). Using this "over-prepositioned phrase" that "triples the direction of the growth" (Jacobs, 1995, p. 5), one asks what it is Winnicott "grew up out of" and further, what he grew up toward.

What Winnicott "Grows Up Out Of"

One notes with interest that the actual phrasing that Winnicott (1968b) used ("suppose") implied some hesitancy to characterize the change in "church reli-gious practice" as growth, although he will conclude that his "religious upbring-ing" was of a kind that "allowed for growing up out of" (pp. 142–143). A reli-gious upbringing that "allowed" for growing up out of reminds one of the freedom that his father gave him to "read the Bible" for himself and find his own answers regarding religious truth (Winnicott, 1978). Goldman (1993) help-fully pointed out that "Winnicott is speaking of growing up out of religious *practice*; he is not referring to abandoning everything that can be associated with a religious outlook" (p. 117).

What practices then does Winnicott identify as those he has grown up out of? The first thing he noted was that he had grown up out of "*church* religious practice." His next statement made it clear that part of what he had grown up out of was church attendance (Winnicott, 1968b). Already noted is that Winnicott may have ceased regular church attendance sometime after his first marriage and his entering into psychoanalysis, although he may have continued regular church attendance into the Second World War. Regardless of when regular church at-tendance ceased, church attendance of a sporadic nature may have continued in Winnicott's adult life. A letter to a correspondent mentioned seeing them at the christening of a friend's child (Winnicott, 1949d). Rodman (2003) described an uncompleted survey sent to Winnicott by Thomas Ssasz in which one of the questions inquired about church membership and attendance. From this survey

one observes that in 1959 Winnicott indicated he held membership in an organized religion and had attended church "less than three times" during the year.
Since this was the last category for attendance, the wording of the questionnaire
could mean he had not attended at all that year (cf. Winnicott, 1959e). The only
other mention of church attendance comes in a comment from an extended case
study of treatment that took place during the years 1965–1968. In the report of
this case there is an exchange about church attendance with his five-year-old
patient in which Winnicott (1977) responded to her question about whether he
went to church with "sometimes" (p. 182).[6]

Winnicott's comment about growing up out of church religious practice
sounds very similar to a remark he made in an unpublished letter to the *London
Times*. In a letter written a little over a year before his death Winnicott said of
himself "I would not describe myself as a practicing Christian, having reached a
degree of maturity appropriate to age" (quoted in Rudnytsky, 1991, p. 97; cf.
Winnicott, 1969f). This remark is similar to his other in that he refers to religious *practice* in both instances. He does not exactly say he is no longer a Christian as some have interpreted this remark (Rudnytsky, 1991; cf. Hopkins, 1997;
Jacobs, 1995), only that he is not a *practicing* Christian.

The possibility that Winnicott might have thought himself a "non-practicing
Christian" reminds one of the phenomena of "non-practicing Catholics." This is
a sociological term designating those who in national polls and census requests
describe themselves as (baptized) Catholics but who do not practice their faith in
any of the obvious ways of religious observance such as attendance at mass
(Coriden, 2007; Edles, 2003; Francis & Egan, 1990). In this sense being a Catholic is more a cultural than religious identity and might be compared to those
who identify themselves as being "Jewish" more as an ethnic than religious designation.

Could Winnicott mean to imply that he is a "Christian" in this socio-cultural
sense; that is, in the way that to be "English" is to be "Anglican"? He is most
likely to have indicated his "religion" as Anglican (a form of Christian identification) on the census even if he did not consider himself a "practicing" one. Furthermore, his ritual of preparing and sending his own privately made and painted
Christmas cards might be interpreted in this way. One notes that the images on
the cards are not particularly religious (Rodman [2003] reproduces one), but
sending them was very much a part of who Winnicott was as a person. So much
so, that when he was recovering from a heart attack in New York and could not
get back to England, his secretary devised a way for him to continue this ritual
(Rodman, 2003). While some aspects of the deep influence of "cultural Christianity" on Winnicott are described in subsequent chapters, this is not likely his
meaning in describing himself as "not . . . a practicing Christian." It is much
more likely that he meant he did not practice Christianity in the "traditional" or
"evangelical" way of his youth (see below and chapter 9).[7]

So, what other "practices" has Winnicott grown up out of? It is clear from
his further remarks to the evangelism conference that part of what he no longer
"practices" are certain "beliefs" (1968b). He noted that his writings on the "ca-

pacity to believe *in*" probably earned him his invitation, and he remarked, "This leaves open the whole question of what you place at the end of the phrase" (p. 143). He questioned whether two beliefs in particular are needed: a belief in miracles and the after-life. Clearly Winnicott is implying that he has grown beyond beliefs in either of these. His lack of belief in miracles is confirmed in a letter to a colleague (Winnicott, 1967f). In this letter, Winnicott seemed to think that these beliefs were required by traditional religion, and having left them behind he did not consider himself religious in this more traditional sense, though as will become clear he still considered himself religious in other ways.

There are several other, more complex beliefs that Winnicott grew up out of (or "into" if one switches to the positive pole), such as the place of "original sin" or the relationship between religion and morality. Several of these more complex connections between his religious upbringing and his theory of human development are dealt with in a later chapter. What is important here is to observe that Winnicott also seemed to imply in the letter to the editor of the *Times* that practicing one's faith belonged to an earlier stage of development and that, as one matured one no longer engaged in such practice. This acknowledgment of a developmental appreciation of religious sensibilities is a theme reconsidered later along with inquiries into Winnicott's consistency with his own theory. At this point it is sufficient to note that this developmental focus is coupled with an attitude that suggested personal growth "up out of."

What Winnicott Grows Up Toward

If Winnicott grew up out of certain practices and beliefs, what did he grow toward in their place? One gets some hint of this at the end of his young adult years with the adoption of a more analytic and principled way of speaking about religion. It is clear that Winnicott began to develop certain attitudes toward and beliefs about science and psychoanalysis. These, in turn, began to cast new light on how he thought about religion (and God).

Starting with his encounter with Darwin, Winnicott began to develop what he would later describe as a "faith" in science, particularly as a method for exploring and understanding the wonder of nature (including human nature). This faith is not a faith in science as a guarantor of knowledge; scientists thrive on questions and doubt. Such doubt Winnicott contrasted with the "certainty" that characterized religion. And yet in a paradoxical way, he noted that science also implied a "faith." What the scientist had faith in was not always clear. What was more important than faith in something particular was a "capacity" for faith. If pushed about particulars he conceded that perhaps the scientist had faith in the "inexorable laws that govern phenomena" (1961d, p. 14; cf. Winnicott, 1969h). Thus Winnicott's faith in the scientific method shifted to become a faith in the underlying laws of nature.[8] More will be said about Winnicott's own work on the capacity for faith or "belief in" and how it relates to his religious upbringing in a later chapter. It is enough for now to note this trend as something he grows toward.

His faith in the scientific method led him to a certain faith in psychoanalysis as a new kind of science for exploring human relationships and problems. "Psycho-analysis turns out to be a fine instrument by which human beings may study themselves and their interpersonal relationships; but it does remain an instrument of scientific research or a therapy, and it never makes a direct philosophical or a religious contribution" (Winnicott, 1945e, p. 133). Winnicott's notion that psychoanalysis did not make a direct religious contribution was a theme he would take up again in other papers where he arrived at a different conclusion (see chapter 8). Similarly, his allusion to a dichotomy between science (in the form of psychoanalysis) and religion was not consistent with his own later theory (see chapter 8).

However, even when being analytic in his views of religion as projection or illusion Winnicott pushed these categories in new and creative directions. For instance, he extended psychoanalysis to provide new insights into the psychological origins of God and religious experience. Some of the developments in Winnicott's understandings of the confluence of psychoanalysis and religion taken up later include his understanding of God as a special type of "object" to which people both "relate" and "use." Winnicott's ideas about the nature of God and changes in these ideas also are explored. Some of these insights show continuity with his Wesleyan Methodist upbringing; others show him diverging from the "simple" faith of his father.

While it is obvious that Winnicott "grew up out of" various aspects of his religious upbringing, Goldman (1993) spoke of a "lingering religiosity" that characterized Winnicott throughout his life (p. 115). In some ways, the next few chapters take up this thesis to outline the nature of Winnicott's religious sensibilities. What "lingers" and what changes? In the language of Phillips (1988), how is Winnicott's work a "continuing" as well as "reacting against" various dimensions of his religious background? Although Winnicott's "cultural Christianity" certainly casts its own deep influence on his work, (and some aspects of this are seen in subsequent chapters), it also has been obvious that the influence of his religious upbringing runs much deeper than this to more personal levels as well. The next several chapters seek to "make plain" the depth and nature of this influence in his adult life and work.

Notes

1.   It is significant that Winnicott's first exposure to Freud came through Oskar Pfister. Pfister was a devotee to the work of Freud, having first become familiar with it through Freud's published lectures and then later through visits to the Freud home. Pfister found in psychoanalysis a helpful tool for understanding his parishioners and engaged in a lively correspondence with Freud about his ideas (Meng & Freud, 1963). As a pastor he was especially interested in Freud's ideas about religion and offered one of the first positive

appraisals and critique of Freud's ideas on this subject. Pfister (1917) had written *The Psychoanalytic Method*, and this book was given to Winnicott by a librarian during his years at Cambridge after he complained that he could no longer remember his dreams (Kahr, 1996; Rodman, 2003). Pfister's analysis of Freudian method does not contain the overly negative critique of religion that is characteristic of Freud's own writings (cf. 1927, 1930). Pfister wrote, "Psychoanalysis in no way violates the claims of truth of the Christian religion as such" (p. 412).

One sees several themes from Pfister's book in Winnicott's letter to his sister Violet. His comments about how therapy can help religious extremists mirrors Pfister's appreciation of the way psychoanalysis can be helpful to certain religious character types who suffer from obsessional rituals and ideas. While this language is reminiscent of Freud's 1907 essay on "obsessional neurosis and religion," Winnicott's comments more likely reflect Pfister's positive slant. "Religion, in favorable cases, guards the libido repelled by the rude, avaricious reality, against conversion into hysterical physical symptoms, and against introversion into anxiety, melancholia, obsessional phenomena, etc." (Pfister, 1917, p. 413). Winnicott's comments about Christ being a psychotherapist reflects Pfister's conclusions as well: "Exactly as Freud heals the obsesssional neurotic individual by winning back the love and affording it appropriate realization, so does Jesus. He taught to love and thereby destroyed the religious obsessional neurosis" (p. 576). Finally, one notes that Winnicott's comments about the role of religion in setting high ethical standards sounds very much like Pfister's comments. "The great prophets, as Amos, Hosea, Isaiah, Micah and Jeremiah . . . favored a transformation of the libido into social activity and thus created the first important social religion in which divine pleasure was made dependent on the preservation of social-ethical sentiment" (p. 574). (Cf. "Stekel also attributes to religion a high ethical mission" [p. 413]).

2.   This handwritten note contains the following reflections: "We are spared our own funerals and for this we may praise God. What else is there for which one can, at 70 years, praise God? Well, for one thing, there's this fact that one has made it. But this immediately introduces the idea of all the others who stumbled or died. If I have got anywhere or contributed anything to the world, then the good includes my friends & contemporaries who were killed in the two great wars, who died of cancer or by accident, or who got into trouble and never caught up again." It is interesting to observe that this particular note has a squiggle that has been turned into a dragon-looking creature on the back of it. It is difficult to know what to make of the squiggle. Is it perhaps a reflection of death for Winnicott? Clare once observed that Winnicott thought of death as a "disaster which you have to put up with because you are human" (Winnicott, 1983, p. 187).

3.   In this regard, one might also note that Winnicott's second wife, Clare, was also the daughter of a very prominent minister (this time Baptist, another evangelical Protestant denomination), and was involved deeply in her church as a young adult. In a lengthy letter to Winnicott written before their marriage, after several pages where she tried to summarize a conversation they had had on the nature of "good" and "belief," she remarked "religion is so important to me that I must get it sorted out a bit" (C. Winnicott, ca. 1941–145). Again, while the choice of any marriage partner involves multiple factors, it is interesting to observe that when marrying, Winnicott chose women who had strong religious backgrounds.

4.   In a breach of confidentiality Strachey did share a few brief comments about Winnicott's analysis in letters to his wife, Alix (Meisel & Kendrick, 1985). Although Rodman (2003) has speculated on what these comments might reveal about Winnicott's relationship with his parents, Strachey's (e.g., 1924, 1925) comments offer no obvious light on the religious dimensions of Winnicott's analysis.

5.   There is a comment from Rodman (2003) that suggests an ongoing religiousness in Winnicott that was manifest in his second analysis with Joan Riviere which occurred during the years leading up to World War II. Rodman quoted from an undated letter from Riviere responding to a letter from Winnicott in which she stated she did not "share your demand for everything to be spontaneous in the sense of inspired." She went on to offer as an alternative that she believed "human beings can sometimes make something good & not that it always has to be God doing it!" (p. 88). If taken at face value, Riviere seems to be saying that Winnicott held the position that God was the ultimate source of all things. Rodman concluded that if true this was an extreme position.

If Riviere has faithfully reported Winnicott's sentiments then this is testimony of a lingering religious sentiment in Winnicott that is quite conservative in nature. However, in the absence of a specific letter from Winnicott to Riviere that includes these remarks, I think one must be cautious in interpreting Riviere's report in this way. A date for the letter might cast some light upon this issue. Rodman seems to think it written sometime after 1941. Although he has not fully developed his ideas around creativity, play, and aliveness, Winnicott (1942) has begun to link these concepts (e.g., "Play is the continuous evidence of creativity, which means aliveness"—p. 150). Perhaps Winnicott is expressing a very conservative religiosity at this point, but it seems entirely possible (and more in keeping with Winnicott's known writings) that by "inspired" he means to say that one must "create" or find an "aliveness" for oneself in one's life and the ideas one adopts. (This certainly seems to be part of his own struggle vis-à-vis the ideas of the Kleinians at this time—Rodman, 2003.) I conclude with Rodman that taking Winnicott's comment about inspiration to only refer to "God doing" the work seems a "supposition" on Riviere's part that misses the mark given the shifting religious landscape in Winnicott's life during this period.

6.   Winnicott seemed thrown off his guard by this question. He acknowledged that he did not know what to say (Winnicott, 1977) and his further comments about what church means to the little girl seems to miss her point about it being connected to her desire to be nearer her parents. He responded by asking her whether church has something to do with God.

7.   With declining church attendance came corollary declines in the practice of the sacraments (cf. Bagenal, 1949). Even the pattern of his weddings indicates his shifting practice. Although his first wedding to Alice was a church ceremony, his second marriage to Clare involved both a religious service at a Baptist church followed by the actual civil wedding ceremony later in the day (Rodman, 2003). One might remember that Clare's father was a Baptist minister and whether this first ceremony was in deference to her family or indicative of some religious sentiment is hard to know at this distance. Perhaps it was a bit of both. Letters from Clare's family indicate interest in God's blessings upon this new union. For instance, Elsie Britton (1951), Clare's sister wrote "I shall pray each day that you may both fulfill God's purposes in your life together." To what extent Winnicott shared these sentiments at the time is unknown. Probably more telling in regard to Winnicott's feelings about church rituals are the arrangements following his death. Although there is a memorial service in which his psychoanalytic colleagues participate, there is no mention of a church funeral. Kanter (2004) said that Winnicott was cremated although he gave no further details about this. In the autobiographical notes where Winnicott shared imaginings about his death there is no mention of a church funeral (Winnicott, 1978).

8.   It is important to note that Winnicott's simple dichotomy between science and religion belies what is known of the relationship between these two phenomena and the larger questions regarding the nature and relationship of objective versus subjective knowing

(Bernstein, 1983; Pruyser, 1983). Schlauch (2007) summarized Pruyser's (1983) contribution (which had drawn upon Winnicott's theory): "One of the primary assumptions that emerged in the context of Cartesian, Newtonian, and Kantian commitments was the contrast of things subjective with things objective. Art, literature, music, and religion were members of the former group, set over against the exemplar of the latter group: science. . . . Pruyser upends these assumptions. Art, literature, music, religion, and science carry out the play of the imagination. They bear a family resemblance. Said more strongly, these enterprises are members of a class—they are styles of illusion-processing" (p. 382).

This dichotomy between science and religion is one repeated in other places (e.g., Winnicott, 1945e; cf. Winnicott, 1967a), and yet further belies Winnicott's own contributions to this question via his paradox of the intermediate area. Winnicott's notion that science also relied on a "faith" is closer to his own position regarding the place of an intermediate area in fostering "creative scientific work" (Winnicott, 1951b, p. 242). A later chapter takes up Winnicott's inconsistency in drawing such a stark contrast between science and religion and his own theoretical contributions to the philosophy of science.

Prayer for the Wesleyan Methodists took several forms. It was personal and individual and involved one in a private prayer time. Yet it also was done corporately, both in the general corporate worship of the congregation in the regularly appointed services, and also in the small groups or bands that Wesley established (Chilcote, 2004). These groups provided opportunity for people to share and be encouraged in their walk of holiness.

Scripture reading was to be done privately during times of devotion, but also was part of corporate worship and the work of the bands. In the band meetings there were often exhortations of various Scripture passages that were designed to help people explore their growth toward holiness (Chilcote, 2004).

Another dimension of Wesleyan Methodist piety that is worth mentioning is the singing of hymns. Charles Wesley, who with his brother John, are the personalities responsible for the Wesleyan revival in England, composed over six thousand hymns, often referred to as theology set to music (Chilcote, 2004; Hoffman, 2004). The Methodists sang their theology as much if not more than they listened to it in sermons or read about it in learned treatises. Singing became a key way in which Methodists imbibed the theology of Wesley. Charles especially seemed to have a deep appreciation for how music burrowed deep into the soul or spirit and sticks with one via the tunes. Singing touched the population in ways that reading did not, and also reached into and stuck in the mind of those that may not have been accustomed to formal learning through reading.

Socially Involved (Love of Neighbor)

Wesleyan piety is personal but also lived out in love to neighbor. It is not isolationist, nor entirely mystical (though it has something of that dimension taken from Wesley's appreciation of Moravian piety). One sees this social dimension at work in two ways: (1) inside the movement (e.g., band meetings, church attendance, participation in the sacraments) but also (2) evident through works outside the society (care for the poor, building schools, hospitals); a concern for the whole person (Chilcote, 2004; Maddox, 1994; Rack, 1983; Runyon, 1998; Semmel, 1973; Turner, 1983).

Wesleyan Methodist Piety and Winnicott's Attitudes toward the Practice of Psychoanalysis

Winnicott was influenced both by his personal exposure to Wesleyan Methodism in his home, especially as a young child, and later by his exposure to the wider Wesleyan Methodist tradition at his boarding school. There are several themes from this piety that influenced Winnicott's life and work, especially in terms of attitudes it fostered. In addition, his personal experience of this piety carried over into an overall positive attitude toward religion.

Goldman (1993) has observed that "it is striking how some of the fundamental doctrines of Methodism were given secular expression by Winnicott" (p.
118). These include "the partnership of ordained ministers and laity in the worship and administration of the church; concern for the underprivileged and the
betterment of social conditions; tolerance for differences of conviction regarding
various theological disputes" among other things (p. 118). This next section
demonstrates that this striking similarity is the result of Winnicott deeply imbib-
ing the ethos and attitudes of the Wesleyan Methodist piety to which he was
exposed. This section shows how deeply the practical dimensions of Wesleyan
Methodist piety helped "form" the very ways Winnicott thought about life, others, even organizations (e.g., the British Psychoanalytic Society).

Inclusion and Valuing of Non-Analytic ("Lay") Groups

An aspect of Methodist piety that seems to have settled deep into Winnicott
is its emphasis on the cooperation between clergy and laity. In Wesley's day this
took the form of gaining spiritual nourishment from taking the sacraments from
the clergy, as well as attending to the growth of the soul through shared testimony in the lay administered "bands" (groups that met to encourage one another in
living more holy lives) (Chilcote, 2004). In later Methodism this cooperation
between professional clergy and laity was formalized through the inclusion of
lay people at the Methodist conferences where clergy had met to discuss matters
of church polity (Turner, 1983). Winnicott would have seen this inclusiveness
lived out through his layman father's deep involvement in the affairs of his local
Wesleyan Methodist congregation and conference.

Winnicott seems to have absorbed this inclusive attitude in both conscious
and unconscious ways. For instance, one sees a counterpart to this type of inclusion and cooperation not only in the speeches Winnicott gave to various groups
of social workers, child-care organizations, parents, teachers, and pastors, but in
his active work with several of these groups. Winnicott was particularly prone to
work with social workers and to see them as adjuncts in the care of those who
were ill (Winnicott, 1984). Those who worked in the residential homes that kept
children war evacuees were treated similarly with great respect as part of the
team. Clare Winnicott (1984), who first became acquainted with Winnicott
through their work together with the war evacuees, spoke of how Winnicott's
role became one of supervising the workers while they performed the actual care
for the children. Similarly, in his practice as a child psychiatrist Winnicott occasionally treated the parents rather than the child so that the parent could carry on
the treatment for the child (Winnicott, 1971g, 1977). Another way one sees this
inclusiveness is in the many popular BBC broadcasts Winnicott gave to mothers
and parents, which went through several editions when published. As Khan
(1975) once observed, for every paper Winnicott gave to a professional audience

he gave "at least a dozen to gatherings of social workers, child-care organizations, teachers, priests, etc." (p. xxii).

Of course, one must ask whether Winnicott's involvement with all these non-analytic groups may derive from other motivations, such as his prohibition from teaching at the British Psychoanalytic Society, given his failure to align with either the Kleinians or (Anna) Freudians (Rodman, 2003). Although this prohibition against teaching certainly contributed to Winnicott seeking speaking opportunities elsewhere, in the light of the obvious influence of his Wesleyan Methodist background upon his life, to attribute his prolific involvement with these other groups primarily to this prohibition seems too constrictive (see also chapter 9). It seems part of his nature that Winnicott did not restrict the insights of psychoanalysis to specialists but shared it with the "laity."

An earlier chapter noted how Winnicott's desire to "speak plainly" to such groups mirrored Wesley's (1746b) desire to speak plainly about God. One of the last groups that Winnicott addressed, about six months before his death, was a group of Anglican clergyman who asked him how they might tell which type of person they could help and which they needed to refer. In a way that reflects this spirit of inclusiveness Winnicott offers a practical rather than technical answer: "If a person comes and talks with you and, listening to him, you feel he is boring you, then he is sick, and needs psychiatric treatment. But if he sustains your interest, no matter how grave his distress or conflict, then you can help him alright" (cited in Khan, 1986, p. 1). As Phillips (1988) observed of this remark, "there is a commitment here, unheard of in psychoanalysis, to affinity between people rather than to a technique of professional help" (p. 25). This commitment to an affinity between people rather than to technique mirrors the Wesleyan Methodist preference for a "practical" theology that speaks plainly to people and their needs (rather than for a systematic theology more concerned with consistency than with distressed parishioners) (Maddox, 1994).

Concern for Poor and Betterment of Society

Concern for the underprivileged and the betterment of social conditions was another clear hallmark of Wesleyan piety (Chilcote, 2004; Maddox, 1994; Runyon, 1998; Semmel, 1973). Such emphases grew out of Wesley's focus on the whole person. "One common thread in that lineage is a holistic concern for the well-being of God's creatures—mind, body, and soul. The Methodist program of medical clinics and interest-free loans, orphanages and schools, housing for the widows and meals for the poor, were of a piece with Wesley's understanding of "love of neighbor" (Heitzenrater, 1995, p. 321). Wesley and his followers were also instrumental in addressing things such as the slave trade in England and the poverty of the lower classes (Runyon, 1998).

Again, Winnicott would have observed this kind of commitment in his father's many church and civic activities such as his work as church Steward (the person responsible for funds to aid those outside the congregation who were in need) and as mayor of Plymouth. That Winnicott himself directly participated in similar religious activities as an adolescent and young adult (e.g., his work with the underprivileged of Cambridge during his school days there) has been noted. This aspect of Wesleyan Methodist piety is seen in other activities in which he engaged. Throughout his life Winnicott wrote letters to the editors of the *London Times* and various professional journals to address various social ills (Rodman, 1987). His efforts on behalf of mental patients that might undergo leucotomy and shock treatments further testify to his concern for the underprivileged and the betterment of social conditions (Winnicott, 1943, 1956e), as does his involvement with the Home Commission on the treatment of child war evacuees (Winnicott, 1984; Kahr, 1996). Kahr (2011) further noted that a period in which Winnicott took certain patients into his home might reflect this Wesleyan focus.

It is important to note that Winnicott not only thought one should be concerned for the underprivileged and the betterment of society, or that one should include other groups as part of the means by which professionals treated those with mental problems, he lived out these attitudes. Thus, his absorption of the deep influences of his Methodist upbringing not only infuses his attitudes but his actions in these instances.

Non-Dogmatic (Valuing Freedom of Thought)

The Wesleyan Methodist tradition placed a high value on freedom to think for oneself, especially about matters of faith and religion. Such a belief was rooted in Wesley's fundamental theology. "The God of love is willing to save all the souls that he has made. . . . But he will not force them to accept of it" (Wesley, 1791, p.148). As Runyon summarized, for Wesley "Depriving human beings of freedom is neither the nature of God's grace nor the nature of God's love" (p. 27). Wesley's valuing of each person's ability to respond to God also contributed to his aforementioned resistance to creating "theological systems" that precluded human action, preferring to keep theology a more practical discipline for shaping people's lives (Maddox, 1994, p. 17).

This understanding that God grants freedom found a further expression in a tolerance of religious differences (Runyon, 1998; Semmel, 1973). "Methodism did not think of itself as *exclusively* in possession of religious truth" (Semmel, 1973, p. 20). Not only had Wesley himself pleaded for tolerance among those with different theological positions, this need for tolerance was long a part of the nonconformist heritage (Runyon, 1998; Semmel, 1973). Wesley's theology is often a case study in finding the truth that lay on both sides of an issue and is sometimes characterized as a theology of the "middle" (Chilcote, 2004; Semmel, 1973; cf. Wesley, 1746c, 1763b).

Winnicott had experienced this Wesleyan Methodist allowance for freedom of thought in his father's admonition to read the Bible for himself and to find his own answers there. Rather than restrict his son to correct answers from a religious tradition, he frees him to find his own way. Thus, Winnicott was well aware from personal experience that religion could encourage free thinking. Though he had been exposed to some ways in which religion might restrict certain behaviors, in his earliest childhood experiences of religion Winnicott seems to have gained an appreciation for this non-coersive quality of religion that allowed freedom of thought. As already noted, this freedom to find one's own answers would have been strengthened by masters such as Balgarnie during his time at The Leys. One sees the deep influence of this aspect of Wesleyan Methodist piety on Winnicott is several ways.

One sees Winnicott absorption of this aspect of Methodist piety most obviously in his preference for ways of being religious (and psychoanalytic) that are not dogmatic. Rayner (1991) said of Winnicott, "factionalism, ideological dogma, reliance on authority and zealous evangelicalism were all alien to his spirit" (p. 9). Rodman (2003) pointed to this anti-dogmatic quality as one of the central defining characteristics of Winnicott's personality, and located its origins in his religious upbringing, a position with which Kahr (1996) concurred. Although the connection between Winnicott's non-dogmatic stance and his religious upbringing may be a bit more complex as noted earlier, the essential point remains true.

As Goldman (1993) has noted, it is important to remember that Winnicott's aversion to dogmatic religion is not an anti-religion stance. Winnicott knows that religion also can be positive. Although he is aware of the ways that religion could be restrictive, defensive, or dogmatic (e.g., Winnicott, 1935, 1968b), his Wesleyan Methodist background also exposed him to a creative, vitalizing potential in religion.

Yet what is true about dogmatic religion for Winnicott is also true about dogmatic psychoanalysis. Winnicott has imbibed deeply the Wesleyan Methodist focus on freedom of thought. One clearly sees his aversion to dogma in psychoanalysis in a letter addressed to Melanie Klein and Anna Freud in which he described himself as one who can "no more stand the falsity of a rigid system in psychology than they can tolerate it in religion" (Winnicott, 1954d, p. 72).

One especially can see Winnicott's concern over dogmatism in psychoanalysis in a letter written to Melanie Klein in 1952. In this letter he spoke with some urgency against what he saw as an encroaching doctrinaire attitude toward Klein's work by factions in the British Psychoanalytic Society. Winnicott was concerned that every paper presented had to be reinterpreted in Kleinian language during the discussions that followed. He wrote about his concern with "Kleinism" and urged Melanie Klein to help purge the Society of this pressure (Winnicott, 1952b, p. 35).

Here one can see Winnicott's aversion to any kind of doctrinaire attitude, to any kind of pressure to speak a certain language in the conveyance of ideas. Said more positively, Winnicott desired a freedom for everyone to find his or her own voice to express understanding of psychoanalytic truths (Winnicott, 1952b). Winnicott's appeal to Klein for tolerance of differences in expression sounds very much like Wesley's comments on differences among Christians when they speak of God. "It is true, believers may not all speak alike; they may not all use the same language. . . . But a difference of expression does not necessarily imply a different sentiment. Different persons may use different expressions, and yet mean the same thing. . . . How then can we be rigorous in requiring others to use just the same expressions with us" (Wesley, 1765, p. 454). Winnicott may not have been familiar with this actual advice from Wesley, but he is imbued with this Wesleyan attitude.

Finally, one might note that something of Winnicott's Wesleyan heritage is visible in Winnicott's work to create a place for the so-called middle group in the British Psychoanalytic Society. Winnicott's efforts to find a place for a psychoanalysis of the middle mirrors in some way Wesley's efforts to articulate a theology of the middle. As a member of this middle group Winnicott tried to appreciate the contributions of those aligned with both Melanie Klein and Anna Freud (while also appreciating how they were both wrong!). Of course, Winnicott's allegiance to the middle left him suspect by the more doctrinaire Kleinians and Freudians, not unlike the suspicion Wesley experienced from the more doctrinaire Calvinists on the one hand and the high Anglicans on the other (Maddox, 1994).

Non-systematic (Practical in Focus)

Another way Methodist piety seems to have influenced the way Winnicott practiced psychoanalysis is in its focus on practical (rather than systematic) structures of thought and action. Several of Wesley's biographers have described him as a "practical theologian" rather than a "systematic" one (Chilcote, 2004; Collins, 2007; Maddox, 1994). Chilcote noted of Wesley's theology that it was "formulated in the saddle and in the context of a ministry among common, ordinary people seeking to be faithful disciples of Jesus—it was eminently practical" (p. 22). Recall Wesley (1746b) himself "design[ed] plain truth for plain people" (p. 104).

Winnicott, much like Wesley, forged his theory in the midst of his work with people. Therapy, Winnicott came to believe did not entail a slavish allegiance to psychoanalytic theory; theory must be adaptable to clinical practice. It was the practical task of helping someone who was suffering that drove the way Winnicott practiced therapy. His theory derived from his clinical work and was shaped and guided by what worked in clinical practice. He held up as a guide "an analyst who challenges everything, who puts clinical evidence before accepted theory, and who is no worshiper at a shrine" (Winnicott, 1953b, p. 413). (This does not mean that Winnicott always attained such aspirations—cf. Mitchell, 1993.)

Thus, like Wesley, Winnicott's thought also lacks a coherent overall theoretical system. As he himself noted, his work would make little sense to those who had not been exposed to Freud first (Winnicott, 1954f). The same might be said of the relationship of Winnicott's thought to Klein's theory (cf. Winnicott, 1963n). So, although Winnicott ends up making several theoretical contributions to psychoanalysis, these emerged from his clinical work rather than from a systematic attempt at theory building.

It is understandable therefore that Winnicott never developed a theoretical "system" around which others had to gather. Furthermore, he steadfastly refused to become a "leader" of the middle group, a move that might have given it more theoretical definition. Although there are multiple reasons for Winnicott's failure to create a psychoanalytic system, including the nature of his own mental processes, part of the reason for his lack of building a system was his desire to let everyone find his or her own voice, a desire deeply resonant with his Wesleyan Methodist background.[1] As a corollary to this lack of system building, Pontalis (1987) once observed that although one could speak of "Klienian" patients he did not think there were any "Winnicottian" ones. One would add that it would not mirror the spirit of Winnicott to find such.

There are other Wesleyan Methodist influences at work in Winnicott's failure to develop a "theoretical system." Winnicott's many presentations to non-analytic groups were earlier connected to the Wesleyan Methodist emphasis on inclusiveness. Here one observes the additional point that Winnicott's presentations to non-analytic audiences reflect a Wesleyan emphasis on speaking practically rather than systematically. Thus, whatever other motivations may have driven them, Winnicott's many speeches on the problems of social management, education, and parenting (in addition to those he gave on clinical problems) reflect a Wesleyan emphasis on speaking practically (plainly) to ordinary people (cf. Wesley, 1746b).

In his focus on practical theory rather than systematic theory, Winnicott seems like Wesley temperamentally. Whether Winnicott's focus on the practical over the systematic is a result of his Wesleyan heritage or merely a way in which he is temperamentally like Wesley is an interesting question. It may be that this lack of system in Winnicott's thinking was a temperamental quality that he would have displayed had he a background different from Wesleyan Methodism. However, it also is interesting to note that William James (1902) had long ago observed that people are drawn to religious traditions that match their temperament, so that what one may have in Winnicott is a confluence of personal temperament and religious background, both reflective of the importance of practical service over theoretical sophistication.

Wesleyan Methodist Piety and the Goals of Psychoanalysis

Not only does Winnicott's Wesleyan Methodist background influence the way in which he practiced psychoanalysis (e.g., as non-exclusive, non-dogmatic), it influenced the way Winnicott thought about the goals of psychoanalysis as well. In Winnicott's descriptions of the goals of analysis one hears further echoes of his religious heritage.

Before turning to specific similarities between the goals of psychoanalysis and religion, it is important to note that the metaphor of "religion" itself seem to be one that Winnicott used several times to frame his work as a psychoanalyst. Use of this metaphor helped him explore similarities and differences between the two approaches. On one occasion he described the work he did to a group of doctors as a "kind of religion" that dealt with external relationships (Winnicott, 1970d, p. 112). What he suggested in this talk was that psychoanalysis was like a religion in the sense that it explored how external relationships help shape who one came to be and further, how these relationships contributed to a sense of meaning and aliveness in life. And while he claimed here that psychoanalysis did not deal with the "religion of the inner experience," in other places (e.g. 1958g, 1961d, 1968b) he pointed out that psychoanalysis did have its own appreciation for and means of exploring the richness of the inner world (including inner religious experience).

One also notes that in the excitement of his initial discovery of psychoanalysis Winnicott (1919) spoke in religious metaphors when he talked about writing plainly so that those "who run may read" (p. 2). This language evoked the religious imagery of the Hebrew prophet who was told to write the word of the Lord plainly so that those who read it may run (Habakkuk 2:2). In his early enthusiasm he is close to likening psychoanalysis to a "revelation" (which is exactly the word Clare [Winnicott, 1983] used to describe his encounter with Darwin). However, one most clearly sees parallels between religion and psychoanalysis when one looks at the goals Winnicott ascribed to each.

A Focus on Cure/Care

In the essay in which he described his work in psychoanalysis and child psychiatry as "a religion of external relationship" Winnicott (1970d) noted that both religion and medicine were interested in "cure," a word that implied "care." Drawing from the *Oxford Dictionary of the English Language* regarding the etymological roots for "cure" (Hopkins, 1997), Winnicott traced changes in the meaning of "cure" from "care" to "remedy" and pointed out that something of the original meaning needed to be retained. It was this common focus as people who "care-cure" and its implications that Winnicott explored in this talk. He concluded by noting that "it is always a steadying thing to find that one's work links with entirely natural phenomena, and with the universals, and with what we expect to find in the best of poetry, philosophy, and religion" (Winnicott, 1970d, p. 120). Thus, for Winnicott religion and psychoanalysis shared a common goal in their interest in care-cure.

Attention to Human Suffering

A second parallel interest and goal shared by psychoanalysis and religion was a focus on helping individuals come to grips with suffering. At the beginning of his psychoanalytic career Winnicott (1935) spoke of this parallel in his paper on "The Manic Defense." He noted that religion helped people deal with depression, to rise up beyond their suffering (to become "ascensive") through religious faith and ritual. He observed that others acknowledged sadness without the aid of religion and perhaps found psychoanalysis able to provide a kind of shared support. (Of course, both people in analysis and religious people may defensively avoid recognizing their sadness). Years later Winnicott re-affirmed this common goal of the alleviation of suffering. Compare his comments on doing therapy with "character disorders" ("Here then is the basis for psychotherapy, because psychotherapy relates to individual suffering and need for help" [Winnicott, 1963l, p. 205]) with his comments regarding the "healing phenomena of ordinary life" ("innumerable environmental failure situations are frozen but are reached and unfrozen by the various healing phenomena of ordinary life, namely friendships, nursing during physical illness, poetry, etc., etc." [Winnicott, 1954h, p. 284]). He clarified in another place that the "etc." included religion (Winnicott, 1961f).

Valuing the Interior Life

A third goal that psychoanalysis and religion shared in common for Winnicott was their respective valuing of the interior life. A previous chapter noted how Wesley's emphasis on personal experience and religious affections was a way Wesleyan Methodism attended to the interior life (cf. Clapper, 1989; Wesley, 1746d, 1746e) and this chapter has observed how an emphasis on personal piety does the same. Winnicott recognized this shared emphasis between psychoanalysis and religion on the importance of the interior life in several places (e.g., 1958g, 1961d, 1968b), writing at one point of their shared recognition of "the importance of the *feelings* of early years" (1931b, p. 7, emphasis added).

Nurturing the Sacred Core of the Person (True Self)

A most intriguing parallel between psychoanalysis and religion in Winnicott comes from examining what became for him the central goal of therapy: an attendance to and nurturing of what he called the "sacred core" or "true self" of the individual (Winnicott, 1960e).

The goals of psychoanalysis have been variously framed by Winnicott. For instance, psychoanalysis "enables the patient to release painful material from repression" (1945e, p. 131); it seeks to bring "to consciousness that which was unconscious" (1954c, p. 60); it "aims simply and solely at undoing the hitch" in the individual's emotional development (1961f, p. 103) so that "the person who is being analyzed gradually comes to feel less and less at the mercy of unknown forces both within and without, and more and more able to deal in his or her own peculiar way with the difficulties inherent in human nature, in personal growth, and in the gradual achievement of a mature and constructive relationship to society" (1945e, p. 133); more characterized by "freedom within the personality," a "capacity for trust and faith," and "freedom from self-deception" (1967c, p. 26).

However, it is obvious that the longer he practiced psychoanalysis the clearer it became to him that a critical goal of analysis was to provide a space in which the sacred core of the person, the true self, might have opportunity to emerge and flourish. A sample of comments makes this clear: "It seems necessary to allow for the concept of the isolation of this central self as a characteristic of health" (Winnicott, 1960i, p. 46; cf. Tuber, 2008). "At the center of each person is an incommunicado element, and this is sacred and most worthy of preservation" (Winnicott, 1963a, p. 187). "The fact remains that the search for the self as a way of feeling real, and of living from the true rather than from the false self, is a task that belongs . . . to a large portion of the human race" (Winnicott, 1964h, p. 491). "I am concerned with the search for the self. . . . It is in playing and only in playing that the individual child or adult is able to be creative and to use the whole personality, and it is only in being creative that the individual discovers the self" (Winnicott, 1971j, p. 54).

Winnicott's description of this sacred core of the individual is reminiscent of theological language used to ascribe an essential, spiritual core to humans. This notion of a central, sacred core in humans is variously spoken of as the "soul" or "spirit" or the *imago Dei* by theologians (Anderson, 1990; Boyd, 1998; Maddox, 1994; Muller, 1990; Rollins, 1999; Wesley, 1788a, 1788b). Nurturing this sacred core is clearly a goal of religion (cf. Wesley [1759]: "You know that the great end of religion is to renew our hearts in the image of God" [p. 185]). Although Winnicott (1964a; cf. 1963a) did not directly mention nurturing this sacred core as a goal of religion, he acknowledged that religion may be a venue in which this happens. Parallels between Winnicott's concept of the true self and a theological understanding of a sacred core in humans are reconsidered in a later chapter.

A Christ-like Therapist

Another way that one sees the influence of Winnicott's Wesleyan Methodist piety on his practice of psychoanalysis comes through his interest in and identification with the figure of Jesus. This interest in the character of Jesus leads to what might be characterized as a goal for the analyst rather than a goal for psychoanalysis as such.

Although Winnicott (1919) had early on shown some interest in the life of Christ in his letter to Violet, his encounter with Robert Graves' reconstruction of the life of Jesus, particularly in the books *King Jesus* (1947) and the *Nazarene Gospel Restored* (Graves and Podro, 1954) sparked a special interest in the life of Jesus for Winnicott during his later years (Hoffman, 2004).[2] He wrote to Bion in 1967 of his fascination with this latter book because it gave him new perspective on the religious stories of his youth (Winnicott, 1967f).

However, Winnicott's interest in the life of Jesus is more than academic; he also identified with Jesus on several levels. As Rodman (2003) observed, "from at least the mid-1940's to the mid-1960's, Jesus Christ was clearly a figure with whom he identified" (p. 291). According to Kahr (1996) Charles Rycroft pointed out that this identification was not necessarily a healthy identification for Winnicott. Kahr cited a personal communication with Rycroft to the effect that "Winnicott suffered from an identification with the martyred Jesus Christ, masochistically torturing himself with more and more tasks" (p. 124). It is possible this masochistic identification compounded certain narcissistic tendencies in Winnicott (e.g., development of a messianic complex). Goldman (1993) quoted a personal communication from Katharine Rees, a psychiatric social worker with Winnicott at Paddington Green Hospital where he worked for forty years to the effect that "it is as if he felt an ounce of Winnicott was worth a pound of pediatric psychotherapy" (p. 10). She concluded that his tendency to see children on an irregular schedule rather than refer them to other therapists who could have seen them on a traditional analytic schedule "short-changed" some of the children.

There were other expressions of Winnicott's identification with the sufferings of Christ. One can be seen in the story of his fashioning a crucifix from matches during one of his sessions with Marion Milner, an analysand at the time. The story as recounted by Milner to Linda Hopkins (2004):

> In one of our sessions, Donald was playing with some matches and an elastic that were here on the table. He made them into a beautiful little crucifix. There were two matches for the cross and then he bent the other one forward like Christ, with the head hanging down. A rubber band held it all together. He left it there, and I always thought he was trying to tell me something." (p. 241)

Hopkins noted three interpretations that have been given to this incident:

> One comes from Milner, who said, "I think it was something about his marriage to Alice." Another comes from Rodman (2003), to whom Milner also told the crucifix story. Rodman interpreted the story as Winnicott's request for help from Milner: "I told . . . [Milner] . . . that it seemed as if he had wanted treatment from her, needed it, and communicated this via the crucifix. . . . He was trapped, I thought, in his Christ situation" (p. 140). Masud Khan had heard Milner's story years earlier, and he had a typically cynical reaction that he rec-

orded in his private Workbook. . . . "Silently to myself, I instantly interpreted
that DWW knew he was crucified on a hopeless predicament." (p. 241)

Regardless of what else may be going on in Winnicott's fashioning of the crucifix, in all three interpretations everyone is agreed that part of the identification is
with the sufferings of the Christ. The fuller implications of this identification are
not so clear; it is harder to say whether the identification with the suffering
Christ exacerbated Winnicott's own suffering or helped him cope. Perhaps it did
a bit of both.

Rodman (2003) noted that Winnicott's identification with Jesus also can be
seen in his poem "The Tree" which he wrote late in his life and that is associated
with his mother's depression. In the context of the larger poem, it is obvious the
tree in the title is the Cross. Rodman interpreted the poem in part as a "privately
stated commentary on his plight as a Jesus figure" who suffered because of and
with his mother (p. 291). However, in the context of the complete poem, the
identification with Christ does not revolve entirely around dealing with his
mother's depression. There also are positive aspects of Winnicott's identification with the Christ figure who not only suffers but gives of himself to bring
hope and love to others (cf. Hoffman, 2004).[3]

Rodman (2003) offered another insight into a possible identification with
Jesus when he described Winnicott as bringing a "New Testament gloss" to the
ethos of the British Psychoanalytic Society in contrast to the "harsh . . . Old Testament" ethos represented by Klein and her constituency. Rodman spoke of
Winnicott as representing the "forgiving attitude of a non-organizational, pre-
Pauline Jesus Christ" (p. 114). This description of Winnicott's identification
with Jesus picks up the non-organizational or non-systematic nature of Winnicott's temperament that has already been noted in his refusal to take a leader-
ship role for the middle group of the British Psychoanalytic Society or to develop a theoretical system. Rodman's connection of Winnicott with a "forgiving"
Jesus evokes another identification that needs elaboration.

The most intriguing way that Winnicott's interest in and possible identification with Jesus shows up is in his last major theoretical paper devoted to the
topic of object usage (Winnicott, 1971k). This is a complex paper and was not
well received (or understood) when first presented (Goldman, 1993; Kahr, 1998;
Rodman, 2003).[4] In this paper Winnicott distinguished object "usage" from object "relating," the former being what allowed the infant to come to see the
world as other than its projections. In order for an object to be "used" it must
survive attempts (in the infant's unconscious fantasy) to destroy it, and do this
without retaliating against the infant. It is the object's survival that makes it "real" to the infant and no longer simply part of its inner world.

Winnicott connected this concept of object usage to therapeutic contexts.
He argued that the nature of successful therapy required that patients not only
relate to their therapists in ways that re-create early object "relating" but that at
some point patients need to encounter an object that is able to survive their aggression in ways that earlier objects did not (i.e., they do not respond in the same

ways to which the patient was accustomed). It is the object's ability to survive the patient's aggression (without retaliating) that permits the patient to "use" the object that has been "psychically destroyed" (in this case the therapist) to construct a new interior life in which objects are allowed their own reality.

Hopkins (1989) pointed out how Winnicott's interest in the survival of the object is clearly mirrored in the death and resurrection of Jesus. That is to say, Jesus becomes the representative of object survival *par excellence*. Healy (2004) has summarized Hopkins position succinctly:

> For Hopkins, two things are central in Christ's story: the human destructiveness Christ absorbed in the Crucifixion, and the Resurrection proof that this destructiveness failed to destroy either Christ's person or his love for his destroyers. For Winnicott [1971k], two things are central in the experience of object-use: infantile destructiveness directed at the mother, and the ongoing demonstration that neither the mother herself nor her love for her child are destroyed by its attacks. (p. 54)

Thus, Christ shows himself to be in his crucifixion and resurrection both a non-retaliating and surviving object.

One notes at this point that Winnicott's insights about object usage may owe some debt to his reflections on the life of Jesus during the same period in which he works on this paper (Hoffman, 2004). Although Winnicott did not include specific religious imagery in his discussion of object usage, he did acknowledge in another place that the movement toward object usage changed the nature of the relating so that one "almost worshipped" the object "in a new way" (Winnicott, 1970f, p. 263).

It is clear in his paper on object usage that Winnicott thought the therapist's ability to make him or herself of "use" to the client signaled an advanced way of working in therapy. He tried to make himself a therapist that patients could use in this way, seeking to survive their aggression in non-retaliatory ways.[5] If, as Hoffman (2004) suggested, this article was connected to Winnicott's reflections on the life of Jesus, one may see here another way that he identified with Jesus. That is, the type of analyst that Winnicott sought to be was one that was a Christ-like figure in that the analyst survived the patient's projections without retaliating (cf. Hoffman, 2011). Winnicott's interest in these Christ-like qualities for therapists is taken up again in chapter 9.

The Theological Heritage of Developmental Psychology

In concluding this chapter on the influence of Winnicott's religious upbringing on the "form" of his thought Susan Kirschner's (1996) thesis that the broad contours of Winnicott's religious heritage shaped not only his thought categories but those of an entire discipline is taken up. Winnicott, like his psychological forebears, Freud (1905) and Klein (1946), offered a "developmental" psychology. That is, he painted a picture of humans as moving from an earlier, less differentiated, more dependent state toward a maturity characterized by a relative "independence," more authentic living, and "higher" level relationships. His use of the phrase "grow up out of" as indicative of this trajectory has been noted. According to Kirschner (1996) this type of teleological vision of humans was indebted to a much older paradigm that found its roots in Christian theology.

Kirschner's (1996) enlightening book on the "religious and romantic origins of psychoanalysis" traced the genesis and transmission of the "cultural narrative" of "development" through four successive phases. Kirschner argued that the cultural roots of a narrative of development had its origins in the Christian story of humans being created in the image of God, their subsequent "fall" from communion with God, and their redemption and restoration to fellowship with God (phase 1). In subsequent centuries this basic narrative structure was reworked through a neo-platonic adaptation that gave the story a more "secularized" and "interiorized" cast (phase 2) that was subsequently deepened by the Romantic movement in Britain and Germany (phase 3). This narrative found its latest embodiment especially in the psychoanalytic versions of human development offered by such theorists as Winnicott (phase 4). Thus, she concluded that "modern theories of human development are heir to much older spiritual . . . structures and themes" (p. 5).[6]

Kirschner (1996) further argued that these "long-standing cultural themes persist not only in the plot structure of psychoanalytic developmental theories, but also in the ends or goals of development as depicted by those theories" (e.g., self-reliance, authenticity, intimacy). More specifically, "these images of the ideal self are secularized versions of Protestant ascetic and mystical visions of the soul's election by God or reunion with him" (p. 5).

Psychoanalytic developmental theories show their religious heritage in yet another way according to Kirschner (1996). Not only are the "plot structure" and "substantive goals" indebted to the Christian narrative, the psychoanalytic vision of the "human condition" sounds very much like its religious forerunner. "Both types of narrative—psychological theory as much as theological doctrine—embody attempts to delineate and address the deepest and most difficult existential issues that human beings face: suffering, loss, frustration, and various forms of moral 'evil'" (p.6). Thus, at least one aspect of both discourses is that they function as "theodicies," that is, as attempts to address the "existence of all forms of human suffering and the imperfections of human life . . . and imbue [them] with meaning. A theodicy constructs the dilemmas of human existence along certain lines and offers the possibility of their resolution (e.g., salvation) or mitigation along similarly structured lines" (Kirschner, 1996, p. 6). Already noted were the common goals between religion and psychoanalysis in Winnicott. Perhaps part of his ease in seeing similar goals is attributable to this common cultural narrative of development.

Kirschner's (1996) is a powerful and well-argued case that helps one appreciate how Winnicott's Christian roots give "form" to his overall theory. One can see that his way of framing human development as a journey from "absolute dependence" and merger, to a "relative dependence" and ability to distinguish "me" from "not-me," to a movement "towards independence" and object usage (Winnicott, 1960i, 1971k), mirrors the Christian narrative structure. In a secularized and interior focused way, his narrative reflects the journey from creation (union with God/Other) to a separation from the Other, to a reconnection with the Other in differently constituted ways.

If one were to connect this teleological narrative more directly to Wesleyan theology, one would note that the maturational goal for humans according to Wesley (1759) is the "renewal of the image of God" (p. 185). This goal of Wesley's fits with the larger Christian narrative just noted; the "renewal" is necessary because humans have "fallen" from their original relationship with God and each other (Wesley, 1756b, 1759).

Thus, one concludes that The Wesleyan Methodist piety that so deeply influenced Winnicott was itself heir to a more general Christian narrative that impacted the whole of Western culture. This "narrative of development" provided a lens by which much of human life came to be structured. The developmental and clinical psychologies especially came to reflect an implicit theological structure (Browning, 1987; Oden, 1978).[7] Chapter 11 will explore more fully the implicit theological dimensions of Winnicott's developmental psychology. Next, attention is focused on ways this larger Christian narrative is also discernable in the way religious language permeated the discourse of the Western world, especially the language of the English Bible. The following chapter explores this influence in Winnicott's writing.

Notes

1.   There is another, more personal reason for this aversion to requiring that psychoanalysis speak a specific language that is connected to Winnicott's temperament and his need to make theory "real" or "alive" for himself (Goldman, 1993). These qualities were expressed in certain workings of his mind that made it hard for him to give due diligence to his intellectual sources (Phillips, 1998; Rodman, 2003). Winnicott was often accused, and justly so, of not citing those from which he drew ideas. He acknowledged this as a weakness in a letter to Balint (Winnicott, 1960g). In a characteristic admission, he once noted that his method of writing did not involve a historical survey that connected his ideas to those of other people; rather, he gathered snatches of insight from various people and places, including his clinical work and formulated his own ideas. Only later, if at all, did he try to acknowledge the connection of his ideas with what others had written (Winnicott, 1945c). Masud Khan (1975) told a revealing story of trying to encourage Winnicott to read an article by Lionel Trilling. Winnicott responded "its no use, Masud, asking me to read anything! If it bores me I shall fall asleep in the middle of the first page, and if it interests me I will start re-writing it by the end of that page" (p. xvi). Late in life Winnicott admitted that in his attempts to find his own language he had neglected the language of other analytic contributions and others had been impoverished by the inabil-

ity to connect his work to other analytic work. He admitted that this failure was a "fault" in his character (Winnicott, 1967h).

2.   Robert Graves is best known as the author whose book was the basis for the popular television series, *I, Claudius*. His novel *King Jesus* (1947) is an imaginative reconstruction of the life of Jesus as one who "dedicates himself to being the zealous enemy of Woman and by doing so becomes one of her heroes" (Phillips, 1988, p. 29). This is a theme that would have appealed to Winnicott's (1950e, 1957d) interest in the cultural "fear of WOMAN."

The Nazarene Gospel Restored (Graves and Podro, 1954) is presented as a non-fictional reconstruction of the historical life of Jesus. Biblical and historical scholars faulted the book for both its distortions and its failure to cite the sources upon which its arguments were built (Nesbitt, 1955; *Time*, 1954). Winnicott (1967f) noted this disfavor of the Christian churches toward the book in his letter to Bion.

3.   The entire poem has been printed several times (Hoffman, 2004, 2011; Rodman, 2003). It is produced in its entirety in chapter 6 of this work.

4.   The paper seems not to have been communicated well either. Winnicott was sick and did not respond substantively to the paper's respondents (Goldman, 1993). Winnicott revised the paper prior to publication to clarify that the object destruction to which he referred occurred in fantasy and not literally, a point that seems not to have been clear in the initial presentation of the paper.

5.   Rodman (2003) told a story of how Winnicott replaced a valuable vase that a patient had broken in a fit of rage before the patient's next session. Winnicott saw the replacement as a means of letting the patient know without verbal comment to the patient that he had "survived" her rage.

6.   Kirschner (1996) extended this argument in discussing the work of William Kessen (1979, 1990). "Kessen points out that in the case of child psychology, the welding of Darwin's non-teleological evolutionary theory to the teleological idea of development and 'progress' borrowed from the moral sciences harkens back to a much older concept, that of Salvation History" (p. 105). This is interesting in particular both for the way in which Winnicott, like others, has changed Darwin's original notion of "devolution" to an upward spiral, and for the way in which this illumines Winnicott's attraction to Darwin. One might argue that what made Darwin so attractive to Winnicott, at least in part, was that Winnicott's particular reading of Darwin had a deep (unconscious?) resonance with a much older paradigm from his own religious tradition (cf. Hoffman, 2004).

7.   Marie Hoffman (2011) has written an insightful articulation of the "mutual recognition" that is possible when the common roots of the psychoanalytic and Christian narratives are acknowledged.

Chapter 6
Scriptural and Religious Allusions in Winnicott

"I am very interested in the way you bring in the Bible story"

Winnicott once disclosed to a colleague that he felt odd when he sat in the president's chair at the British Psychoanalytic Society because "I *don't know my Freud* in the way a president should do; yet I do find I have Freud in my bones" (quoted in Grosskurth, 1986, p. 401). Winnicott's more intuitive approach to appropriating Freud (as well as Klein and other psychoanalytic authors) has been noted by several scholars; they attribute this approach to his need to make the theoretical writings of psychoanalysis "real" to him, and not something mechanically adopted (Goldman, 1993; Kahr, 1996; Phillips, 1988). They also note that this approach often caused Winnicott to be remiss in citing the sources for his own ideas, a habit that sometimes earned him the ire of colleagues (Phillips, 1988; Rodman, 1987, 2003).

Goldman (1993) has noted further the wide range of intellectual influences on Winnicott's ideas, many of which go without specific citation. In addition to the psychoanalytic ideas of Freud and Klein, Goldman noted that the literary and intellectual sources of Winnicott's work included thinkers "as diverse as the Romantic poets such as Wordsworth and Keats, the British empiricists, Lewis Carroll, Darwin, the fourteenth-century Lollards, and John Wesley" (p. xxvii).

As broad as this list might be, this chapter will argue that another source for Winnicott's thought is the English Bible and the ethos it engendered in British culture. In one way, this chapter reinforces Kirschner's (1996) thesis that the Christian narrative permeated English culture. One evidence of this is the ubiquity of scriptural and religious allusions in English discourse. This influence is especially notable in Winnicott's writing.

As Winnicott did with most sources, he did not clearly identify the English Bible when used. Despite the lack of citation however, one finds ample illustrations of scriptural and religious allusions in Winnicott's writings. Given the influence of the Christian tradition and the English Bible on British culture one might expect to find some citations of this sort in any educated Englishman. However, so frequent is this type of allusion, that one could make the case that Winnicott not only had "Freud in his bones," he also had the English Bible (and his Wesleyan Methodist heritage) "in his bones." He certainly acknowledged his interest in how scriptural and religious concepts compared with psychoanalytic ones in a letter to Bion writing that he was "very much interested in the way you bring in the Bible story in your paper on catastrophic change and also quite frequently when you are talking" (Winnicott, 1967f, p. 170). A means by which one can discern the influence of Winnicott's religious upbringing on his thought is in the way scriptural and religious allusions flavor his writings.

This chapter might be thought an extended illustration of the influence of Winnicott's religious heritage on the form of his thought. However, one also shall discover that to a lesser extent, it also influenced the content of his thought.

Scriptural Allusions in Winnicott's Writings

True to his more intuitive style Winnicott only directly cited a scriptural source once; all other occasions when he appealed to Scripture are allusions without specific notation as to where the language or thought originated. Sometimes these allusions were to specific verses; other times they simply illustrated the use of language steeped in the English Bible. At times the allusions only appropriated the wording from Scripture to illustrate a point already made, much like one might quote a poet. At other times, his appeal to Scripture was more substantial and actually made his point or extended his thought.

Direct Quotations from Scripture

The one occasion in his published writings where Winnicott specifically quoted the Scripture as Scripture is a reference to the book of *Ecclesiasticus*. In a discussion of the "split-off intellect" (a concept associated with the False Self) he noted that it was the person who was able to "assimilate" or integrate his or her bodily and mental experiences that truly could achieve wisdom. By contrast, "the intellect only knows how to *talk about* wisdom. You might quote: 'How can he get wisdom whose talk is of bullocks?' (Ecclesiasticus 38:25)" (Winnicott, 1968i, p. 60) (emphasis added). Here Winnicott's citation was more to illustrate his point than to extend it.[1]

Allusions to Specific Verses without Citations

Although the above example is the only specific citation of Scripture in Winnicott's published writings, this absence of specific quotations nevertheless misses a rich and varied reference to Scripture found in Winnicott's writings. Much more common is his allusion to Scripture without specific citation. Again, the chief way in which he made use of Scripture in this fashion was to illustrate a point or to give an apt, perhaps familiar phrase, to his thought.

For instance, in comparing the damage done in leucotomy (a type of brain surgery to correct "mental" problems) to that done by severing motor nerves in the upper limbs to correct tendencies to masturbation or theft, he noted how "unthinkable" the latter. Of such patients he remarked, "perhaps the victim might have said 'forgive them, for they know not what they do!'" clearly a reference to the prayer of Jesus from the cross in Luke 23:34 (Winnicott, 1951a, p. 549). The allusion made a poignant point, but did not appreciably extend his argument.

Other examples of this illustrative use of Scripture abound. In commenting on the infant's ability to rest after making reparative gestures to the mother Winnicott (1954c) stated: "The breast (body, mother) is now mended, and the day's work is done. Tomorrow's instincts can be waited with limited fear. Sufficient unto the day is the evil thereof" (p. 72). The latter sentence is a quotation from Matthew 6:34 from the Sermon on the Mount. The quotation adds a familiar phrase that reinforced the previous sentence regarding tomorrow's anxiety. His comment on how the adolescent must learn to cope with newly found powers of aggression is similar. Of such powers he noted, "It is like putting new wine into old bottles" (Winnicott, 1961a, p. 80), a phrase that mirrored Jesus' comment about not putting new wine in old wineskins lest the new wine break the old container (Matthew 9:17), an evocative description of the adolescent's struggle with aggression. Another example of this use of Scripture is the opening lines of his review of a book by Searles where he noted: "Ideas, like the Word, can fall on stony ground, or they can be received into good soil and so bear fruit" (Winnicott, 1963g, p. 478). This reference clearly calls to mind the parable of the sower and the seed told by Jesus where the seed (the word of God) is said to fall variously on stony ground, among thorns, and on good ground (Matthew 13:1–9; Mark 4:1–9; Luke 8:4–8). He wished Searles' ideas to fall on good ground. He made two other references to the parable of the sower and the seeds, both of which were illustrative (Winnicott, 1936b, 1970g).

Winnicott's self-description when criticizing medical doctors is a final example of this illustrative use of Scripture to emphasize a point with a familiar phrase. He remarked, "I assure you I know all about the beam in my own eye" (Winnicott, 1970d, p. 114), an allusion to Jesus' comments about the need to pay attention to the larger shortcomings in oneself before commenting on the smaller shortcomings of others (e.g., the "beam" (log) in one's own eye versus the "moat" (splinter) in another's eye: Matthew 7:5). One notes at this point Winnicott's preference for citing the language of the King James translation, and for a clear familiarity with the Sermon on the Mount (three allusions here; six altogether).

A slightly different use of allusion to a specific Scripture can be found in a talk on autism. There Winnicott commented on the difficulty that the parents of an ill child had in that they were apt to be uncritically blamed for the child's condition. He noted that "it is easier, however, if society can get the idea that the illness is due to fate, or an act of God. Even the sins of the fathers will do quite well" (Winnicott, 1966d, p. 213). Here Winnicott's allusion to Scripture also points to wider cultural reflections concerning the explanation of suffering. The Scriptures, like a variety of cultural writings offer several answers, including the notion that one's suffering is not always due to one's own action. Punishment for the sins of the fathers is a concept noted several times in the Hebrew Scripture (e.g., Psalm 79:8, Isaiah 65:7; Jeremiah 32:18). What Winnicott seemed to suggest through appropriating this concept was that parents might be thought less at fault for a child's autism if there were a biological or genetic cause. Although this meaning is not entirely absent from the Scripture, the passage alluded to more likely makes the opposite of Winnicott's point. That is, a father's action may be blamed for a son's suffering. So, although Winnicott shows familiarity with the language of Scripture, this familiarity did not always demonstrate adequate textual understanding of the passages to which he alluded.

On one occasion Winnicott used scriptural allusion to offer counterpoint to his psychoanalytic point. He re-appropriated (might one say "used") Jesus' comments about asking and receiving from the Sermon on the Mount (Matthew 7:7). He is speaking of how transitional objects are a bridge toward reality thinking. Though unquestioned as to their own reality, they are essential to the infant's attempts to relate inner and outer reality. Winnicott remarked of such objects: "Not 'ask and it shall be given', so much as 'reach out and it shall be there for you to have, to use, to waste'" (Winnicott, 1970e, p. 50). This familiar turn of phrase helped make his point about the nature of such objects and their use. For Winnicott, it is only through the use of such objects that people come to understand the real world and their relation to it.

General Allusions to the English Bible

There are other allusions to Scripture in Winnicott that give a sense that the language that comes readily to his mind is steeped in the language of the English Bible. Again, one often has the sense that the allusions are illustrative, and not used to make a specific connection to or extension of an analytic concept.

An example of this use of phrasing that evokes the language of the English Bible can be found in his advice to those who work with pre-school children to "harden your hearts" (cf. Deut 15:7; 1 Sam 6:6) toward the potential delinquent and remove them from other children (Winnicott, 1936a, p. 76). Another example is his advice that there are different kinds of children, some who need treatment and some who may be left "to work out [their] own salvation" (cf. Phil 2:12) (Winnicott, 1936b, p. 90). Similarly, Winnicott's description of the melancholic who "strikes her breast with her fists and says: 'Woe is me!'" (Winnicott, 1958e, p. 55) bears a striking resemblance to the story of the tax collector who beat his chest and prayed "God be merciful to me a sinner" (Luke 18:13).

So common is this type of reference in Winnicott that it is not difficult to multiply other examples. When he referred to the physician's obligation, he noted, "included in the oath is the promise that we do not commit adultery with a patient" (Winnicott, 1960c, p. 160), evoking the phrasing in the seventh commandment (Exodus: 20:14). A reference to dreams as "daily bread" for the analyst (Winnicott, 1964f, p. 47) was an allusion to the Lord's Prayer (Matthew— "give us this day our daily bread"). Even Winnicott's comment that "the unforgivable sin in the cultural field is plagiarism" (Winnicott, 1971e, p. 99) alluded to scriptural comments about unforgivable sin (cf. Matthew 12:31–32).

Winnicott also appropriated scriptural phasing in the opening of his essay on "the place where we live" (Winnicott, 1971h, p. 104). He wrote that in seeking to emerge from the "muddle" of sorting inner from outer reality one looked for a place to rest. Such a place may be likened to finding port in a storm or "when I am on dry land I look for a house built on rock rather than on sand; and in my own home, which, (as I am English) is my castle, I am in a seventh heaven" (1971h, p. 104). This convoluted phrasing combined reference to Jesus' words from the Sermon on the Mount (Matthew 7:24) with a possible allusion to St. Paul's writings (2 Cor 12: 2 cf. "third heaven"), both merged with the English proverb about the nature of an Englishman's home (Titelman, 1996). One should note that the reference to "seventh heaven" is a common English phrase referring to paradise or bliss adapted from traditions about multiple heavens in Judaism, Christianity and Islam (Segel, 1999). This over-combination of allusions might be thought to "muddle" his opening point, but more likely was intended as a "playful" attempt to invite his reader into that playful area "where we most of the time are when we are experiencing life" (Winnicott, 1971h, p. 104).

There is one appropriation of scriptural phrasing by Winnicott that deepened his contrast between the type of knowing available to science and that available in religion. Winnicott contrasted science, with its openness to observation, to bringing preconceived ideas, a kind of "knowing in advance" that foreclosed openness and was anathema to science (and Winnicott). He stated "anyone who knows the answers in advance, who has seen the light, so to speak, is not a scientist, and must be out of place among scientists" (Winnicott, 1967a, p. 236). Here the allusion to "seeing the light, so to speak" evoked the story of St. Paul being struck down by a light on the road to Damascus (Acts 9: 1–9). Such revelations from outside or above were clearly in contrast to the kind of knowing that science brings. Winnicott strengthened this allusion to religious knowledge by revelation by stating that "knowing in advance belongs to poetry" (p. 237; and poetry is akin to religion for Winnicott [1945e]).

One also might note that Winnicott's well-known introduction to the concept of transitional phenomena seems to have the language of the English Bible in the background. Winnicott (1951b) wrote: "I am here staking a claim for the intermediate state between a baby's inability and his growing ability to recognize and accept reality. I am therefore studying *the substance of* illusion . . ." (p. 230, emphasis added). Hopkins (1989) noted that Winnicott's definition of transitional phenomena echoed the definition of faith found in the New Testament "the substance of things hoped for, the evidence of things not seen" (Letter to the Hebrews 11: 1).[2]

One might note before leaving this section that these same patterns are present in Winnicott's published letters. An illustration of Winnicott's acquaintance with specific scriptures comes from an early letter to his sister Violet in which he explained to her what psychoanalysis was about. He said he wished to be able to speak plainly and simply about psychoanalysis because he hoped one day to introduce these ideas to the English so that "who runs may read" (Winnicott, 1919, p. 2). Phillips (1988) noted how Winnicott's desire to speak plainly and simply mirrored John Wesley's ambition ("I design to speak plain truth for plain people"—cf. Wesley, 1746b, p. 104). Jacobs (1995) called attention to the scriptural allusion in Winnicott's words. The words are an inverted reference to Habbakkuk 2:2 which reads "And the Lord answered me and said: 'Write the vision; make it plain upon tablets, so he may run who reads it" (RSV). Clearly, one can see that Winnicott's desire to speak simply and plainly has behind it the prophet's admonishment to write plainly and clearly.

Another illustration of Winnicott's familiarity with specific Scriptures is found in comments to a colleague about the impact of his work on a certain case. Here Winnicott inverted a proverb cited by the Hebrew prophets Jeremiah (31:29) and Ezekial (18:2), a proverb interestingly enough that the prophets said would undergo a similar inversion: "The fathers have eaten sour grapes and the children's teeth are set on edge." Winnicott wrote: "In other words the mother had eaten grapes that were not sour and it was the child's teeth that ceased to be set on edge" (Winnicott, 1969e, p. 191). Both Jeremiah and Ezekial noted that there was to come a day when people "shall no longer say" this proverb because everyone would give an account for him or herself.

One also sees in Winnicott's private letters several illustrations where his acquaintance with scriptural language is such a part of who he was that his phrasing mirrored that of Scripture. To one colleague he compared depression to "carrying the sins of the whole world" (Winnicott, 1940, p. 5), a phrase that evokes the description of Jesus as the one who takes the sins of the whole world (John 1:29; 1 John 2:2). To another colleague he wrote that drawing conclusions from quantitative survey data is "like building a house on sand, to use a rather old-fashioned simile" (Winnicott, 1963h, p. 140), an allusion to Jesus' comments in the Sermon on the Mount (Matthew 7:26). When he wrote to John Wisdom that "I have done some important work out of the sweat of my psychoanalytic brow" he alluded to the verse about Adam's curse in the garden (Genesis 3:19) to emphasize his point that he did not wish his work to be overlooked (Winnicott, 1964e, p. 146). In a letter to Donald Gough about Gough's research into eye contact in infants, Winnicott (1968f) remarked: "I love to think of all the clinical observations that are waiting for us to make but it is a question of he who hath eyes to see let him hear!" (p. 176), a somewhat whimsical conflation of scriptural admonitions about seeing and hearing (cf. Matthew 13:13 "seeing they do not see, and hearing they do not hear." Cf. also Matthew 13:9; Revelation 3:22: "he who has ears, let him hear"). Finally, one might note Winnicott's letter to Michael Balint in which he observed that "it is certainly important for the Society to be reminded over and over again that man cannot live by bread alone—bread here meaning verbal interpretations," an allusion to Jesus' response to the devil's temptation in Matthew 4:4 (Winnicott, 1957c cited in Rodman, 2003, p. 239). One wonders if Winnicott did not think interpretations the temptation offered to analysts! His appeal to this verse certainly reaffirmed his conviction that one must not assume a dogmatic attitude toward the use of interpretations.

There also are scriptural allusions in Winnicott's unpublished papers and letters (cf. 1965b, 1970i, n.d.1). Probably the most striking illustration of scriptural allusions in Winnicott's unpublished works is his poem, "The Tree." Written late in his life, this poem provides an illustration of Winnicott's identification with the suffering Christ (Rodman, 2003). Hoffman (2004) has noted over two dozen scriptural allusions in this poem.[3]

Scriptural Allusions That Expand Psychoanalytic Ideas

Winnicott's allusions to Scripture to illustrate various points or to punctuate the point with a familiar phrase are clearly indicative of the deep influence of his religious upbringing, if only in their number. However, what is of more import in terms of demonstrating the lingering influence of his religious heritage are those occasions in which Winnicott actually used reference and allusions to Scripture to deepen or extend his psychoanalytic thought.

For instance, Winnicott evoked the creation story of Genesis to describe the infant's "creation" of a world ready to be found or created. According to Winnicott the infant, like a god, feels him or herself to be omnipotent. The mother facilitates this creation, and Winnicott's (1970e) comparative evocation that "each baby starts up with a new creation of the world. And on the seventh day we hope that he is pleased and takes a rest" (p. 49) clearly has the biblical account in mind. In addition to the positive appropriation of this imagery, Winnicott also employed it as counterpoint. Illustrative of this latter use is his comment that, "It is not necessary to postulate an original state of chaos. Chaos is a concept which carries with it the idea of order; and darkness too is not there at the beginning, since darkness implies light. At the beginning before each individual creates the world anew there is a simple state of being" (Winnicott, 1954c, p. 135). Chaos only arrives if the facilitating environment is not responsive and reliable.

Another use of reference and allusion to Scripture to deepen a psychoanalytic idea was Winnicott's reference to the Hebrew name for God (translated I AM) and his discussion of the importance of the attainment of the "unit state," or a sense of individuality (Winnicott, 1968i, p. 57; cf. 1955b).

Before integration the individual is unorganized, a mere collection of sensory-motor phenomena, collected by the holding environment. After integration the individual IS, that is to say, the infant human being has achieved unit status, can say I AM (except for not being able to talk). . . . I suggest that this I AM moment is a raw moment; the new individual feels infinitely exposed. Only if someone has her arms round the infant at this time can the I AM moment be endured, or rather, perhaps, risked. (Winnicott, 1955b, p. 148)

Winnicott saw achievement (and maintenance) of the I AM stage as a key marker in human development (1968i) and specifically related this achievement of individuality or unit status to the Hebrew name of God (I AM) (Winnicott, 1964g). He further connected this development into an "individual" to the emergence of monotheism in culture. "Does not this name (I AM) given to God reflect the danger that the individual feels he or she is in on reaching the state of individual being? . . . So when people first came to the concept of individuality, they quickly put it up in the sky and gave it a name that only a Moses could hear (Winnicott, 1968i, pp. 56–57). Because the I AM achievement is precarious and fraught with danger, he observed that in religious history one finds this developmental achievement handed over to God (Winnicott, 1954i). This sense of "personal existence" can be so anxiety producing that human defenses against this include retreat to some sort of unity or oneness with God (Winnicott, 1963e). This movement toward "self-assertion" (p. 95) that takes one away from the earlier merger with the environment (mother) sounds very much like the Judeo-Christian story of the separation from God told in Genesis. In achieving one's own sense of I AM, one has taken on characteristics of the One known by a similar name (Exodus 3:14).

A final example of the use of scriptural references to underscore a point Winnicott wished to make about psychoanalytic theory can be found in his paper on Klein's "depressive position." Winnicott (1935) quite clearly and consciously appropriated a part of the Christian tradition to speak about defenses against "depression" (not to be confused with the "depressive position," [Klein, 1946] a Kleinian term that referred to a stage of growth). Winnicott drew from the Christian tradition of the Ascension of Christ (cf. Acts 1:9–11) to argue for an "ascensive" movement as a way to cope with depression. If, as he suggested, Good Friday represented being in touch with the depths of sadness and Easter Sunday a manic response to such sorrow, then the Ascension represented a more balanced response that signaled recovery from one's depression (see chapter 8). Although he does not return to this imagery in other writings, Winnicott's familiarity with the Scriptures of his religious background is very much in evidence in this, his first psychoanalytic paper given on the occasion of his admission to membership in the British Psychoanalytic Society.

Religious Allusions in Winnicott's Writings

In addition to his allusions to Scriptures, which seem to convey some awareness of his source, Winnicott's writing also incorporated language that showed the deep indebtedness of Western culture to the influence of the Judeo-Christian tradition. Such influence is seen in the pervasive references to religious history, concepts and practice; it also is obvious in the way "religious" language is used to speak moralistically. One might attribute such references to having been schooled in the West, but the number of religious allusions again shows Winnicott to have imbibed more of this tradition than one might attribute to a general education. Thus one concludes that these references and allusions are further illustrations of the deep influence of his evangelical upbringing in the Wesleyan Methodist tradition. Of particular interest is his intentional use of religious allusions to draw parallels between psychoanalytic concepts and religious concepts and practices.

Religious Allusions as Part of Western Culture

Winnicott, like many of his countrymen, used language rich in allusions to religious concepts. From his use of these terms, it is not always clear whether he was aware of the specific religious background for such terms, though he would likely have known of their religious origin in a general way. Often these religious allusions are such a part of Western culture that they permeate the language almost unnoticed. An illustration of this might be Winnicott's (1970g) references to a child being assigned the role of "scapegoat" in the homes that kept evacuee children during the war (p. 227). The "scapegoat," of course, is a reference to aspects of ancient Hebrew practices connected to the Day of Atonement, where a lamb that was to represent the sins of the people was banished to the wilderness (Leviticus 16). Similar examples include his references to the child who danced like a "possessed" person in an attempt to control inner phenomena (Winnicott, 1946b), or his comment that one patient's use of guilt was rather like "sackcloth and ashes" without an outcome (Winnicott, 1966a, p. 164). Dancing or moving as though possessed is noted of both the prophets of Baal (1 Kings 18) and the afflicted man from Gerasene (Luke 8:29), while sackcloth and ashes were rituals connected to biblical traditions of mourning and repentance (cf. Ezek 27:31; Matt 11:21; Luke 10:13). Another example of this type of allusion would be Winnicott's reference to "onanism," an older way to refer to masturbation (Winnicott, 1934, p. 158; 1977, p. 160). The original reference is to Onan, who according to the Hebrew Scriptures sinned by "spilling his seed upon the ground" (Genesis 38:9). Although "spilling seed" is more likely a reference to coitus interruptus than masturbation (Hamilton, 1995), "onanism" was often used to designate the latter.

Although the prevalence of such terms in the English language may partly reflect Winnicott's Wesleyan Methodist background they may simply reflect the way scriptural terms have been absorbed in Western language and culture. In addition to the above kinds of words and concepts that have scriptural origins behind them, one can point to other ways that the Christian religion in particular has influenced the language and thought of the West. For instance, when Winnicott (1951b) referred to transitional objects being relegated to "limbo" (p. 233), he used a metaphorical re-appropriation of an originally religious concept that referred to the Catholic doctrine regarding the estate of the souls of infants who died unbaptized (V. Brown, 1990). Similarly, when he illustrated the futility of trying to separate the influence of the environment on a child's development from what is happening in the child's internal world he likened it to "trying to count the number of fairies on the end of a pin" (Winnicott, 1967h, p. 580). This remark is an allusion to esoteric medieval theological discussions about whether several angels could occupy the same space at once (cf. Aquinas, 1981).

In like manner one would attribute Winnicott's allusions to more specific Christian events in England to the pervasive influence of Christianity in English culture. The references to John Bunyan and his *Pilgrim's Progress* would be illustrative (Winnicott, 1945b, 1958g), as would Winnicott's rephrasing of a very well-known English proverb attributed to the English reformer and martyr John Bradford (1510-1555). Bradford is reported to have said about a fellow Tower of London prisoner going to be executed, "there but for the grace of God goes John Bradford." Winnicott (1959c) observed that "when we see a psychotic patient we feel 'here but for the grace of God go I'" (p. 72). Similarly, when Winnicott (1969d) observed at James Strachey's memorial service that "intellectual honesty in living leads to the stake" (p. 509), one cannot help but recall that most famous of Englishmen, Thomas Cranmer, whose burning in the streets of Oxford is linked with such honesty.

However, in addition to these general allusions to religion that one might attribute to any educated English subject, one finds certain other religious allusions that are more indicative of Winnicott's evangelical background. In this regard one might point to his reference to a leucotomy patient as being freed from "missionary zeal" (Winnicott, 1951a, p. 552), a comparison clearly drawn from an activity associated with evangelical religion. One also might point to his use of "sin" as a term of moral condemnation (to be elaborated on below). In reflecting upon the influence of Winnicott's religious background it is interesting to note that when he defined the word "devoted" in one of his popular BBC talks on the "ordinary devoted mother" it was an illustration from religious life that he used. "You have the job of doing the altar flowers for your church at the end of every week. If you take it on you simply do not forget" (Winnicott, 1966i, p. 4).

Finally, one might note that the influence of Winnicott's religious background is evident in the frequency of allusions or references to religion and religious practices that Winnicott made. It seems he was never short on religious examples for the points he was making. He spoke of children born in "holy wedlock" (Winnicott, 1960b, p. 471), of the appropriateness of requiring "grace before meat" and "no swearing" if these are the rules of one's house (Winnicott, 1944, p. 89), and "prayers at school" (Winnicott, 1931b, p. 16) as one of several things that cause young children to faint. He noted Ernest Jones was "no saint" (Winnicott, 1958c, p. 406); he commented on monogamy (Winnicott, 1964k) and the absence of divorce (Winnicott, 1950b) as somewhat problematic Christian beliefs. He remarked on the helpfulness of the monarch's "belief in God" (Winnicott, 1950e, p. 255), and his raising the question of whether "God has saved the Queen" (Winnicott, 1970f, p. 261) identified a particularly English conundrum connected to belief in God and the monarchy. He spoke of the terror experienced when "sacred objects" are threatened in dreams (Winnicott, 1964i, p. 95), of "consulting a priest" when one questioned one's goodness (Winnicott, 1958e, p. 52), and how a narrow definition of the conflict between Catholics and Protestants in Northern Ireland left little room for those who were agnostic (Winnicott, 1969b). He often spoke of the connection between "act of God" and the concept of fate (Winnicott, 1931a, pp. 3–4; 1966d, p. 213; 1970h, p. 276; 1971c, p. 36) and there is his comparison of the different interpretations of the Christian Eucharist to illustrate the relationship of symbolization to transitional objects (Winnicott, 1951b; cf. Flew [1978]).

Use of Religious Language to Speak in Moralistic Terms

Another way that allusions to religion and religious practice showed up in Winnicott was his association of religion with moralistic judgment. For instance, he contrasted the kind of moralizing associated with religion with the more accepting, non-moralistic attitude characteristic of psychoanalytic understanding. An example of this is his reference to parents who understand the unconscious reasons behind the child's (petty) theft as an expression of hope or a claim on the mother's love and thus, do not demand "confession" (Winnicott, 1964j). Similarly he advised that too much strain can be placed on children if one conveys the idea that to "make a mess is a sin, and to smear the wall is sacrilege" (Winnicott, 1936a, p. 67). This same contrast between psychoanalytic approaches and more religious ones stands behind Winnicott's (1964a) desire to speak about the False Self without appearing to "preach a sermon" (p. 65). Finally, he spoke straightforwardly that one should not link clinical symptoms with sin (Winnicott, 1970g). Similarly, he wrote that telling ill people that they were wicked was unhelpful (Winnicott, 1970d).

What is interesting, given the contrast Winnicott made between the moralizing of religion and the non-moralizing of psychoanalysis is his appropriation of religious language when he himself wished to moralize! For instance, when Winnicott wished to condemn a practice he often used religious language or evoked religious imagery. Examples include his observation that failing to heed clinical facts in medicine was a sin (Winnicott, 1931a); similarly, he compared shock treatments to attempts in the middle ages to rid people of evil spirits (Winnicott, 1943). Other examples of this use of religious allusion include his noting that patients are not to be sacrificed on a scientific altar (Winnicott, 1964f) and his praise of Fairbairn as "no worshipper at a shrine" because he valued clinical evidence over accepted theory (Winnicott, 1953b).

One encounters a similar use of religious allusion in his comment that over-rigidity regarding infant feeding schedules signifies the modern "puritan" (Winnicott, 1945a). His appropriation of a remark by James Baldwin to liken medical students' inability for empathy to the "sin" of being unaware (Winnicott, 1970d) functions in a similar way. This appropriation of religious language to speak in moralistic tones may simply reflect the general influence of religion on Western culture. However, one cannot fail to note that Winnicott's Wesleyan Methodist background would have reinforced such language and his inability to divest himself of such moralizing language (even when he so desires) is another lingering effect of his religious heritage.

In addition to using religious language as part of Western culture or to speak in condemnatory and moralistic tones, there is yet another way in which Winnicott employed religious allusions. As with his use of scriptural allusions, this involved allusions to religious ideas and practices to illustrate or explain psychoanalytic concepts.

Use of Religious Language to Explain Psychoanalytic Ideas

Winnicott also employed allusions to religion and religious practices to draw attention to parallels between certain religious ideas or practices and psychoanalytic concepts. Sometimes the references are more direct and not simply allusion (as with the use of the name of God [I AM] noted above under Scripture uses).

With only a couple of exceptions, the parallels Winnicott drew were positive in their intent. One of these exceptions was Winnicott's (1958g) agreement with Freud that an obsessional neurosis can generate rituals that are similar to if not a caricature of religion. A second exception is when Winnicott (1971b) noted that Klein's articulation of the death instinct appeared to be a re-introduction of the notion of original sin. Winnicott (1952c, 1956b, 1968h, 1969l) did not find the death instinct a helpful psychoanalytic concept because of this ascribed parallel, and considered the formulation of the death instinct to be an error on Freud's (cf. 1920) part. Winnicott (1963j) thought the concept of original sin overshadowed an appreciation of "original goodness" present in human nature (see chapter 11).

In addition to the reference to scriptural allusions regarding "ascensive" defenses, Winnicott alluded to religious practices to illumine another modified Kleinian concept. In his discussion of gratitude Winnicott pointed out that gratitude was not an easy emotion to understand. He noted that gratitude, especially in exaggerated forms, involved avenging forces in need of "propitiation" (Winnicott, 1970d, p. 118). Propitiation is a religious concept connected to satisfying the gods; in the Christian tradition the death of Jesus is said to be propitiation for the sins of humanity (1 John 2:2; 4:10). Winnicott further elaborated on the complexity of gratitude with a reference to religious care for the poor. He noted that caregivers need those cared for as much as those cared for need care. He reminded those who cared for others that they did not do their work to receive gratitude from those helped. Rather, "in a sense it is you who are grateful to them" (Winnicott, 1970g, p. 227). He then cited a quotation from St. Vincent de Paul to the effect that those who served the poor might well ask the poor to forgive them for helping! In both of these illustrations Winnicott drew upon religious understandings of gratitude to help illuminate his psychoanalytic point that gratitude is a complex feeling intertwined with varying motivations, both conscious and unconscious.

Twice Winnicott drew upon religious concepts to illustrate his concept of transitional phenomena. On one occasion he referred to the doctrine of transubstantiation and the symbolization of the Eucharist wafer as a way to understand how the use of transitional objects is wrapped up with the ability to use symbols (Winnicott, 1951b, p. 234). On the other occasion he spoke of the dialectic between spontaneity and form and quoted from the *Book of Common Prayer* the phrase "whose service is perfect freedom" to illustrate that creativity ("freedom") emerged through form ("service"), not unlike Shakespeare's creative use of the sonnet form (Winnicott, 1970c, p. 278).

Another passing allusion to religious practices and transitional phenomena is found in Winnicott's notion that religious beliefs and moral codes, like transitional objects, should be left lying around by parents and society to be "created" or discovered rather than imposed. Even the "revealed" morality of religion will be adopted by the infant if made available in a non-coercive way. "With luck, the morality we have adopted as 'revealed' will appear in all those who are not endowed with too much of something which could be called original sin." He further noted that "the only morality that counts is what comes from the individual. After all, the 'revealed' morality . . . was built up over the centuries, or millennia, by thousands of generations of individuals, helped by a few prophets" (Winnicott, 1966c, p. 107).

Another way in which Winnicott used religious allusion to illustrate a psychoanalytic concept was his appropriation of the religious metaphor of "everlasting arms" to flesh out his point about the need for a general capacity to "believe in" prior to acquiring specific beliefs. In an essay on morals and religious education, Winnicott (1963j) had made the point of the absurdity of trying to induce religious values by force (cf. the story of professor Keate who had told a student he would believe in the Holy Ghost by 5 o'clock or be beaten). In his articulation of a capacity to believe in Winnicott wanted to "get behind" the specific ideas and beliefs one might have to inquire how one developed a capacity to believe in anything (p. 93). The development of this capacity was rooted in the quality and consistency of the child's early care-giving environment. If the early environment showed itself dependable then the child came to have a faith in itself and its environment. However, if this prior capacity was absent, Winnicott made the point that there was little personal psychic value in espousing beliefs in compliance to external expectations. Yet if a child had this prior capacity to believe in, then a wide variety of things to believe in could be appropriated based in the child's personal experience. If a child had experienced consistent care (e.g., "holding"; "good enough mothering"), Winnicott (1968b) thus reasoned by way of illustration:

> Let's take my suggestion that the whole of the preverbal expression of love in terms of holding and handling has vital significance for each developing baby. Then we can say that on the basis of what has been experienced by an individual, we may teach the concept of, say, everlasting arms. We may use that word 'God', we can make a specific link with the Christian church and doctrine, but it is a series of steps. (pp. 148–149)[4]

Here Winnicott clearly connected the quality of the mother's holding and handling with the child's later ability to conceive of and experience a loving God.

Thus, as with his use of scriptural allusions, one can see the influence of Winnicott's religious background in the number of allusions to religious concepts and practices scattered throughout his writing. This influence included the more general impact of the Judeo-Christian religion on English culture, reinforced by Winnicott's own Wesleyan Methodist heritage, including his use of religious language to speak in moralistic tones (Goldman, 1993; Kirschner, 1996). However, the influence of Winnicott's religious upbringing is especially seen in the employment of religious concepts and language to illumine or extend various psychoanalytic points, including minor ones such as those regarding gratitude or transitional objects and symbols. So frequent are his allusions to Scripture and religious concepts that he does indeed seem to have the English Bible in his bones.[5]

Summary and Evaluative Conclusion

This review of scriptural allusions in the writings of D.W. Winnicott has identified approximately thirty allusions in his published essays and letters.[6] This list does not include another twenty-plus allusions found in his poem "The Tree." Although the allusions come from over a dozen books of the Bible, he shows a clear preference for the gospels, with almost half of the allusions being found in St. Matthew's gospel (and the parallel passages in St. Mark and St. Luke). Jesus's Sermon on the Mount is the source of six different allusions, making it the most frequently used source. The frequency of the allusions seems to follow that of his publications; they are scattered throughout his writings over the years, including both essays and letters. There were three allusions in his published work before 1940, plus two allusions in subsequently published letters from this period (e.g., Rodman, 1987). There were five allusions in his writings from the 1950s, one of which was in a letter. There were eleven allusions from the 1960s, three of which come from letters, and seven from 1970 until his death in 1971, all in published essays. From the number of allusions identified it is clear that the English Bible was a source for Winnicott's thoughts and writing, along with the rich array of other sources Goldman (1993) enumerated. No doubt Winnicott's acquaintance with the Bible was due in large part to his religious upbringing in the Wesleyan Methodist church, an evangelical type of faith where knowing the Scriptures would have been important.

Similarly, numerous allusions to the larger Judeo-Christian tradition and its practices were noted in Winnicott. The various functions of these allusions was indicative of the influence of this tradition on the Western intellectual heritage in which Winnicott was schooled, especially when he wished to speak in moralistic tones. One should also note that although Winnicott (cf. 1949a) occasionally spoke of Eastern religions and practices, it is important to remember that when he spoke of religion and religious practices it is primarily the Christian religion (with its roots in a particular interpretation of its Jewish heritage) that provided the background for his comments. The version of Christianity most obvious in Winnicott is of course his Weselyan Methodism.

Up until this point this chapter has been primarily illustrative rather than evaluative; now some implications of this material must be explored. For instance, one must ask, despite the numerous references to Scripture in Winnicott's writing, whether he made use of the Bible in a way that accorded it personal significance? Does his use of Scripture add anything to illumine the particulars of his lingering religiosity? Did Winnicott's appropriation of Scripture and religious concepts have significance beyond their illustrative value for Winnicott? One might further inquire what these allusions reveal about Winnicott's view of God (e.g., akin to fate?) or human nature (e.g., original sin), or about his epistemology (e.g., differences between religious and scientific "knowing"). These latter questions are taken up in subsequent chapters. This chapter concludes with reflections on what Winnicott's use of Scripture says of its significance to him.

It is obvious that he alluded to the Bible in ways that are not that different from quoting a poet. On these occasions it functioned as a source of literary allusions that his audience would have been familiar with (much like he used Shakespeare or Wordsworth). This use of the Bible as a literary source was the most frequent way that Winnicott used Scripture and might lead one to conclude that the Scriptures did not have a particularly personal relevance for the adult Winnicott. However, such an assessment would be pre-mature. Even though most of Winnicott's uses of the Bible did not rise above literary allusion, one concludes that there is a deep familiarity with the text of scripture that extended beyond what an educated Englishman would have had, a familiarity that must be attributed to his religious exposure as a child. Furthermore, the number of positive allusions to Scripture by an analyst of Winnicott's stature is surely notable, given Freud's (1927) negative view of religion and the long shadow he cast over psychoanalysis.

However, even more important in assessing the relevance of the Bible for Winnicott are those occasions where he used the Scriptures to illustrate psychoanalytic concepts. These occasions demonstrate an underlying attitude that the Scriptures contain a wisdom that the analyst could appreciate. The most obvious are his articulation of the I AM state and the achievement of individuality, the "ascensive" defenses against depression, and the infant's "creation" of objects.

Winnicott's use of the I AM imagery from Scripture deliberately drew a parallel between the achievement of individuality and God's self-identification and self-expression. Humans become like the "Great I AM" in their achievement of self-expression and identification. Furthermore, this achievement of individuality is connected to health and maturity (Winnicott, 1960i, 1967c). Winnicott's characterization of the human as self-expressive being via this analogy reveals not only his dependence upon the broader Christian narrative (Kirschner, 1996) but his positive appropriation of a specific scriptural vision of God and humans that could be drawn from no other source (i.e., he specifically connected this vision of God as I AM to the rise of monotheism in the Judeo-Christian tradition (Winnicott, 1968i, p. 56).

Winnicott's use of the Ascension narrative from Christian scripture indicates that he also saw within this tradition unique resources for understanding and dealing with sadness and grief (a goal he saw shared by psychoanalysis and religion). One observes that Winnicott also has thought sufficiently about this aspect of the Christian tradition to offer a psychoanalytic justification for the inseparability of doctrines long seen as inseparable theologically. Similarly, Winnicott's appropriation of the creation story from Genesis is used to provide insight into the emotional development of the infant. Winnicott's understanding of the story of creation helps him envision how gratifying yet frightening omnipotence can be for the dependent infant, and thus the eventual desire to be divested of it (Winnicott, 1966c, 1968d, 1968i).

Winnicott's use of religious allusion follows a similar pattern to his use of scriptural allusion. Some allusions are simply illustrations of psychoanalytic concepts (such as his reference to the Eucharistic wafer and symbolic thought); other allusions illumine and enrich these concepts. For instance, gratitude is understood to include not only as a sense of gratefulness, but as evoking a sense of guilt, even fear of the anger of the gods or those served. Although Winnicott drew upon Klein (1948, 1957) for some of this understanding, the religious tradition regarding propitiation enriched his argument. Similar was his use of religious tradition to illumine the concept of holding. The powerful image of God as "everlasting arms" gave a cosmic significance to the mother's holding even as the mother's holding made possible one's ability to appropriate this image. Either image without the other is impoverished. It is doubtful Winnicott could have fashioned as powerful a metaphor of the mother's holding without his knowledge and appeal to this religious allusion.

Those occasions where Winnicott drew from his religious tradition to enrich and illuminate various psychoanalytic concepts help one evaluate the question of the personal significance of these allusions. One concludes from the prevalence and richness of Winnicott's use of scriptural and religious allusions that these had significance for him beyond their usefulness as literary allusions. One senses a deep personal significance as well. Regarding his religious heritage he had disclosed to Bion: "I have no desire to throw away all that I listened to over and over again and tried to digest and sort out" (Winnicott, 1967f, p. 170). One will see that although his understanding grew and changed, trying to "digest and sort out" his religious tradition retained a deep influence on him. Winnicott clearly saw the Bible and his Christian heritage as a source of important wisdom about human development and drew from them in unfolding several of his key ideas.

Notes

1.   It is of interest to note that Winnicott's only specific quotation from Scripture is from *Ecclesiasticus*, a book that is considered part of the *Apocrypha* in the Methodist tradition in which Winnicott was reared. The *Apocrypha* is a group of writings not generally included in bound editions of the Protestant Bible although these books did appear in the original "King James" Bible and often appear in Bibles read by the Church of England. That Winnicott quoted from an Apocryphal book may imply a familiarity with the Scriptures that extended beyond that which he would have gained from his traditional Wesleyan Methodist upbringing.

2.   This contrast between a religious "knowing in advance" and scientific knowing is an important distinction that is not always consistently argued or observed by Winnicott. A later chapter will return to this issue and its implications.

3.   The poem "The Tree" used by permission of The Marsh Agency Ltd on behalf of The Winnicott Trust. The poem appeared in Rodman (2003) and was reproduced by Hoffman (2004, 2011) with identification of scriptural allusions. Both are reproduced here. Hoffman's identifications appear in brackets. The poem in its entirety clearly shows Winnicott's identification with the suffering Christ that was noted in a previous chapter.

The Tree [Written November 4, 1963]

Someone touched the hem of my garment	[Mt. 9:20, 36]
Someone, someone and someone	
I had much virtue to give	[Mk 5:30, Lk 6:19]
I was the source of virtue	
the grape of the vine of the wine	[John 15]
I could have loved a woman	
Mary, Mary, Mary	[Mark 15:40–41]
There was not time for loving	
I must be about my father's business	[Luke 2:49]
There were publicans and sinners	[Mt. 9:10,11]
The poor we had always with us	[Matt. 26:11]
There were those sick of the palsy	[Matt. 4:24]
and the blind and the maimed	[Matt. 15:30]
and the widows bereft and grieving	[Lk 7:11–15]
women wailing for their children	[Jer.31:15,Mt.2:18]
fathers with prodigal sons	[Luke 15:11–32]
prostitutes drawing their own water	[John 4:7–30]
from deep wells in the hot sun	

Mother below is weeping   [John 19:25–27]
      weeping
      weeping

Thus I knew her

Once, stretched out on her lap   [John 19:17–25]
    as now on a dead tree
I learned to make her smile
    to stem her tears
    to undo her guilt
    to cure her inward death

To enliven her way my living

So she became wife, mother, home   [Mark 6:3]
The carpenter enjoyed his craft   [Matt. 19:13–15]
Children came and loved and were loved   [Mark 10:13–16]
Suffer little children to come unto me

Now mother is weeping
She must weep

The sins of the whole world weigh less than this   [John 1:29]
    woman's heaviness

                             [Legendary site of
O Glastonbury   first Christian
                            church in England]
                            [Legend of the
Must I bring even these thorns to flower?   thorn (Rodman,
    even this dead tree to leaf?   2003, p. 411)]

4. It is possible that the metaphor of "everlasting arms" should be treated as a scriptural allusion rather than as a more general religious allusion. The background for this comment by Winnicott is unclear. There is a verse of Scripture in Deuteronomy 33:27 that spoke of "everlasting arms" underneath and holding humans and Winnicott couched this illustration in the context of the mother's holding. However, this verse gave birth to a well-known hymn "Leaning on the Everlasting Arms" as well and Winnicott's love of Methodist hymns has already been noted. Whether this was one of them is unknown. Thus, it is hard to say which of these, the hymn or the Scripture verse, may be uppermost in Winnicott's mind in this allusion. What is clear is that aspects of his religious background are present in such an allusion.

5. This chapter has focused on Winnicott's published papers and letters. There also are unpublished notes and letters that further attest to the influence of the English Bible on Winnicott. However, much of this material serves simply to further affirm points made from the survey of published materials. For instance, there are two letters to his secretary that allude to scriptural passages; one used the story of Noah's preparations delaying the flood (Gen 6-7) to illustrate his recognition that disaster would not come if he delayed work for a holiday (Winnicott, n.d. 1), and the other was a humorous free association

about her vacation that involved a reference to oxen "kicking against the pricks" (i.e., yoke; cf. Acts 26:14 KJV) (Winnicott, 1965b). These allusions showed his familiarity with Scripture without being additive to the points he made. Also telling in terms of demonstrating Winnicott's familiarity with Scripture are some handwritten notes on the typed manuscript of his talk "This Feminism" (Winnicott, 1964b). There he quotes from Psalm 103:15, Isaiah 40:6-7, and James 1: 10-11 on the brevity of life (i.e., "all flesh is grass"). Also indicative of Winnicott's familiarity with scripture are more Gospel quotations in an unpublished manuscript for a presentation to the Christian Union at St. Bartholomew's Hospital reviewed in some detail in chapter 9 (Winnicott, n.d. 3).

In addition to these Scripture references one also finds several religious allusions similar to those already noted such as a reference to "preaching to the converted" to acknowledge that the recipient of his letter was in agreement with Winnicott's (1961b) point and an allusion to resurrection as a sign of new life (Winnicott, 1950d). Of a different nature is his repudiation of a reference to his being a "Madonna" figure, an over-idealized image of mother/woman that Winnicott thought distorted both him and his work (cited in Goldman, 1993, p. 42; cf. Winnicott, 1966h). Of more import for understanding the significance of religion for Winnicott are reference to the Lollards and the ideals of Christ in these unpublished papers. Where these and other unpublished references contribute further insight into Winnicott's religious sensibilities they are quoted or cited at appropriate places throughout the book.

6.   As an aid to the reader, below is a summary table of scriptural allusions in Winnicott's published writings.

Genesis 2:2	"on the seventh day...rest"	1968b: 49
Genesis 3:19	"sweat of...brow"	1964e: 146
Exodus 3:14	"I AM THAT I AM"	1964g: 112
Exodus 20:14	"do not commit adultery"	1960c: 160
Jeremiah 32:18	"the sins of the fathers" (cf. Isaiah 65:7; Psalm 79:8)	1966d: 213
Jeremiah 32:29	"fathers eat sour grapes...the children's teeth are set on edge" (cf. Ezekiel 18:2)	1969e: 191
Jonah 2:10	"spewed out upon land"	1971e: 96
Hab. 2:2	"he may run who reads"	1919: 2
Ecclesiasticus 38:25	"How can he get wisdom whose talk is of bullock?"	1970e: 60
Matthew 4:4	"cannot live by bread alone"	Rodman, 2003: 239
Matthew 6:11	"daily bread" (cf. Luke 11:3)	1964f: 47
Matthew 6:34	"Sufficient unto the day is the evil thereof"	1954c: 72
Matthew 7:5	"the beam in my own eye"	1970d: 114
Matthew 7:7	"ask and it shall be given" (cf. Luke 11:9)	1968b: 50
Matthew 7:24	"a house built on rock" (cf. Luke 6:48)	1971e: 104 1963h: 140
Matthew 7:26	"building a house on sand"	1961a: 80
Matthew 9:17	"putting new wine into old bottles"	1971e: 99
Matt. 12:31	"the unforgivable sin" (cf. Mark 3:29; Luke 12:10)	1963g: 478

Matt. 13:1-9	"the Word, can fall on stony ground, or…good soil and so bear fruit" (cf. Mark 4:3-9; Luke 8:4-8)	cf. 1970g:221 cf. 1936b:80
Luke 23:34	"Forgive them for they know not what they do"	1951a: 549
Acts 1:9-11	(the Ascension of Christ)	1935: 135
Acts 9:1-9	"seeing the light" (St. Paul's experience)	1967a: 236
Phil. 2:2	"work out their own salvation"	1936b: 90
	Other Possible Allusions	
Deut. 15:7	"harden your hearts" (cf.1 Sam. 6:6)	1936a: 76
Deut. 33:27	"everlasting arms"	1968b: 149
Matt. 13:13	"who has ears, let him hear" (cf. Mark 4:9; Luke 8:8; cf. also Matthew 13:9; Revelation 3:22)	1968f: 176
Luke 18:13	"strikes breast…God be merciful to a sinner"	1958e: 55
John 1:29	"carry the sins of the world" (cf. 1 John 2:2)	1940: 5
2 Cor. 12:2	(multiple heavens)	1971h: 104
Hebrews 11:1	"the substance of (faith)"	1951b: 230

Chapter 7
Wesleyan Methodist Piety and the "Content" of Winnicott's Thought

"It is always a steadying thing to find that one's work links with . . . the best of poetry, philosophy, and religion"

About two months before he died Winnicott (1970d) gave a presentation to doctors and nurses in St. Luke's Church in Hatfield. In this speech he talked about some of the common interests that doctors and nurses share with clergy and a previous chapter discussed his central point: a shared interest in cure as care. Near the end of his talk Winnicott noted that the ability to be caring people as adults owed its origins to having been cared for by a "good enough mothers" at the beginning of one's life. He thus reflected on the notion of a great cycle in the life processes. He took satisfaction in the thought that he had devoted considerable attention in his career to understanding the processes by which each new generation learns to be caring. He concluded his talk by noting "it is always a steadying thing to find that one's work links with entirely natural phenomena, and with the universals, and with what we expect to find in the best of poetry, philosophy and religion" (p. 120). Thus, once again Winnicott reflected on how his work as a pediatrician and psychoanalyst echoed certain themes from his religious background. This chapter elaborates on the connections and similarities between ideas and themes from Winnicott's religious heritage and central concepts from his theoretical work as an analyst.

This chapter may be thought of as complementing chapter 5. That chapter demonstrated how Winnicott's religious background influenced the "form" of his thought (Goldman, 1993). This chapter takes up Goldman's additional claim that it also influenced the "content" of his thought. Goldman further noted that Winnicott's "lingering religiosity is probably most evident in how akin so many of his ideas are to religious categories" (p. 122–123). He is not alone in observing how similar Winnicott's most popular concepts are to religious discourse (Eigen, 1981; Gay, 1983; Jacobs, 1995; Lambert, 1987; Reiland, 2004). This chapter focuses on two ways in which the lingering influence of Winnicott's religious background showed up in the content of his thought: key questions in which he was interested and religious corollaries to several of Winnicott's key concepts.

An Interest in Theologically Oriented Questions

An earlier chapter focused on how the influence of Winnicott's religious up-bringing was evident in certain attitudes he held as well as actions in which he engaged. This section explores how it is seen in his lifelong interest in questions that have religious overtones. Although Winnicott's interests range much more widely than the themes elaborated here, this section focuses on several theologi-cally oriented questions that clarified both his interest and his theory.[1] It looks briefly at these questions as well as Winnicott's answers. The further implica-tions and evaluation of his answers are addressed in later chapters. The goal of this section is primarily descriptive.

What Makes Life Worth Living

Abram (2007b) has observed of Winnicott's work that "all his questions, from very early on, are to do with the meaning of life and what it is within that makes life worth living" (p. 5). Similarly, Rodman (1987) stated that Winnicott "was the first to approach in an analytic fashion a question that had not been considered by psychoanalysts before him: what is it that makes life worth liv-ing" (p. xxxii). Winnicott (1971e) himself contrasted a psychology focused on illness with one that needed to explore "what life itself is about" (p. 98). He was clear that the absence of illness was not the same as health.

Questions regarding the purpose of life, what gives it meaning and what makes it worth living have long been questions raised by theology (Kirchner, 1996). Wesley's (1759) reference to the purpose or "great end" of religion (p. 185) has been noted. In the last two centuries these traditional theological ques-tions also were raised by existential philosophies and the psychologies influ-enced by these movements (Kirschner, 1996). Browning (1987) has argued that the clinical and developmental psychologies all contain implicit, if not explicit visions of what people can and should be (and achieve), areas that clearly extend psychology into theological terrain. As both a clinical and developmental psy-chology, Winnicott's work not only moves into theological territory because of its vision for what humans can be, but also by the nature of the very questions he wanted to explore.

Winnicott stated that his own push toward raising the question of "what life itself is about" had come from working with psychotic patients, a class of pa-tients for whom the traditional psychoanalytic answer that satisfaction of instinc-tual desires drove human behavior was not satisfactory. What people were after according to Winnicott was not simply satisfaction of instinctual needs, but a sense of feeling "real" or "alive"; that life was worth living (Winnicott, 1971e). Winnicott (1960e) had made an earlier comment about a patient with a "caretaker self" who at the end of her analysis had come to the "beginning" of her life because she finally felt real and wanted to live (p. 148).

However, Winnicott's interest in and answers to the question of what makes life worth living did not find its origin only in his clinical work. Nor was it a question of mere intellectual interest. The need to feel alive and make things real was a defining personal quest for Winnicott, as much an aspect of his own personality as it was a theoretical concept (Goldman, 1993; Phillips, 1988; Rodman, 1987, 2003). It is seen in Winnicott's struggle to "be himself" (Rodman, 2003) and to make the writings and theories of others "real" to him through his own unique appropriation of them (Goldman, 1993; Khan, 1975). This tendency often resulted in his inadequate acknowledgment of his sources and his indebtedness to them (Winnicott, 1967h). Winnicott's need to feel real or alive was such a part of his character that even in death he wanted to feel alive. He began the autobiographical notes he penned near the end of life with a prayer: "Oh God, may I be alive when I die" (Winnicott, 1978, p. 19). He went on to imagine what happened after he died as a way to make even his death real to him.

Thus, Winnicott's interest in this religiously tinged question is both clinical and personal. His lifelong exploration of the answer not only defines his character but also colors his theoretical contributions. This quest to feel real or alive is inextricably bound up with the processes of growth and is thus interwoven with several of Winnicott's key concepts (e.g., holding, true self, play) that are explored later.

How Do People Come to Believe

Another religiously oriented question with which Winnicott dealt at some length is that of how people come to believe, including having a belief in God. Smith (1963) traced the long association and deep connection of "belief" to religion and its practices. Winnicott's interest in this question clearly shows indebtedness to his religious tradition, as is seen in the many examples he drew from in articulating his answer.

Winnicott framed this question of believing as a more generic question that explores the origins of a capacity to "believe in" that precedes any specific beliefs, including a belief in God. Once the capacity for belief in is present, then specific beliefs such as belief in God (or society) can be bequeathed to the child. However, for the child who lacked this prior capacity, movement to a "belief in God" became problematic (Winnicott, 1963j).

For Winnicott, a capacity for belief or belief in is a general human quality rooted in consistent child care: "We are believing people because we are started off well by somebody" (Winnicott, 1968b, p. 147). "The infant and small child is usually cared for in a reliable way, and this being cared for well enough builds up in the infant to a belief in reliability. . . . To a child who has started life in this way the idea of goodness and of a reliable and personal parent or God can follow naturally" (Winnicott, 1963j, p. 97). Even science, with its insistence on observation, implies a "faith" or at least a capacity for faith (Winnicott, 1961d).

This capacity to believe in is very similar to trust (Winnicott, 1966e). Thus, through the mother's consistent, reliable care the infant comes to trust the environment and its provision and so develops the capacity for belief. The development of such trust also is connected to the capacity to be alone. "Maturity and the capacity of be alone implies that the individual has had the chance through good enough mothering to build up a belief in a benign environment" (Winnicott, 1958a, p. 32).

However, the development of this general human capacity for belief is not something everyone accomplishes. If one did not get "started off well" then problems in the capacity to believe develop. Winnicott (1963j) also is clear that such problems cannot be overcome simply by offering the child beliefs (even belief in God); there is no substitute for consistent, reliable care by another human being. Thus, people develop the capacity to believe, including belief in God, because of the quality of their early relational interactions. Winnicott's answer to and interest in this question draws one back to his own early religious environment. In asking how it was one developed any kind of faith, one wonders if Winnicott was at some level trying to understand the nature of his father's simple faith (and perhaps in the process how one might come to more complex faith).

Also noteworthy is how similar Winnicott's concept of belief in is to certain traditional religious concepts of faith. Religious discussions of faith often distinguish between faith as a noun (i.e., the content of what one believes) and faith as a verb (i.e., the processes of believing) (cf. Fowler, 1981; Smith, 1963). Wesley, for instance distinguished between faith *in which* (i.e., the content or object of faith) and faith *by which* (i.e., trust or the internal, subjective processes of faith) one believes (Chilcote, 2004; cf. Wesley, 1738c). Winnicott's concept of *belief in* is very similar to these religious distinctions regarding the processes of faith or believing.

Are Humans "Naturally Good"

Another question with which Winnicott was deeply concerned was that of whether humans were naturally good or not. This was a question discussed in Christian traditions since the Apostle Paul who quoted from more ancient texts in the Psalms and Hebrew prophets (cf. Romans 3:10). One clearly sees the influence of Winnicott's (1963j) religious background in his interest in what he considered an explicitly theological question. Yet this question of whether humans are naturally good or not was one that Winnicott thought to be of great importance for those interested in children's emotional development.

Winnicott's answer to this question is bound up with his evolving under-standing of the origins of aggression. Because Winnicott struggled with the ap-propriate expression of aggression at a personal level (Rodman, 1987), it is not surprising that he made it a focus of theoretical attention as a psychoanalyst. An early paper (Winnicott, 1939) was devoted to this topic and it was a central theme in his last theoretical paper on object usage (Winnicott, 1971k). Although it is not always easy to follow his argument regarding aggression (cf. Abram, 2007b) two things are clear: (1) aggression is a developmental achievement, something that arises out of the interaction between infant and its environment, and (2) there are two dimensions to aggression.

Klein (e.g., 1948) had argued that aggression was inborn, a manifestation of the death instinct. Winnicott (1971b), by contrast came to see Klein's position regarding the death instinct as a secularized version of original sin, explaining human destructiveness through reliance upon the idea of inherited aggression. As an alternative, Winnicott put forth the position that aggression was a devel-opmental achievement (cf. Abram, 2007b). Winnicott (1963j) wanted to account for his observations of innate tendencies toward development of a moral sense, what he called "original goodness" (p. 94).

Winnicott (1964c) often contrasted this innate moral tendency with an "im-posed" or "implanted" morality.

> There are two ways in which a child can be introduced to . . . morality, and lat-er to religious and political beliefs. One is for the parents to implant such standards and beliefs, to force the baby or child into accepting them, making no attempt to integrate them with the developing personality. . . . The second way is to allow and encourage the innate tendencies toward morality. (p. 96)

It is important to note at the outset that Winnicott did not speak so much of an innate morality in infants as of innate moral *tendencies*. These innate moral tendencies, in contrast to an imposed morality, do not have to be taught (Win-nicott, 1954b).

When Winnicott (1939, 1954a, 1964i, 1968h) explored the origins and de-velopment of these innate moral tendencies he saw their beginnings primarily in the quality of the mother's care. For Winnicott, the mother's reliability provided a foundation for the growth of the infant's innate moral tendencies. Deficits in the mother's care at these critical early encounters deprived the infant of an en-vironment in which these innate moral tendencies could grow (Winnicott, 1958f). However, consistent care and attunement to the infant's developmental needs and timing provided the environment in which these innate tendencies could emerge and the infant could find or "create" its own moral direction with-out having to comply with an implanted one (Winnicott, 1963j).

Although Winnicott placed the emphasis on the role of the environment in facilitating these innate moral tendencies, he nevertheless acknowledged that development of these tendencies involved a series of complex maturational steps, including the infant's developing imagination and the movement toward separation of self from environment. Because the infant is not able to separate "me" from "not me" in the beginning, Winnicott argued that early on aggression did not include the intent usually implied by this term. At the beginning aggression is better defined as motility or spontaneity; Winnicott (1950a, 1958f) thought confusion arose because people often used the term aggression when it was these latter terms that were meant. Although these spontaneous movements might harm by chance, only later can one attribute intent to harm to these movements.

At the beginning when there is no intent and no separation of self from environment there is only spontaneous movement and utter abandon to one's need. Infant and world are one; the world is there to satisfy the infant's needs because the infant created it. There is a sense of aliveness and excitement that is vitalizing in this aspect of aggression. However, to retain such a view of self and world is to remain in an illusion. Health demands recognition that the world is other than one's projections.

The movement toward separation of self from environment necessarily involves recognition of difference. For instance, the baby who thought it created the breast finds it reacts when bitten! With this recognition that the breast is more than his or her projections the infant also recognizes that its spontaneous gestures can inflict harm on this that is other than self. The infant must now confront its potential to harm. This is a developmental achievement according to Winnicott.

A step in coming to terms with its potential to harm involves the infant's projections of its dawning internal feelings onto the caregiver generating "crude fears of retaliation" (Winnicott, 1958f, p. 11); what Winnicott (following Klein) called "talion dread" or the fear that one's own ruthless abandon would be visited back upon oneself (cf. Winnicott, 1939, 1963j). The fears associated with these projections are part of natural developmental processes and play their own role in moving the infant toward nascent experiences of remorse and a desire to repair the fantasized damage. In normal development (i.e., in an environment that is not overly reactive) the innate tendencies toward good in the infant manifest as guilt or concern for the other at this stage. This involves a desire to protect the other from one's harmful potential as well as reparative gestures for real or imagined harm. Again, the sensitive mother does not preclude destructive ideas from forming in the child, thus facilitating the child's innate guilt to blossom (Winnicott, 1949j). Her "survival" of these imagined aggressions is an important part of the infant's journey toward learning to understand the nature of and to manage these fantasies and toward recognizing self and environment as separate (Winnicott, 1971k). Where the infant does not reach the stage of concern one has the possibility of aggression with intent to harm and thus the possibility of more pathological forms of development.

Thus, Winnicott articulated two dimensions to aggression along with a developmental pattern for its expression (cf. 1950a). On the one hand, aggression has a vitalizing, imaginative quality, devoid of intent to harm that is associated with health. On the other hand, there is a more intentional and actual destructiveness associated with pathology (cf. Abram, 2007b). Winnicott (1939) once framed these two aspects by observing that aggression belonged both to love and to hate. Similarly, in his paper on object usage he contrasted a destructiveness carried on in unconscious fantasy that is related to health with a destructiveness in actuality that is associated with anti-social actions and illness (Winnicott, 1971k). However, it is important to note that although he acknowledged an actual destructiveness in humans, Winnicott emphasized the positive nature of aggression and its role in furthering healthy maturation. Furthermore, Winnicott (1960a, 1960e, 1967d) noted that in health one is able to integrate one's aggressive tendencies without splitting them off. Otherwise one becomes a compliant self, devoid of the vitalizing qualities that belong to aggression or else one becomes given entirely to destructive aggression and cannot function in society.

Before leaving this section, one notes that Winnicott also connected this natural goodness evident in the child's innate moral tendencies to the growth of the true self. More will be said of the true self shortly, but note at this point that it refers to a potentiality at the core of each person; a source for the creative possibilities that lie in humans. Failure to let the infant or child become aware of its own moral gestures impinged upon the development of the true self. Imposing a morality to which the child must comply without discovery of its own creativity and goodness created the potential for "immorality" according to Winnicott (Winnicott, 1963j). Furthermore, Winnicott (1968b) pointed out that early interventions to correct behavior can rob the other person of the opportunity to sort through his or her impulses. The person either complies or rebels with neither response permitting the person's innate capacity toward morality to emerge. Conversely, if one is to nurture the true self, Winnicott argued that the original goodness that lies in humans must be acknowledged and honored.

Winnicott's (1963j) reflections on this topic of a natural goodness in humans was one area in which he thought himself at odds with traditional religion opinion. A later chapter explores to what extent this is true by comparing Winnicott's views on this question with various theological ones.

What Is the Nature of the Soul

Yet another explicitly theological question that interested Winnicott was one that concerned the nature of the soul. His interest in this question clearly reflects the influence of Winnicott's religious background. "Soul," though variously defined is a term often linked to religious or spiritual qualities in humans (Boyd, 1998; Moon, 1999; Muller, 1990; Osterhaven, 1984; Rollins, 1999) and a term and concept to which Winnicott devoted considerable attention. He entertained several questions regarding the nature of the soul including its relationship to the psyche, to the mind and to brain function as well as questions on whether the soul might "develop" (Winnicott, 1954c).

Winnicott's interest in this topic also may reflect his awareness that the nature of the soul was a matter of some debate and disagreement in religion. His interest in the soul caused him to inquire in one place about the "philological origins" of the word in terms of its connection with the word "breath" (Winnicott, 1954c, p. 162). In another essay Winnicott revealed an interest in words and their etymology, pointing to the need not only to understand the history of a word but its current usage (1968j), noting on another occasion that words sometimes struggled to "establish and maintain identity" (Winnicott, 1970d, p. 112). This is certainly true of the word "soul." Even theologians, for whom the word is de rigueur, cannot agree as to its precise nature. For instance, is it a "substance" or a "relationship"; is it "material" in nature or non-material or does it participate in both somehow; is it "immortal" (cf. Anderson, 1982; Boyd, 1998; Muller, 1990; Moreland & Ciocchi, 1993)?

Winnicott shared this lack of clear usage; that is, he used soul to refer to several aspects of human nature. Nevertheless, his several statements about the soul show his grappling with the religious dimensions of this concept. In terms of the philological associations of the word soul with the word "breath" (Winnicott, 1954c, p. 162), Winnicott also observed (1945c) that one of the interesting things about breath was that it was hard to decide whether it was primarily an inner or outer movement. It is this elusive quality which pointed to the notion of "spirit, soul, anima" (1945c, p. 154). The Hebrew and Christian Scriptures also connect the word soul to the word breath (Grudem, 1994), where "breath" (*ruach, pneuma*) is connected to God's spirit (or breath) which is breathed into humans (cf. Genesis 2:7, "God . . . breathed into his nostrils the breath of life and man became a living soul").

In addition to his interest in the philological origins of the word soul, Winnicott was particularly interested in the psychological origins and qualities of the soul. For Winnicott the nature of the soul was such that one did not come into being with a soul that was fully developed, but with one that had potential and was in the process of growth. The soul could develop or grow because of its connection to the "psyche-soma," Winnicott's (1954c) designation for the emerging psychosomatic unity that expressed itself fully in the experience of individuality. This was a complex process with a series of steps so that its attainment was an "achievement" dependent both on the mother's care and the infant's response. Winnicott argued that the "psyche" was an imaginative elaboration of physical functioning. That is, one began with an awareness of physical motility or a bodily sense of self. The psychological sense of self (psyche) emerged from these early spontaneous bodily movements. "Out of the material of the imaginative elaboration of body functioning . . . the psyche is forged" (Winnicott, 1954c, p. 52).

However, the critical point for Winnicott is not the distinctions between the psyche and soma but the unity of these aspects of one's nature. Viewing them as separate aspects is a matter of perspective. "The whole person is physical if viewed from one angle, psychological if viewed from another. There are the psyche and the soma" (Winnicott, 1954c, p. 11). Thus, though Winnicott distinguished soma and psyche (and later mind), he was careful to note the fundamental unity between them.

The point to grasp in terms of the soul is that Winnicott saw the soul as integrally involved with the emergence of these processes. He described the soul as a "property of the psyche" (Winnicott, 1954c). This made the soul not only dependent upon brain function but subject to illness as well. Winnicott thus conferred a strong physical or material basis to the soul and its growth. He then noted "I know that this is a personal view that is counter to the teaching of almost every religious system" (p. 52).

This idea that the soul depended on brain function also meant that the soul could be injured when the brain was damaged. This had practical import to Winnicott (1954c) because of the use of leucotomy (a type of brain surgery involving destruction of certain brain tissues) to relieve "suffering in the psyche."

> For me who holds that the term 'soul' (if it means anything at all) means something that grows in the individual, the deliberate distortion of healthy brain functioning is and must remain a price too big to pay for relief of suffering, since it alters irrevocably the basis for the existence of the psyche, soul included, and there is after the treatment, no longer a whole person, psyche or soul, left. (pp. 52-53)

Thus, for Winnicott destruction of the brain tissue also damaged the "soul," changing the suffering person to something not fully human. Furthermore, the soul is necessary to a sense of wholeness; damage to the "psyche, soul included" left one less than whole, a "part-human."

In thinking further about the implications of leucotomy for the relationship of the soul to the psyche-soma Winnicott once asked whether a new baby started "at par" or "above par" with regards to the soul, noting that deep religious convictions attended such questions. He observed that most people prefer to assume an implanted soul (analogous to preferring to think of God as perceived by rather than conceived of by humans) (Winnicott, 1951a, p. 552). Although it is not entirely clear what he meant by "par" or "above par," his reference to the notion of the soul being implanted implied a contrast with the notion of the soul emerging from developmental experience and also reminds one of similar contrasts he made about implanted morality versus a naturally emerging morality.

In addition to his comments about the reliance of the soul on the psyche-soma, Winnicott also spoke of the soul as referring to the interior life of the person. "After all, human beings are not animals; they are animals plus a wealth of fantasy, psyche, soul, or inner world potential or whatever you will" (Winnicott, 1949h, p. 44). Note also that in this quotation from a presentation to a less professional audience that Winnicott did not distinguish between the psyche and the soul as he had in the previously quoted lecture which was directed to professionals (Winnicott, 1954c). One notes that this way of referring to the soul places less emphasis on its physical or material basis. In this second quotation psyche and soul become two of several words used to refer to one's inner life. A poem by Winnicott called "Sleep" is of interest here; in it he connected the life of the soul to the unconscious interior life:

Let down your tap root
to the centre of your soul
Suck up the sap
from the infinite source
of your unconscious
And
Be evergreen
(quoted in Winnicott, 1978, p. 32; Used by permission)

This usage of the word soul to refer to one's inner life is similar in some respects to certain religious uses (cf. Rollins, 1999).

Winnicott's connection of the soul with the inner life, along with his previous connection of the soul with the word breath brings up a final point to make regarding Winnicott's view of the soul, and that is his connection of the soul to the establishment of the true self. "[W]hen the patient is concerned with the establishment of a true self as the place from which to live and the settlement of this true self in the body[,] it is here that the philological link between the word soul and the word breath becomes sensible" (Winnicott, 1954c, p. 162). Similarities between the soul and the true self are taken up below.

This section concludes by noting that Winnicott's varied comments on the soul do not consistently define its nature. Though he tried to shed light on a much-debated topic in religion that was of interest to him, he left much unclear and unresolved. A later chapter returns to Winnicott's ideas about the soul and contrasts them with various religious ones.

What Is the Role of Religion in Life and Culture

Another question that Winnicott was interested in had to do with the overall role of religion in life and culture. This in turn led to corollary questions about how psychoanalysis might contribute to religion. These questions occupied a large part of Winnicott's work and a complete chapter is devoted to his answers (see chapter 9). At this point, it is sufficient to note his interest in such questions.

Although these five questions are by no means all the ones that Winnicott raised that have religious implications (see chapter 11), they are sufficient to make the case that the content of his thought was often informed by his religious tradition. Many of his ideas and interests clearly mirror traditional theological concerns often revealing the musings of an "amateur theologian" (Winnicott, 1963j, p. 95). A later chapter is devoted to fleshing out the theology implicit in such questions and musings.

Theological Echoes in Winnicott's Psychoanalytic Concepts

Another way that one can see the influence of Winnicott's religious background on the content of his thought is in the similarity between several of his key concepts and certain religious ideas. For instance, Goldman (1993) has suggested that "holding, personalization, the capacity to be alone, [and] the True Self" are all "akin . . . to religious categories" (p. 123). Given Kirschner's (1996) thesis (see chapter 5) this is not surprising. Even when Winnicott thought in psychoanalytic terms, it is as though his religious background stood as the backdrop. As already noted, religious examples came readily to mind when he spoke of the baby's creativity or the achievement of a sense of individuality (I AM state). This section explores several key analytic concepts from Winnicott that have interesting parallels with religious ideas.[2]

The Capacity to Believe In and Faith

The section above devoted to Winnicott's interest in religiously oriented questions observed how closely his concept regarding the capacity to believe in is to certain aspects the Christian concept of faith. That material might well have been presented in this section re-framed as a similarity between Winnicott's analytic ideas and religious ones. Clearly, here is an analytic concept influenced and informed by Winnicott's religious background and it is reiterated here to acknowledge the parallel between this concept in Winnicott and religious ideas.

The Mother's Holding and God's Loving Grace

Several authors have called attention to how closely Winnicott's description of the mother's "holding" of her infant mirrors descriptions of God's loving interactions with humans (Goldman, 1993; Hansen & Drovdahl, 2006; Hoffman, 2004). Winnicott (1968b) himself connected the quality of the mother's holding with a subsequent ability to experience a God who holds with "everlasting arms" (p. 149).[3] The Christian doctrine of a loving and gracious God was a hallmark of Wesley's thought; some have called it the centerpiece of his theology (e.g., Wynkoop, 1967). A comparison of Winnicott's description of the mother's holding and Wesley's theology of a loving, gracious God reveals just how closely Winnicott's language comes to Wesley's.

Holding is Winnicott's metaphor for the totality of the mother's care for her infant (a metaphor that further widens to include other aspects of the environment) (Winnicott, 1967g). Holding takes in several related ideas including Winnicott's concepts of primary maternal preoccupation, absolute dependence, and the illusion of omnipotence. Exploration of these processes will make the connections between holding and God's loving grace clearer.

For Winnicott the infant is born into a holding environment that begins before birth with the mother's emotional preparation to welcome her baby. Her heightened sensitivity to the new life growing within her continues for a period after the infant's birth in a state that Winnicott (1956f) dubbed "primary maternal pre-occupation" (p. 300). This term refers to the mother's prescient attunement to her child and its needs during its state of "absolute dependence" (Winnicott, 1960i, p. 42), a time in which the infant is not able to distinguish itself from the world, nor its wishes and desires from reality. The journey toward individuality involves several steps aided by the quality of the mother's interactions with her infant.

In the state of absolute dependence one of the mother's tasks is to create an illusion of omnipotence in the infant. Initially, this occurs when the mother is able to present to the infant the object of its desire just at the time he or she is searching for such an object (e.g., a breast when the hungry infant imagines an object to satisfy its hunger). Although this illusion of omnipotence is short-lived and must be "disillusioned"—i.e., replaced with more realistic encounters with the world as the infant builds toleration for delay of gratification, it is a necessary early step on the journey to individuality.

In further describing the journey toward the infant's ability to distinguish "me" from "not me" (Winnicott, 1962b, 1963f), Winnicott (1966i) described an earlier step in this process as one in which the mother loaned something of her ego to the infant until the infant's own separate ego was sufficiently established to integrate its experiences. This ego support happens in part through what Winnicott called the "mirror role" of the mother. In this role the mother conveys to the infant her view of the infant as a unit so that the infant comes to see itself in terms of what it sees in the mother's eyes. Winnicott (1967g) summed up the result of such an exchange: "When I look I am seen, so I exist. I can now afford to look and see" (p. 114; cf. Winnicott, 1965g).

Another step along this journey of differentiation of self from world is the infant's coming to see itself as dwelling in a body so that it experiences itself as a psychosomatic unity ("personalization"—cf. Winnicott, 1954c). The mother's sensitivity in handling and holding her infant facilitates this process, helping the infant recognize the limits of its body (e.g., its own skin as a limiting membrane between it and the mother—cf. Winnicott, 1947a). Proper holding allows the baby to experience (and contain) its feelings and emotions (both positive and negative) without becoming overwhelmed (Winnicott, 1956f). Furthermore, proper holding is of such a nature that it does not "impinge" on the baby's needs by substituting the caregiver's needs; it recognizes the child as a person in its own right (Winnicott, 1956f).

Holding also permits the infant to develop trust in the reliability of its environment (Winnicott, 1968b, 1968d). Conversely, a failure in holding causes the infant to feel "dropped," one of several "primitive agonies" that result from inadequate holding (Winnicott, 1963e). Thus one sees that the quality of the mother's holding is crucial to healthy development; failure in this area risks "infantile psychosis" in which the infant cannot integrate its experience and the developmental processes are delayed or thwarted (Winnicott, 1955b). Proper holding allows for the emergence of the true self (Winnicott, 1960e).

However, proper holding is dependent upon the mother's devotion to her infant, to a loving identification and temporary pre-occupation with the infant's need during this early stage (Winnicott, 1955b). This type of care is possible in part because the mother remembers her own being cared for when she was an infant (Winnicott, 1966i), showing a clear social link in the chain of human development. Through the nurture provided by others during its early development the infant can become its own separate self that is able to relate to and care for others (as well as provide self-care and soothing). This care for others expresses itself initially in the infant's "concern" for the mother in terms of its (fantasized) attacks on her (Winnicott, 1950c). Later it will manifest in the infant's ability to relate to the mother as a separate person, and will eventually develop into the child's capacity to relate to mother, father, and others as people who are separate and who have their own needs.

Several convergences emerge from a comparison of Winnicott's concept of holding with a Wesleyan perspective on God's abundant grace (Wesley, 1733, 1739). The first comparison is drawn between Wesley's concept of God's prevenient (preceding) grace and Winnicott's notion of the mother's prior action in facilitating the emergence of the infant's separate sense of self. By prevenient grace Wesley (1739, 1785) meant to convey the idea that God had made the first move toward humanity prior to any attempt by humans to move toward God. It was this prevenient grace on the part of God that made any subsequent move by humans toward God possible. This notion of a preceding move on the part of God that permits the emergence of a movement on the part of humans is reminiscent of Winnicott's description of the mother's prior movements (e.g., primary maternal preoccupation, creation of illusion of omnipotence, loaning of her ego) that make possible the emergence of the infant's nascent self. Parker (2008) has noted how the sense of self or identity conferred on the infant by the mother's care mirrors a similar process attributed to God.

Winnicott's premise that a belief in God's reliability is built upon a prior experience of the mother's provision of a reliable and facilitating environment reflects a similar idea. Winnicott's description of the mother's holding making trust possible is very close to Wesley's notion that it is God's prior action (God's prevenient grace) that makes trust in God possible. Winnicott's (1968b) premise even provides a rationale for the psychological origins of such a belief (cf. Goldman, 1993) further noting that such a belief could never be given as a substitute for the prior experience of a reliable environment (Winnicott, 1963j).[4]

A second similarity between Winnicott's ideas about the mother's holding and God's loving grace is the non-impinging quality of God's grace. According to Wesley (1745, 1772) God's grace gives humans the freedom to respond to God in either a positive or negative way; God does not coerce people into service. Although Wesley's position on this point was the source of criticism from other Christians (Maddox, 1994; Runyon, 1998), his point accords well with this aspect of proper holding. Hansen and Drovdahl (2006) have further pointed out that the nature of grace for Wesley is such that human cooperation and participation are necessary. This is not because of a lack of sufficiency in God's grace but because another aspect of God's character is not to override the "liberty" of choice God gives to humans. This allowing a "role for human cooperation and participation" reinforces the idea that God's holding has a non-impinging quality that includes a "respect for persons in their own right" (p. 58).

Another parallel that might be drawn between the mother's holding and God's loving grace is the ability of both to "hold" not only the positive but also the negative experiences that characterize life. Hansen and Drovdahl (2006) summarized this kind of connection between Wesley and Winnicott: "God's prevenient grace extends to all humanity and is sufficient to hold both our positive and negative affects: fears and failures, disinterest and disdain, sins and shortcomings. . . . Since God's grace is a safe environment, trust can be placed in the God who holds, who initiates, and who leads in love" (p. 58).

One also could say this characterization of God as able to hold all one's affects is similar to Winnicott's (1965g, 1967g) description of the mother's "mirroring" of the baby. That is, in looking into the "face" of this gracious, loving God to see how one is viewed, one sees reflected back that one is loved. John Wesley's (1748a) description of "spiritual respiration" expressed a very similar idea. "God's breathing into the soul, and the soul's breathing back what it first receives from God . . . an unceasing presence of God, the loving, pardoning God, manifested to the heart and perceived by faith" (p. 442).

A final comparison between Winnicott's description of the mother's holding and Wesley's depiction of God's loving grace centers on the question of whether Winnicott's idea of primary maternal preoccupation might find a corollary in Wesley. The mother's stage of primary maternal preoccupation refers to a period in which the mother forgoes her own needs while being hyper attentive to the newborn's needs (Winnicott, 1956f). Whether there might be a parallel process in God raises theological questions regarding God's self-limitation (cf. Moltmann, 1981), a term used to express ideas that a being traditionally described as omniscient, omnipotent, and omnipresent does not always appear to act so. Moltmann (1981) for instance spoke of God's self-limitation in creating a space for the world to occupy. This self-limiting act on God's part is seen as a self-chosen act of love toward the creation. The language of God's self-limitations takes one deep into theological territory where answers differ (cf. Pinnock, 2001; Ware, 2008). The extent to which Wesley might have subscribed to such descriptions of God's self-limitation is a matter of debate (cf. Maddox, 1994; Ware, 2008). Although Wesley used the more traditional descriptions of God (e.g., omnipresence), he nevertheless spoke movingly of God's love for creation, especially humans (e.g., Wesley, 1733, 1786). Does it stretch things too far to suggest a parallel between the mother's state of primary maternal preoccupation and God's abundant, loving grace toward creation? Though one cannot offer a definitive answer, it is interesting to speculate whether this aspect of the mother's holding also mirrors an aspect of God's loving grace (cf. Parker, 2008). Following Kirschner's (1996) thesis, holding might be seen as a secular way to speak of what theologians mean by grace (see also chapter 11).

True Self and a Sacred Core in Humans

Winnicott's concept of the true self is another idea that sounds very much like a religious one. Hoffman (2004) has noted how closely Winnicott's description of the true self resembles that of the soul created in the image of God. Others have made a similar point (Goldman, 1993; Phillips, 1988; Rodman, 2003), and Winnicott (1960e, 1962d) himself acknowledged that his reflections on the true self (and its counterpart the false self) drew upon religious tradition.

The true self represents that which is authentic and real for Winnicott (1960e). It makes one feel alive. It is a wellspring of creativity and moves one toward health. "Only the True Self can be creative and only the True Self can feel real" (p. 148). It originates in the infant's early physical motility. "The True Self comes from the aliveness of the body tissues and the working of body-functions, including the heart's action and breathing" (p. 148). These early spontaneous physical movements are met and received by the mother. In providing a facilitating environment to receive these spontaneous gestures the mother grants the infant its temporary sense of omnipotence, allowing the true self to emerge. As Winnicott (1960e) noted, it is the mother's "repeated success in meeting the infant's spontaneous gestures" or illusions that permit the true self to become "living reality" (p. 145).

If the mother is unable to adequately meet and receive the infant's spontaneous gesture, a false self emerges. This occurs because instead of meeting the infant's gesture, the mother "substitutes her own gesture which is to be given sense by the compliance of the infant. This compliance . . . is the earliest stage of the False Self, and belongs to the mother's inability to sense her infant's needs" (p. 145). The infant recognizes that only some of its gestures are welcome and acceptable and develops a compliant (false) self that denies core elements of the true self. For instance, its spontaneous "aggressive" gestures may engender reactionary response from the environment such that the infant splits these off and is not able to integrate them into its personality. Thus, the false self develops to deal with impingements made too early upon the nascent self. In doing this, the infant loses the vitalizing quality this can provide and rather experiences the deadness, the sense of futility or feeling "unreal" that characterizes the false self. Although the false self is understood as a betrayal of the true self in some sense, Winnicott noted that it did have a salutatory role in that it arose to protect the true self.

Winnicott called attention to similarities between these concepts and religious ones by observing that the concept of the false self appears in various religious and philosophical discourse (1960e). Similarly, he noted that poetry and philosophy often portrayed a true self and saw its betrayal as something to be avoided (1962d). He further strengthened his association between the true self and religious categories when he spoke of the sacredness of an incommunicado core in each person (1963). This sacred "core," this "true self" (p. 187) is to be respected and approached with reverence, for if not so treated, it will resist and retreat from violation or alteration. His idea that therapy involved the discovery of this core or true self gives it a sacred cast as well. He noted that therapists must be aware of the "sacredness" of therapeutic encounters (1965f); of a patient's openness to share something of his inner world, Winnicott (1968a) once noted that he felt the patient had entrusted him with something sacred. Furthermore, he noted that therapists must anticipate certain resistances because of the person's feelings that a sacred area has been breached (Winnicott, 1969i).

In comparing Winnicott's comments about the true and false self with religious ideas several parallels emerge. The notion that there is some sort of sacred core in humans is very characteristic of Winnicott's Wesleyan Methodist heritage. As noted above, several have called attention to the similarity between Winnicott's notion of the true self and the religious concept of the soul (Goldman, 1993; Hoffman, 2004; Phillips, 1988; Rodman, 2003). Soul is one of several terms used by Wesley (cf.1788a, 1788b; Maddox, 1994) and other religious thinkers to speak about an essential, sacred core in humans. Whether it is the best religious concept with which to compare Winnicott's ideas regarding the true self is debatable[5] and a point taken up in a later chapter. However, in its common use soul clearly denotes ideas similar to Winnicott's notion of a sacred core in humans.

Another parallel between Winnicott's description of the true self and religious ideas is that of the true self as the vitalizing force in humans. The sense of aliveness and realness that exemplifies the true self is reminiscent of the Wesleyan Methodist focus on the new life or new birth that comes when the soul is renewed in the image of God (cf. Wesley, 1746f, 1760a). Through the imparting of the Holy Spirit, the human spirit is enlivened (Wesley, 1767). This renewal of life belongs to the core of religion for Wesley (cf. 1759).

The sense of aliveness or realness that belongs to the true self also brings to mind the Wesleyan focus on a personal experience of God. This emphasis on personal experience was such a hallmark of Wesleyan piety (Clapper, 1989; Semmel, 1973) that Wesley had to defend himself occasionally, affirming that "true Christianity cannot exist without both the inward experience and outward practice of justice, mercy and truth" (Wesley, 1792, p. 174). An earlier section noted how Winnicott's need to feel real and alive was a defining aspect of his personality, one that he imaginatively tried to extend to his death. It is clear that Winnicott's religious upbringing fits well with this aspect of his character and likely contributed to it; Winnicott and Wesley shared a penchant for personal experience both temperamentally and theoretically.[6]

Another way Winnicott's description of the true self parallels Wesley's religious teaching is through the focus on authentic living. This idea is frequently taken up by Wesley under the rubric of hypocrisy (cf. "hypocrisy, then or insincerity, is the first thing we are to guard against in prayer" [Wesley, 1748d, p. 575]). In this regard one also notes that among the functions of the Methodist "bands" (small groups) that Wesley inaugurated was the encouragement of honesty and openness about sharing the day-to-day successes and struggles in living a holy life (Chilcote, 2004; Runyon, 1998).[7]

A final parallel between Winnicott's concept of the true self and Wesley's theology already noted is Winnicott's (1960e) account of the mother's role in facilitating the emergence of the true self. Without the mother's facilitating environment the true self remains hidden. Similarly, for Wesley (1739, 1785), the ability for humans to flower into the creation God has desired and destined them to be begins with God's first movement toward humans via prevenient grace.

Transitional Space and the Mystical

Winnicott's description of transitional phenomena is yet another place where his language evokes religious concepts. This section looks at how closely Winnicott's descriptions of transitional phenomena come to religious descriptions of the mystical (cf. Eigen, 1981, 1998).

For Winnicott (1951b), transitional phenomena point to a step in the infant's growing ability to distinguish itself from the world. Like several colleagues at the British Psychoanalytic Society, especially Klein (cf. 1935, 1946), Winnicott saw the infant beginning life in an undifferentiated state in which self and world, inner and outer reality, were not distinguished. Only gradually over the first few months did the infant attain the ability to separate these. What Winnicott proposed was that there is an intermediate area on the journey from fusion with one's environment to being able to distinguish the "me" from the "not-me." This intermediate area is a "transitional space," a place populated by various "transitional phenomena" that help one negotiate the journey from merger to individuality (Winnicott, 1951b).

This intermediate or "potential" space (Winnicott, 1971e,) is a middle ground for sorting through and inter-relating the realities of one's inner and outer worlds. It is a place of great imaginative possibilities where the infant can experiment with letting go of its illusions and develops the ability to tolerate delays in need satisfaction. "I am here staking a claim for an intermediate state between a baby's inability and growing ability to recognize and accept reality. I am therefore studying the substance of illusion, that which is allowed to the infant, and which in adult life is inherent in art and religion" (Winnicott, 1951b, p. 230).

Furthermore, this intermediate area goes unchallenged. Thus, this creation of an intermediate space where inner and outer worlds, internal and external reality, co-mingle provides a safe place in which the infant can experiment or "play" with its emerging ability to sort the real, external world from its own internal fantasy world. It therefore is a place where creative ideas can emerge as one negotiates the never-ending task of sorting reality from fantasy (Winnicott, 1951b).

The transitional nature of religion itself is developed more fully in a subsequent chapter. This section explores various ways Winnicott's description of transitional phenomena evoke religious ideas of the mystical. Although an often maligned and misunderstood term thought to encompass the irrational, the mystical is especially associated with religious experience and points to a realm where the temporal and eternal, the finite and the infinite, the human and divine meet; where creative, imaginative encounters between the objective and subjective, the known and the unknown occur (James, 1902; Tinsley, 1983). Mystical experiences transcend the bounds of time and space and tend to be unifying and healing (Meadow, 1999). According to Otto (1923) such encounters lie at the heart of living religion, continually opening up new possibilities. Descriptions of the creative, imaginative possibilities that characterize transitional phenomena and space sound very similar to certain qualities of the mystical (cf. Eigen, 1998).

In addition, mystical experience has an "in between" quality to it. In his classical treatise on *The Idea of the Holy* Otto (1923) described mystical or numinous experience as an encounter with something "wholly other" (p. 25) that inspired both attraction and apprehension (a *mysterium tredmendum et fascinans*). Such encounters evoked a sense of awe as well as the awful. They are experiences "in between" fascination and fear, desire and dread. They are experiences that defy easy circumscription and that disappear if pursued with too much rationalism. Transitional phenomena and space have a similar in-between quality. Although there are differences between Otto's portrayal of the numinous and Winnicott's account of transitional phenomena (e.g., Otto's notion that the numinous is "felt as objective and outside the self" [p. 11]), this in-between quality of the experience is very similar.

Another way that Winnicott's account of transitional phenomena and space is similar to descriptions of the mystical is in the similarity of both to Victor Turner's (1969) comments on the liminal quality of religious ritual. Liminality defines the time or space in between structure and differentiation. Liminal phenomena are "unstructured or rudimentarily structured and relatively undifferentiated" experiences. Liminal phenomena (e.g., rituals) facilitate the transition from one state to another (e.g., the bar mitzvah recognizes a transition from child to adult in relation to the Torah) and are a "moment in and out of time" (p. 96). Thus, there are creative possibilities attendant to such moments. Liminality is further defined in terms of a series of "binary oppositions" (e.g., absence/presence, sacredness/secularity, silence/speech, simplicity/complexity, acceptance/avoidance) (p. 106).

Winnicott's depiction of transitional phenomena gave them a liminal quality. When he (1951b) described transitional phenomena (including space) as between "creative activity and projection of what has already been introjected," as between "unawareness of indebtedness and the acknowledgement of indebtedness," as between the baby's "inability and growing ability to recognize and accept reality" (p. 230) he presented his own list of binary oppositions. That transitional objects are extensions of both the mother and the self, that they are "outside, inside, at the border" and that they are not challenged further testifies to their liminal characteristics (p. 230). Similarly, Winnicott's (1971l) clarification that it is "not the object . . . that is transitional" but rather that "the object represents the infant's transition from a state of . . . to a state of . . ." (p. 14) also points to the liminal nature of transitional phenomena. Thus, transitional phenomena share with liminal moments the potential for new creative possibilities to emerge.

In addition to the similarities between Winnicott's descriptions of transitional phenomena and broad ideas from the Judeo-Christian tradition, which both Otto (1923) and Turner (1969) acknowledge as influencing their arguments, there is one particularly Wesleyan Methodist similarity to be noted. It is found in Winnicott's emphasis on maintaining the tension between form and creativity in the intermediate area. According to Winnicott (1971j), the intermediate area is located somewhere between form and formlessness, a space in which the spontaneous impulse or creative gesture could emerge. Winnicott spoke of this tension between form and spontaneity in several ways. In an essay on "The Location of Cultural Experience" he observed that "it is not possible to be original except on the basis of tradition" (Winnicott, 1971e, p. 99). He made a similar point about the relationship of form to art and the use of the sonnet form by poets to express creative gestures. He further noted that those who were religious found that "service" allowed "freedom" (Winnicott, 1970c, p. 278).

Holding the tension between form and creativity was very much a part of Wesleyan religious expression. For instance, it is seen in the inclusion of both liturgy and extemporaneous prayers during worship (Goldman, 1993). This dialectic of form and creativity is also seen in Wesley's emphasis on the need to combine the "*form* and the *power* of godliness" (cf. 2 Timothy 3:5). This was an oft-repeated theme for Wesley (cf. 1743b, 1750, 1763a; cf. 1741, 1748b, 1767). Chilcote summarized Wesley's position:

> His experience had taught him that people tend to hold on to the external forms of religion without ever experiencing its power. But he also observed that whenever Christian people begin to neglect the practice or form of religion—in other words, whenever they stop praying or going to church or sharing in fellowship with other Christians—they quickly lose the power as well. He wanted to guard against this at all costs. The point was to hang onto both. . . . Either was deficient without the other. An emphasis upon order and an appreciation for the past can become lifeless if not celebrated presently in the Spirit; the celebration of the Spirit as the animating force within the life of the church can become divisive and self-serving if not rooted in the timeless heritage of faith. (p. 56, 62)

This desire to maintain the tension between the form and the power kept Wesley in his own day from separating from the Church of England to form his own denomination. Instead his followers were a network of "societies," neither church nor sect but something in between that allowed for creativity within the established church. Certainly the informality of the society meeting allowed for spontaneous testimonies and creative gestures (Chilcote, 2004; Runyon, 1998).

An earlier chapter noted how this Wesleyan Methodist emphasis influenced the form of Winnicott's thinking, perhaps in ways not fully known to his awareness. Here one sees that this Wesleyan emphasis may have echoes in Winnicott's language about the intermediate area as a place where form and formlessness live in tension.

Capacity to Be Alone and the Presence of God

Winnicott's notion of the capacity to be alone is another of his concepts that seems to echo religious categories. Both Goldman (1993) and Hoffman (2004) called attention to parallels between this capacity and the traditional religious teaching on the presence of God.

The capacity to be alone is a hallmark of health (and is distinguished from a withdrawn state); like other core ideas in Winnicott it has its origins in the early mother-child relationship. It is built on the paradox of being alone in the felt presence of the mother: "it is only when alone (that is to say, in the presence of someone) that the infant can discover his own personal life" (Winnicott, 1958a, p. 34). Although the mother is present, she does not make demands of the child, thus freeing it to discover its own desires at its pace. In providing these conditions the mother creates a space in which the infant can experience feeling real.[8]

At this stage of development the infant is trying to come to terms with the mother's presence and absence, with her continued existence. It is the mother's reliability that allows the infant to tolerate being alone for brief periods (Winnicott, 1958a). Being alone in this way involves an "assumption that the person who loves and who is therefore reliable is available and continues to be available when remembered after being forgotten" (Winnicott, 1971i, pp. 47–48).

Winnicott's thoughts regarding the capacity to be alone evoke religious ideas of experiences of the presence of God. One thinks, for instance, of meditative traditions in which one "practices the presence of God" (Lawrence, 1968). Such activities might well be described as exercises in being alone in the presence of an Other, an experience made possible according to Winnicott by this similar prior experience. Winnicott (1963a) once observed that psychoanalysis has often overlooked the positive aspects of this kind of "mysticism," which can include an increase in the sense of "feeling real" (pp. 185–186).

Winnicott's thoughts on the capacity to be alone also invite comparison with the traditional distinctions between God's "immanence" versus "transcendence." God's transcendent quality is that which defines God as "wholly Other," as different from God's creation, the human. It is God's transcendent Otherness that creates a sense of awe and distance (cf. Otto's [1923] *mysterium tremendum et fascinans*). God's immanent quality is that which allows God to be experienced as close and like the creation in some way, as personally present. While acknowledging both qualities, various theologies tend to emphasize one over the other.

Wesley's (cf. 1786) emphasis fell on God's immanence. He preached that God's loving grace is present to all people at all times (prevenient grace). Though transcendent, God was primarily experienced as a loving, gracious Presence. Hoffman (2004) called particular attention to the parallels between Wesley's theology of God's immanent presence and Winnicott's acheivement of the capacity to be alone.

> For Winnicott, the loving, immanent relationship between a caretaker and an infant is strongly in the foreground, with the mother's "otherness" (as seen in her hatred and her own subjectivity) emerging as a background theme. Whether one speaks of the "holding environment," "good-enough mothering," or the "facilitating environment," this foreground figure—a good object who is loving—is central to his theorizing. In similar fashion, the aspect of God that predominates in the Wesleyan narrative is the loving God, one whose grace is good enough and whose maternal provision is bountiful. God's own subjectivity, His "otherness," remains a known but less focused-on theme. (p. 788)

One also notes, as does Hoffman (2004), that Winnicott's description of the mother's quiet presence without demands, a presence that allows momentary forgetting, could describe a "transcendent" dimension to her presence. That is, she is present but "over there" in the infant's view; like the ground in a figure-ground display. She, of course, is ready to receive the child's gesture to make her presence manifest as the figure. Thus, in some ways Winnicott's description of the mother in relationship to the child's emerging capacity to be alone mirrors both the transcendent and immanent qualities of God's presence, though the emphasis for Winnicott, like for Wesley, falls on the latter quality.

According to Winnioctt (1958a) the capacity to be alone involves the infant's coming to terms with both the presence and absence of the mother. This too has parallels in religious reflections on the experience of God's absence and presence (Parker, 2008; Underwood, 1986). For instance, St. John of the Cross (1959) wrote of the "dark night of the soul" as an aspect of one's spiritual journey. Underwood appealed to Winnicott's work to argue that it is experiences of God's absence that permit one to experience God as "real," that is, as other than one's projections. He argued that the ability to deal with perceived experiences of God's absence is as much a matter of spiritual health, if not more so, than the ability to deal with experiences of God's presence (cf. Parker, 2008). Thus, Winnicott's work on the capacity to be alone, like his work on the mother's holding, is richly suggestive not only in terms of psychological factors involved in one's perceived experiences of God, but also offers criteria for maturity, both natural and spiritual.

Object Usage and the Crucifixion and Resurrection

An earlier chapter noted that Winnicott's concept of object usage evoked the images of the crucifixion and resurrection of Jesus. There the concept of object usage was elaborated on in the context of Winnicott's interest in and identification with Jesus. Similar to the summary regarding the commonality between belief in and faith, the previous material on object usage and the crucifixion and resurrection need not be repeated at length but is briefly reiterated here as another key construct with similarity to theological ideas.

Object usage refers to a stage in emotional development in which the child is able to accord to others a separate existence apart from the child's imaginings and illusions. On the way to this stage the child fantasizes destruction of the object which through its survival emerges as a subject in its own right and thereby moves the child along in its coming to terms with the real world. This destruction of the object in fantasy is a way Winnicott spoke of the positive dimension of aggression. The non-retaliating survival of the object (destroyed in fantasy) can now be "used," thus facilitating the movement to more mature relating. Recall Winnicott's (1971k) notion that the therapist must become an object for use in this way arose in tandem with a special interest in the life of Jesus and reflected at some level his own identification with Jesus.

Hopkins (1989) drew attention to Jesus as the representative of survival par excellence; that is, in the crucifixion and resurrection Jesus showed himself to be a non-retaliating, surviving object. Similarly, Hoffman (2011) has recently argued that the therapist's ability to survive a patient's projections and become an object that can be used in the way Winnicott depicted mirrors the Christian theme of crucifixion. She pointed out that through "surrender to a process that will lead to unavoidable enactments, [therapists] experience firsthand the devastation that our patients have been forced to live through. At times we suffer unjustly for the crimes of others, a morass that echoes Freud's [Meng & Freud, 1963] remark to Pfister that 'the transference is indeed a cross' (p. 39)" (p. 106). Although there is no obvious religious language in Winnicott's depiction of object usage, the ideas articulated clearly provide another example of the ways Winnicott's central concepts echo theological ones.[9]

Concluding Summary

This section argued that several of the key concepts in Winnicott's work seemed to have aspects of his religious heritage as backdrop. Often Winnicott made the religious background obvious by various examples used to illustrate his concepts. Even when he did not expressly mention religion, his religious background provided both categories and language for unfolding his ideas.

The comparison of central concepts in Winnicott's thinking with similar theological categories suggests a kind of implicit theology in Winnicott to the extent that these central concepts reveal answers to questions of the human condition and teleology (Browning, 1987; Kirschner, 1996). Winnicott's concepts of the mother's holding, the intermediate area, creativity and play, the true self, feeling real and the capacity to be alone provide insight into Winnicott's particular "attempts to delineate and address the deepest and most difficult existential issues that human beings face" (Kirschner, 1996, p. 6). A later chapter is devoted to making explicit the contours of the theological vision implicit in the comparisons of this and other chapters.

Notes

1.   It also is important to note that several letters addressed to Winnicott refer to religious topics. Although there were no corresponding letters in response the letters attest to the frequency with which friends and family addressed religious topics with Winnicott and give further indication of his interest in such topics. A few of these letters are cited throughout the book at appropriate places.

2.   There are other concepts in Winnicott besides those covered here that also have theological echoes though they are less obviously similar to religious concepts than those covered here. For instance, Goldman (1993) and others (Green, 2005; Lambert, 1987) have suggested that Winnicott's concept of personalization evokes the religious language of incarnation. Although I find the connections between personalization and incarnation less compelling, I note this connection made by others. Additional concepts with less obvious theological echoes are noted in the chapter on Winnicott's implicit theology.

3.   It is noteworthy that Winnicott's idea that the psychological origins of an experience of God as having everlasting arms resided in an experience of the mother's holding evokes images of Otto's (1923) description of the experience of the numinous or holy. Such experiences inspire both attraction and dread (a *mysterium tremendum et fascinans*). It was this dual fascination and fear that characterized living religion for Otto. Winnicott's (1963c) descriptions of the infant's trying to bring together its varying experiences of the mother's care (i.e., the "object mother" of excitement and the "environment mother" of reliability) are evocative of the dualities Otto set forth. The section on transitional phenomena takes up further similarities between the numinous and Winnicott's ideas.

4.   Although Wesley would share some commonality with Winnicott here regarding the psychological origins of ideas (and experiences), Wesley would call attention to reciprocal processes in such beliefs and experiences. That is, he would see ideas about human reliability (including a mother's) having their roots in God's prior reliability (God's first gracious move toward humanity) (cf. Hansen & Drovdahl, 2006; Maddox, 1994).

5.   Although it clearly points to some kind of "sacred" core in humans, soul is not the easiest term to circumscribe (Cousineau, 1994), having been variously defined and described in Christian theology (Boyd, 1998; Moreland & Ciocchi, 1993; Rollins, 1999). Generally, soul is used to refer to an essential quality of humanity; however, the nature of this essential quality is often debated (Anderson, 1982; Boyd, 1998; Moreland & Ciocchi, 1993; Myers, 1978). For instance, a common contrast is to distinguish the soul from the body, the former referring to some immaterial or spiritual essence, while the latter refers to the material or physical properties of humanness. Although such distinctions create their own problems from a religious perspective (e.g., is the soul some "substance" hu-

mans possess; is the body "non-spiritual"—cf. Anderson, 1982; Myers, 1978), soul continues to be widely used in theological discourse. It is most commonly used to speak about the holistic nature of humans. According to Rollins (2007), historically and etymologically the English word soul seeks to capture both Hebraic and Greek notions of "the total of conscious and unconscious life in the human personality" (p. 25). In religious contexts, soul is often used to ascribe a "spiritual" quality to humans (Anderson, 1982; Moon; 1999; Muller, 1990); in this sense soul is often compared to similar concepts such as "spirit" (Osterhaven, 1984) or the *imago Dei* (Anderson, 1982; Ingram, 1999. Note that this latter term also was included in Hoffman's [2004] quotation about the similarity between the true self and the soul.)

It is not the purpose here to resolve all the questions that arise from the use of the term soul or to offer refined distinctions between various theological concepts that speak to the "spiritual" nature of humans. A later chapter devoted to the topic of Winnicott's implicit theology will further address these topics. For now, the more limited purpose is simply to acknowledge how closely certain key concepts in Winnicott sound to religious ideas.

6.   Using Smith's (2009) categories one could argue that Wesleyan spirituality is an "embodied" spirituality given its affective, experiential quality (cf. Wesley's [1738a] comment that his heart was "strangely warmed" at Aldersgate). That Wesleyan theology was more likely learned from singing than didactic learning (cf. Chilcote, 2004; Hoffman, 2004) further testifies to its embodied nature. Winnicott seems to have had an especial affinity to embodied experience as well. He once commented about his clinical work that he listened with his throat, noting that his larynx followed the sounds he heard especially the voice of someone talking to him. He also stated that this had always been a noticeable characteristic for him (Winnicott, 1963m). This resonance with embodied experience might also be a temperamental quality that Winnicott shared with Wesley. In addition to its function as transitional phenomena Winnicott's singing of Methodist hymns might also tap this temperamental affinity with the embodied experiential quality of his Wesleyan Methodist heritage.

7.   The following is a list of five questions that were to be asked at every band or small group meeting:
    1.   What known sins have you committed since our last meeting?
    2.   What temptations have you met with?
    3.   How was [*sic*] you delivered?
    4.   What have you thought, said, or done, or which you doubt whether it be sin or not?
    5.   Have you nothing you desire to keep secret? (Wesley, 1738b, p. 78).

8.   Because of the central role that Winnicott ascribed to the mother in the infant's early development, one notes that several of his concepts overlap (Abram, 2007b). For instance, the noted aspects of the capacity to be alone share common ground with ideas encountered in the articulation of holding and the true self.

9.   As a different point but relevant to the discussion of object usage and its similarity to religious discourse, one might note that just as the mother only becomes "real" through surviving the infant's fantasized destruction, it is only as God is allowed to be other than one's projections that God can become real (cf. Parker, 2008; Ulanov, 2001). Similarly, without a prior experience of a moment of illusory omnipotence, this real God could not emerge without the previous imaginative capacities to project God.

Chapter 8
Religion as Creative: Winnicott's Psychoanalytic Vision

"I am therefore studying the substance of illusion"

In giving his qualifying paper for acceptance into the British Psychoanalytic Society Winnicott (1935) paused for a brief aside on the question of religious beliefs and practices. Although it is not surprising that Winnicott addressed the topic of religion, given his background, what is surprising is the way in which Winnicott came to the defense of religion among colleagues that did not tend to view religion in a very positive light. Although acknowledging that religion sometimes can be employed as a psychological defense, Winnicott quite characteristically, turned the tables on his psychoanalytic colleagues to suggest that too much railing against religion also can be a form of defense. What is significant about this paper is that Winnicott was not content to simply repeat Freud's (1927) negative view of the defensive character of religion as something to be overcome; Winnicott actually spoke favorably regarding the role of religion in helping cope positively with depression. In the course of developing his own contribution to psychoanalytic theory Winnicott (1951b, 1970e, 1971h) would reverse much of Freud's argument regarding the pathological quality of religion, often using established psychoanalytic theory to advance his own challenges to the accepted psychoanalytic wisdom about religion. It is significant that this tendency began with his first formal psychoanalytic paper.

Previous chapters have looked at how Winnicott's religiosity showed up in his use of scriptural language and allusion, in the way he explicated certain psychoanalytic concepts, and in the way certain aspects of his Wesleyan Methodist tradition were present in the way he practiced psychoanalysis (e.g., his inclusiveness, his non-dogmatic stance). This chapter attends to Winnicott's overt reflections on the nature and role of religion in life and culture. In some ways this chapter affirms Goldman's (1993) claim of a "lingering religiosity" in Winnicott by demonstrating a lifelong interest in the positive role of religion. In stark contrast to the traditional psychoanalytic perspective on the pathological role of religion, Winnicott lays the foundation for a psychoanalytic view of religion that sees it as one of the most creative and adaptive of human experiences. This positive view toward religion owed much to his religious background.

However, in exploring Winnicott's thoughts on the nature and role of religion one will see that the influence of Winnicott's religious upbringing on the way he viewed his work is not one-directional. This chapter also looks at the way Winnicott's exposure and adoption of psychoanalytic categories influenced his view of religion. It will trace changes in Winnicott's psychoanalytic views on religion from his early appropriation of Freud's perspective to his more mature and reflective view on the role of religion in life and culture.

Winnicott's Exposure to Psychoanalysis and Its Influence on His View of Religion

Winnicott's first exposure to psychoanalysis came through his reading of a book by Oskar Pfister (1917), a Swiss Reformed pastor who had adapted Freud's ideas to his ministerial work. Winnicott had been troubled by his inability to recall his dreams and after consultation with a librarian ended up with Pfister's introduction to Freudian psychology. Winnicott (1919) wrote of this early encounter with Freud's ideas in a letter to his sister Violet sent while he was still in medical school. This letter was revealing in several ways. First, it showed Winnicott's grasp of Freud's early model of the mind with its various regions of consciousness. It also showed his attempt to apply Freud's ideas to his work with patients in his medical studies. However, more significantly, one notes that Winnicott's early evaluation of Freud's ideas also repeated Pfister's assessment regarding the role of religion.

In Freud's (1907, 1913, 1927, 1930) own writings about religion he tended to focus on the contribution of religion to pathology. Pfister (1917), in adapting Freud's ideas, also acknowledged that religion may be used by individuals in unhealthy ways. For instance, religion may function very much like an obsessional neurosis, with repetitive religious acts looking much like the repetitive rituals of obsessive compulsive disorder. Yet, as a pastor, Pfister argued that religion also served a positive function in society. One such function is that it provided ethical guidelines. One sees both of these sentiments about religion reflected in Winnicott's letter to his sister. He is aware that religious obsessions can correspond to various disorders of the mind yet finds religion useful in establishing ethical standards (Winnicott, 1919).

This early penchant for valuing both the negative and positive critique of religion would continue to characterize Winnicott's use of a psychoanalytic lens throughout his career. And although Winnicott was not blind to the ways in which religion could contribute to an individual's pathology (as noted below), the hallmark of his own psychoanalytic theory included a clear argument for the positive role of religion in life and culture. However, before attending to Winnicott's unique contribution to psychoanalytic theory and its implications for the positive role of religion, it will be beneficial to explore some of his other statements about religion.

Winnicott's First Formal Psychoanalytic Paper

Winnicott's (1935) inaugural paper for admission into the British Psychoanalytic Society was titled, "The Manic Defense." This paper was a tribute to Melanie Klein, one of Winnicott's mentors and supervisors, and dealt primarily with applying and extending her insights about a person's experiences of fantasy and reality (Klein, 1935). What is of interest here are several comments that Winnicott made about religion in this paper. Although not the central thrust of the paper, the disclosures nevertheless give glimpses into Winnicott's developing psychoanalytic view of religion.

Religion and the Inner World

One might first note that Winnicott acknowledged that religious behavior, like many other behaviors, can be a "manic defense," a kind of flight from the anxieties of the inner world. Yet, this evasive quality is not what Winnicott dwelt upon. Even as he further acknowledged that psychoanalysis might explain the Christian concepts of the Crucifixion and Resurrection as "symbolic castration with subsequent erection" Winnicott (1935) was quick to offer his rebuttal of this view as not only unsatisfactory to the Christian but as analytically deficient as well, since it focused on only one analytic dimension of this belief and practice (p. 135). What is significant in Winnicott's comments is that although he demonstrated his familiarity with analytic concepts and a psychoanalytic interpretation of religious behavior, he was not content to simply endorse these. Rather, he subjected them to critique, not only from a Christian viewpoint, but from the viewpoint of adequate analytic theory. Conversely, what Winnicott offered in their stead were reflections on the positive contributions of religion.

One of these positive contributions is that religion, far from aiding one's flight from the anxieties of the inner world, actually makes one more aware of the deep emotions in life. Religion, through its rituals, can both remind people of deep emotions such as sadness, as well as help them cope with such deep affect. He wrote, "each year the Christian tastes the depths of sadness, despair, hopelessness, in the Good Friday experiences" (Winnicott, 1935, p. 135). However, because "the average Christian cannot hold the depression so long . . . he goes over into a manic phase on Easter Sunday" (p. 135). What Winnicott proposed was that the Christian add to the Crucifixion (which ritualized recognition of sadness, depression) and the Resurrection (which ritualized manic flight from sadness and depression) a re-appropriation of the "Ascension" of Christ: a way to ritualize the "recovery from depression" without simply a manic flight. Winnicott contrasted this religious way of recognizing and potentially coping with deep emotions with a tendency among those of an analytic persuasion to lapse into a manic defense against "sadness, guilt, hopelessness" inasmuch as their disparagement of religion hid a failure to recognize these deep emotions. Thus, according to Winnicott certain religious doctrines and rituals prevented people from suffering the illusion that life is always "nice" and thwarted a manic defense that would deny life's sadness.

There are other things of interest in this argument about religious doctrine and ritual and its relation to the inner world. First, one notes that Winnicott was able to turn analytic thought upon its head so that it became self-critical. That is, not only can psychoanalytic theory offer reflections on the psychological role of religion; when wielded by someone like Winnicott, it can reflect upon the nature of its own reflections about religion, and find them wanting. (This tendency to turn analytic theory upon its head was characteristic of Winnicott and is delightfully seen in a letter to a colleague in which Winnicott amusingly pondered "what is the penis symbolical of"—an interesting question indeed for those accustomed to seeing phallic symbols behind every pillar and post [Winnicott, 1956c, p. 99].) Second, one notes Winnicott's deep understanding of Christian doctrine and ritual. He reflected upon these doctrines and practices both as a psychoanalyst and as an "amateur theologian" (Winnicott, 1963j, p. 95). As psychoanalyst, he offered new and illuminating comments on the unconscious significance of Christian doctrine and ritual. These comments acknowledged both the negative and positive potential of these practices, but one notes that the emphasis was on the positive. As an amateur theologian, one notes that Winnicott's acquaintance with the Christian religion was of sufficient depth for him to suggest that the common focus on the Crucifixion and Resurrection might be inadequate theologically. His re-appropriation of the Ascension rituals pointed to other theologically (and psychologically) important dimensions of Christian teaching and ritual.

The role of religion in appreciating the depth of the emotions was a theme seen throughout Winnicott's life. In an early work he spoke of religion (along with art) as one of the social forms for recognizing the importance of early feelings (Winnicott, 1931a). And although at one point he pondered in a letter to a friend whether theology had embraced the notion of the unconscious (Winnicott, 1949e), he later affirmed that religion shared with psychoanalysis an appreciation of this dimension of our humanity (Winnicott, 1968b). In two other essays, he affirmed the connection between depressed mood and the struggles with the deepest conflicts of the "inner nature" (Winnicott, 1958g, p. 25), noting that such common human struggles were well known to religion, art and philosophy (Winnicott, 1961d).

In addition to his reflections on religion's role in appreciating the depth of emotions, Winnicott offered another reflection on religion in this paper that will be significant in his later writings. It is in this first formal psychoanalytic paper that Winnicott lays the groundwork for what will be known as "God images." Although this concept is explored in detail later, a brief comment is in order.

God Images

In this first psychoanalytic paper Winnicott (1935) made several comments on the psychological origins of a person's "God" that are worth noting. He recognized that "God" can be an "internal object" in the same way other significant persons (and parts of others) become internalized as "objects"—personal mental representations of external phenomena overlaid with idiosyncratic imaginings and strong affect. Similarly, Winnicott was aware that "God" sometimes is the symbol for various projections (such as that of a fierce father or a place to put goodness and badness). For instance, people often attribute the good they see in themselves to "God," not recognizing their own contribution to such internalized images. However, Winnicott also argued that therapists must not force such recognition, nor treat such internalized objects as merely a projection or fantasy when working with religious clients; rather the therapist should let a person's recognition arise gradually as therapy progresses.

In assessing Winnicott's (1935) comments in this essay, one might note that this way of speaking of God is indebted to Klein's (e.g., 1935) theory, and that Winnicott later tended not to speak of internal objects in this rather reified way, in part because he thought Klein's emphasis on internal objects omitted the role of the external environment. Although Winnicott recognized a personal contribution to a person's "God," there is a hint that the personal origins of a person's "God" did not provide a complete understanding of God. A later chapter returns to the concept of God images.

Other Significant Reflections

Winnicott continued throughout his professional career to comment on the role of religion from a psychoanalytic framing. Though few of his published essays are devoted directly to the role of religion, it is never far from his thinking and he continued to reflect on its positive and negative qualities. As noted in a previous chapter, Winnicott struggled with how to define the relationship between psychoanalysis and religion. Over the years he reflected on both what religion can offer the individual and society, as well as whether and what contribution psychoanalysis might make to the study of religion (Winnicott, 1936a, 1951b, 1963j). In some of his earlier writings he took the position that although psychoanalysis was an instrument to study human relations, it offerred no religious contribution (Winnicott, 1945e). Even while repeating a similar thought,

Winnicott (1961f) also affirmed that there must remain no reserved area in a patient's life if he or she is to profit fully from an analysis. This included a person's religious life. Winnicott (1963j, 1966f) later concluded that psychoanalysis can indeed offer a religious contribution.

Religion's Contributions to Society

As noted above, in his early letter to his sister Violet, the young Winnicott (1919) remarked that one of the positive and proper contributions of religion to society is that it offered "high ethical standards" (p. 3). Winnicott continued to affirm this aspect of religion throughout his life but almost a half century later, he offered a much more nuanced reflection on how religion ought to do this. One of the few extended statements that Winnicott made about religion is found in his essay on "Morals and Education" written in 1963, an essay that repeated several themes from earlier essays on guilt and the innate morality of the child (e.g., 1944, 1949b, 1958g, 1962a). In this essay he made several statements about religion, including some of his most critical comments. Given that Winnicott's overall psychoanalytic project affirms the positive role of religion in life, it is important to note the nature of the rather strident critique of this essay.

In many ways the points he made in this essay are derivative because the chief focus of the paper was about moral development. Recall that in this essay he contrasted an innate moral development with the imposed morality that was often associated with religion. Winnicott's chief complaints against religion were its tendency to impose morality without appreciating the "original goodness" in humanity and its insensitivity to developmental processes and timing in acquiring moral standards. Because religion tended to impose morality onto the child before it was developmentally ready, religion could stifle the child's own creative impulses, foreclosing on the child's moral creativity and discovery.

Winnicott argued that when religion inculcated morals, rather than being sensitive to the child's own moral discovery, it lost the high ground in its provision of ethical guidelines. Thus, Winnicott's early remarks that religion had a role in setting high ethical standards, became modified in his later thought to suggest that religion was a source for ethical guidelines, perhaps even a key one, but one that must not impose these ethical standards so much as make them available for use. That is, for them to become truly internalized and "real" (so that one does not need a personal policeman to accompany him or her), these standards must be personally discovered or "created" through appropriately timed developmental processes.

In contrast to the idea that morals need to be implanted in children, Winnicott argued that morality arose naturally out of consistent care during infancy, a point he had made in earlier essays (e.g., Winnicott, 1958g). The acquisition of moral standards involved complex processes of early mental and emotional development. Even when things went well in terms of early child care, the infant was still confronted with its own mental fantasies about its impulses. Lacking experience in this regard, the infant must find its own way, building a sense of self and other out of its experiences, often with some frightening missteps, a point he had made more than twenty-five years previously. There he observed that it is not that a child has no innate control over its impulses; rather problems arise because these early "crude and vicious" methods of impulse control are so well used that the child needs rescue from them (Winnicott, 1936a, p. 74).

One positive contribution of religion in this respect is its ability to "humanize" the fierce innate morality of the child (Winnicott, 1963j, p. 101; cf. 1949b, 1946a, p. 74). However, even though religion can help humanize the fierce morality of the child, morality is not something to be implanted in the child through religious teaching. Developmentally, there will come a time when the child is ready to adopt a less demanding moral code and Winnicott argued that there ought to be some lying around for the child to pick up (cf. 1964c). His argument was one of developmental timing. That is, moral teaching (and by extension religious teaching) serve the person well only when introduced at the appropriate time developmentally. To hand or impose a moral code on the child too early is to impinge upon the development of the true self (cf. Winnicott, 1962a, 1968b) and deprive the child of its own ability to arrive at moral decisions.[1]

What Psychoanalysis Can Contribute to Religion

According to Winnicott (1963j) the chief contribution that psychoanalysis could make to religion was to help it remember this. If religion forwent implanting morality and instead allowed the creativity that belonged to finding one's own internal morality, psychoanalysis might help religion recover a place in culture by helping it regain a creativity that was lost if morality or religion was imposed upon the person. More specifically, Winnicott argued that psychoanalysis might restore the creativity involved in imagining God as a repository of goodness that theology or imposed morality tended to erode. Psychoanalysis makes this contribution in part by reminding religion of the importance of the mother's early care (e.g., the quality of her holding provides the basis for an experience of "everlasting arms" [Winnicott, 1968b]): Winnicott (1963j) argued in another place that although religion generally acknowledged the importance of family life, it was psychoanalysis that placed the importance of the mother's care at center stage.

This, of course, is not the only contribution that psychoanalysis can make to religion. Winnicott argued in another place that certain psychoanalytic concepts might help those who struggle with the concept of miracles find a new way to think about these. For instance, he drew upon his concepts of "belief in" and "transitional phenomena" to reflect upon the child's emerging use of symbols (Winnicott, 1966f). One way these analytic concepts help is by allowing one to reflect on the symbolic significance of miracles. Winnicott seems to have expanded on this idea in a letter to his brother-in-law for the latter wrote back: "I want to say how much I liked your last long scribble about religion. . . . I don't think much about miracles: perhaps I ought to think more. I simply think of them as honorific myths. But of course here again there is the question, why mere stories? And I must admit that some of them give immense satisfaction. (But here I think I am simply picking up clues of yours)" (Britton, 1967). The discussion continued by exploring the role of biblical miracles as expressions of concern for justice. A later chapter returns to Winnicott's personal engagement of religious symbols; this section continues with his psychoanalytic contributions to understanding religion.

Despite these important and significant statements about religion, Winnicott's greatest contributions to the psychoanalytic understanding of religion did not come from his speaking directly about religion.[2] Although he argued that religion was an important cultural source for ethical standards when offered at the appropriate developmental time (Winnicott, 1963j), his greatest contribution to the psychoanalytic understanding of religion arises out of his most unique contribution to analytic theory: his concept of transitional objects and transitional phenomena. It is from understanding this contribution to psychoanalytic theory that one comes to see Winnicott's strongest argument regarding the positive role of religion for the individual and society.

Winnicott's Expansion of Psychoanalytic Theory: Implications for Religion

Arguably Winnicott's most singular contribution to psychoanalytic theory is his concept of the transitional object and its correlate, transitional phenomena. The transitional object is the most recognized concept of Winnicott's theory, one which Anna Freud noted had "conquered the analytic world" (cited in Rodman, 1987, p. xix). Winnicott (1951b) first published his formal essay on this topic in 1951, though he had made observations about these phenomena in several previous essays (Winnicott, 1945c, 1948a, 1949i, 1950b). It was a topic that he continued to refine for the remainder of his life, publishing a revised edition of the essay in his last edited book which appeared posthumously (Winnicott, 1971l). This central concept has important implications for how religion is to be understood and became the cornerstone for Winnicott's argument regarding the positive role of religion in the life of the individual and in culture.

Transitional Objects and Transitional Phenomena

The concept of transitional phenomena arises from Winnicott's consideration of the question of how it is infants come to see themselves as separate and distinct from their world. For Winnicott (1951b) the infant began life in an undifferentiated state, unable to distinguish self from world. Only gradually over the first few months did the infant gain the ability to separate internal from external reality. Winnicott proposed that on the journey from merger to differentiation of self and object there is an intermediate area. This intermediate space is populated by "transitional objects" or "transitional phenomena" so that one might even speak of the intermediate area as "transitional space." This "potential space" between mother and infant, between subjective and objective experience is a creative realm where the infant "plays" and experiments with its illusions while learning to sort its inner and outer realities. It is an unchallenged middle ground that provides a respite from the strains inherent in coming to terms with a world that does not comport with one's wishes.

To aid the transition from the inability to distinguish the world from one's wishes or illusions to the ability to clearly differentiate the two, certain objects in the infants world take on a special significance because they have the capacity to traverse the gap between the infant's fantasy world (where needs are perfectly met, creating an illusion of omnipotence), and the external world of reality where the infant's needs are sometimes frustrated. These special "transitional objects" occupy this intermediate area where their "reality" is a combination of what the child brings to the object by way of its fantasy and imagination and "external" qualities the object may possess. Because the child has taken these objects into imagination and invested them with unique qualities, they may be said to have a reality for the child not accessible to an outside observer. However, it also is the nature of such objects that they are never challenged. That is, the parent knows not to say to the infant, "did you create this teddy bear or was it bought at a store?" The truth lies in between. The teddy bear is an object purchased at a store, but this objective object is not what the infant interacts with. The infant interacts with a more subjective object to which it has attached feelings and motives and actions. Thus, on one level, this particular teddy bear with which the infant interacts was "created" by the infant.

Transitional objects are transitional in the sense that they help the infant move from one emotional state to another. They assist the infant in navigating through those times of the mother's absence because they create an illusion of her presence by virtue of her connection to the transitional object. Transitional objects are thus involved in the growing ability to self soothe. However, because transitional objects belong to a "potential space" between the mother and the child, a space that is "outside, inside, on the border," they also have a special relation to fantasy and illusion (Winnicott, 1951b, p. 230). Yet unlike Freud (1913), who thought illusion an infantile defense, Winnicott viewed illusion as a positive aspect of development. That is, rather than being an obstruction to reality illusion leads to the ability to play, and play is what allows for the emergence of culture, art and religion (Winnicott, 1971i).

It is this creative dimension of transitional phenomena that draw one to them throughout life. "Come to think of it, do we any of us grow right up out of a need for an intermediate area between ourselves, with our personal inner world, and external or shared reality?" (Winnicott, 1956g, p. 19). Furthermore, Winnicott (1942) argued that play, art, and religion all can move one toward greater integration of the personality. The significance of this transitional space—and the chief reason it belongs to health (Winnicott, 1951b)—is that it allows for the tapping of the creativity that belongs to play (Winnicott, n.d. 5). In adult life one encounters transitional phenomena particularly in art and religion. Both of these can create an in between space in which the boundaries between reality and fantasy can be suspended. At the theater or a profoundly moving liturgy one becomes aware that (for the moment) one is in a special place that is neither purely objective nor subjective. The actors are on the stage but one's ability to enter into the drama is something that one has helped create from what was "lying around" on the stage. For Winnicott, this ability to play, to fantasize and create, is what allows new, original, sometimes surprising possibilities to emerge.

Religion as Transitional Phenomena

A central implication of Winnicott's (1951b) concept of transitional phenomena is that religion and its associated practices can be creative and adaptive rather than defensive (Jones, 1991; Meissner, 1984; Rizzuto, 1979). That is to say, religion arises within a psychic space that allows for and promotes creativity and growth. Transitional phenomena are creative because of their connection to play and imagination and this connection allows new possibilities to emerge and in adulthood produces art, religion, and culture. As transitional phenomena religion is no longer understood simply as a process of defense against anxiety, but as a creative psychological process. As transitional phenomena religion becomes part of the creative, adaptive responses humans can make to life and continues throughout life. Winnicott's argument does not mean that religion cannot also be defensive, but it opens up the possibility that religion can be a genuinely creative response to life.

To fully appreciate what Winnicott has done with this psychoanalytic perspective on the role of religion, one must note how his argument diverges from Freud's position. In his 1927 book, *Future of an Illusion*, Freud argued that religion was an "illusion" rooted in infantile wishes for a protective father to preserve one from a cruel and capricious cosmos. These protective qualities are projected outward onto "God" and become internalized as religious (or "oceanic") experiences. Thus, the essential Freudian perspective on religion is that it is the result of infantile wishes that a more mature, consciously aware person would abandon; it is a defense against the anxieties of death and a cruel world. Although Freud formally distinguished illusion from delusion in this essay, because he saw illusion as rooted in infantile regression he did not consider participation in illusionary activities a hallmark of maturity. Even art was illusory for Freud, though he tolerated indulgence in artistic pursuits and its appreciation better than religious ones. Freud (1930) would later blur this distinction between religion as illusion rather than delusion in his essay on *Civilization and Its Discontents*, writing there that religion served humanity's need to "procure a certainty of happiness and a protection against suffering through a delusional remolding of reality" (p. 81).

It is obvious when one reads Winnicott that he is aware of Freud's negative position toward religion, and even agreed in several places with Freud's interpretations of religion. In the letter to his sister Violet he noted, much as Freud himself had argued in his 1907 essay, that religion can function much like an obsessional neurosis (Winnicott, 1919). Winnicott certainly knew from some of his patients that prayer and other religious rituals could take on an obsessive quality (cf. 1931a, 1958g, 1965a, 1977). Furthermore, Winnicott knew that religion could be used as a defense, particularly against the fears associated with death, noting that religious beliefs in the after-life helped to calm concerns about the unpredictable nature of life (1931a, 1963e)—reflections that also echo Freud's position. Winnicott added his own extension of this line of thought by noting that religion might be used as a defense against the fears that accompany the attainment of individuality (1968h).

Winnicott also understood that religious beliefs could be projections onto the cosmos. For instance, in his work with one client he discussed how the client's images of a fierce father were projected onto the client's musing about the God represented in the religious wars of seventeenth century England (Winnicott, 1968c). Winnicott also saw Jung's dream of God defecating on the cathedral as illustrative of Jung's projecting aspects of his father onto God (1964h). (That people project images of the earthly father onto God was a central theme of Freud's *Future of an Illusion* and these projections were what gave religion its illusory quality.)

Winnicott even shared Freud's understanding of religion as "illusion."[3] What Winnicott did not share was Freud's view that illusion was a sign of pathology. Here in his view of illusion Winnicott significantly diverged from Freud (cf. Turner, 2002).

By re-interpreting the nature of illusion, Winnicott turned Freud's argument about the pathological quality of religion upside down. Although religion participates in illusion, if illusion belongs to maturity and creativity, this opens up a way to view religion as belonging to creativity and adaptation and not to pathology. Thus, in Winnicott's view religion can be mature, and not simply projective defense (1945e). As Gay (1983) summarized, for "Winnicott . . . the task is not to control one's overwhelming urges towards satisfaction; it is to assemble a completed 'self,' an agency that can feel urges, overwhelming or not. For Freud, civilization is a necessary evil that induces neurotic conditions; for Winnicott, civilization, including religion, is an indispensable source of solace and hope, without which the ego slips into schizoid terrors" (p. 372).

Creative Role of Religion

As transitional phenomena religion is one of the means by which adults tap into their creative potential (Winnicott, 1951b). The special nature of transitional objects is that they draw both from external reality and the creativity of the person's inner world. They point to an area, revisited often in the journey of the self, that is necessary to mental health (relief from the "strain of relating inner and outer reality"—p. 240). Far from being infantile in a regressive pathological way, transitional phenomena allow the adult to move into the realm of play and from there to creativity. They are thus, one of the most creative, adaptive aspects of human development. "Out of these transitional phenomena develop much of what we variously allow and greatly value under the headings of religion and art and also the little madnesses which are legitimate at the moment, according to the prevailing cultural pattern" (Winnicott, 1954c, p. 107). Furthermore, religion and the arts assist adults in negotiating the never-ending demands of "reality-testing and reality-acceptance" (Winnicott, 1952d, p. 224).

In addition, religion becomes one of the ways in which transitional phenomena can be shared and provides a common ground for gathering into groups (Winnicott, 1951b). Furthermore, "in religion and in the arts, we see the claim socialized so that the individual is not called mad and can enjoy in the exercise of religion or the practice and appreciation of the arts the rest that human beings need from absolute and never-failing discrimination between fact and fantasy" (Winnicott, 1954c, p. 107). Nevertheless, in this sharing one must not place too great a claim upon others. To do so is a kind of "madness"; but if one can refrain from such claims one may find those with similar intermediate areas and perhaps share art or religion with them (Winnicott, 1951b).

In noting that childhood transitional objects (e.g., teddy bears, security blankets) give way to art and religion in adulthood, it would be a singular mistake to think of religion or art as a substitute security blanket or teddy bear. Such an analysis is too reductionistic and does not appreciate the nuanced argument Winnicott made about the nature of transitional phenomena. Transitional objects are not simply comforters, but reflect complex processes that reveal the creative imagination needed to navigate the vicissitudes of life. Winnicott wrote of several ways that this creative and adaptive aspect of religion as transitional phenomena showed up in the lives of individuals and in culture.

Fosters Integration of the Personality

One of the ways that religion as transitional phenomena functions creatively is that it fosters integration of the personality. It does this by opening up a space for engagement of the imagination; it becomes a kind of "play" in Winnicott's use of the word.[4] "Play, and the use of the art forms, and religious practice, tend in various but allied ways towards unification and general integration of the personality" (Winnicott, 1942, p. 151). In fostering integration of the personality, religion contributes to maturity which for Winnicott included the ability to identify with and contribute to a group or cause outside oneself, such as religion (Winnicott, 1959b).

The integration of the personality for Winnicott began in the early mother-infant relationship. Winnicott spoke of integration as connected to the mother's ability to "hold" (1955b) her infant, to provide a "good-enough" (1952a, 1963k) response to the infant's needs so that a sense of self or individuality (I AM) is able to emerge. Since the establishment of the sense of I AM can produce anxiety, Winnicott (1962b) also spoke of the ability to relax and "unintegrate." Thus, the maturity inherent in integration of the personality for Winnicott includes the ability to pull together various bodily and psychic experiences, to be able to distinguish self from other, internal from external reality while still relating the two, and the ability to relax from this stress, to trust and to thus engage in and enjoy cultural pursuits, including religion.

Facilitates Therapeutic Repair

Yet another way that religion functions in a creative and positive way for Winnicott is in its potential for therapeutic repair. Certain religious practices and relationships have the potential to provide a kind of therapy for Winnicott. Religion, like certain kinds of friendships or nursing care can provide conditions in which the "extreme dependence" needed for therapeutic repair can occur (Winnicott, 1961f, p. 106). Religion is able to facilitate this kind of therapeutic healing because it helps "unfreeze" environmental failures and allows them to be healed.

> It is normal and healthy for the individual to be able to defend the self against specific environmental failure by a *freezing of the failure situation.* Along with this goes an unconscious assumption (which can become a conscious hope) that opportunity will occur at a later date for a renewed experience in which the failure situation will be able to be unfrozen and re-experienced, with the individual in a regressed state, in an environment that is making adequate adaption. The theory is here being put forward for regression as part of a healing process. (Winnicott, 1954h, pp. 281–282; emphasis in original)

One might ask at this point, how it is that religious experience can help unfreeze these environmental failures. By providing opportunity for the "regression to dependence" that healing requires, religion becomes one of the "healing phenomena of ordinary life" through which "environmental failure situations . . . are reached and unfrozen." Other healing phenomena of ordinary life include "friendships, nursing during physical illness, poetry, etc., etc." (Winnicott,

1954h, p. 284). Since some of this potential for unfreezing environmental fail-ures lies in some types of friendships, religion may provide opportunity for a person to come into contact with the kind of reliable, consistent friend that makes healing possible (Parker & Davis, 2009). Perhaps, it is not too much of a stretch to imagine that a religious person can even think of God as such a friend.

Certainly the psychological mechanisms for such imagining can be under-stood in Winnicottian terms. One might think of certain religious experiences as providing opportunity for the experiencing of an absolute dependence (on God), and such regression allows for the failure situation to be unfrozen and re-experienced (cf. Ulanov, 2001). At a psychological level, one would explain this by saying that a certain portion of the psyche is able (through its projections onto God) to take on and provide the missed mothering function. (If one were to further assume that there is a real God [though not provable and inaccessible to psychological investigation], then the notion that such relationships can foster healing must be entertained. There may be realities other than psychological ones to account for in the healing process.)

Provides a Venue for Expression of the True Self

Another way that religion can be creative is that it can become a venue for the expression of the true self. One might recall that for Winnicott the true self represents the spontaneous vitality of the infant, conveyed in a sense of alive-ness or realness (Winnicott, 1960e).

For Winnicott, the true self is counter-point to the false self, which has its origins in the failures of the early care-giving environment. The false self is characterized by compliance, futility, and reactivity rather than spontaneity. "From this one can formulate a fundamental principle of existence: that which proceeds from the true self feels real (later good) whatever its nature, however aggressive; that which happens in the individual as a reaction to environmental impingement feels unreal, futile (later bad), however sensually satisfactory" (Winnicott, 1954h, p. 292).

Winnicott noted that religion (as well as other areas such as science or poet-ry) can become an area for true self living, an area for no compromise or com-pliance with the false self; furthermore, everyone sets aside some area for no compromise (Winnicott, 1964a). Similarly, Winnicott observed that mystical experiences can contribute to one's capacity to feel real. "In thinking of the psy-chology of mysticism, it is usual to concentrate on the understanding of the mys-tic's withdrawal into a personal inner world of sophisticated introjects. Perhaps not enough attention has been paid to the mystic's retreat to a position in which he can communicate secretly with subjective objects and phenomena, the loss of contact with the world of shared reality being counterbalanced by a gain in terms of feeling real" (Winnicott, 1963a, pp. 185–186).

It is important to note that science and poetry can also become venues for the expression of the true self and one might propose that psychoanalysis as a kind of science was a way in which Winnicott attempted true self living. The next chapter expands on this idea.

Contributes to God Images

Yet another way the creative dimension of religion shows up for Winnicott is through a person's God images. Religion, like all transitional phenomena, is both created and given. To make this point Winnicott spoke of listening to a Beethoven quartet.

> This quartet is not just an external fact produced by Beethoven and played by the musicians; and it is not my dream, which as a matter of fact would not have been so good. The experience, coupled with my preparation of myself for it, enables me to create a glorious fact. I enjoy it because I say I created it, I hallucinated it, and it is real and would have been there even if I had been neither conceived of nor conceived. This is mad. But in our cultural life we accept the madness. (Winnicott, 1959d, p. 58)

And perhaps share them at times!

In a similar way people can create gods. That is, out of the various ideas and images that parents and culture leave "lying around" the person is able to weave an image of God (Winnicott, 1963j). These images, like all transitional phenomena, draw from both internal and external reality including early relational connections and the emotions associated with them (cf. Parker, 1996; Rizzuto, 1979). As transitional phenomena they have a creative quality. People create all kinds of images of God: as powerful, loving, embracing, hateful, vengeful, terrorizing, and any number of other characteristics. This point about creating "God" is bound up with recognizing a developmental pattern in children for Winnicott (cf. 1963j). That is, there are a series of steps in acquiring a belief in God (e.g., it is rooted in an earlier capacity to believe in; this capacity itself arises out of human nature, that is to say, out of reliable interactions with caregivers). The gods thus created are never simply subjective or objective; they are both. Thus, as Winnicott (1935) noted, it is dangerous for a therapist to think of or to treat a person's image of God as simply a fantasy object.

To think of God as a transitional object is to understand both the creative potential that lies in one's imaginings of God as well as to appreciate the maturity possible in learning to relate to God with the same level of maturity one brings to other relationships. God images have the potential to move one into new directions and provide alternate meaning and motivation. They both challenge one's narrowness and sustain one in stress. When one imagines God as powerful, sustaining, rescuing, or ever present, one can find strength for daily living; strength that allows one to move beyond one's internal fears. When one images God as creator of all life, one is opened to a new relationship to others and the earth and its resources.

There is another way that one can speak of the creative vitalizing qualities of religion. Although Winnicott himself did not directly apply his insights about the vitalizing potential of destructiveness or aggression to his reflections on the creative potential of religion, certainly an argument could be made in this regard. This is seen most clearly in his argument regarding the creative "destruction" of the object (in unconscious fantasy) that permits one to move toward object usage. Object usage was Winnicott's way to speak of the most mature kinds of human relating. In object usage one moves beyond the fantasy that others are created by and for one's own desires (an infantile state) to recognize the objectivity of one's environment and to interact with others in ways that acknowledge the other as a person in his or her own right (a mature state). When applied to religious contexts this destruction means God (religious objects) can become an object for "use." The dawning sense of their otherness and survival permit religious objects to become "real" (and thus vitalizing) in a way not possible when there is only "object relating" in interaction with these objects. Thus, in one's imaginings of God, there is the possibility to move beyond relating to God as simply a projection of one's wishes to consider things larger than one's own desires and to respond accordingly (cf. Ulanov, 2001).

Provides a Source for Valuing Freedom of Thought

Before leaving these reflections on religion as transitional phenomena one might note another way in which Winnicott saw the creative potential of religion contributing positively to life and culture. Religion for Winnicott provided the creative cauldron from which arose the English tradition of valuing freedom of thought. As noted already, Winnicott valued freedom of thought and resisted any kind of dogmatism or indoctrination. And although he recognized that religion could be quite dogmatic, it is significant that he favorably quoted Ernest Jones who credited religion as one of the sources for the English tradition of free thinking (Winnicott, 1958d). A letter to Ian Rodger made a similar point: "I want to meet you and discuss the way in which the Lollards laid the basis for liberal thinking in England and Europe" (Winnicott, 1969g). Goldman commented upon this letter, "Perhaps Winnicott saw in the Lollards a way of expressing his own iconoclastic defiance of and unconscious bond to his religious upbringing" (p. 122).

Thus, in his arguments about religion as transitional phenomena Winnicott saw a way that psychoanalysis could contribute to religion gaining a new relevance for those who may have laid it aside because it required too much in the way of dogmatic affirmation. In Winnicott's (1966f) mind, thinking of religion as transitional phenomena could allow those turned off by the dogma of religion to re-engage the religious question. The next chapter explores Winnicott's particular form of this re-engagement.

Notes

1.   Compare his argument noted earlier that interventions to correct behavior that are made too early rob people of the creativity involved in the growth of their innate moral tendencies (Winnicott, 1968b).

2.   In regards to Winnicott's indirect contributions to a psychoanalytic understanding of religion, Goldman (1993) made an interesting observation in conjunction with his remarks on how closely Winnicott's concepts come to religious ones (a point developed in the previous chapter). Goldman suggested an argument could be made that several of Winnicott's concepts "rather than demonstrating Winnicott's affinity for religious thought indicate how he was explicating the developmental origins of religious ideas" (p. 123). Winnicott (1963j, 1968b) himself observed such possibilities in his remarks that a belief in God found its psychological origin in an experience of the mother's reliable care. He similarly suggested that the psychological origins of a belief in monotheism arose from the experience of individuality (Winnicott, 1968h). Although this suggestion regarding the psychological origins of religious ideas remains underdeveloped in both Goldman and Winnicott it is intriguing to speculate on how the concepts covered in the previous chapter might contribute to understanding the psychological origins of various religious beliefs. For instance, a belief in an omnipotent God might find its origins in the infant's own temporary experience of omnipotence or as Goldman suggested a belief in a God who became incarnate might find its origins in the experience of personalization—a psyche coming to indwell a soma and the subsequent experience of being a unified being. Similarly, McCarthy (2010) saw the origins of the "religious imagination" in transitional phenomena. Speculation on the psychological origins of such beliefs provides a complement to Winnicott's reflections on psychoanalytic contributions to religion and need not be in and of itself reductionism (though it can be if taken as the only way to understand the origins of such religious beliefs).

3.   In addition to these shared reflections on the psychology of religion, Winnicott also shared Freud's visceral aversion to the more dogmatic qualities of religion. This common aversion to the dogmatic qualities of religion is especially seen in both men's understanding that religion represented an anti-science stance; hence the need for a clear contrast between "science" (including psychoanalysis) and "religion" (Winnicott, 1946a, 1947d, 1961d, 1967a). A previous chapter noted Winnicott's (1961d) contrast between the "questions" and doubt of science and the "certainty" of religion (an ill-worded contrast that does justice to neither Winnicott's view of science nor religion as a later chapter makes clear).

4.   In thinking about the creative, playful dimension of religious worship, one might consider Guardini's (1935) characterization of the church liturgy. According to Guardini there is a playful dimension to the liturgy in that it "is life pouring itself forth without an aim, seizing upon riches from its own abundant store, significant through the fact of its existence. . . . It unites art and reality in a supernatural childhood before God. . . . It is in the highest sense the life of a child, in which everything is picture, melody and song" (pp. 179–181). Baer (1976) made a similar comment about a very different type of worship: Pentecostal glossolalia. "More and more I am impressed with the element of playfulness in glossolalia, the sheer childlike delight in praising God in this manner." He noted that this worship "almost always had about it a releasing quality" and was "thus ultimately healing and redemptive" (pp. 158–159). What both the liturgy and glossolalia shared in common, according to Baer was that both these practices "permit the analytical mind—

the focused, objectifying dimension of man's intellect—to rest, thus freeing other dimensions of the person . . . for a deeper openness to divine reality" (p. 152). Neither of these experiences was to be understood as dissociation but an experience more like the "flow" one feels when dancing after having mastered the formal dance steps. There is a point in which one moves to the music without continuing to think about one's feet. The descriptions of worship by Guardini and Baer are very reminiscent of the creative freedom Winnicott attributed to play.

Chapter 9
Religious in His Own Way

"I was not myself religious in their . . . particular way."

In the summer of 1954 Winnicott responded to a letter from Michael Fordham who had written to him about a paper Winnicott had given. Fordham had taken Winnicott to suggest that art and religion were "spare time amusements" and Fordham thought such a position would upset religious people. In his response, Winnicott (1954g) wrote:

> [I]f you look at this again I do not believe that you will be able to substantiate your suggestion. One must be able to look at religious beliefs and their place in psychology without being considered to be antagonistic to anyone's personal religion. I have found others who thought that I was anti-religious in some of my writing but it has always turned out that what they were annoyed about was that I was not myself religious in their own particular way. (p.74)

In acknowledging that he was not religious in the way some people wanted him to be, Winnicott implied that if he considered himself religious, it was in his own particular way. One purpose of this chapter is to explore in some detail the particulars of Winnicott's way of being religious.

A second purpose of this chapter is to ask whether one can discern in Winnicott's work as a child psychiatrist and psychoanalyst a deep sense of purpose that connects to his way of being religious. That is, does Winnicott's chosen life's work become a "vocation"—a sense of calling for him? Even further, does it become a way for him to depict transcendent values or to voice certain religious sentiments? Did psychoanalysis come to fulfill the functions of religion for him? These are the questions that occupy the latter part of this chapter.

An Irony in Winnicott's Religiousness

This chapter begins by reflecting upon an irony in Winnicott's life: his positive view of religion did not translate into his own life in terms of religious practice.

Winnicott argued that religion can be creative and adaptive in several ways: it can be instrumental in freeing one from "frozen" relationships (1954h); it can provide a healing therapy (1961f); it can foster an integration of the personality (1942); it can become a venue for the expression of the true self (1964a); it can humanize the fierce morality of the child (1963j). He argued that religion is part of an intermediate area that none outgrows (1956g). Yet, in his own life, he spoke of having grown up out of religious practice; practices that no longer belonged to a person who had reached a maturity appropriate to age (letter to the *London Times* [cited in Rudnytsky, 1991, p. 97]; Winnicott, 1969f).

An earlier chapter noted that religious practices he had grown out of were church attendance and a belief in miracles and the after-life (Winnicott, 1968b). He also thought himself to have departed from traditional religious teaching about the soul (Winnicott, 1951a) and original sin (Winnicott, 1963j). This inability to subscribe to certain traditional beliefs from his religious background, coupled with the absence of church attendance, caused Winnicott to no longer describe himself as a "practicing Christian." Yet in an unpublished manuscript to be reviewed below he defined a Christian as one whose "life and thought" are "turned to the activity" and "ideals . . . of Christ" and seemed to fit this description to himself as one who had "the cause of Christ very much at heart."

What is one to make of this ambivalence in identifying himself as a practicing Christian? Does he simply mean he no longer attended church, a practice he seemed to have ceased sometime between the end of the Second World War and his marriage to Clare Britton? Or does he mean more than this? Is it possible that Winnicott has not entirely grown out of his adolescent understanding that "practicing Christians" are those who adhere to the more traditional, evangelical Christianity of his youth (who perhaps have the "simple" faith of his father)? That those who have "matured" toward the more "liberal Christian" views he seemed to hold as an adult (Rudnytsky, 1991) are somehow not practicing Christians in his mind? Similarly, might his ambivalence about identifying himself as a practicing Christian be connected to his life-long struggle with the appropriate expression of his aggression (cf. Rodman, 1987)? Given the Wesleyan emphasis on the sinfulness of anger (cf. Wesley, 1777) did Winnicott think the expression of anger and aggression something practicing Christians did not do (a holdover of the religious expression in the Winnicott household? Cf. Goldman, 1993). The juxtaposition of his statements about being one devoted to the ideals of Christ, yet not a practicing Christian presents a paradox that needs exploring.

In considering this paradox, one might first inquire as to the reasons for Winnicott's decreasing participation in church religious practices despite his obvious continuing interest in religious ideals. Several possibilities suggest themselves given the time frame in which the decrease seems to have occurred.

It may be that Winnicott's decreased involvement in conventional religious practice is simply a result of approaching mid-life. This seemed to be his assessment: he had reached another stage of development where he had grown up out of religious practice (Winnicott, 1968b). Fowler's (1981) charting of "stages of faith" noted that mid-life can become a time of religious passivity and withdrawal for some, especially those who have become disillusioned by the "paradoxical understanding of truth" (p. 198). One could interpret Winnicott's questioning of traditional religious beliefs as indicative of his grasp of the paradoxical dimensions of truth. His characterization of transitional phenomena also testifies to his appreciation of the paradox that belongs to coming to grips with reality (Winnicott, 1951b). These observations seem to point to developmental issues connected to his arrival at mid-life that contributed to Winnicott's decreasing engagement in religious practices. However, given his continued and increasing interest with religious questions and ideals, coupled with his refusal to "settle down to lukewarm late middle life philosophy" (Winnicott, n.d. 3), this does not seem to be a sufficient answer.

Similarly, Winnicott's questions about the relevance of various Christian doctrines (miracles, after-life, original sin) may have contributed to his decreased interest in religious practice. Again, Fowler (1981) has pointed out a "stage of faith" characterized by an intensification of questions about the faith, often "precipitated by a change in primary relationships, such as a divorce" (p. 181). Winnicott experienced the death of his father and separated from his first wife, Alice, within the span of about a year (1948-49, see Rodman, 2003).[1] Such life changes and their attendant questions can bring about both cognitive and experiential changes in the way religious practices and symbols are understood and engaged according to Fowler.[2]

Another possible contributor to Winnicott's decreased involvement in religious practice may have been the Second World War. The closing years of the war seem to have been a turning point in this regard. Whether the war itself brought a reexamination of his faith is not known, although the malevolence and destructiveness of this war raised questions of faith for many (cf. Dietrich, 2003; Rubenstein, 1992). Perhaps his close involvement with the evacuated children affected by this war brought some questions as to the efficacy and meaning of religious practices for Winnicott, though this seems unlikely as well given the absence of any remarks by Winnicott that might suggest this. The loss of several friends during the First World War left Winnicott with some lingering questions about his own survival and the meaning of life (Winnicott, 1978). Yet, by his admission, the Second World War seemed to have brought him some relief from this survivor guilt. In the review of his life given at his retirement from Paddington Green there is a note about this. "The war [WWI] left its scar. With most of his contemporaries dead, he felt it wicked to be alive, a sense of guilt that was not expiated until the next war when he worked in London throughout, except for one day a week when he was psychiatrist in charge of hostels for evacuation failures in the County of Oxford" (Winnicott, 1961c, p. 137).

Yet another possible contributor to Winnicott's declining interest in conventional religious practices may have been his affair with Clare Britton which began sometime in 1944 (Rodman, 2003). One gathers from the letters he and Clare exchanged that he suffered some guilt over their involvement (cf. Rodman, pp. 100-102). The nature of the guilt is complex involving not only his sense of self and self-ideal, but his sense of obligation to his wife, Alice, with her many problems (Rodman, 2003). Whether his guilt also involved his thoughts about the teachings of the church is less clear. Twenty years later in an essay on feminism and envy of the opposite sex he remarked about how difficult monogamy was in practice; he mused that perhaps it was impossible, "a bit of Christian teaching that ignores too much?" (Winnicott, 1964k, p. 190). One does not know if this is a bit of self-disclosure or not. Research indicates a negative correlation between marital infidelity and church attendance (Atkins & Kessel, 2008; Burdette, Ellison, Sherkat, & Gore, 2007). Whether this was an actual factor for Winnicott is not known.

Finally, one notes that a contributing factor to the decline in Winnicott's involvement with formal religious practice could be his various understandings of "God." Winnicott made few direct statements about God in his writings (Ulanov, 2001) and in reviewing the actual comments, a mixed picture emerges. The next chapter specifically addresses Winnicott's view of God; it is sufficient to note here its potential contribution to the decline in his formal religious practice.

Before leaving this section on the irony of Winnicott's claims for the creative functions of religion not translating into his own religious practices, one should note that there is an exception to this. One recalls that Winnicott continued to sing the Methodist hymns of his youth all through his life (Kahr, 1996). He seems to have found a certain vitality in the singing of these songs. Thus, this aspect of his early religious practice continued to evoke the intermediate area and allowed him to manage the tasks of being an analyst.

Whatever may be the reasons and contributing factors for Winnicott's declining religious practice, one concludes that he continued to see himself as religious in his own way. He even seems to have thought of himself as a Christian at times (though not an "orthodox" or "practicing" one). Although Winnicott seems to have remained a Christian in a liberal Protestant way (cf. Rudnytsky, 1991), having known what it meant to be a Christian in the evangelical tradition, there are other times he shows discomfort with this language. Still, he is not willing to "throw away" everything either (Winnicott, 1967f, p. 170). Thus, Winnicott's particular ways of being religious bear exploring.[3]

In What Ways Was Winnicott Religious?

Several of those who have written of Winnicott have commented on the importance of his religiosity (e.g., Phillips, 1988; Rodman, 1987, 2003). Rudnytsky (1991) spoke of Winnicott as a "believing skeptic"—one who was able to fuse "liberal Christian values with free thinking" and who thus retained a positive attitude toward religion throughout his life; an attitude rooted in the positive memories of the early walks home from church with his father (p. 96). Eigen (1998) has written of Winnicott as a "psychoanalytic mystic" whose "work resonates with a sense of the sacred" (p. 15). This was not an "other world mysticism" since "the real of this world was more than enough" for Winnicott (p. 15). Yet, according to Eigen, there abided in Winnicott a deep appreciation for aliveness and that which freed the true self. Thus there is both a "mystical" and "muted sacramental current" in Winnicott's insistence that realness involved an intermediate area beyond the "three dimensional material world" (p. 15).

Most notably Goldman (1993) spoke of a "lingering religiosity" in Winnicott that is evident not only in the content of Winnicott's writings, but in the very form these take (pp. 115, 122). In many ways this book can be seen as an extended articulation of the ways in which Winnicott's religiousness lingered. Previous chapters have looked at several of these ways: his use of religious categories and language to speak of analytic concepts, his interest in religious questions, his interest in articulating a positive role for religion in life and culture. Goldman further argued that Winnicott "remained a religious person in the sense that he maintained a capacity for wonder and reverence for the objects of wonder" (p. 117). One sees this particularly in Winnicott's (1961d) "faith in the inexorable laws that govern phenomena" (p.14). Such laws are part of the fabric of reliability of the external environment that is first known through the mother's care (1963j, 1966e, 1968b). Yet beyond this, life (a sense of aliveness) is a gift to be honored and cherished. That such vitality is "sacred" reveals a lingering religious dimension to life for Winnicott (1971e, p.103).

Yet aside from these assessments from others, one must ask whether Winnicott continued to see himself as religious? And if he did, in what ways did he do so? The question is framed this way initially because the answer takes some interesting turns.

The first thing to note in response is that Winnicott was not always sure that he was religious! For instance, he wrote to Edith Stengal (Winnicott, 1954e) to clear up some misinformation she had received that he had been a parson: "I have never been a parson; in fact I think it could be said that I am not really a religious person. This is not to deny that I was religious as an adolescent, because I certainly was." And in an unpublished letter to the *London Times* written a little over a year before his death Winnicott said of himself, "I would not describe myself as a practicing Christian, having reached a degree of maturity appropriate to age" (cited in Rudnytsky, 1991, p. 97; cf. Winnicott, 1969f).

Is one to conclude from such comments that, as an adult, Winnicott did not think himself religious? A very interesting exchange of letters in 1966 adds fuel to such speculation. A correspondent had written to Winnicott stating:

I have been asked by *The Observer* to write an article on "dying without God",
largely to bring into open a subject affecting an increasing number of people
but which does not seem to receive the attention it should.

Crowded as your days are, I wonder if you would be prepared to talk to
me about your own personal feelings towards death and how you have come to
terms with the concept, as I think a symposium of views of a few eminent ag-
nostics and atheists who have thought deeply about the subject could be a great
help to the public.

I would be most grateful if you would consider contributing in the way I
have suggested. (Dobie, 1966)

Winnicott responded by asking if they might meet for lunch to discuss this. At
the meeting, Winnicott shared with him the poem he had written entitled "The
Tree," and indicated in a second letter that he would like to meet again to "go on
with the conversation we started up . . . I hope that your work on this very important subject is progressing well" (Winnicott, 1966g). What is one to make of
these remarks? At least two things stand out. One, Winnicott was very much
interested in the topic of "dying without God"; two, it is unclear whether Winnicott thought himself as fitting this category and hence an agnostic or atheist.
Given his disclosure about his poem which is clearly religious in tone and in
which Winnicott identified with the Christ figure, one must assume that he
brought some discussion of religion into this conversation about dying without
God. So the question is did Winnicott identify as one "without God" or is he
simply acknowledging his interest in the topic? Since one does not know anything more about the role he would have assigned to religion in these conversations it is difficult to know whether he identified himself as an agnostic (or atheist), or simply as one interested in the overall topic. Given Winnicott's overall
positive assessment of religion, if one were to think of Winnicott as an agnostic
or atheist, he certainly does not seem to be one in the conventional sense.

Despite these tantalizing hints that Winnicott may not have thought himself
religious, one is confronted with considerable evidence that there are other times
that Winnicott not only showed a deep interest in things religious but seems to
have thought himself religious. In 1967 his brother-in-law responded to a "long
scribble about religion" that Winnicott had sent which seemed to have discussed
how and why it is people believe, the question of miracles, and prayer (Britton,
1967). That same year he wrote to Wilfred Bion "I, like you, was brought up in
the Christian tradition (Wesleyan) and I have no desire to throw away all of
what I listened to over and over again and tried to digest and sort out. It is not
possible for me to throw out religion just because the people who organize the
religions of the world insist on beliefs in miracles" (Winnicott, 1967f, p. 170).

So, if it is not possible for Winnicott to "throw out religion" because some
require beliefs to which he cannot ascribe, in what ways did he consider himself
religious? An earlier chapter noted that his neglect of religious "practice" does
not imply a complete lack of religious sentiment. There seem to be several ways

that Winnicott either remained religious or thought himself religious, despite his comments that he might have grown up out of certain religious practices.

Preserving a Role for Free Thought in Religion

It is very clear from what Winnicott wrote that if he was to be religious, it must be a religion that fostered the ability to think freely. He had written to Anna Freud and Melanie Klein in 1954 about the factionalism in the British Psychoanalytic Society that he could "no more stand the falsity of a rigid system in psychology" than he could "tolerate it in religion" (Winnicott, 1954d, p. 72). Winnicott struggled against dogmatic systems wherever he found them. His rebellion against an enforced conformity of belief lay behind his late life self-identification as a "modern day Lollard" (Goldman, 1993).

Winnicott was appreciative of the role that non-conformist religion had played in conferring upon the English people a deep valuing of freedom of thought. He had written to Ian Rodger, a playwright who had given a series of presentations about the Lollards on BBC radio, "I am glad to be in touch with you, and sometime or other I want to meet you and discuss the way in which the Lollards laid the basis for liberal thinking in England and Europe. It seems to me that but for the early Lollards and Wycliffe all these people who come to England to be accepted and to find refuge would not have had anywhere to go" (Winnicott, 1969g). As part of the early non-conformist tradition in England, the Lollards had stood firmly against certain dogmas of the Catholic Church, especially the doctrine of the infallibility of the pope (Semmel, 1973). Winnicott's interest in the Lollards not only showed his continuing interest in religious questions and answers, his identification with the Lollards provided him a means to think himself religious in a similar way. Being able to stand against the imposition of dogma (whether in religion or psychoanalysis) became an area of "no compromise" for Winnicott.[4]

This tendency to anti-dogmatism has been connected to Winnicott's religious exposure as a child (Winnicott, 1983). Rodman (1987) even suggested that some unspecified religious crisis in adolescence or young adulthood strengthened his resolve against dogmatic approaches to life. That religion sometimes insisted on affirmation of certain beliefs made Winnicott suspicious and distrustful of religion in its dogmatic forms. When religion insisted on certain beliefs and practices Winnicott (1963j) felt that it tended to rob humans of their own creative discovery of values and goodness. As it specifically applied to religion, Winnicott resisted the notion that religious people had to ascribe to certain dogmas such as a belief in miracles. If such beliefs were required to be religious, then he was not. However, by his way of thinking not only could one be religious without such dogmas, the exercise of free thought regarding religious questions made for a better religiousness. His would not be a "simple" faith (as that of his father?). It would not be one with the "certainty" that belonged to traditional religion (1968b, p. 14); he eschewed the kind of "knowing in advance" (1967a) associated with certain kinds of religion. Winnicott's way of being religious retained a critical place for questions, no matter how sacrosanct a belief seemed to be.

To these religious questions he wanted to bring the kind of critical thinking he associated with "science" (Winnicott, 1968b). Late in his life, one sees this in his interest in the book *The Nazarene Gospel Restored* (Graves & Podro, 1954).This was a book designed for a popular audience that tried to pull together certain scholarly works devoted to recovery of the original message of Jesus. Although this book was not the best example of careful historical scholarship (Nesbitt, 1955; *Time*, 1954), what Winnicott saw in this book was an attempt to bring critical, "scientific" thinking to questions of Christian origins. Although he noted that Christian churches looked with disfavor upon this attempt to reconstruct the original story of Jesus we wrote with excitement to Bion that he found a "study of this book fascinating and very important for the understanding of the Bible story that we came to know so well" (Winnicott, 1967f, p. 170). His extension of this kind of thinking to explore the "natural" vs. "revealed" nature of religion might be cited as another way that Winnicott exhibited scientific questioning in his religiosity (Winnicott, 1968b, p. 143).

Winnicott's desire for a religion that maintained room for free thought reflects a deeply ingrained value of his Wesleyan heritage. For instance, Wesley, like the Lollards, emphasized human freedom as a necessary defining characteristic of what it means to be truly human. Regarding salvation he noted that God could act in such a way that God's grace would be irresistible, but if God chose to give humans no choice in responding to such grace, "then man would be man no longer; his inmost nature would be changed. He would no longer be a moral agent, any more than the sun or the wind, as he would no longer be endued with liberty, a power of choosing or self-determination" (Wesley, 1783, pp. 488–489). Thus, it belongs to the heart of Wesleyan thought that a manifestation of God's grace is the granting of "free will," the ability to think and choose for oneself (Wesley, 1739). When Winnicott's father encouraged him to read the Bible for his own answers, his father's advice was very much in the Wesleyan spirit. Again, this Wesleyan value (and the larger non-conformist tradition and its valuing of freedom of thought) was one that Winnicott had deeply absorbed into his character, a quality that defined his way of being religious.

Preserving Religious "Ideals"

A second way that Winnicott remained religious centered in his attempt to preserve and embody certain religious "ideals," in particular certain of those associated with Christ. Insight into this aspect of Winnicott's religiousness is seen especially in an unpublished (and incomplete) manuscript for a presentation at Bart's Hospital (St. Bartholomew). The talk seems to have been to the Christian Union there and is undated.[5] Winnicott began by stating

> My object this evening is to plead for a Christianity which is more nearly related to Christ than the Christianity which is represented by the Bart's Christian Union, indeed for a Christianity which is—as it should be—the working out of the Christ ideals in life. You will wonder why I presume to pose as a preacher, who am so deficient in the Christ ideals in my daily life. I own that I do fail in this, the great test. But I offer no apology to you; for although I fall short of what I would be I have the cause of Christ very much at heart. (Winnicott, n.d. 3)

He proceeded to criticize a Christian "orthodoxy" that would unreflectively reject the findings of science.[6] He thought such orthodoxy an "insult to God." In contrast, everyone "has a right to a development of himself in the direction of his own temperament and talent; indeed it is his duty to his Creator to use all his powers to develop all his parts—bodily, mental and spiritual—in a beautiful proportion." He continued that everyone should be growing and noted that such growth meant "we must set aside what we have been taught and each of us examine Christ for himself."

He then made a distinction between Christianity and religion. Religion is an "attitude of mind," a "psychological pose" that helped shore up a person's "confidence and sense of security." It also "points toward the ideals (be they Christian or otherwise) which that man or woman has chosen." Christianity on the other hand is the living out of those ideals "in the crudest most integral elements."

> Only in so far as the resulting life is altered, only in so far as the old ideals and ambitions have changed is that man become a better man. If the new ideals are those of Christ and the man's life becomes imbued with the virtues which some see in Christ—then it may be said—as a matter of terminology, that that man has been converted to Christianity. But he may not believe any of the orthodox views about the Resurrection, the Virgin birth and other very interesting problems. The question is—Does his future life and thought become active and turned to the activity of Christ? (Winnicott, n.d. 3)

Winnicott then made the point that if the lack of belief in such dogmas meant one is not a Christian in the eyes of certain orthodox people, then so be it. He likened himself to a person in the New Testament whom the disciples forbade to do good because he was not one of their company (cf. Mark 9:38–41). "Our Lord was only too eager to reprove them and hastened, with the words, 'He that is not against us is on our side' to place that man on an equal footing with the disciples." Thus, one sees in this exchange something of Winnicott's claim that he is religious, a Christian even, but not in an unquestioning, "orthodox" way. He concluded the extant portion with comments on prayer. Here he paid special attention to a psychological explanation for prayer and connected part of its efficacy to his notion of "belief in" noting (as he had about the need for scientists to have faith) that

> These properties of prayer require faith, be it in the god to whom the prayers are offered or in the laws of nature—which after all are also God—which promise a fruitful issue to your meditation. It is according to what you consider is the name of the factor behind all these laws. In other words the answer to prayer is the same to a true believer, be he an atheist, a worshipper of idols, a Christian mystic or a fun scientist. The only essential factor is belief. (Winnicott, n.d. 3)

This unpublished and incomplete manuscript gives us one of the adult Winnicott's clearest statements about his relationship with Christianity as an organized religion. This manuscript is important in several ways, both as to its consistencies with Winnicott's other statements about religion and his work in general and its particular clarifications of his desire to articulate something of the "Christ ideals" for himself and for others.

In terms of his consistency with prior thoughts regarding religion, one notes several reiterated here. For instance, he devalued unthinking dogmatism where ever found (whether in religion or psychoanalysis), and valued thinking for oneself (cf. Winnicott, 1954d). The emphasis on ethics restated one of his earliest themes from his letter to Violet with its own echo of Pfister's (1917) thesis (Winnicott, 1919). There are further consistencies with his larger work in his emphasis that people are always growing. Two other themes from his larger work that he had connected with religion are given a specifically religious context here as well. His argument (Winnicott, 1963j) that belief or "belief in" was a common denominator that preceded the ability to believe in something specific (such as God) is restated here in his comment about the commonness of belief whether one is atheist, believer, or "fun scientist." In addition, his comment about it being one's duty to develop in the direction of one's temperament sounds very much like his remarks about the true self (Winnicott, 1960e, 1964a).

One might also note that his remark on the need for a real change (altered life) sounds very Wesleyan,[7] and even echoes a sermon from his days at The Leys. As noted in an earlier chapter, on the day that Winnicott won first place for his contribution (a recitation from Antony), the speaker for the day made special note in his talk on the need for real change. The school paper recorded part of the sermon as emphasizing that

> It is easy to substitute conduct for character, outward purity for inward cleanness. This temptation is overcome when Christ reigns in the heart, and so we might say that the prophecy symbolizes three things: First, it tells of the transformation of the unreal into the real. Here Mr. Lees made a fine appeal for gen-

uine decision for Christ, which would make all character and work genuine to the highest degree. (*The Leys Fortnightly*, V. 38 # 279, July 14, 1914)

Although it is impossible to know to what extent if any Winnicott retained anything from this sermon, one is struck by the similarity of its central idea with Winnicott's comments years later. Perhaps, again, he has retained more of his Wesleyan Methodist ethos than he realized.

In looking at Winnicott's attempt to extract and preserve some of the "Christ ideals" one also must acknowledge some of the shortcomings in the argument Winnicott offered in this manuscript. In presuming "to pose as a preacher" Winnicott revealed some of his deficiencies in this regard. For instance, his analysis of the relationship between orthodox Christianity and science is superficial and overdrawn; something of this inconsistency of treatment was noted in his acknowledgement that science also has a faith (Winnicott, 1961d, 1969h). His distinction between Christianity and religion is similarly flawed and superficial. Religions are not merely "attitudes of mind," nor does describing Christianity as a living out of religious ideals exempt it from being a religion. Finally, one notes that he does not seem to take into account his own point that images of God and Christ are built up from one's experiences with early caregivers, coupled with one's own imaginings (Winnicott 1963j, 1968b); thus, everyone tends to fashion images of God or Christ based on his or her personal experiences (cf. Parker, 1996, Rizzuto, 1979).

Despite these shortcomings, one purpose is clear in Winnicott's argument: he wanted to make a distinction between "living" out one's religious ideals and simply affirming them as "orthodox" beliefs. In this he tried to distinguish between "Christ" and "orthodox tradition." He would align himself very much with the "cause of Christ" but not with orthodox traditions. This distinction mirrors similar distinctions he made between a religion that required a belief in miracles and one that did not (1967f, 1968b).

There is an interesting phrase in this paper that takes us back to the question of Winnicott's identification of himself as religious. In citing Jesus' renunciation of those who would exclude those who live out the Christ ideals even though they may not affirm all the orthodox traditions about Christ, Winnicott used the phrase "our Lord" (vs. the Lord). What is one to make of this phrase? This seems to be its only occurrence in Winnicott's writing. Is its singular use to be attributed to a specific audience? This seems unlikely since Winnicott occasionally spoke to clergy and other religious audiences. Does this singular use imply that Winnicott thought of himself as Christian at times? It seems he did, though not consistently so. What is clear is that he is not willing to exclude himself from those who identify with Christ's ideals, even if others might exclude him from such company.

What were these ideals and how did Winnicott try to follow them in his own life? In this unpublished manuscript Winnicott seemed to identify at least two. From the tone of the paper and certain examples offered one of these ideals is what he labeled "the precious gift of free thought." To fail to think for oneself, to subsume this ability to some unthinking orthodoxy was to disdain "as sacred a gift as the bible" he wrote. As seen in previous chapters, valuing freedom of thought not only characterized the Wesleyan Methodism of Winnicott's youth this particular value became a hallmark of Winnicott's adult life (Winnicott, 1954d). It was the quality he prized in the Lollards and early dissenters in England (Goldman, 1993). He himself tried to live out this Christ ideal in his fierce determination to avoid uncritical, dogmatic thinking both in religion and psychoanalysis; as he writes in this unpublished paper, he would "examine Christ for himself." In words from this unpublished essay he would not "violate the sacred shrine of his temperament" by giving up "the precious gift of free thought" to "settle down to lukewarm late middle life philosophy."

Another Christ ideal Winnicott identified in this unpublished manuscript is "doing good" from "unselfish motives," an ideal without specific examples in the portion of the manuscript surviving but one which Winnicott seemed to have taken to heart. Winnicott may have tried to identify with the Christ ideal of doing good from unselfish motives in the way he attempted to give of himself to his patients. He clearly desired to be a therapist his patients could "use" without their having to fear his retaliation or destruction (Winnicott, 1971k). Even a comment to his audience at Bart's that he wanted to give them "definite handles by which [they] may grasp [him] at the end and tear [him] to bits" echoes his desire to be an object they can use. Chapter 5 demonstrated that the development of his concept of object usage coincided with a late life interest in Jesus and that the biblical story of Jesus' Crucifixion and Resurrection presents Jesus as a clear exemplar of object usage (cf. Hoffman, 2004; Hopkins, 1989). It was suggested there that Winnicott's desire to be a therapist his patients could use reflected some identification of himself as a Christ-like therapist.

Although there are only two clearly identified Christ ideals in Winnicott's unpublished manuscript one cannot help but wonder if there were other values he thought of similarly. For instance, in connecting the valuing of freedom of thought to ideas concerning the true self and an area of no compromise Winnicott (1964a) may be pointing to the Christian concern with authentic living as another Christ ideal.

Winnicott's attempt to separate the Christ ideals from the less reflective engagement of Christianity raises the related question of how he went about this task. One gains some insight into this from his letters to friends and family. For instance, in his letter to Bion noted above he mentioned the book on the restoration of the "Nazarene gospel." It seems that Winnicott was influenced by this project in the sense that he wanted to recover what the original message of Jesus might have been before it was overlaid with so much "tradition." At least part of Winnicott's attraction to such a project was the use of critical "scientific" thinking. Thus, one way Winnicott sought to separate the Christ ideals from the "traditions" about Christ was through a study of the scientific research about the historical Jesus.

One gets a further glimpse into how Winnicott might have gone about the task of separating ideals from tradition from a letter that his brother-in-law sent in response to a "long scribble about religion" from Winnicott (Britton, 1967). It is obvious from this letter that Winnicott's "scribble" had included a discussion of miracles. Comments in several published manuscripts reveal that a belief in miracles was something Winnicott (1968b) felt he had "grown up out of" (p. 143). Yet one glimpses something more of his thoughts on miracles from the brother-in-law's response. The brother-in-law comments on the "mythic" quality of miracles "I simply think of them as honorific myths. But of course here again there is the question why mere stories? And I must admit that some of them give immense satisfaction. (But here I think I am simply picking up clues of yours)" (Britton, 1967). Since one gets Winnicott's reflections second-hand, it is not entirely clear what he meant here. From the brother-in-law's comments one might infer that part of Winnicott's reflections on miracles was to interpret them, not as an abrogation of the laws of nature, but as "stories" or "myths" having a symbolic (or idealistic) intent. For instance, his brother-in-law mentioned that biblical miracles "sometimes seem to be splendid examples of poetic justice" (though not in a consistent way—the story of Balaam's talking ass [Numbers 22] is noted). Thus, it may be that Winnicott thought the symbolic nature of miracles to point to ideals such as justice. As "myths" of this kind he did not want to reduce their ability to convey meaning to "second class citizen[ship]" in intellectual thought (Winnicott, 1968b, p. 143). However, in another context Winnicott (1966f) connected the symbolic interpretation of miracles to his concept of transitional phenomena. Thus, this symbolic interpretation of miracles may not imply the reductionism of the justice example. It is possible that Winnicott meant the symbolism of miracles also to include something of the paradox of transitional phenomena. He noted that taking his concept of transitional phenomena seriously might "perhaps put religion once again into the experience of those who in fact have grown up out of the concept of miracles" (Winnicott, 1966f, p. 134). Although it is not clear which meaning was intended in the missing letter to his brother-in-law, one gathers from the brother-in-law's response that another way Winnicott sought to separate the Christ ideals from the later traditions was through "symbolic" interpretations of things like miracles.

This section concludes by observing that a general way Winnicott seemed to live out this distinction between religious "ideals" and the more narrow ways that religion might be used was through his project to preserve a positive place for religion in life and culture. Despite the negative contributions that might come from religious dogma and tradition, Winnicott sought a way to preserve the good that religion offers.

Psychoanalysis as Vocation

In addition to being religious by preserving a place for free thought and by trying to live out certain religious ideals, there is yet another way to reflect on the
nature of Winnicott's religiousness. Although he did not use the theological language of "vocation" to speak of his life's work, nevertheless this language
seems a relevant way to reflect on Winnicott's way of being religious. Originally, vocation (from Latin *vocatio*) meant a "calling" (*vocare*; to call) and found
its root meaning in the scriptural usage of a call to serve God (Davies, 1983). In
the Middle Ages vocation was restricted to those who had taken up monastic
orders, but with the Reformation the term was expanded to include the various
roles in society that one might fulfill (e.g., parent, shopkeeper, governor) as
ways to render service unto God. In contemporary times, the term has been expanded even further so that it means little more than occupation to most people
(T. Brown, 1990).

What is proposed in applying this term to Winnicott's work is a recovery of
something of the meaning of the term as used by the Protestant reformers, particularly Martin Luther. Luther saw all aspects of life as a way to respond to "the
call to servanthood before God and neighbor" (T. Brown, 1990, p. 1308). As
Brown summarized, for Luther "a vocation is a position or station which by its
nature is helpful to others. The presence of service and love determined whether
the station qualified as a vocation. These could be part of any serviceable work
and there was no secular order from which God was excluded" (p. 1308). Brown
pointed out that there is an echo of this theological meaning in contemporary
uses of the word vocation to designate work from which one derives meaning
and purpose beyond simple economic livelihood. One sees something of this
meaning of the term in Rudnytsky's (1991) brief biographies of Rank and Winnicott: *The Psychoanalytic Vocation: Rank, Winnicott and the Legacy of Freud.*

In speaking of psychoanalysis as vocation, what is proposed is that Winnicott saw it as much more than a source for economic livelihood. One even
hears echoes of this language of vocation in the description of his work as a
quest to understand the "ordinary devoted mother." "I suppose that everyone has
a paramount interest, a deep, driving propulsion towards something. If one's life
lasts long enough, so that looking back becomes allowable, one discerns an ur-
gent tendency that has integrated all the various and varied activities of one's
private life and one's professional career" (Winnicott, 1957d, p. 141). Psychoanalysis became a way for Winnicott both to find meaning and to stay "alive" in
his own life while concurrently helping others find meaning and aliveness. Thus,
one might say that psychoanalysis became one way for Winnicott to be religious
in his own particular way. It provided a way for him to ask questions of ultimate
meaning (cf. Emmons, 2003; Tillich, 1952). It is obvious from Winnicott's writings that he felt psychoanalysis was a way for him to be of service to (used by)
others. Furthermore, psychoanalysis seems a means by which Winnicott nur-

tured a "call" to become more fully his true self, a concept with religious over-tones for him (Winnicott, 1960e).[8]

In speaking of psychoanalysis as Winnicott's vocation one must note that the use of psychoanalysis in this way is as an umbrella term that takes in the various ways in which psychoanalysis impacted Winnicott's career. He was both pediatrician and psychoanalyst and he felt each aspect of his work informed the other. His quest to understand the emotional development of the child was informed both by his pediatric cases and his training and work as an analyst (Winnicott, 1945c, 1971f). Even when not doing formal analysis with children, Winnicott still thought analytic categories the best way to understand what was going on in his young patients (cf. 1971f). He seemed most content to blend these two aspects of his work with children by referring to himself as a child psychiatrist (1963j).

How then does psychoanalysis as vocation work its way out in Winnicott's life? Several means by which it allowed Winnicott to be religious are worth noting.

Provides a Means to Re-frame His Religious Interests

This point has been expounded in a previous chapter and is only summa-rized here. Not only did psychoanalysis give Winnicott a way to continue his pursuit of religious questions, it gave him a means to translate religious concepts into analytic language.[9] Already noted for instance is how his description of the mother's holding evokes qualities long attributed to God in the Hebrew and Christian scriptures (Hansen & Drovdahl, 2006). His use of "I AM" to designate awareness of individuality is correlated by Winnicott (1964g, 1968i) himself to the biblical use of I AM to designate God and the emergence of monotheism. His reference to the "true self" in religion was noted as well (and more is said about this below).

Psychoanalysis also provided Winnicott a means to argue for a creative role for religion in life and culture. By locating religion in the intermediate area of experiencing—"the place where we live"—Winnicott (1971h) affirmed its con-tribution to human vitality. Winnicott's lifelong interest in the positive role of religion is very much like a calling or vocation for him. Finding a way to articu-late a creative, adaptive role for religion seems to have been a project that con-tributed to what made life worth living for Winnicott (see below).

Perhaps this sense of calling arose psychologically from his tendency to re-sist being put in a box. That is, he could no more capitulate to the accepted psy-choanalytic dogma regarding the pathology of religion any more than he could capitulate to any dogma. The beginnings of this project to recover a positive role for religion in psychoanalysis is seen in his first psychoanalytic paper where in the midst of acknowledging the then current analytic position regarding the defensive nature of religion, he pointed out that fighting too vigorously against religion can be its own defense (Winnicott, 1935). Through his concept of transitional phenomena Winnicott (1951b) was able to turn much of the traditional psychoanalytic view of religion as pathological upon its head and to construct a psychoanalytic argument for the creative potential that he had observed in religion as a child.

Provides a Means to Explore What Makes Life Worth Living

A previous chapter has elaborated on this point; it is simply noted here that psychoanalysis provided Winnicott a means to continue his exploration of what makes life worth living. Rodman (1987) argued that Winnicott was the first person to ask this question in an analytic setting. Yet what is striking about this question is how religious it sounds. By using psychoanalysis as a means to explore what makes life worth living, Winnicott created a particular way to be religious.

Winnicott's several references to the loss of his friends, particularly in the First World War seems relevant to this question of what makes life worthwhile. That he survived while others did not is a question that haunted him throughout the remainder of his life and became a source of guilt for him. There is a great mystery here for him. Recall his mention of this upon his retirement from Paddington Green (Winnicott, 1961c). It seemed especially on his mind during the last years of his own life. Clare (Winnicott, 1978) mentioned that it occupied a place in his autobiographical notes (he mentioned it in the place where he imagined his own death). In reflecting on his prayer that he might be alive when he died, he remarked "this makes me feel awful because so many of my friends and contemporaries died in the first World War, and I have never been free from the feeling that my being alive is a facet of some one thing of which their deaths can be seen as other facets; some huge crystal, a body with integrity and shape intrinsical to it" (Winnicott, 1978, p. 20). In another brief autobiographical comment in an address in 1970 he remarked "To finish off my brief autobiography, I spent the first two decades of my life half drowned in a perpetual sense of guilt, from which psychoanalysis rescued me, except that I can never escape from the sense that I ought not have escaped the death that eclipsed the careers of so many of my friends in the 14-18 war" (Winnicott, 1970i). His career in psychoanalysis seems to have helped Winnicott come to grips with his own life purpose as noted in the retirement comment. However, his achievements continued to owe a debt of memory to his dead friends according to another unpublished note written around his 70th year. In a note entitled "An Allotted Spanner in the Works" he wrote "if I have got anywhere or contributed anything to the world, then the good includes my friends & contemporaries who were killed in the two great wars, who died of cancer or by accident, or who got into trouble and never caught up again" (Winnicott, 1966b). Thus, one sees that Winnicott's reflection upon the question of what makes life worth living is not an intellectual exercise, but is rooted deeply in an existential sense of loss and reflection upon the great mystery of life.

There are a few places where Winnicott seems to reflect upon life as a gift of God. Because this is not prominent in his published writings, one must not overstate the case, but it is worth noting these remarks and their contexts. In one of his posthumously published talks, "The Pill and the Moon," Winnicott (1969k) offered a bit of doggerel that arose out of unproductive time spent thinking about his talk. It is a brief "poem" entitled "The Silent Kill" and begins: "O silly Pill for folks not ill! Why not wait till you know God's will?" (p. 196). Though he made little use of this, because it seemed to belong to a time of free associating, he hinted that conception of a child is a gift of God. Even more telling in terms of a statement about life as a gift of God are some comments in an unpublished manuscript entitled "Rabbi Ben Ezra" (Winnicott, n.d. 6). It is unclear what Winnicott's intent was in this manuscript since no introduction or context is given. It appears to be a running prose restatement of the poem by Robert Browning, interspersed with the briefest commentary. Thus, it is not clear whether Winnicott is necessarily endorsing certain thoughts in the manuscript or simply trying to restate them. For instance, to the opening lines that include the words

> Our times are in his hands
> Who saith 'a whole I planned,
> Youth shows but half; trust God . . .

Winnicott wrote "we are all in the hand of God, who, as he made us planned for each his life. God planned the whole and youth is only half. Then put trust in God." And to the closing lines of the poem that state

> But I need, now as then,
> Thee God, who mouldest men. . . .
>   . . .
> [T]ake and use Thy work . . .
>   . . .
> Perfect the cup as planned!

Winnicott wrote "But God is in need now as much as ever he was when he molded us. God must take and use us, having fashioned us." Since Winnicott's intent is not clear, one should not be overly quick to read these statements as endorsements, but that he felt the poem worth restating gives some indication of a positive attitude toward the sentiments of the poem that life is a gift of God.

Finally, two other unpublished comments are noteworthy. In the talk to the Christian Union at Bart's Winnicott (n.d. 3) spoke of one's "duty to his Creator to use all his powers to develop all his parts" and in the unpublished note, "An Allotted Spanner in the Works" (Winnicott, 1966b) he remarked "what else is there for which one can, at 70 years, praise God? Well, for one thing, there's the fact that one has made it." One concludes that Winnicott in his more personal moments did occasionally think of life as a gift from God, though this is not a sentiment that appears plainly in his published works. Nevertheless, one surmises that as a way to explore the question of what makes life worth living psychoanalysis provided Winnicott a way to be religious.

Provides a Means for Expression of the True Self

Yet another way that psychoanalysis provided Winnicott (1963a) a way to be religious was in allowing for the expression of his true self, that "sacred" (at times incommunicable) core of aliveness and vitality that makes life worth living. Psychoanalysis provided this vitalizing expression of Winnicott's true self in several ways: it allowed him to continue his focus on the interior life and the value of feelings; it provided him a venue to develop his capacity to "believe in," and it provided him a way to be involved in care/cure (Winnicott, 1963j).

One way a vocation in psychoanalysis nurtured Winnicott's true self was through allowing his continued focus on the value of the interior life, especially its unconscious expressions. Winnicott was not always convinced that valuing the unconscious life was common ground between religion and psychoanalysis. In a letter about the value of expiation for criminals he wrote of theological reluctance to embrace findings about the unconscious (Winnicott, 1949e). However, about ten years later he wrote that both psychoanalysis and religion reveal and deal with the deep conflicts of the inner life (Winnicott, 1958g), and later wrote that investigation of the "defenses" was an unparalleled way to explore the kind of human struggles with which philosophers, artists and religion dealt (Winnicott, 1961d). Thus, Winnicott came to understand that psychoanalysis and religion share a common interest in the significance of the interior life.

Winnicott's exploration and articulation of the value of the interior life is carried forth in two ways: Winnicott's own self-analysis and growth throughout his life, and his work in helping his patients focus on and explore the richness of their interior lives. Rodman (1987, 2003) observed that being a practicing psychoanalyst allowed Winnicott to continue his own growth through providing him a means and opportunity to deal with his own aggression and narcissism. As a method of treating psychological distress, Winnicott (1967c) saw psychoanalysis not only as a means for uncovering the deep conflicts in his patients, but also as a means for nurturing the yearning for health that also was present both in himself and in his patients.

A second way that his work in psychoanalysis vitalized Winnicott was through providing him a venue in which to develop his capacity to believe. The capacity for belief was prior to any particular beliefs for Winnicott, and without this prior capacity the question of belief in God, for instance, was moot (Winnicott, 1963j). This capacity to believe was rooted in the quality of early infant care and was a precursor to maturity in the developing individual (Winnicott, 1958a, p. 32). Even the scientist needed this capacity for belief (Winnicott, 1961d). Thus, psychoanalysis became a way for Winnicott to exercise his capacity to "believe in"; to exercise his belief in "the inexorable laws that govern phenomena" (Winnicott, 1961d, p. 14). He even likened these laws to belief in God in his speech to the Bart's Christian Union. One might even say that Winnicott's faith in these "inexorable laws" reflects his sense of wonder (Goldman, 1993).

However, psychoanalysis gave Winnicott other ways to exercise his capacity for belief and some of the things he came to believe in had religious overtones. For instance, his belief in the ability of science to help cure human ills evoked a common connection with religion for him (Winnicott, 1961f, 1970d). Psychoanalysis also allowed him to develop his belief in the creative, adaptive role of religion. Psychoanalysis even helped Winnicott develop his capacity to believe in the original goodness of humans, despite the many problems he encountered in his patients (though one would also note that his childhood and Wesleyan background also contributed to this belief in the goodness of others. See chapter 7).

Psychoanalysis allowed Winnicott to be religious through his involvement in what he called "care/cure" (Winnicott, 1970d). In a talk to doctors Winnicott compared psychoanalysis and religion arguing that psychoanalysis and religion both shared an interest in cure as "care" as opposed to the emphasis on cure as "remedy" that was sometimes encountered in medicine. Remedy here pointed to a non-holistic approach to the person, a supposed notion that cure can be arrived at without attention to the inner workings of the person, or through some quick fix of the physical components of a person's illness. Cure as care recognized a complexity in humans and the attachments and dependencies they make to their physicians (transferences). Winnicott argued that cure as care exhibited several qualities: the physician was non-moralistic, truthful, reliable, accepting of the patient's love and hate, without being provoked or cruel. He acknowledged that both doctors and parsons can be either of the care/cure type or remedy/cure type. (One might note that remedy is not all bad for Winnicott; he noted that without a focus on remedy some of the breakthroughs in medicine such as penicillin would not have emerged.)

A further dimension of the shared interest in care/cure in psychoanalysis and religion is the focus of both on the relief of human suffering. As Winnicott (1935) noted in his paper on the manic defense, religion for centuries had helped people recognize and cope with deep feeling such as sadness. Similarly, he wrote that what gives psychotherapy its basis is that it too "relates to the individual suffering and need for help" (Winnicott, 1963l, p. 205).

Before concluding this section on psychoanalysis as vocation for Winnicott, one should note a further aspect of Winnicott's attitude toward his life's work. Although Winnicott did not think all therapy or mental health work to be psychoanalysis, he did not think the insights from psychoanalysis as method should be restricted to psychoanalysis as treatment. He thought social workers, residential care coordinators, and other health care workers could profit from and help facilitate the kinds of mental health care that psychoanalysis lacked the resources to provide, especially "management," a type of supportive therapeutic work focused on stabilizing one emotionally as distinct from work focused on insight into unconscious processes (Winnicott, 1959a). He also saw parents as able to carry on this kind of therapeutic work for their children. This attitude of sharing psychoanalytic insights with non-analysts was one he both talked about and wrote about and lived out in his many presentations to parents, nurses, educators, social workers, residential care workers, pastors, and magistrates. It also drew criticism from his psychoanalytic colleagues that he did not always make sufficient distinctions when he gave these talks (Rodman, 2003). Nevertheless, this "taking psychoanalysis to the masses" seems to have been a deeply felt conviction for Winnicott, perhaps yet another way he lived out of his true self and in doing so made psychoanalysis a vocation and a means to be religious in his own way. [10]

In arguing that psychoanalysis was a way for Winnicott to be religious, I have suggested that it came to fulfill some of the functions of religion for him (e.g., conveyed a vitalizing aliveness and sense of purpose, attended to the interior life). This is not the same as saying that psychoanalysis became Winnicott's religion. Although both Hoffman (2011) and Kirschner (1996) have argued in slightly different ways that psychoanalysis became a secularized version of earlier religious narratives, a substitute means by which the religious pursuit of truth or visions of growth were given new relevance, the point here is different. Although psychoanalysis provided Winnicott a means to live out many of the ideals of his religious background, one must not lose sight of the fact that Winnicott also remained religious in *religious* ways. Though he no longer attended church services or ascribed to certain beliefs from the religion of his youth, he remained religious in his desire to live out the Christ ideals, in his preservation of that most cherished Wesleyan tenet of free thought, and in seeing the "temperament" (true self) as sacred, a gift of "his Creator" to which he tried to be true. One notes that this way of being religious had much continuity with his Wesleyan roots. I conclude that although he was not always comfortable to describe himself as religious, he nevertheless thought himself religious in his own way. I further conclude that in addition to the vitalizing force that Winnicott found in psychoanalysis, a deep personal interest in religion also continued to vitalize his life and work. [11]

Notes

1.   Rodman (2003) argued that Winnicott was only able to find the strength to separate from (and later divorce) Alice after the death of his father. Such a claim suggests that Winnicott's decreasing religious practice may also be tied to the death of his father. If the death of his father freed him to make decisions regarding his unhappy marriage it also may have freed him to be more self-determined regarding church attendance. The extent to which Alice may have contributed to his regular church attendance is not known.

Kahr's (2011) recent article called attention to the numerous tensions Winnicott felt with his family and in his personal life as well as with certain troublesome patients during the mid to late 1940s. These personal tensions may have contributed to the decline of his church attendance in ways not yet known. Kahr also noted that Winnicott began to see patients on Sundays during this period, a practice he continued throughout his life.

2.   Fowler's model provides an interesting window on certain developmental aspects to Winnicott's fluctuating attempts to integrate his religious interests with his psychoanalytic training. Though much more cognitive in tone than Winnicott's own approach to development, James Fowler's (1981) "stages of faith" offer one way to reflect upon Winnicott's religious journey. One can chart a common pattern of religious growth outlined by Fowler in Winnicott. In his early adolescence Winnicott seems to have accepted the religion that was passed on to him (a "synthetic-conventional" faith according to Fowler). One could see his service with the scouts as an extension of this allegiance to the faith in which he was brought up. However, beginning with his time at The Leys, and certainly obvious by the time he became involved with psychoanalysis, Winnicott had begun a process of questioning his former religious context in an effort to arrive at a more personal and reflective way to hold the faith (the movement to what Fowler called "individuative-reflective" faith). One sees in Winnicott's questioning of central dogmas of the Christian faith his attempt to come to a new understanding of the faith; one in which he can embrace some things but must let go of his belief in others things such as miracles and the after-life. Such questionings can cause those of one's previously authoritative religious groups to wonder whether one has "lost" the faith.

Having arisen in late adolescence or young adulthood, this style of questioning faith seems to have remained with Winnicott for the remainder of his life. One may see the beginnings of the movement that Fowler calls "conjunctive" faith in the last years of Winnicott's life with his renewed interest in religious characters such as Jesus and the Lollards. Not that he has ever lost his interest, but his reflective period seems to have made him more aware of religious ideals, though less involved in the interpersonal qualities of religion such as church attendance with others. The increased interest in ideas and ideals, religion as the embodiment of principles, is characteristic of individuative-reflective faith. However, with the renewed interest in religious people one may see the beginnings of conjunctive faith with its desire to join together the more reflective approach to religious ideals with the neglected interpersonal dimensions. What one does not see however, is a full movement to this stage. Although Winnicott wants a faith that allows questions, he does not seem to have moved to a place where he can bring his questionings into a peace with his being a "practicing Christian." He does not seem able to integrate his former religious intensity with his questionings, but rather seems to hold them in separate compartments. He does not engage religion personally in the high/mature way he outlined in his argument for religion as creative and adaptive. There is no way to know whether he would have moved further toward a conjunctive faith had he lived longer. Perhaps, but Fowler (1981) is clear that such movement only happens with a minority of adults.

3.   In reflecting upon the inability of Winnicott to integrate fully his theoretical position about the positive role of religion in life and culture and his own religious practice, one wonders if he might have identified with the contemporary distinction between religion and spirituality (cf. Frame, 2002)? In this distinction, religion is much more associated with the institutional structure and practices of religious organizations, while spirituality refers more to an animating force, often divorced from such structures. Winnicott's desire to question and to be interested in religious things without being one who attended church functions or participated in church dogma is very much in keeping with such distinctions. However, in his argument for the creative role of religion in life and culture, Winnicott holds out a hope for religion that included organized religion. Thus, there also are arguments in Winnicott where the religious sentiment stays closely tied to organized structures.

4.   One might compare Winnicott's rejection of a belief in miracles (1968b) with his rejection of the death instinct (1968h). Both were "traditional" beliefs for religion and psychoanalysis respectively. Winnicott would not ascribe to either simply as a matter of accepted belief. In this way he thought himself very much in the spirit of the Lollards.

The Lollards were a radical non-conformist sect that pre-dated Wesley by two centuries (Heitzenrater, 1995). Associated with John Wycliffe, a fourteenth-century translator of the Bible into English, the Lollards had denied such doctrines as transubstantiation and the authority of the Pope long before the rise of Protestantism (Goldman, 1993; Heitzenrater, 1995). In a series of letters to Ian Rodger, Winnicott spoke of an interest in the word "Lollard" and described himself as a "natural Lollard [who] would have had a bad time in the 14th and 15th centuries" (quoted in Goldman, 1993, p. 119). Phillips (1988) suggested Winnicott may have thought himself a Lollard because the word derived from "lollen" meaning to "mew, bawl, or mutter" and Winnicott had a special interest in the development of infants who "mew, bawl" and eventually "mutter" (p. 38).

More convincing in the light of Winnicott's comments to Rodger about the Lollards is Goldman's (1993) suggestion that Winnicott's interest in the word Lollard had to do with its derivation from the Dutch "lollaert" meaning "mumbler." This was "a term applied to certain European groups suspected of combining pious pretensions with heretical belief." (p. 120). Goldman argued that Winnicott's interest in the Lollards involved several levels.

On one level was his interest in the Lollards as non-conformists. Winnicott was appreciative of the radical non-conformism of the Lollards, perhaps because he too saw himself as a radical non-conformist. Goldman speculated:

> Why did Winnicott, late in his life, see himself as a "natural Lollard"? Did he see himself as a "heretic" or "nonconformist" within his own movement? Was it because of his contempt for certain trends within psychoanalysis that, in his mind, smacked of subservience to authority and secular idolatry? Was he fearful that psychoanalysis might degenerate into an ossified belief system, built upon a stagnant cannon [sic] inaccessible to the common man? One wonders if there isn't, perhaps, a disguised allusion here to his own struggles against both the dogmatic Kleinians and the Freudian canonizers. Is it not likely that Winnicott saw a connection between the demands for compliance imposed upon the early heretics and his notions of the True Self and False Self?" (Goldman, 1993, p. 121).

On another level Winnicott valued the contributions of the radical non-conformists tradition to the growth of English freedoms. Goldman quoted Winnicott's appraisal that "it was persecuted religious heretics who . . . had the tolerance and sensitivity to 'lay the basis for liberal thinking in England and Europe'" (p. 120). Winnicott's personal valuing of these freedoms manifested itself in his aversion to coercive religion or psychoanalysis.

5.   The extant portion of the manuscript is reproduced as an appendix. It is hard to date in its unfinished form. Internal evidence such as correspondence with published ideas that it seems to replicate (e.g., the true self, object use) suggest a date sometime in the 1960's. Further evidence for a date in the 1960's is the version of the Bible from which a scripture quotation comes. The wording is that of *The New English Bible*, a translation authorized by a Joint Commission of the major Protestant churches in Great Britain and appearing in 1961 in the first edition of the New Testament.

6.   His example was of those who believed the earth to have been created around 4000 B.C. This was the date offered by Archbishop Ussher in 1650 from his calculations of the age of the earth using Bible verses (Ford, 2004). This notion that science and religion could coexist for the thoughtful person had long been an influence of Winnicott's Wesleyan tradition. Recall his days at The Leys where he was a member of both the Biology club and the Christian Union (chapter 3). Winnicott (1964d) made a similar point in an unpublished letter to the *London Times*, stating that Christianity need not denigrate Freudian thought in order to establish its own tenets.

7.   Winnicott's comments on religious practice versus true inward change are reminiscent of comments from one of Wesley's sermons on the "new birth."

> Go to church twice a day, go to the Lord's table every week, say ever so many prayers in private; hear ever so many sermons, good sermons, excellent sermons, the best that ever were preached; read ever so many good books—still you must be born again. None of these this will stand in the place of the new birth. No, nor anything under heaven. Let this, therefore, if you have not already experienced this inward work of God, be your continual prayer, "Lord, add this to all thy blessings: let me be 'born again.'" (Wesley, 1760a, pp. 200-201)

8.   Whether Winnicott would have been comfortable with an overtly religious reference to his work, an early note from his father was not reluctant to speak of his son's work as a doctor in this way. In a letter dated January 21, 1934 he wrote:

> Am afraid present conditions must make things very trying for you but your letter seemed to show that you are still fairly occupied in your endeavour to give relief to people needing your help—there can be no holier service and I often pray that you may receive Divine guidance and that your patients may find relief and that God's blessing may be with you in your work." (J.F. Winnicott, 1934)

It is interesting to compare this letter from Winnicott's father with a note from Freud's father that was inscribed on the inside cover of a special Hebrew Bible that Freud's father gave to him on his 35th birthday. His father implied a divine destiny for Freud when he wrote "it was in the seventh year of your age that the Spirit of God began to move you to learning" (cited in Jones, 1953, p. 19).

9.   In making this point, I note its difference from similar ones articulated by Hoffman (2011) and Kirschner (1996). Hoffman argued that psychoanalysis became a secularized version of the religious concern with the pursuit of truth (i.e., bringing the dark and hid-

den into the light). She argued that Freud had to obscure the religious roots of his methods given the confluence of Enlightenment rationality and the anti-Semitic context in which his ideas were forged. Similarly, Kirschner argued that psychoanalysis was a secularized version of the biblical narrative of development and redemption. In noting that Winnicott translated religious concepts into psychoanalytic ones I recognize both a different context and intent on his part. The commonality between Winnicott's concepts and religious ones cannot be understood simply as a conscious attempt to substitute secular language and ideas for religious ones, though if Kirschner and Hoffman are correct there would have been deeper, less conscious processes at work (an argument advanced in this book regarding the influences of Winnicott's Wesleyan heritage). Although Winnicott shared an interest in making religious concepts more acceptable to a secular audience, he was just as interested in the converse. One must remember that his motivations in finding consistency between religious and psychoanalytic ideas also involved more personal motives rooted in his need to make ideas real to himself. Nevertheless, Winnicott does seem to have found in psychoanalysis a way to live out many of the ideals associated with his religious background.

10. As noted previously, in suggesting such a possibility, one must ask whether Winnicott spoke so often to nurses, doctors, social workers, pastors, and others because he was not allowed to teach at the British Psychoanalytic Society (BPS). Or was there something in Winnicott that would have pushed him to do this anyway? Certainly, one can speculate that had he been more directly involved with the BPS early on that he might have been more insular regarding psychoanalysis, but the fact that he was not more centrally involved was from his own choice and character. There was something about Winnicott that refused to let him align with either the Anna Freud or Klein factions. So, even had he been allowed to teach at BPS one suspects that Winnicott still would have held the position that psychoanalysis should not be so restrictive with its wisdom, and that all kinds of caregivers could facilitate healing in others.

11. An interesting question arises at this point as to whether the hundreds of Winnicott's personal squiggles housed at the Wellcome Library, London give any insight into his way of being religious. This is hard to judge since there are so few with overtly religious themes, though this in itself might be telling. However, of the four with obvious religious themes, three of these are framed (whereas less than a fourth of the total collection is framed). The four squiggles with clear religious themes include one entitled "Prayer and Fasting" of a saint (including circle around his head) kneeling at an altar in prayer. The three framed squiggles include a picture of a fish (an early Christian symbol) with the word ICHTHUS (fish) in both Greek (ΙΧΘΥΣ) and English characters inscribed. Another framed squiggle is of a nun and is titled "Nun such," an example of his humor; the final framed squiggle is entitled "A believer experiencing levitation at the Last Trump" and is dated "1-7-57." It depicts someone being lifted up into the sky. Whether other squiggles deal with religious themes or not depends on the extent to which one might read unconscious aspects into them (e.g., there are "monsters" aplenty in the collection) and is not taken up here.

Chapter 10
Winnicott's God Images

"Man continues to create and re-create God"

The earliest glimpse one has into the life of the young Winnicott is from a story he recounted in his autobiographical notes (Winnicott, 1978). There he told a story involving his father and a doll named Rosie. The doll had belonged to one of his sisters, but the young Winnicott had become attached to the doll and this attachment had become a source of teasing from his father. One day when he was three, following one of these times of teasing, Winnicott's wrote that he took a croquet mallet and smashed in the doll's nose. Winnicott remembered feeling both pleased and troubled by his actions; however, his father's subsequent actions also left a lasting impression. His father took a series of matches, and warming up the wax of the doll's face, was able to reshape the doll's nose.

One does not have access to all the emotions, tensions, and reactions that must have surrounded this event. Whether the sisters reacted by crying that the doll had been ruined or whether the father benignly smiled at the outrage of his three-year-old son is unknown. What one has are Winnicott's reflections on the event through the lens of the analytic theory he had developed in the intervening 70 years. "This early demonstration of the restitutive and reparative act certainly made an impression on me, and perhaps made me able to accept the fact that I myself, dear innocent child, had actually become violent directly with a doll, but indirectly with my good-tempered father who was just then entering my conscious life" (Winnicott, 1978, p. 23).

This story of Winnicott's interaction with his father is revealing in several ways. As an early memory, it gives insight into the father's way of relating with his son. Though described as "good tempered" the father also showed some insensitivity to his young son's feelings. This incident sits in contrast to the story of the young Winnicott walking home from church with his father. The good natured father, who can treat his son with special favor, can at times taunt him.

Similarly, this incident gives some insight into the son's reaction and relationship to his father. Although one can never make too much of a single incident, the fact that it is remembered so vividly by Winnicott suggests that it may be representative of a more ingrained pattern of relating and interacting. His father's treatment leaves Winnicott feeling alternately special and angry.

The story also is significant in revealing how Winnicott read his later developmental theory back into his early life. Winnicott even saw in this incident, precursors to his development of a sense of responsibility for his aggressive actions. The infant's restitutive gesture and development of a capacity for concern are contributions of Winnicott (1963c) to the understanding of early development. Learning to understand and come to terms with one's early aggression and need for reparative gestures extends into adult life. Understanding aggressive tendencies (e.g., "hate") was a focus in both Winnicott's (1939, 1947c, 1950a, 1964i, 1968h) theoretical work and his personal life (Rodman, 1987, 2003).

The story also is significant at this point because it is the earliest insight into Winnicott's relationship with one of his parents. This is significant for the present chapter, because Winnicott (1963j) and others write of the formative impact of one's earliest relationships (especially with parents) in shaping understanding of God (Jones, 1991; Parker, 1996; Rizzuto, 1979; St. Clair, 1994). One's ideas of and feelings about God find their building blocks in the quality of the earliest interactions with one's care-givers coupled with one's own imaginative sorting of the inner and outer worlds. This incident with one of Winnicott's parents (along with others to be described) gives an early glance into feelings and thoughts that Winnicott will associate with God.

Winnicott (1963j) argued at one point that people are constantly creating and re-creating God. By this he meant that people were constantly building up new ideas of God from various experiences with inner and outer reality beginning with their earliest illusions of omnipotence. By projecting a variety of good (and bad) qualities, people create (and re-create) their understandings of God.

Although he acknowledged this process in the formation of one's understanding of God (1963j), Winnicott never spoke directly to his own efforts in this way. In fact, direct statements about God are actually rare in his writings (cf. Ulanov, 2001). The purpose of this chapter is to explore how this psychic process of creating and re-creating God was present in Winnicott's own life. What images of God did Winnicott form? Even more interesting, can one trace the sources for his God images in his developmental history? Thus, in some way this chapter seeks to use Winnicott's own theory to understand this aspect of his emotional development.

God Images and Concepts

Freud (1913) argued that the cultural origins of religion arose from aggressive acts of sons against the father; guilt for these acts led to setting up totemic objects in memory of the slain father as reparation. At the individual level religion arose from deep yearning regarding the lost father. "God" thus represented projected wishes for a cosmic father protector (Freud, 1927).

Winnicott's interest in the psychological origins of religion lay not so much in the projections or beliefs that one might have about God but in the prior question of how the capacity to have such projections or beliefs arose (1963j, 1968g). According to Winnicott the development of the capacity for a belief in God began in the earliest interactions of the infant with its care-giver. If these interactions were "good enough" the child began to build up a sense of the reliability of the external world. If a child had acquired this sense of reliability, other perceptions became possible. Winnicott spoke most directly regarding the process in a 1963 essay on "morals and education." There he noted "the infant and small child is usually cared for in a reliable way, and this being cared for well enough builds up in the infant to a belief in reliability. . . . To a child who has started life in this way the idea of goodness and of a reliable and personal parent or God can follow naturally" (Winnicott, 1963j, p. 97). The conceiving of the idea of a reliable other called God began with these earliest experiences of reliability in care giving and was an extension of the idea of a reliable parent (Winnicott, 1963j).

It is important to remember that Winnicott is describing a process here. At the beginning of the process the infant cannot yet distinguish itself from its environment. In the earliest phases the sense of reliability arises from the mother's highly attuned responses to the infant's needs (Winnicott, 1956f). This period of "primary maternal preoccupation" allows the infant a momentary illusion of being omnipotent, of thinking it is the creator of its environment. Yet with good enough mothering the infant also experiences a disillusionment when it begins to realize that the environment is other than its wishes. This emerging capacity allows the infant to perceive the mother as "not me" substance, and from this growing capacity will come the ability to perceive the environment more widely (i.e., as peopled with fathers, and grandmothers and nurses for instance).

If one seeks to implant a concept of God prior to the child's readiness for the idea of God one disrupts the natural creativity connected to the personal contribution to such concepts (Winnicott, 1963j). When Winnicott spoke of the child's "creating" a God, he also drew upon his arguments concerning transitional objects and phenomena (cf. Winnicott, 1951b). As noted in an earlier chapter, the transitional object draws its special qualities from the fact that it is not simply an object of the external environment but is an object that the infant has imbued with its own psychic fantasies and imaginings. In this way the infant "creates" the object it perceives; such objects thus participate in both external and internal realities. These creations contain both "ideas" and "feelings" which can get associated with God (Winnicott, 1963j). Thus, for Winnicott one's "idea of God" or "concept of God" has both affective and cognitive dimensions; furthermore, such concepts or ideas draw from both internal and external experience.

In the last three decades a literature that draws upon Winnicott's theory about the formation of one's understanding of God has developed, but in ways that more closely demarcate the affective from the cognitive dimensions of such understandings. For instance, Rizzuto (1979) distinguished God *images* (or representations) from God *concepts*. God images or representations are the more emotional, affect-laden, and unconscious experiences of God, closer to what

Winnicott called inner experience (1951b); whereas God concepts are understood as the more cognitive, culturally mediated ideas about God, taking on
more of what Winnicott referred to as outer experience. In this model, God images draw from interactions with and share qualities similar to one's significant
others (or objects). By contrast, God concepts draw from cultural ideas (e.g.,
theology) to shape one's understandings of God. Although both of these ways of
thinking about how people form a belief in God were present in Winnicott's
thought, this specific distinction was not one Winnicott himself made. The term
God concept embraced both affective and cognitive associations and draws from
both inner and outer reality for him.

Winnicott's Explicit Statements about God

To explore the concepts of God that Winnicott constructed it will be helpful first
to detail the various ways Winnicott spoke of God in his writings. Although
Winnicott rarely spoke of God directly, even in his writings on the role of religion, one finds four ways in which the term God turned up in his work.

God as Social Convention

Several times when Winnicott spoke of God, the sense seems to be little
more than use of a social convention; he did not seem to be offering intentional
thoughts on God's nature. When he remarked that his father encouraged him to
read the Bible for his own sense of the truth to be found there he concluded, "I
was left, thank God, to get on with it myself" (Winnicott, 1978, p. 23). The reference to God here seems hardly more than social habit. Similarly, when he remarked that a patient's "complaint is not the statement of God's truth," the addition of God in this sentence seems more a social convention designed to
emphasize what is true than a statement about God (Winnicott, 1938, p. 37). If
such a thought is there it is implied rather than intentional. Although it also
could imply more, perhaps the opening to his autobiographical notes, "Prayer:
Oh God! May I be alive when I die," simply employed the cultural understanding of God as the one to whom prayers were directed (Winnicott, 1978, p. 19).

God as Projection of Internal Qualities

A second way Winnicott used the term God was to designate projections of
internal qualities, a use that shared common ground with Freud's (1927) notion
that God was a projection of the father. For Winnicott (1963j, 1969b), God becomes a projection of one's internal badness and/or goodness.

Badness

This quality gets projected onto God in several ways. Similar to Freud's (1927) ideas, God might become a repository of a person's hostility in the form of a fierce father, as Winnicott (1968c) once noted in the case of a patient: "for this man . . . God could be used as a substitute for the absence of a fierce father" (p. 237). According to Winnicott, one way the projection of badness onto God showed up culturally was in the notion of a punishing God. There were several times when Winnicott appealed to this common cultural understanding. For instance, when he mentioned that a young child had given him a warning that the child was "God" Winnicott (1954c) stated, "I knew therefore that I was to expect to be used as a bad person who ought to be punished" (p. 90). He also made references to this idea in a more playful vein: "The spirochete and the gonococcus are no longer (as they were certainly felt to be fifty years ago) agents of a punishing God" (Winnicott, 1961a, p. 82). Similarly, he remarked that because of advances in modern medicine "we can no longer leave it to God, so to speak, to kill everybody" with the diseases that plagued humanity prior to these advances (Winnicott, 1969k, p. 204).[1]

On a more individual level, Winnicott noted that God can represent a place where persecutory elements are projected: "In the inner psychic reality . . . help is afforded by the fact that benign elements can be exported, or projected, and so also may persecutory elements. In this way human beings are always inventing God and are always organizing disposal of dangerous waste products" (Winnicott, 1969b, p. 223). Although this thought is similar to the idea of a punishing God here is the added thought that projecting these hostile feelings onto God aids in the ability to manage persecutory thoughts and feelings. This idea of God as a means to manage persecutory feelings seems to be the meaning behind an interpretation given a patient who did not know where to put her anger. Winnicott suggested that perhaps she had put it in God (Winnicott, 1971a).

Goodness

Badness was not the only internal quality that was projected onto God for Winnicott; goodness also was. "Man continues to create and re-create God as a place to put that which is good in himself" (Winnicott, 1963j, p. 94). However, in projecting goodness onto God, humans tended to overlook their own "original goodness": "Religions have made much of original sin, but have not all come round to the idea of original goodness, that which by being gathered together in the idea of God is at the same time separated off from the individuals who collectively create and re-create this God concept" (p. 94). Furthermore, such attributions failed to recognize the human contributions to such visions of God (Winnicott, 1941b). Thus, God also can be an external projection of the goodness that lies within humans. In projecting these various internal qualities onto God Winnicott pointed out that humans forget the role they themselves played in the constructions of their ideas about God. However, in acknowledging these internal contributions to people's ideas about God, Winnicott did not mean that

God was somehow reduced to these projections; only that these projections and their origins were the focus of Winnicott's (cf. 1935, 1968g) attention.[2]

God as Impersonal Principle

A third way Winnicott spoke of God was as a representative (a projection) of various impersonal principles or qualities. Some of these have a positive connotation though they do not generally convey more personal qualities to God. For example, in projecting goodness onto God, God comes to represent the principle or ideal of goodness.

Fate

One way Winnicott used the term God to designate an impersonal principle was in portraying God as equivalent to fate or chance. This idea emerged in comments about accidental traumas such as fractures, lacerations, concussions, burns, or drowning as "acts of God" (Winnicott, 1931a, pp. 3–4). Similarly, Winnicott (1970h) equated another patient's spina bifida to what was often called an "'act of God' or the "operation of chance" and asked if there was any "logic" to a "feeling of blaming God" (p. 276). In interpreting another patient's dream he noted that she was struggling with "God or fate" (Winnicott, 1971c, p. 36). Thus, one picture of God that emerges from Winnicott is that of a distant, uninvolved God who lets things happen according to chance or "nature." Such a picture is strengthened by Winnicott's (n.d. 3) comment to those at Bart's Christian Union regarding "the laws of nature—which after all are also God."

External Reality

A similar use of this are places where Winnicott spoke of God as equivalent to the principle of external reality. In speaking of the disillusionment that must follow the illusion of omnipotence Winnicott (1968d) noted that such movement can only occur if there has been this prior experience of omnipotence: "Is it not from *being God* that human beings arrive at the humility proper to human individuality?" (p. 101; emphasis in original). Once the baby has had this illusion of omnipotence, he or she can relinquish it as a personal quality and recognize this as a quality that belongs outside the self. Omnipotence can now be turned over to "external reality" or to "a God-principle" (Winnicott, 1966c, p. 111).

Analogical Uses

The fourth use of the term God occurs in a series of what might be called analogical comments. These are occasions where God is mentioned or alluded to in passing comparison to other concepts. There are three such comparisons that help illumine Winnicott's understandings of God.

A Holding Environment

The first analogical use is Winnicott comparison of God to the mother's holding. It is this comparison that led to earlier observations of how closely this concept resembled God's loving grace (see chapter 7). Recall that holding is Winnicott's metaphor for the totality of the mother's interaction with her infant (Winnicott, 1961f). The mother "holds" the infant because the infant is not yet a "unit," and thus not psychologically able to hold itself or integrate its various experiences (Winnicott, 1954j). Through proper holding the infant is able to progress along the continuum of development that eventually allows the infant to distinguish self from environment.

This notion of the mother as a good enough holding environment, is a concept that can be applied to God as well.

> Let's take my suggestion that the whole of the preverbal expression of love in terms of holding and handling has vital significance for each developing baby. Then we can say on the basis of what has been experienced by an individual, we may teach the concept of, say, everlasting arms. We may use that word 'God', we can make a specific link with the Christian church and doctrine, but it is a series of steps. (Winnicott, 1968b, p. 148–149)

Thus, Winnicott presented an image of God that evoked the mother's loving care and holding of the infant.

Achievement of Individuality

A second analogical use of the term God comes in a series of statements regarding the achievement of individuality. Becoming an individual is an achievement that is part of larger developmental processes. "By good enough child care, technique, holding, and general management the shell becomes gradually taken over and the kernel (which has looked all the time like a human baby to us) can begin to be an individual" (Winnicott, 1952a, p. 99). Winnicott saw in the designation of God as "I AM," not only a cultural inheritance regarding monotheism, but an important way to speak about the psychological achievement of individuality.

God is seen as a representative of this process. "It is difficult for us to remember how modern is the concept of the human individual. The struggle to reach to this concept is reflected, perhaps, in the early Hebrew name for God. Monotheism seems to be closely linked to the name I AM" (Winnicott, 1968i, p. 57). The use of the language of I AM to designate the achievement of this stage along the integration path was an intentional reference to the Hebraic designation of God and made it clear in this instance what God Winnicott had in mind.

A related aspect of this analogical reference to God as representing individuality is seen in Winnicott's (1971j) statement to a patient regarding the difficulties with its achievement. "I referred here to God as I AM, a useful concept when the individual cannot bear to BE" (p. 62). Here God further represents the principle of being and is associated with the kind of care already reflected in God's ability to hold one when one cannot yet hold oneself.

Illusion of Omnipotence (Creativity)

A third analogical use of the term God comes in statements regarding the infant's illusion of omnipotence. Following a brief but necessary period of feeling omnipotent, Winnicott said this "uncomfortable function" is turned over to God (1970e, p. 49). Thus, in this comment God is representative of the function or principle of omnipotence. In one sense this means that God alone is to retain this quality; failure to relinquish omnipotence for Winnicott (1969l) is to remain emotionally immature, making others extensions of one's own subjectivity (cf. Hoffman, 2011). Yet the more interesting connection to the experience of omnipotence for this comparison is the analogy Winnicott made to God's creating the world. According to Winnicott, the mother's attunement to the infant's nascent gestures allows the infant a temporary experience of omnipotence; that is, it permits the infant an experience of "creating" the objects it is ready to "find." The end result is that "each baby starts up with a new creation of the world. And on the seventh day we hope that he is pleased and takes a rest"(Winnicott, 1970e, p. 49). Thus, God does not simply represent some principle of omnipotence but is associated with creative activity. Like God the infant "creates" the objects it desires and creativity throughout life retains something of this early infant experience of being able to create the world.

Summary Conclusions

From these various uses of the term God one draws two main conclusions. This section elaborates these along with a corollary question that arises.

One's Creations

Although God might represent some external quality or principle for Winnicott (e.g., fate), God is more often representative of inner qualities projected outward (e.g., "original goodness," badness). Thus, the concept of God that one forms has personal dimensions that get overlooked. "The idea of God is at the same time separated off from the individuals who collectively create and re-create this God concept" (Winnicott, 1963j, p. 94). Note that although God concepts draw from "collective" interactions in this ongoing process, there also is an "individual" element in shaping these ideas. It is these inner experiences that give God concepts a personal character. In projecting these internal qualities onto God, God to some extent becomes one's own creation.

Winnicott (1963j) further observed that in shaping a concept of God one came to understand one's own internal life better.

The saying that man made God in his own image is usually treated as an amusing example of the perverse, but the truth in this saying could be made more evident by a restatement, such as: man continues to create and re-create God as a place to put that which is good in himself, and which he might spoil if he kept it in himself along with all the hate and destructiveness which is also to be found there." (p. 94)

As noted earlier this fashioning and re-fashioning an understanding of God helps one come to terms with both one's sense of goodness and badness.

Whole Objects

In Winnicott's analogical use of the term God he once noted that God might come into awareness as a whole object, much as the father might. In elaborating his thoughts on God as representative of the stage of individuality he connected the emergence of monotheism to the infant's dawning awareness of the father. Unlike the mother, who begins as a part object in the infant's awareness, the father can be the child's first encounter with a whole or integrated object. From this association Winnicott (1969l) noted that one might easily move to the concept of monotheism or one God. Winnicott made it clear that in making this argument he was not reiterating Freud's notion that monotheism was a projection of repressed ideas about the father but rather that both ideas (monotheism, having a father) were humanity's earliest recognitions of individuality. What is significant here is that in connecting the God of monotheism to the notion of the father as a whole object, Winnicott provided a way to think about God as a whole object. This does not mean that God cannot continue to be related to as part object at times, but this way of understanding God creates the potential for a more mature way of relating to God. That is, God has the potential to take on qualities other than one's projections, to be an object with its own reality.

The movement toward the ability to experience and interact with whole objects Winnicott (1971k) tied to his concept of object usage and the object's survival of the infant's fantasized destruction. Object usage refers to the infant's developing ability to perceive the external world as more than his or her projections onto it. By "use" Winnicott meant the opposite of utilitarian or narcissistic use. Object usage means the object is granted its own subjectivity and reality; it is no longer simply the object of one's fantasies and projections. Thus, the ability to "use objects" signals maturity in the person and in his or her relationships. One recalls that the mother's ability to survive her infant's needs and fantasies is another aspect of her care that can be transferred to God (cf. Hopkins, 1989). Like the mother who survives and thus becomes "real" in her own right (an object for use), so God can come to be seen in similar manner (cf. Ulanov, 2001). Though Winnicott does not develop the connection between object usage and God in an explicit manner, the implication for such identification is there and may have been part of his interest in the character of Jesus.

In thinking about the possibility of God being a whole object it is important to note that God is not presented simply as representative of good or bad, but as projections of both. Although such projections could engage in splitting, with God being alternately good or bad for a given person, that God may hold both projections further opens up the possibility to engage a more complex view of God as whole object rather than part object.

Is God "Real"?

If God is a projection, a creation that partakes of one's inner world, this raises the corollary question of whether God is real for Winnicott; that is, more than a psychic projection. As seen above, Winnicott primarily referred to God in terms of psychological processes: the "idea" of God, projections, the capacity for "belief in"). This is what one would expect from the psychoanalyst. Unlike the theologian, one does not anticipate that the psychoanalyst would deal with more than the psychic reality of God. And yet it is an interesting question. Did Winnicott ever express a specific belief in God?

Goldman (1993) observed that Winnicott once expressed value in a belief in God when he remarked in comments about democracy how helpful it is when the sitting monarch proclaims a belief in God (Winnicott, 1950e). Although it is obvious that Winnicott affirms the monarch's belief in God as important, such a belief is couched in terms of its social utility or function. Thus, the remark provides little insight to specific beliefs Winnicott may have held about God.

There is only one place where Winnicott takes up the question of whether there might be a real God apart from the ideas of God that one constructs. In a discussion of transitional objects and phenomena he expands upon the paradox that the baby created the object that was found:

> [I]n theology the same thing appears in the interminable discussion around the question: is there a God? If God is a projection, even so is there a God who created me in such a way that I have the material in me for such a projection? . . . [T]he paradox must be accepted, not resolved. The important thing for me must be, have I got it in me to have the idea of God? – if not, then the idea of God is of no value to me (except superstitiously). (Winnicott, 1968g, p. 205)[3]

There are several ideas here: that God can be a projection; that having an idea of God is preceded by having something in one prior to this that makes it possible (i.e., the capacity for "belief in"); that there is a paradox in the very question because God is both external and created by the infant.

Winnicott (1968g) was clear that simply acknowledging God as a certain kind of psychic reality (i.e., a projection), did not allow one to dismiss the larger question of whether there was "a God who created me in such a way that I have the material in me for such a projection" (p. 205). Winnicott's answer to the question of the reality of God was to acknowledge a complexity in the very question itself. There is a paradox here that must be accepted and not resolved. God, even as psychic phenomena, inhabits the intermediate area of transitional phenomena where it becomes impossible to answer the question: did you create this or was it given? As they do with teddy bears and security blankets, parents and culture leave lying around images of God which the child can pick up and make creatively its own, much like the child does when he or she turns a handed over teddy bear into a true transitional object. Further pressure to explain the reality of this intermediate area that takes contributions from both the external environment and internal experiencing must be resisted for Winnicott. Thus, even the question of whether there is an ontological God over against one's psychological God seems misguided to him.

Thus, one understands that an image of God is not simply subjective reality; neither is it entirely an object of external reality. From the cultural object "God" the child constructs a particular "God" that includes its own creative imaginings. It is a mistake to think of such a God as simply a psychic fantasy (cf. Winnicott, 1935). It is just such a God that allows one to feel alive and real because this God participates in both "realities" (and might later become an object for use) (Ulanov, 2001).

Winnicott's God Images and Concepts

If people are continually creating and re-creating God in the personal psychological way Winnicott described (apart from whatever God may be otherwise), one can assume that Winnicott also participated in this process. However, given his position on God's realness and the paucity of direct statements about God one acknowledges that any attempt to construct Winnicott's God concepts is heavily inferential. Nevertheless, it is useful to try and the following reflections summarize the portraits of God that emerge from the uses of the term noted above. Given the complexity of this ongoing process of creating and re-creating God is it not surprising that there are several, rather different pictures from Winnicott.

Distant, Impersonal

On the one hand the God Winnicott portrayed was an emotionally distant God, not unlike fate or nature. As the equivalent of fate or chance such a God might be thought to punish (i.e., "acts of God") in the same way fate might be thought cruel. (Though there is a way in which a punishing God might be thought immanent, this is not the implication of these connections in Winnicott.) Even when God is seen to represent qualities or principles such as goodness this idea of God hardly comes across as personal.

Loving, Close

On the other hand one sees a picture of God as loving and close; a God who provides the kind of holding environment that a good mother provides; who survives; a being who assists human beings toward integration and wholeness; a God who confers a specialness and grants freedom to think. A Creator before whom one "has a right to a development of himself in the direction of his own temperament and talent; indeed it is his duty to his Creator to use all his powers to develop all his parts—bodily, mental and spiritual—in a beautiful proportion" (Winnicott, n.d. 3).

Creative, Playful

A third portrait from Winnicott is that of a creative, playful God. One can see the creative dimension in the analogical references to the God of creation. And yet because creativity is connected to play (a feeling of aliveness), one also infers a playful dimension to God for Winnicott. That is, God represents a sense of aliveness or "being" (Winnicott, 1971j). I would even suggest that Winnicott found a sense of aliveness in the playful way he spoke of God. For instance, the God he so drolly thanked in his comment about being able to get on with thinking for himself following his father's advice indicates playfulness in the way Winnicott thought about God. There also is a playful aspect to the prayer that Winnicott offered to start his autobiographical notes: "Oh God! May I be alive when I die." Even the free association poem about birth control, "The Silent Kill," playfully points to a God who is involved in bringing (unexpected) children into being.[4]

Surviving, Whole

One also sees a God who represents the principle of being and the achievement of individuality; a God who survives aggression and can be a whole object, thus facilitating integration and the achievement of wholeness in others. A God who thus allows one to relate with others as whole objects in turn.

Developmental Sources of Winnicott's God Images and Concepts

According to Winnicott, one's concepts of God have their origins in early caregiving encounters as well as in later encounters with one's cultural environment. Although Winnicott did not go so far as to say that one should be able to point to the origins of a person's God concept, Rizzuto (1979) has sought to extend Winnicott's concepts of transitional objects in the direction of trying to uncover the developmental sources in the formation of one's images of God. Might such a process help illuminate the sources of Winnicott's concepts of God as well as extend one's thinking on the nature of his God concepts? One might think of this last section as an attempt to turn the lens of Winnicott's theory with its implication regarding the formation of God concepts onto his own development. What can one discern regarding the sources of Winnicott's understanding of God? Do incidents from his early development suggest any links with the portraits of God one encounters in his life and work?

Although Winnicott says very little about how his religious upbringing may have shaped his concepts of God, it is obvious from his own work on child development, that his interactions with his parents, the wider household, and his Wesleyan Methodist tradition, would have influenced these. However, since there is little information on the quality of the interactions between the infant Winnicott and his parents, and not much more on the interactions between the child Winnicott and his parents, any comments about this influence have a speculative quality. Similarly, even though Winnicott himself noted that access to the earliest infant-parent interaction was rarely accessible and that psychoanalysts actually placed more faith in a person's analytic re-constructions for understanding the psychic impact of those interactions (cf. Winnicott, 1947b), there is no clinical data available on Winnicott to help re-construct this process (Rodman, 2003). Nevertheless, if one keeps in mind the conjectural nature of the project undertaken in this section, the effort should bear some fruit.

His Mother

For all of Winnicott's writing on the role of mothers and their infants, he says too little about the relationship with his own mother. Already noted was his remark that his lifelong devotion to explaining the role of the mother was in some sense a way to acknowledge the debt to his own mother (Winnicott, 1957d). Yet, Winnicott's feelings about his mother are tinged with ambivalence. He wrote in one place that he seemed to have had too many mothers and too much mothering; "things never quite righted themselves" (Winnicott, 1978, p. 24). So, although he is grateful for his mother, there was a price to be paid as well.[5] It is striking that in his autobiographical notes Winnicott recounted several memories of interactions with his father but none with his mother.

From the various sources that give insight into the quality of Winnicott's relationship with his mother, the overriding fact seems to be her depressions. Rodman (2003) noted that Winnicott told Marion Milner, a longtime associate, that his mother was depressed. An earlier chapter observed how Winnicott's poem "The Tree" indicated that he felt it his task to enliven his mother's depression. Clare's (Winnicott, 1978) report of a letter sent from boarding school one Mother's Day gives the impression of a young boy trying to cheer up his mother and one wonders if Winnicott's tendency to "play the clown" as an adult (with his pratfalls and other physical humor) was not a carryover of his learning to enliven his mother. Writing news to cheer one up is a recurrent theme in letters between Winnicott and his family and friends.[6]

Growing up with a depressed mother whom he felt it his business to enliven reminds one of Winnicott's remarks about the false self that one constructs to meet the gestures required by one's caregiver when one's own gestures are not met. Rodman (2003) has connected Winnicott's struggle to feel real and alive to some deficiency left by a depressed and emotionally unavailable mother. He was left upon her lap as though on a dead tree. Furthermore, the identification with the sufferings of the Christ in his poem "The Tree" may concurrently indicate some identification with his mother's sufferings (Rodman).

Does growing up with a depressed mother influence Winnicott's understanding of God as like fate or chance? Is the emotionally distant God of fate reflective of a depressed and emotionally unavailable mother? Such an inference is reasonable. A mother who is intermittently depressed would convey a sense of God who is not reliably present—perhaps even a God to grow up away from.[7]

Although a depressed mother may have contributed to notions of a distant, impersonal God, might his mother also have contributed to Winnicott's images of God as loving and creative, as able to "hold" one psychologically and emotionally; one who is able to nurture expressions of the true self; a God with whom one can playfully interact, who is connected to creativity in humans. Clare (Winnicott, 1978) described Winnicott's mother as "vivacious and outgoing" (p. 21). Although Clare had never met Winnicott's mother one assumes that her descriptions derive, at least in part, from conversations with her husband (and perhaps with his father and siblings). It is hard to know at this distance the extent to which these qualities may have characterized interactions between Winnicott and his mother, but if present these qualities would have contributed to Winnicott's concepts of God's loving presence.

Perhaps the contributions to the images of a loving, creative God come from the wider circle of "all [Winnicott's] mothers" (Winnicott, 1978, p. 24). Though not without his problems as an adult (after all, Winnicott underwent fifteen years of analysis), his biographers concur with Kahr (1996) that "on the whole, Winnicott seems to have enjoyed a fairly solid and predictable childhood" (p. 7; cf. Phillips, 1988; Rodman, 2003). The overall security of his childhood contributed to his ability to attribute to God qualities not only of holding but of surviving attacks as well; he can envision a God who is there for "use"—to be created and re-created—and yet who creates people in such a way as to have these projections. One must attribute at least part of this way of understanding of God to "good enough" mothering from someone who got Winnicott started off well.

His Father

Whatever the image of God as loving and creative, as able to hold and survive, owed to Winnicott's mothering, his interaction with his father also seems

Whatever the image of God as loving and creative, as able to hold and survive, owed to Winnicott's mothering, his interaction with his father also seems to have contributed to this understanding of God. The positive association between Winnicott's relationship with his father and his understanding of God can be seen in the privileged position given to Winnicott in the walks home from church with his father. These walks conferred specialness on Winnicott, not only in the eyes of his father (Winnicott, 1978), but perhaps in the eyes of his father's God as well. For instance, in the presentation to the Bart's Christian Union (Winnicott, n.d. 3) one glimpsed a portrait of God as conveying specialness and giving one the freedom to think.

Winnicott also associated with his father images of survival and reparation that seem to transfer to God. In his telling of the incident with the Rosie doll, Winnicott stated he learned of his father's ability to survive, even repair the effects of, his childhood aggression. These seem to be qualities Winnicott also applied to God. Recall that an object's survival contributes to its movement beyond the fantasied relationships that belong to part objects to become a whole object. That Winnicott connected this survival and reparation with his father reminds one that the father as a whole object can be associated with God as a whole object. Since the infant generally experiences the father as a whole object the infant draws from this experience to understand God as "one" (Winnicott, 1969l).

However, as with his mother, Winnicott's stories of his encounters with his father also reveal ambivalence in their relationship. The story of being told to read the Bible for himself, while conveying the gift of freedom to think for himself, also has a dismissive quality to it (see chapter 2). Even more telling is the story of the "pained look" in his father's face when Winnicott said "drat" at the dinner table, an incident that figured in his memory of being sent away to boarding school even though Winnicott judged this to have been for his good.[8] Another incident recorded while Winnicott was at The Leys School also is revealing of the quality of the relationship between father and son. Rodman (2003) told of Winnicott's asking a school friend to inquire about his father's feelings about Winnicott pursuing medicine as a career rather than joining his father in the family business. One gathers from a letter to the friend (cited in Rodman) that Winnicott found his father hard to approach; he seemed to have anticipated that his father would not receive this desire very well. Although one must not make too much of single incidents, one wonders if this event reveals a more general attitude that Winnicott experienced in relationship with his father. What one sees in this story is a son who did not know how to interact with his father's reaction, or perhaps how to bear his father's negative judgment. Would this desire be experienced as another disappointment to his father? However, the letter is also revealing in that one saw a son who seems to anticipate that his father would probably come round to the son's desire, though he clearly felt the need for an intermediary to check out his father's attitude.

Is a father who is hard to approach reflective of a distant and hard to approach God, a God akin to fate or chance? Does a father who is alternately sen-

seems Winnicott also takes from his father images of God as distant, emotional-ly uninvolved, hard to approach.

It is important to point out that when one compares Winnicott's images of God with his interactions with his parents, there is not a simplistic, one-dimensional correspondence. This is as one would expect. One's interactions with caregivers are never one-dimensional but what is hoped for is that the pleasant, reliable interactions will outweigh the bad experiences. That is, that there is enough consistency in attending to one's needs in this early care-giving that it is "good enough" to get one started well. Thus, one anticipates that both pleasant, reliable experiences with both parents would be wedded to experiences of failed attunement and that both kinds of experiences would contribute to one's ideas and feelings about God.

His Religious Tradition

Winnicott (1963j) argued that one's concepts of God also draw upon cultur-al traditions about God; sometimes these are "implanted" but in the more opti-mal situation, are left "lying around" for the person to pick up when develop-mentally ready for such concepts. This section looks at how Winnicott's background in Wesleyan Methodism may have contributed to his God images.

First, one would note that the picture of a distant, impersonal God, little more than the laws of nature, is very foreign to Wesley's thought (Collins, 2007; Maddox, 1994). Although Wesley sought to balance God's otherness or tran-scendence with God's communion and closeness to humans, one senses Wesley emphasized God's immanence (cf. Hoffman, 2004, 2007; Wesley, 1786).

This is not to say that there are not elements in Wesleyan Methodism that may comport with Winnicott's concept of a punishing God. For instance, Wes-ley contrasted the holiness of God with the sinfulness of humans, the latter de-serving punishment. "Nothing is more frequently or more expressly declared in Scripture than God's anger at sin and His punishing it both temporally and eter-nally" (Wesley, 1756a, p. 345). It is probably this aspect of Wesleyan Methodist tradition (and Christian tradition in general) that Winnicott had in mind when he spoke of a punishing God. Similarly, Winnicott's struggle over original sin probably draws from this aspect of Wesleyan Methodist tradition.

However, to simply focus on God's punishment is to miss an important di-mension of how Wesley presented the concepts of holiness. Though God pun-ishes sin for Wesley, this is not a sign of God's distance or lack of involvement. God's holiness is never separated from God's love in Wesley (Collins, 2007). The God who calls one to holiness of life empowers this possibility. It is only when God's holiness is divorced from God's love that one gets an image of God as punisher. When the two are held together in a Wesleyan fashion, one sees that it is God's gracious character that triumphs. God is "a God of unblemished jus-tice and truth: but above all is his mercy" (Wesley, 1790b, p. 62).

It is this latter quality of God's mercy that points one to the dominant image of God in Wesleyan Methodism and that is of a loving God, who graciously calls all to a life of holiness made possible by God's indwelling presence. Wesleyan scholars agree that the chief defining quality of God for Wesley was God's love (Collins, 2007; Maddox, 1994; Runyon, 1998; Wynkoop, 1967). God's love for Wesley was "his reigning attribute, the attribute that sheds an amiable glory on all his other perfections" (Wesley, 1755b). This love was a holy love but also a gracious love available to all. The connection between God's loving grace and Winnicott's concept of holding has been noted. God, like the mother, makes the first move toward the dependent child. God, like the mother, survives the child's aggression and fantasies, and reflects back to the child that it is loved.

God's loving grace is manifest in several ways. It is found in the freedom to think and chose for oneself. Human freedom for Wesley was a gift of God; it was in the nature of the way God created that God gave freedom of choice (cf. Wesley, 1745, 1791). Wesley grounded this notion of human freedom in God's character as loving and gracious. One also would connect God's loving (and non-coercive) grace to Winnicott's (n.d. 3) understanding that God gave space for expression of the true self. God (as I AM) gives a person permission to be the true self that he or she is. The human can "be" because God is "being" (Winnicott, 1971j). The new life made available by God's indwelling spirit manifests both God's creative ability as well as God's loving grace. In calling people to a life of holiness, Wesely made it clear that response to such a call also was a gift of God's grace. Furthermore, the ability to follow a life of holiness was possible only because the indwelling "holy Spirit" of God transformed one by love. The "infinite and eternal Spirit of God . . . is . . . the immediate cause of all holiness in us" (Wesley, 1749, p. 82).

Thus, one sees that Winnicott's Wesleyan Methodist tradition also influenced his understandings of God. On the one hand, it contributed to the notion of a punishing God, though Winnicott's portrayal of this aspect of his tradition seems one dimensional and not an idea he appears to endorse (at least in the one dimensional way he presented this image). Perhaps he is only acknowledging a common cultural understanding of God with this language. On the other hand, Winnicott's seems to have drawn upon his Wesleyan tradition in his understanding of God as able to hold, to survive aggression, to grant freedom of choice, and to nurture the expression of the true self.

Thus, Winnicott's concepts of God present one with a mixed picture. From experiences with his parents and his religious tradition he has constructed concepts of God with both positive and negative qualities. There is a distant God who is a repository for the accidents, diseases, and misfortunes that befall humans, a God akin to fate or perhaps the laws of nature. Conversely, one encounters a God who can survive one's anger, who can hold like a mother, and who grants freedom to think. It is not surprising that a concept as complex as God should include such varying pictures; it would be more surprising if it did not. What is more relevant is to ask whether any of these images seemed more dominant for Winnicott. That is a harder question and impossible to answer with any certainty. From the material he has left, it seems the adult Winnicott struggled with the idea of God. As with his feelings of his parents, one encounters ambivalence about God in Winnicott (and this ambivalence may contribute to the previously noted ambivalence regarding his identifying himself as a practicing Christian. See chapter 9). Perhaps a freedom-granting God, like his father, is also dismissive. There is a part of him that finds God less available. Perhaps he found it difficult to relate consistently to God as a "whole object." However, his ambivalence runs both ways. Even in his affirmation of a God who is equivalent to the laws of nature one recalls that these laws held a certain fascination and wonder for Winnicott. There is that part of him, perhaps so deeply influenced by his early care-giving experiences, that knows of the potential for a loving, caring, freeing God. And he seems to have some experience of this God in the freedom he finds to think for himself. Perhaps the best one can do is to point to some of the sources for this ambivalence in his early background and leave it there.

Notes

1.   These comments, especially about the cultural assumptions of a punishing God lead one to ask whether Winnicott also accepted the idea of God as punishing? One gets a sense from the playful quotations that he was poking fun at such an idea rather than embracing it. That Winnicott's own understanding of God was different than this is seen more clearly in a comment made in the manuscript for his talk at Bart's Christian Union (Winnicott, n.d. 3). There he remarked "what is the cunning distinction between the attributing to God of vengeance and the will eternally to torment, and the vulgar anthropomorphism of the heathen worshipper of wooden gods and gods of stone?" As a "man of deep thought" Winnicott did not see this as a vision of God that reflected "the life and teaching of Christ."

2.   It is interesting to note that Winnicott (1935) addressed this idea of the psychological origins of a patient's God in his very first psychoanalytic paper, noting that people often deny their contribution to these internalized objects. Although Winnicott would continue to be interested in the psychological origins of people's concepts of God, it is important to point out that in later references he moved away from the Kleinian influenced language of "internalized objects," in part because he thought Klein's emphasis on internal objects omitted the role of the external environment. Thus, Winnicott is more apt to speak of God as projection of internal qualities (e.g., a fierce father or place to put original goodness). God is more like a transitional object than an internalized object for Winnicott.

3.   The reference to the "superstitious" value of God referred to the defensive uses of God bound up with inner anxieties. "For in superstition we have no confidence in external reality since it becomes so readily invested with feelings that belong to our inner life" (Winnicott, 1936a, p. 73).

4.   Before leaving this section on Winnicott's explicit statements about God, one needs to ask whether, given his Christian background, he made any explicit statements about Christ that have relevance to this discussion. As with direct references to God, Winnicott

actually spoke directly of Christ very rarely. The only reference to Christ in his published writings occurred in his paper on transitional objects where he referred to the controversy over the nature of the wafer used in the Eucharist and its symbolism of the "body of Christ" (Winnicott, 1951b, p. 234) as a conundrum that might profit from his thinking on transitional phenomena. Even his paper on the "Manic Defense" with its references to the Crucifixion, Resurrection and Ascension as Christian practices only implied Christ without direct mention (Winnicott, 1935). His mention of Christ in his early letter to his sister Violet (Winnicott, 1919) is the only occurrence in his published letters, though he did speak of the life of Jesus in his letter to Bion (Winnicott, 1967f). In his unpublished papers and letters his talk to the Christian Union at Bart's is a rare exception in its attention to Christ (Winnicott, n.d. 3). (He may have mentioned Christ or Jesus in the letter to his brother-in-law about miracles, given the subject matter, but in the absence of the letter, one cannot say with certainty.)

In evaluating Winnicott's references to Christ (or Jesus) it is significant to note that his remarks fall short of treating Christ as an alternate designation for a divine being. In fact, it is clear from his address to the Christian Union at Bart's that he harbored questions about the divinity of Christ, and tended to speak of Christ in that paper as a representative of good deeds without selfish motives. Similarly, Winnicott identifications with Christ (Rodman, 2003; see also chapters 5 and 9) are an identification with the suffering and self-giving of the Christ. Although his remarks about the Eucharistic wafer, the Crucifixion, Resurrection and Ascension, and his comments to Violet that he might be thought blasphemous for describing Christ as a psychotherapist suggest a time when Winnicott thought of Christ as more than a supra-ordinate human this idea is never fully developed. Thus, Winnicott's images of Christ do not cast direct light on his images of God.

5.   Strachey, Winnicott's first analyst, in a breach of ethics reported some dream material from Winnicott in which the mother was seen as a "castrating" presence. Strachey interpreted this as displaced father aggression in Winnicott (Strachey, 1925, p. 330).

6.   Winnicott's letters often have the sense of trying to entertain the reader. One correspondent mentioned receiving a letter from Winnicott that he and his wife read on the way home from the post and ending up laughing so hard that people in the street began to stare (Ede, 1940). Rodman (2003) reprinted a lively letter written to his mother from boarding school in which Winnicott recounted a rugby match complete with drawings of his injuries. Rodman also suggested that the Mother's Day letter with its detailed instructions on how to find the gift he had left for her before returning to school showed a boy's sensitivity to the need to enliven a mother prone to depression. His tendency to play the clown, a trait he was known for in his adult life, may have been learned early on as a way to enliven his mother. Khan spoke of his playing the Charlie Chaplin role at a dinner with Princess Marie Bonaparte and spilling her plate on her lap (Willoughby, 2005). Clare also told stories of his riding his bike with his feet on the handlebars, and driving his car with his walking cane to illustrate his ability to play the clown (Winnicott, 1978).

7.   One might find here an additional reason for Winnicott's drifting away from church religious practice to be religious in his own way. He perhaps tried to avoid reproducing in his religious life what he had to produce in relationship to his mother. That is, he wanted to make his own gesture, even in the realm of religion; he did not want to give the gestures required by the church (e.g., belief in miracles). He wanted to feel real and did not see that happening if he merely repeated the words of the church without somehow coming to his own understandings of theological themes (like the soul, original goodness, and the Jesus story).

8.   Winnicott (1978) also attributed a positive dimension to this event in the sense that he saw in his father's actions a recognition by his father that being left "too much to all [his] mothers" was throwing the young Winnicott's development askew (p. 24). Although Winnicott told the story in a way that affirmed his father's judgment that his new friendships would have led him astray, Phillips (1988) questioned whether such an assessment showed too much deference to the father's actions and failed to appreciate that the story also revealed a father who not only conveyed but felt disappointment in his son. He also raised the question of whether the event is more telling of a general attitude present between father and son. It is interesting to note that the source of all these stories is Winnicott's autobiographical notes. Since they are all remembered rather late in his life and are noted in the same source, they may be illustrative of a theme of ambivalence about the relationship with his father since similar themes are repeated in all three memories (of the Rosie doll, saying drat, being told he was free to find his own answers in the Bible).

Chapter 11
Winnicott's Implicit Theology

"So far I have spoken as an amateur theologian"

In a presentation on "morals and education" to the University of London Institute of Education Winnicott remarked that in the early part of the paper he had spoken as an "amateur theologian" but would now speak as a "child psychiatrist" (1963j, p. 95). In an introduction to a presentation to a conference on family evangelism, he made a similar remark stating that he hoped he had not been invited to speak as a "religious teacher" but as someone long interested in the issues with which humans struggled (1968b, p. 142). These remarks indicate some awareness on Winnicott's part that what he did as a professional had theological implications. Even if he was not always comfortable to speak as a religious teacher or amateur theologian, he recognized the similarity of his interests.

Previous chapters have noted this kind of overlap between Winnicott's interests and religious ones and have pointed to his religious background as playing a key role in such interests. This chapter seeks to place Winnicott's various comments about human nature and the world in which people live into more overt theological categories. Browning (1987) argued that modern psychologies, especially the clinical or psychotherapeutic ones, share much in common with traditional religion in that both "provide concepts and technologies for the ordering of the interior life" (p. 2). That is, they both address at some level questions of "the nature of the world, the purpose of life, and at least some of the basic principles by which life should be lived" (p. 5). (Kirschner's [1996] thesis that developmental psychologies are secular versions of older theological themes is a corollary claim. [cf. chapter 5].) Browning proposed that by asking these kinds of questions modern clinical psychologies have strayed into territory once seen as the exclusive domain of theology. Thus, he concluded that modern clinical psychologies have an "implicit theology" that can be uncovered and described.

This chapter seeks to make explicit the implicit theology to be found in Winnicott's vision of human life. An earlier chapter demonstrated how several of Winnicott's central concepts bear similarity to theological ones (chapter 7) and provided insight into his answers to the kinds of questions Browning noted. This chapter further identifies and elaborates his answers to such questions.

193

Winnicott occasionally spoke directly to these issues; however, most of his work was not concerned with explicit theological questions. Thus, his answers to overtly theological questions often must be discerned from discussions of other concerns. Given the attention that has been drawn to the Wesleyan character of his thought (cf. Hardy, 2003; Hoffman, 2004, 2008; Phillips, 1988), this chapter also compares Winnicott's implicit theology with a traditional Wesleyan one.

As a scholarly discipline, theology covers a wider area than the "study of God" that might be assumed by a simple rendering of the term. Certainly theology takes up the question of the existence and nature of deity, but it also encompasses other questions such as how one can know about such things (epistemology) and the nature of human life and experience (theological anthropology).[1] The former question regarding the sources and means of knowing is often bypassed in psychology with its assumption that knowledge is acquired via the "scientific method" or empirical observations. It is taken up here because of Winnicott's (1945e, 1947d, 1961d, 1967a) oft-repeated distinction between scientific and religious knowing. However, it is the latter area of theological anthropology that especially overlaps with the interests of psychology. This area often leads to reflections on the "human condition" and recognition that things are not as they ideally could be imagined and asks how such gaps might be traversed. Theology treats this last question under the rubric of soteriology. Although there are other areas addressed in a "systematic" approach to theology (cf. Grudem, 1994), the categories enumerated here (cf. Browning, 1987), are sufficient to the task of outlining Winnicott's implicit theology.

Winnicott's Epistemology

Since Winnicott was not a theologian or philosopher there is no place in his writing where he laid out a formal epistemology or systematic attempt to describe how it is people come to know. Nevertheless, he made certain observations with epistemic implications. One can discern Winnicott's epistemology through various comments he made contrasting scientific and religious knowing, in his comments about psychoanalysis as a science, in various comments on the value of intuitive knowing, and through his essay on transitional phenomena.

Scientific vs. Religious Knowing

One often encounters in Winnicott a contrast between scientific and other more "intuitive" (e.g., poetic or religious) ways of knowing. Science, in contrast to these other ways of knowing, was the accumulation of knowledge based on observations (Winnicott, 1957a). "There is some point in making the study of human nature a science, a process characterized by observation of facts, by the building of theory and the testing of it, and by modification of theory according to the discovery of new facts" (Winnicott, 1945e, p. 127). Science is further distinguished from these other ways of knowing in its toleration of "gaps" in knowledge; it can be content with ignorance.

Another way scientific knowing differed from more intuitive ways of knowing according to Winnicott (1947d) was that science tended to exclude judgments based on "feelings" and therefore came to be a bulwark against superstition and magic. He argued that doctors, as practitioners of science, must not fill their gaps in knowing with "magical relief" just because this might make the patient feel better at the time (p. 534). Science, with its basis in "objective observation" rather than feelings became "the modern way of dealing with superstition" (Winnicott, 1957b, p. 71). Part of Winnicott's (1949c) objection to leucotomy (a type of brain surgery used to relieve psychiatric symptoms) was its lack of scientific support; he thought leucotomy a procedure on the "borderline between science and superstition" (p. 547). This observational knowing that belonged to science is contrasted with the intuitive knowing that belonged to poetry and religion (Winnicott, 1945e). In intuitive knowing, one can grasp "a whole truth in a flash" (a very valuable asset in some contexts) while scientific knowing never reaches the whole truth (p. 127).

On occasion Winnicott painted the difference between the two ways of knowing in especially stark terms. For instance, in a presentation to a scientific gathering he reprised an earlier argument noting that science was able to tolerate gaps in knowing, while religion, with its desire for certainty, supposedly was not. (Paradoxically, he also noted that the scientist's ability to tolerate not knowing implied a kind of faith on the scientist's part [Winnicott, 1961d].) Similarly he argued on another occasion that intuitive knowing was a kind of "knowing in advance" that was anathema to scientific knowing. Science, unlike religion, was "free from affiliations" and anyone who knew in advance, who had "seen the light" (a religious metaphor) might know in the way poets know but was far removed from the way science knows (Winnicott, 1967a, p. 236).

The sharp contrast that Winnicott tried to draw between religious and scientific knowing relied upon an older understanding of science rooted in the philosophical movements of empiricism and logical positivism (Bernstein, 1983). These movements highlighted the role of observation and experience of the world through the senses and as an Englishman, Winnicott would have been exposed to this tradition in British education, especially in his medical training (cf. Goldman, 1993). Although such positions were deeply engrained in Winnicott, and strengthened by his exposure to Darwin's thought, Winnicott's defense of such a position became problematic and led to inconsistency in his statements about the different ways of knowing. This inconsistency was especially apparent when Winnicott took up the issue of psychoanalysis as a science. There his defense of the kind of knowing that characterized science became inconsistent with what he said about the scientific nature of psychoanalysis.

Psychoanalysis as Science

The term psychoanalysis covered a great deal of territory for Winnicott. It was a "method for investigating" psychological problems (Winnicott, 1945e, p. 131; 1961d, p. 16), a "treatment" for helping redress those problems (1945e, p. 131) and a "theory" about how those problems developed in the first place (1958b, p. 116; 1961d, p. 13). It is clear that Winnicott (1945e) wanted to argue that psychoanalysis was a "science" (p. 125), but he also was aware of certain problems that attended to this enterprise. He noted that psychoanalysis was distinct from other sciences in a peculiar way: "With our minds we are examining the very minds we are using, and with our feelings we are examining our feelings" (pp. 129). He further acknowledged that many people felt that psychoanalysis could never be a science given this methodology. Nevertheless, Winnicott (1956d) argued that psychoanalysis tried to study human behavior objectively and therefore was disliked by some people because this objective study of human behavior "invades the realms where previously belief, intuition, and empathy held sway" (p. 321).

Because of these problems, although he occasionally spoke of psychoanalysis as a science (cf. Winnicott, 1945e, p. 125), Winnicott was more comfortable to characterize psychoanalysis as an "instrument of scientific research" or "a therapy" but not a science strictly speaking (p. 133). Rather, psychoanalysis might be described as an "applied science," an undertaking dependent on the kind of "scientific research" Freud did (Winnicott, 1961d). What Winnicott argued was that while psychoanalysis as a therapy or treatment was not a science in itself, merely the application of science, it drew upon information (theory) gathered through a scientific method of investigation.

Value of Intuitive Knowing

However, one begins to see holes in Winnicott's reasoning when one looks at how the scientific method of "objective observation" was portrayed when used in psychoanalysis. It underwent a strange twist in meaning. Here direct observations of the external world must defer to psychic realities. "Indeed it may be possible sometimes by direct observation to prove that what has been found in analysis could not in fact exist at the time claimed because of the limitations imposed by immaturity" (Winnicott, 1957e, p. 112). Rather than the "modification of theory according to the discovery of new facts" that supposedly characterized science (cf. Winnicott, 1945e, p. 127), Winnicott argued here that "what is found repeatedly in analysis is not annulled by being proved to be wrong through direct observation" (1957e, p. 112). This inconsistent application of the scientific standard in psychoanalysis is strengthened even further by an earlier statement that implied psychoanalytic theory, or at least the "collective experience of analysts" (Winnicott, 1965d, p. 175), was to be given precedent over external evidence: "Direct observation does not confirm the degree of importance given to the oedipus complex by the psycho-analyst. Nevertheless, the psycho-analyst must stick to his guns, because in analysis he regularly finds it, and regularly finds it to be important" (Winnicott, 1947b, p. 155). This is an odd view of the scientific basis of psychoanalysis.

One thus arrives at a curious juxtaposition in Winnicott's epistemology. Despite his protests that scientific knowing is to be preferred to religious knowing, he actually valued the kind of intuitive knowing that belongs to religion over scientific knowing. The above remarks show Winnicott was not a strict adherent of positivist empiricism (cf. Goldman, 1993) but more an interloper in these fields. Although he argued that "scientific inquiry" must be an "alternative to poetic truth" (Winnicott, 1965d, p. 173) in trying to establish the value of psychoanalysis, in the end he gave precedence to personal clinical experience over what might be objectively observed outside the analysis. "Certain concepts ring true from my point of view when I am doing analysis, and yet ring false when I am looking at infants in my clinic" (Winnicott, 1957e, p. 112). He is more the pursuer of poetic truth than he was comfortable to admit and his admiration of Freud as one always ready to let a "poet or philosopher or his own intuition open up the way for phenomena that had not been covered by the metapsychology of the time" (Winnicott, 1969l, p. 241) betrayed his bias for intuitive knowing.

One especially sees Winnicott's appreciation for intuitive ways of knowing in the many comments he made to mothers about their natural ability to care for their infants. He once compared mothers to artists in that both are often the least able to articulate the purpose of what they do even though they do it exceedingly well (Winnicott, 1949f). He concluded by noting that "if you did it [mothering] all intuitively, probably that was the best way" (p. 5). In another place he observed that intuitive knowing permitted a view of the whole person whereas science often missed this perspective (Winnicott, 1965d).

Thus, there is an inconsistency in Winnicott's valuation of these two ways of knowing. He cannot quite bring together the "scientist-pediatrician" observer of infants with the "applied scientist-analyst" treating his patients. One concludes that Winnicott's dissimilarities between religious and scientific ways of knowing are overdrawn. The disparity between science and religion in which, oddly enough, it is the scientists who have a "faith" in contrast to the certainty that characterized the religious is, of course, a caricature of religion. In addition, when Winnicott spoke of the faith of the scientist, he further blurred the distinctions he was trying to draw. When asked what the scientist had faith in, he was vague, suggesting perhaps in nothing. However, "if there must be faith in something, then faith in the inexorable laws that govern phenomena" (Winnicott, 1961d, p. 14). Faith in the inexorable laws that govern phenomena implies that science also has its "certainty" in the sense of basic convictions about lawful processes. Such a position is much closer to contemporary observations that all epistemological perspectives, including science, have a priori assumptions from which they proceed (Bernstein, 1983; C. Smith, 2003, 2010; J. Smith, 2010).

Transitional Phenomena and Limits of Objective Knowing

Not only are Winnicott's statements about religion a caricature, his remarks about science also fail to reflect some of his discussions of the complexity of knowing. For instance, in his paper on transitional objects and phenomena Winnicott (1951b) confronted the inadequacy of empirical knowing. He introduced the idea of an intermediate area of experience as a way to address the philosophical issues attached to the questions of the relationship of inner (subjective or psychic) and outer (objective or external) reality, the very questions raised by a strict empiricist or positivist view of knowing. If one takes Winnicott's arguments about this intermediate area seriously, then the strict distinctions he tried to draw between scientific and religious ways of knowing collapse. Instead, he offered one a land of paradox where such questions must be allowed and tolerated without simple resolutions. As he summarized near the end of his life: "to some extent objectivity is a relative term because what is objectively perceived is by definition to some extent subjectively conceived" (Winnicott, 1971b, p. 66). Nevertheless, he did not always reflect this more mature sentiment as can be seen from the repetition of some of his earlier distinctions between scientific and religious knowing as late as four years before his death (Winnicott, 1967a).

Summary Statement

Winnicott's distinctions between scientific and religious ways of knowing are overstated. Relying on an older philosophical paradigm (logical positivism), Winnicott failed to acknowledge the commonalities behind all epistemological perspectives (e.g., an appeal to a priori convictions and a reliance on metaphors and narratives to structure human knowing; see Barbour, 1974; Bernstein, 1983; McFague, 1982), as well as his own work on the inadequacies of objective knowing (cf. Winnicott, 1951b). Furthermore, he was inconsistent both in his attempts to keep such ways of knowing separate and in his preferred valuation of scientific knowing. Both the scientist and the religious person are dependent on a prior "capacity" to have faith and despite his occasional trumpeting the superiority of scientific over religious knowing, one actually discovers in Winnicott a clear preference for the intuitive ways of knowing that religion encompassed. His answers to how people come to know and what counts for knowledge demonstrate a heavy dependence upon personal experience, whereby he tried to account for both objective observations of the \ sonal, intuitive insights about these observations.

Comparison with Wesley's Epistemology

If one compares Winnicott's approach to epistemology with ..esley's there are some interesting convergences. For instance, one can find concourse between Wesley's and Winnicott's epistemology in the attention each gives to the role of personal experience in knowing. In some ways, Wesley's (cf. 1738a) emphasis on personal experience (e.g., his doctrine of assurance) has an affinity with Winnicott's appreciation for "intuitive" knowing. Winnicott actually deferred to this kind of knowing as an analytic practitioner, thus undermining the strict, simplistic distinction he was wont to draw between religious and scientific knowing. One might even think of Winnicott's (1951b) concept of the intermediate area as a way to honor the "personal experience" of the infant in addition to whatever external realities are allowed. Such a position echoes Wesley's emphasis on the knowing available through such experience.

One sees other similarities between Winnicott's and Wesley's epistemology in Winnicott's (1961d) reference to the "faith" that scientists have. Winnicott's acknowledgment that scientists also have a faith drew from his reflections on the capacity to "believe in" that preceded any specific beliefs (Winnicott, 1963j). This capacity is rooted in the mother's early reliability which allowed a basic sense of trust (cf. Erikson, 1968) to arise in the infant. In making this kind of statement about the faith of the scientist Winnicott placed all kinds of knowing (including scientific) on a developmentally earlier and similar basis. This approach to epistemology is much closer to post-modernist arguments regarding the social-contextual origins of all knowing (including science) than Winnicott's sharp contrasts allow (cf. Bernstein, 1983; C. Smith, 2010; J. Smith, 2010).

Furthermore, in his admission that the faith of the scientist lay in "the inexorable laws that govern phenomena" (Winnicott, 1961d, p. 14), Winnicott revealed that science and not just religion relied on a priori convictions. This aspect of scientific "faith" is not so different from Wesley's point that Christian faith is rooted in prior convictions about the truthfulness of God (Wesley, 1743a). Wesley of course differed from Winnicott in his openness to more content for one's faith. In addition to a "faith *by which*" one believed, there was a "faith *in which*" one believed for Wesley. Chilcote (2004) summarized this distinction when describing Wesley's focus on the need to join the "form" with the "power" of the Christian life: "each of us needs not only a faith *in which* we can believe (the external, objective aspects of the Christian faith, such as its creeds, its story of Jesus and its forms of worship); we also need a faith *by which* we can believe (the internal, subjective action of the believing self in relation to Jesus)" (p. 59). The description of a "faith by which" one believed before there are spe-

...fic things "in which" one has faith is similar to Winnicott's (1963j) point about a prior capacity for belief in before one has specific beliefs. However, the faith in which one believes points to more specific content of one's faith for Wesley.

In drawing attention to the similarities between Winnicott's and Wesley's epistemology the most significant difference to account for is the one Winnicott tried to draw between the "faith" that belonged to science and the "certainty" (Winnicott, 1961d) and "knowing in advance" (Winnicott, 1967a) that belonged to religion. What is the nature of this distinction for him? What Winnicott specifically had in mind in dissociating faith from religion is not clear. Perhaps his reference to the certainty of religion disparaged the kind of "simple faith" his father held though this is far from clear. That he cared little for an unquestioning, dogmatic religion is clear (Winnicott, 1954d); that his father's faith was of this nature is not so clear (see chapter 2). Perhaps he had in mind the Wesleyan emphasis on "assurance," a doctrine by which Wesley sought to affirm a kind of knowing or certainty about one's salvation that was rooted in personal experience (cf. Clapper, 1989), though this too seems doubtful.[2] More likely he was thinking of the religious notion of revealed knowledge, one of the chief ways that theologians address epistemological questions (e.g., sources and means of knowing). When speaking of Wesley's epistemology, scholars often note the sources Wesley offered for defending religious convictions: Scripture, reason, "tradition," and experience (the so-called Wesleyan Quadrilateral, see Maddox, 1994; Outler, 1985). Although each of these means play a role in Wesley's epistemology, he saw Scripture as the primary source for establishing the truth of Christian doctrine and the definitive source for understanding the gracious revelation of God's nature and work (cf. Wesley, 1786). Winnicott's reference to the knowing in advance that can characterize religion is most likely a reference to this Wesleyan notion of the "revealed" knowledge in Scripture and this would be an area of difference in Winnicott's and Wesley's epistemologies.

However, there also are several similarities between Winnicott's and Wesley's epistemologies: in their appreciation for personal experience, their use of a priori convictions, and their metaphors of a "faith" or "belief in" that precedes specific faith content. Thus, despite Winnicott's attempts to make stark distinctions between religious and scientific knowing, one sees that there are more similarities between religious and scientific knowing than Winnicott would admit at times and that his "practical" epistemology was not as far removed from his Wesleyan Methodist heritage as he might have thought (or wished).

Winnicott's Anthropology

The turn to theological anthropology takes up several related questions. In theology the subsection devoted to anthropology seeks to answer two basic questions: what is the essential nature of the human, and what is the nature of the human "condition." This latter question addresses the recognition that humans are not all that they could be or aspire to be and inquires how this condition arose. Theological anthropology is closely related to the category of soteriology (to be taken up in the next section) in that the latter offers answers to the "problem" of the human condition.

Because questions regarding the essential nature of humans and the conditions in which they find themselves are the areas in which psychology and theology overlaps the most (cf. Browning, 1987; Oden, 1978), it is in his reflections on these questions that one finds some of Winnicott's most overtly theological statements. This section takes up Winnicott's thoughts on the essential nature of the human, including the nature of the soul as well as his reflections on the nature of the human condition which takes in his thoughts about original sin and original goodness among other topics. This section draws from Winnicott's explicit statements about these topics as well as from comments about human nature made in other contexts to summarize his key ideas regarding human beings. These views are then compared with a Wesleyan anthropology.

The Essential Nature of the Human

Winnicott's thoughts on the essential nature of the human are found in various comments on how a sense of self as separate from the environment comes to be, the potential of the true self, the nature of the soul, and whether humans have choices or are determined. His reflections on these topics are taken up under the headings of the social-relational nature of the human, the concepts of a psychosomatic unity and a sacred core in humans, and the question of human agency.

Humans as Social/Relational Being

The social/relational dimension of humans is critical to Winnicott's anthropology and is a foundational assumption to several other key ideas including his thoughts on the true self and the integration of the personality. Winnicott (1952a) gave clear articulation to this dimension of human nature in his famous statement that "there is no such thing as a baby" (p. 99). As he further disclosed:

> I was alarmed to hear myself utter those words and tried to justify myself by pointing out that if you show me a baby you certainly show me also someone caring for the baby, or at least a pram with someone's eyes and ears glued to it. One sees a "nursing couple." In a quieter way today I would say that before object relationships the state of affairs is this: that the unit is not the individual, the unit is an environment-individual set up. (p. 99; cf. Winnicott, 1947a, p. 137)

For Winnicott (1960i) each new human begins in "absolute dependence" upon another, though this dependence is not initially recognized. Only through the good-enough ministrations of the m/other is the new individual, this "kernel (which has looked all the time like a human baby to us)," able to emerge and later perpetuate the cycle (Winnicott, 1952a, p.99). Without this crucible of social and relational connections, the new individual never emerges from the "shell."

However, human life does not just *begin* in a social matrix (a "facilitating environment") it also finds its *fullness* in relationships with others. Although Winnicott paid particular attention to the earliest stages of human development and its contingencies, he also made it clear that healthy individuals are those who can have meaningful relationships with others as "whole objects" and not simply as projections of their own desires and needs; this level of human interaction he called "object usage" and for him it represented the highest level of relational maturity (Winnicott, 1971k). Object usage did not mean exploitation for Winnicott but designated mature relating in which both self and other had their separate existence. One further sees this emphasis on the social/relational nature of the human in Winnicott's (1958a) observation that even the capacity to be alone (another indicator of mature emotional development) owed its emergence to one having first learned to be alone in the presence of another.

A Sacred Core in Humans

Another essential quality in humans for Winnicott (1963a) was the presence of a sacred core. A previous chapter noted that several scholars called attention to the similarity of this idea to religious concepts of the soul (e.g., Goldman, 1993; Hoffman, 2004; Phillips, 1988; Rodman, 2003). It is important to remember that although Winnicott was interested in the nature of the soul, it is not his reflections on the soul that best describe this sacred core for him. Rather, he gravitated to his notion of the true self to speak of this sacred core in humans.[3] He described the true self as something inviolable in humans, a sense of aliveness and realness that made life worth living, a sacred center that was incommunicable (Winnicott, 1963a). It represented the creative potential of humans; a desire to be who they truly were rather than comply with external impositions (Winnicott, 1960e, 1964a). Although he connected the soul to the true self on one occasion (Winnicott, 1954c, p. 162), it was clearly the latter term that best described the sacred core that he saw as an essential quality of the human. In his presentation to the Bart's Christian Union (Winnicott, n.d. 3), he even argued that striving to be one's true self was an obligation owed to one's Creator.

The true self originated in early infant movements ("spontaneous gestures" [Winnicott, 1960e, p. 148]); as these spontaneous gestures were appropriately attended to by the mother, the true self emerged as the center of aliveness and realness for the infant. A failure to respond appropriately to these early gestures, either through neglect or through asserting the mother's needs over the infant's, caused a compliant false self to arise (Winnicott, 1960e). Thus, although the true self lay within the human as a potential it did not always emerge. Nevertheless, because it was present as potential in everyone, Winnicott saw it as an essential quality of human nature.

Unity of the Psyche-Soma

Winnicott (1954c) also saw a deep psychosomatic unity in humans. The psyche was "the imaginative elaboration of somatic parts, feelings, and functions; that is, of physical aliveness" for Winnicott (1949g, p. 244). Thus, the psyche was dependent upon somatic functioning, including brain functioning (Winnicott, 1954c).[4] This fundamental unity between psyche and soma was an early and necessary step toward health for Winnicott. Its absence left one open to "unthinkable anxieties" (Winnicott, 1962b) and "primitive agonies" (Winnicott, 1963e). Although Winnicott variously spoke of this unity as the "psyche indwelling the soma" (1954c), the achievement of "unit status" (1960i) or "personalization" (1970a) what he sought to convey was the absolute necessity of this "integration" of psyche and soma for health and maturity (1964f). Furthermore, Winnicott (1962d) saw this striving for integration of the personality as a chief motivation in humans.

Free vs. Determined

Another quality of humans often discussed in theological anthropology is the extent of human freedom and choice over against destiny and determinism. Surprisingly, this is a quality about which Winnicott says very little. His most obvious comment came in a discussion of the roots of psychoanalysis. In acknowledging his debt to Freud (and Darwin) and thus to a naturalistic approach to human nature Winnicott (1969c) noted that any theory of emotions and personality, especially those indebted to Freud, began with deterministic assumptions. According to Winnicott, these theories were extensions of the findings from biology, chemistry and physics. This assumption of naturalistic determinism is reinforced by Winnicott's (1961d) comment that the scientist had "faith in the *inexorable laws* that govern phenomena" (p. 14, emphasis added). Similarly, Winnicott's (1966d, 1967e, 1970a, 1971c, 1971d) several references to "fate" imply a deterministic universe.

Although he recognized determinism as a philosophical problem, Winnicott was much more concerned with practicalities than with theory (cf. Phillips, 1988; Rodman, 2003). At the practical level he noted that most people have a sense of being able to choose most of the time and this experience of feeling free to choose made the theory of determinism irrelevant (Winnicott, 1969c). In health people experienced themselves as able to choose; it was the lack of a feeling of choice that made some "psychiatrically ill" (p. 230). Winnicott described a sense of freedom in which people felt as if and acted as though they were free to choose despite his concurrent belief in naturalistic determinism. Practically, this made determinism more a psychological than a philosophical problem for him. Thus, although Winnicott spoke of determinism as a reality of the natural world, the kind of determinism he described is one that philosophers describe as "soft determinism" (Butterfield, 1998; Kapitan, 1999; Strawson, 1998).

Soft determinism means that humans have real choices in some areas (e.g., choosing to read this book) while recognizing that human choice is not un-bounded (e.g., one could not choose to fly unaided). Thus, Winnicott's com-ments about this practical sense of freedom are very close to this philosophical position regarding soft determinism. Certainly, he himself lived "as though" he had choices and his practice as a therapist would have been meaningless had he not held some hope that clients could make different choices.

Even the emergence of limited choice for humans owed its origins to the processes of early development for Winnicott. As noted above, early develop-ment begins in a social-relational matrix in which the mother-infant dyad pre-cedes any sense of the infant as a "unit" in itself (Winnicott, 1952a, p. 99). Thus, any later sense of choice or agency could only arise if the infant got "started off well" via the mother's attendance to the infant's need (Winnicott, 1968b). If the environment was not sufficiently facilitative, a healthy sense of self and thus choice did not emerge. For Winnicott (1956f, 1960i), whatever sense of agency one has is indebted to appropriate responses by one's early care-givers.

The Nature of the Human Condition

A second set of questions that theological anthropology deals with are those that inquire into the human "condition," by which is meant that one recognizes that all is not as it could be with the human, that there is greater potential than is currently manifest. Thus, to speak of the human condition is to address some-thing of the limits that humans experience. In theology this usually takes in questions regarding the purposes for which humans were created and the reasons for failing to achieve these purposes. This latter condition is often addressed under the rubric of being "fallen" (cf. Grudem, 1994), a way to speak of the bro-kenness and alienation that humans experience. The search for this dimension of Winnicott's anthropology takes one to his reflections on original goodness vs. original sin and on the nature of the environment in which one finds oneself.

Original Goodness vs. Original Sin

Insights into Winnicott's view of the human condition are gained from re-calling his ideas concerning an original goodness that belongs to humans. As observed in chapter 7 Winnicott (1963j) argued for an original goodness that was tied to his ideas about innate moral tendencies in infants. These tendencies were an expression of a creative potential in humans that developed toward an ability to care (be concerned) for those who in their turn were providing con-sistent, reliable care that allowed such innate tendencies to flourish in the child. Winnicott contrasted this view of an original goodness in the child with religious traditions that assumed an "original sin" that required "implanting" morality in children. This contrast of original goodness with original sin was one of the few overtly theological remarks Winnicott made and invites further investigation in order to better understand the distinction Winnicott thought himself making.

There are only three occasions where Winnicott (1963j, 1966c, 1971b) specifically mentioned the concept of original sin and in none of these places did he expound upon its meaning beyond an assumption that it pointed to some "inherited" quality of badness that overshadowed an innate goodness. For Winnicott, the doctrine of original sin was a place where religion had gotten things wrong, failing to appreciate an innate goodness that was more the norm in human development.

However, Winnicott's position on original goodness did not mean he was unaware of times when these innate tendencies toward goodness did not flourish. Especially through his work with his patients Winnicott saw various failures of the innate goodness to flower in manifestation of the false self (1960e), in aggression that was motivated to hurt (1964i, 1968h), and in various psychotic and self-disorders (1955b, 1959-1964, 1963b, 1965e, 1967b).

However, such brokenness and alienation were not the norm for Winnicott. He wanted not only religion, but psychoanalysis to embrace this idea of an innate goodness. It was his stress on original goodness over against an inherited badness that caused Winnicott (1971b) to so strongly object to Klein's (cf. 1948) position regarding the centrality of the death instinct. He saw her as arguing that the roots of aggression were hereditary; for him this argument was akin to reintroducing the doctrine of original sin. In contrast, Winnicott (1958f) argued that before there was aggression properly understood, there was simply "motility"—an original, spontaneous gesture without intent to harm; a gesture that pointed to an original creativeness and goodness in humans.[5]

Benign vs. Impinging Environment

Corresponding to this original goodness in the infant, Winnicott (1963j) also assumed the presence of a benign or favorable environment that met the infant's innate tendencies to goodness. Even though Winnicott spoke of the world as fated or determined, it was not malevolent. It is clear that Winnicott (1968b, 1969i, 1970a) thought the typical environment one that met the infant's needs in a good enough manner. Substantial environmental impingement and failure, although clearly obvious in some cases (e.g., 1950b, 1958e, 1958h, 1963e), was the exception and not the norm for Winnicott. Those who had suffered such impingements and failures he saw aplenty in his practice, but the larger population did not need therapy or analysis because the norm was the "ordinary devoted mother" (1966i) who provided reliable care that started most people off well.

Thus, Winnicott's description of the primary maternal environment posits an essentially benign world. That is, people generally experience the environment as more beneficent than malevolent, more reliable, more satisfying of needs, than not (cf. Strenger [1997] on Winnicott's hopeful vision of the world). Recall his comment that one need not assume an original state of chaos for the infant: "At the beginning before each individual creates the world anew there is a simple state of being" (Winnicott, 1954c, p. 135). Because he assumed a benign environment as the norm, even "antisocial tendencies" were a sign of hope for him (Winnicott, 1967d). Antisocial tendencies, in contrast to outright delinquency, were an attempt to regain something once had but now lost (i.e., a good enough environment). If someone could recognize this and respond in a way to help the child recover some sense of a reliable environment, antisocial tendencies need not become hardened into antisocial disorder sustained by various secondary gains such as easily gotten goods or revenge (Winnicott, 1950b, 1956a).

Summary Statement

It is in the area of anthropology (view of the human) that theology and psychology overlap the most. Anthropology takes up questions of the destiny and purpose of humans, their essence, and their potential and limits. Winnicott's answers to these questions portray the human as a social-relational being, with a psychosomatic unity and sacred core. Humans have a limited though practical freedom to choose and an innate or original goodness. They are destined to be their true selves and even owe it to their Creator to be so (Winnicott, n.d. 3).

Comparison with Wesley's Anthropology

This section compares Winnicott's and Wesley's views of the human in order to explore the depths to which Winnicott's view has been shaped by a Wesleyan view of human nature and destiny. It extends previous discussions of the influence of Winnicott's Wesleyan Methodist heritage on both the form and content of his thought by making explicit the theological vision of the human that guided and played counterpoint to Winnicott's own. One discovers both expected and unexpected convergences and divergences.

Social-Relational Being

Winnicott's characterization of the human as social-relational being has its counterpart in Wesley's theology. Wesley saw the creation narrative of Genesis portraying humans as created for relationship with God and with others (Collins, 2007; Maddox, 1994; Runyon, 1998). Thus, it belongs to the essential nature of humans that they are made for and thrive through connections and relationship with the Other/other. In this paradigm, one understands the results of the disobedience of the first couple to be not simply guilt over the broken commandment, but a breach in the relationship both with God and with each other (Maddox).

Wesley drew attention to this social-relational dimension by pointing to the central command in Christianity to love God and love neighbor (cf. Mt 22:37-39; Wesley, 1743a, 1777). Wesley further recognized that the Christian life flourished in a social context. This can be seen in his emphasis that Methodists should meet in small groups to encourage one another in their quest to live holy lives. Wesley spoke of Christianity as a "social religion" by which he meant both the living out of holiness in love of neighbor, but also the social connections of the societies in encouraging one another in the life of holiness. "Christianity is essentially a social religion, and that to turn it into a solitary religion is indeed to destroy it. . . . I mean not only that it cannot subsist so well, but that it cannot subsist at all without society, without living and conversing with other men" (Wesley, 1748c, pp. 533–534).

However, Wesley also was clear that the perfection of love in humans did not belong to human effort alone. The activation of such love came through the Spirit of God who communicated God's love toward us. "We must love God before we can be holy at all; this being the root of all holiness. Now we cannot love God till we know he loves us. . . . And we cannot know his pardoning love to us till his Spirit witnesses it to our spirit" (Wesley, 1746d, p. 274). Thus empowered by such love, humans cannot but help love others; "Nay, the love of God constraineth those in whose hearts it is shed abroad to love what bears his image" (Wesley, 1733, p. 334).

It is interesting to note some connections between a Wesleyan anthropology and Winnicott's view of the social-relational nature of humans. First, Wesley's argument that the love of neighbor resulted from first being loved by an O/other, reminds one of Winnicott's (1956f, 1968d) descriptions of the mother's role in facilitating the emergence of a separate sense of self, a necessary step to being able later to relate to others in healthy and mature ways. Second, for Winnicott (1960i) the social-relational nature of humans meant that each new person began life in "absolute dependence" on another. Wesley (1739) saw a similar correspondence regarding human dependence on divine grace. Ulanov (2001) pointed to this absolute dependence at the beginning of life and its connection to the deepest of religious yearnings.

> Religion in its liturgy and its disciplines of spiritual direction encourages us to return to the gaps in ourselves, to go back for what we missed, to look for the dependence that someone failed to meet, and to bring our needs to God. Christian tradition endorses this searching as right behavior; it enjoins us to search for the lost sheep, to scour our house to find the missing mite, to welcome the prodigal son home, to eat with the tax collector, to receive the whore. Not only is dependence not to be avoided or defended against; we are urged to acknowledge it. (pp. 119-120)

She concluded by noting "religion urges us to recognize our dependence as creatures on a Creator as our true state. Religion puts dependence right at the center of authentic living" (p. 120) by reminding one that one's existence was and is dependent upon connection to an O/other.

Sacred Core in Humans

Winnicott's notion that there is a sacred core in humans directly echoes his Wesleyan Methodist background. Although Winnicott showed a general reluctance to attribute this quality to a divine source, to speak of anything as sacred (as he did of the true self—cf. Winnicott, 1963a) is to invoke religious symbolism.

A previous discussion pointed out how closely Winnicott's concept of a sacred core in humans was to similar religious concepts in Wesley (chapter 7). Both used a variety of terms to speak of this sacred center, including "soul" and "spirit." One would add here that Winnicott came to prefer the term "true self" to speak of this dimension of human nature while Wesley was more apt to speak of the *imago Dei* to capture this aspect (e.g., Wesley, 1746f, 1759, 1760a; cf. Maddox, 1994). One further observes that a difference between Winnicott and Wesley's view of this sacred core is the latter's greater openness to attributing it to a supernatural source, although in his unpublished manuscript for the audience at the Bart's Christian Union Winnicott (n.d. 3) acknowledged that pursuit of the true self is something owed to one's Creator.

Psychosomatic Unity

These comments on a shared belief in a sacred core in humans point to another area where Winnicott's thoughts on human nature seem to have been influenced by Wesley's theological anthropology. Wesley, like Winnicott, had argued for a psychosomatic unity in humans. There are differences in the way each articulated this unity, but the similarity makes one wonder if Winnicott may have been sorting through ideas from his religious background as he reflected on this aspect of human nature. For instance, both Wesley and Winnicott used the term "soul" to refer to the interior life and then to argue for the dependence of these interior functions on organic functionality (Wesley, 1782, 1788b; Winnicott, 1951a, 1954c).[6] One might also recall that Winnicott's resonance with embodied experience has a corollary in Wesley's affinity for an embodied spirituality.

However, in noting these similarities one also must observe a key difference in the way Winnicott and Wesley characterized the psychosomatic unity of humans. For Winnicott, as a scientist, human functioning, including emotional and mental functioning, remained grounded in the material (somatic) functions. Although Wesley acknowledged a material foundation for mental functioning, he also made it quite clear that his articulation of the psychosomatic unity embraced non-material (i.e., spiritual) aspects of the human as well. Thus, Wesley's anthropology differed from Winnicott's in that Winnicott did not venture into the realm of "non-material" being. One sees the practical implications of this difference by observing that damage to the soul for Winnicott (1954c) derived from brain damage. For Wesley, damage to the soul would include one's alienation from God (cf. Collins, 2007; Maddox, 1994). One is left to conclude that although Winnicott's and Wesley's notions of psychosomatic unity share common ground in an appreciation for the unity of the emotional and physical life, Wesley saw a further unity between the material and non-material that Winnicott did not embrace.

Choice and Freedom

Perhaps the clearest difference between Wesley's and Winnicott's view of the human is found in their positions on human agency. Wesley's robust defense of human choice and freedom as a gift of God's gracious nature seems far removed from Winnicott's soft determinism. Wesley argued his position on human agency so strongly that he was often accused of having diminished God's sovereignty (cf. Maddox, 1994, Runyon, 1998). However, Wesley (1739, 1772) was convinced that to see God as not granting humans freedom would have been a travesty of God's nature.[7] Similarly, Wesley's emphasis on human freedom grants humans a clearer role in contributing to their own brokenness than Winnicott's corresponding emphasis on the role of environmental failure.

Nevertheless, despite the philosophical differences between Winnicott's soft determinism and Wesley's resounding argument for human freedom, at the practical level, one sees a strong influence of this Wesleyan teaching on Winnicott's life. He argued that freedom to think for oneself was the great legacy of the religious reformers like Wesley on the ethos of England (Winnicott, 1969g) and that without this freedom to pursue one's own ideas, one lost vitality whether a religious person or psychoanalyst!

Original Goodness

Winnicott's thoughts on original goodness take one to those aspects of theological anthropology that inquire into the purpose and destiny of the human. What were humans created for and what has happened to them (the human condition)? His beliefs in this area were clearly a place where Winnicott (1963j) felt he diverged from his Christian roots. In comparing Winnicott's thoughts with Wesley's in this area one discovers that he is correct about his divergence, though not as much as Winnicott seems to have thought.

Comparing Winnicott's position on original goodness with Wesley's requires a small detour to its theological counterpart: original sin. One would never know from Winnicott's (1963j, 1966c, 1971b) cryptic comments that the doctrine of original sin has a long and varied history in the Christian tradition. It dates at least to the time of Augustine, who seems to have been the first to use this term (Jacobs, 2008), and has become a shorthand to refer to what happened when the first parents sinned. Thus, it deals not only with the "origin of sin," it reflects upon what was lost as a result. The answer to this latter question is contingent upon descriptions of the primeval environment. For Augustine, humans not only lost "life" (i.e., the consequence of death for eating the forbidden fruit), they lost an original state of perfect goodness and righteousness. Thus, all subsequent humans inherited a willfulness that manifested in continued disobedience to God's commandments. The result was that all of human nature (will, reason, passion) was corrupted by this loss (cf. Hughes, 2004; Thomas & Parker, 2004; Vawter, 1983). This Augustinian view of original sin became the dominant view in the Western church and culture and seems to be the one Winnicott had in mind when he used the term original sin.

However, in the Christian churches of the East a different picture of what got passed on (or not passed on) as a result of the sin of the primordial couple arose based upon a different understanding of the nature of creation prior to this first or original sin. Whereas Augustine viewed the world as a place of perfection prior to the sin of the first couple, Irenaeus of Lyons believed God to have placed the first couple into an imperfect world by design so that God might facilitate their spiritual development (cf. Brown, 1975; Minns, 1994; Steenberg, 2004; Thomas & Parker, 2004). Thus, while for Augustine the first sin concerned disobedience and the loss of original goodness, in the Eastern churches, the emphasis fell upon the couple's loss of the intimate relationship with the God who created them. Because Irenaeus painted a picture of a God who created imperfect and immature creatures who needed an ongoing relationship with their Creator to mature, the nature and consequences of the first sin were cast in a more developmental frame. That is, while human nature has suffered as a result of this sin, the nature of the "fall" is not understood in such stark terms as Augustine framed it, because the starting point was different. If there was no perfect, idyllic state to fall from, only an immature state from which to progress forward, then one might inquire as to whether some goodness remained in God's creatures after this "ancestral (vs. original) sin" (cf. Hughes, 2004), and if so, how it might be described.

When one explores Wesley's position on original sin, it may not be surprising at this point to find he offered a mediating position between the Western and Eastern views. Although humans are flawed creatures and not able by good intentions or willpower to do what is pleasing to God for Wesley, nevertheless, in his view one might still speak of "goodness" in humans in two ways: (1) humans are good in that they are creatures of God, made in God's image, and (2) being in the image of God they manifest something of "conscience," though only dimly (Maddox, 1994). Although this dim awareness of God's moral standards is a gift of God's prevenient grace and not properly considered a "natural" quality for Wesley, because everyone is the beneficiary of prevenient grace (at least in some measure), Wesley can state that "everyone has . . . good desires, although the generality of men stifle them before they can strike deep root or produce any considerable fruit. Everyone has some measure of that light, some faint glimmering ray" so that "no man sins because he has not grace, but because he does not use the grace which he hath" (Wesley, 1785, p. 207). Thus, Wesley's doctrine of original sin emphasized the goodness that may yet reside in humans despite their fallen nature; however, he also was clear that such goodness never rose to the level of commending humans for salvation (Williams, 1960).

However, the chief way in which Wesley created space for some remaining goodness in humans is his understanding of the "image of God" in which humans are said to have been created (cf. Gen 1: 26-27). Creation in the image of God was a very fulsome concept for Wesley. For him the *imago Dei* was at the heart of the uniqueness of the human. Created in the image of God, humans had at their core a spiritual element that made them spiritual beings like the God who created them. Being in the image of God meant humans also had deep affections and longings to be reunited with the Creator from whom they had been separated. The image of God in humans was like a beacon that drew them back to their source. For Wesley (1746f, 1759), the goal of humanity was the restoration of the image of God. To speak of the image of God in humans is thus to speak of their central purpose and design, their unique nature. The image of God in humans unites them to their source; it is descriptive of what they truly can be: for Wesley, reflections of the God who created them.

Although Winnicott never addressed the notion of the *imago Dei* directly in his writings, one cannot help but recall his characterizations of the true self when reading Wesley's comments. For Winnicott (1960e), the true self was an ideal state that pointed to what humans could truly be. It longed to find its expression, unhampered by the adaptive compromises that emerged in relationships. Thus, while different from Wesley's understanding of the *imago Dei* in important ways, Winnicott's description of the true self nevertheless evokes similar ideas about the nature of the human. Thus, when Winnicott had the true self in mind it is plausible that what stood behind this idea were certain theological concepts that were very much a part of his Wesleyan Methodist heritage.

One of the central commonalities is that Winnicott (1963j) associated his ideas about original goodness with the creative potential in humans. Original goodness was not so much an innate quality as an innate potential, a capacity that could be developed (or thwarted). The goodness in humans needs another to flourish for both Winnicott and Wesley. Thus, Winnicott's actual articulation of original goodness is not that far from certain ideas in Wesley. Wesley also spoke of the creative potential that is present in humans as a result of God's prevenient grace. The specific potential that humans have to respond positively or negatively to God's invitation pointed to a wider freedom and creativity that belonged to their being in the image of a creative God.

In his argument about whether there is an original goodness in humans (as opposed to original sin), Winnicott (1963j) saw himself at odds with the religious consensus on this position. Although he is correct about being at variance with the predominant, Western view of original sin, he is closer to a Wesleyan position than he himself seems to know. Thus, Winnicott's notion regarding an original goodness in humans reflects an affinity with certain Eastern Christian beliefs that also influenced Wesley (Maddox, 1994). It may be that Winnicott's position on original goodness was mediated by Anglo-Catholic influences of his Wesleyan roots in ways that escaped his conscious mind. Although Wesley would not have agreed with Winnicott's point that such goodness is present un-aided by God, his doctrine of prevenient grace and his understanding of the *imago Dei* create a space in which one can talk about tendencies toward goodness that remain in humans. Winnicott would have valued such a space.

Graced Environment

When one reflects on Winnicott's (1968b, 1969i, 1970a) notion of a benign environment as the norm, one cannot help but recall that the central quality of the world for Wesley is that it is graced by God. Of all the qualities Wesley as-cribed to God (e.g., omnipotence, omniscience, omnipresence, justice, right-eousness, holiness, mercy), love was above all else God's defining attribute (Wesley, 1755b). This love manifested itself as grace toward the world and it inhabitants. Furthermore, God's grace was multi-dimensional for Wesley. Grace meant that God was for humans (rather than against them); it meant that God had made the first step toward the creation. Furthermore, grace characterized the life of God's people from beginning to end. There was prevenient (or preceding) grace, there was present or saving grace, and there was sanctifying (or complet-ing) grace. Thus, grace preceded encounters with God, defined encounters with God and continued to provide empowering presence in one's ongoing journey with God. Even the creation of the world was an expression of God's loving grace (cf. Collins, 2007; Maddox, 1994, Wesley, 1786). Thus, Winnicott's as-sumption about a benign environment as the norm seems to draw again from a Wesleyan perspective on the world.

A Contrast

Nevertheless, despite a common perspective on creating a space for good-ness in humans and seeing the world as a graced environment, one must note a key difference between Winnicott's and Wesley's anthropology. This difference is found in their varying characterization of the human condition and draws up-on an earlier difference regarding the nature of human freedom.

It is hard not to read Winnicott's comments on original goodness and a be-nign environment as overstating the potential for human goodness. Winnicott so favorably characterized human beginnings and the normative environment that images of human brokenness are the exception for him. The human condition seems quite bright for Winnicott.[8] In contrast, religion retains a more somber perspective on human fragmentation and alienation through its ideas of original sin. In trying to rid himself of hereditary understandings of original sin, Win-nicott has muted the imagery and language for speaking about human broken-ness and intractability. By contrast, Wesley is much more appreciative of this dimension of human life. In retaining a doctrine of original sin that blends ideas from both Western and Eastern Christianity, Wesley is able to preserve a vision not only of the goodness in humans and the world, but a way to speak of the absence of goodness as well. Wesley's description of the human condition was that of "fallen" (broken and alienated) creatures whose goodness was insufficient apart from God's grace. Furthermore, humans had a hand in creating this condition through their not using the grace that was available to them. In contrast to this, Winnicott saw a faulty environment to blame for failures of human goodness. Thus, because he emphasized human freedom less than Wesley, Winnicott saw less personal contribution of humans to their condition than Wesley.

Winnicott's Soteriology

The nature of the human condition points to further questions regarding what needs to be done to remedy it (if anything). In theology this is the area of soteriology, the question of a need for salvation or a savior. Thus, soteriology is connected to anthropology in that the nature of the human condition circumscribes what one needs saved from and how such salvation is accomplished. In Christian theology, including Wesley's, this connection between anthropology and soteriology is seen in the use of the traditional metaphors of "creation, fall, and redemption" (cf. Kirscher, 1996) to gather together thoughts on these questions. Thus, Wesley (1746f, 1759, 1760a) described humans as created in the image of God, yet fallen into sin and thus in need of God's grace to renew the image of God in them. This comes more specifically through the person and work of Christ (Collins, 2007; Maddox, 1994). An inquiry into Winnicott's soteriology asks what it is one needs saved from for him, and what form that salvation takes.

Although the metaphors of creation, fall and redemption are helpful as a general paradigm for developmental movement (cf. Kirscher's [1996] thesis that developmental psychology, including Winnicott, borrowed this trajectory from "salvation history"), since Winnicott tended to focus less on what was lost (i.e., less on the fallen state) and more on what remained, this paradigm is modified to reflect upon his ideas regarding what humans aspire to, what thwarts these aspirations, and what helps restore humans to what they aspire to be. This shift also addresses corollary questions of how and why humans experience themselves as incomplete or less than what they could or should be and how they got that way.

What Humans Aspire To

This section corresponds to theological questions gathered under the rubric of creation. Theologically, the category of creation ties to anthropology via

questions regarding human destiny and purpose. Since these questions were previously addressed, only a brief recapitulation is offered. There are two ways
Winnicott spoke to these questions. One was his answer to the question of what
made life worth living; the other involved his vision of health and maturity.

Winnicott's (1971e) answer to the question of what made life worth living
was the feeling of being alive or real. This quest to feel real or alive is a complex
concept that is interwoven with several of Winnicott's key ideas. For instance, it
is connected with the emergence of a sense of "self," or a "subjective sense of
being" (Abram, 2007b, p. 296). According to Abram, Winnicott's chief project
as a developmental psychologist focused on explaining "what constitutes the
sense of self and how it comes into being" (p. 11). Much of Winnicott's (e.g.,
1970e, 1971b, 1971h,1971j) work was devoted to unfolding the richness of this
concept of feeling alive or real and its connection to a sense of "being," to creativity, to an ability to "play" and surprise oneself. The richness of this yearning
to be alive led Winnicott (1960d) at one point to remark that "we are poor indeed if we are only sane" (p. 61). Real life is more than the absence of problematic symptoms. Winnicott (1960e) also spoke of this quest to feel real and be
alive in his work on the true and false self. People yearn to be the true selves
they feel themselves to be. The true self, with its inviolable, yet fragile core that
must be protected and whose gestures must be nurtured is a way to feel real.

An earlier chapter noted how this quest to be real and alive worked its way
out in Winnicott's personal life in terms of his reading of others theories and his
attempt to restate these theories in his own language. Also observed was his
beginning his autobiographical notes with a prayer that he "may be alive when
[he] die[d]" (Winnicott, 1978, p. 19). Even at death Winnicott wanted to feel
"alive" or "real" and went on in his notes to imaginatively construct what it was
like for him to die, thereby trying to live out the prayer. Thus, for Winnicott,
humans aspired to feel alive and real.

Winnicott also provided insight into his vision of what humans aspired to in
his various ideas about health and maturity. That is, in noting various qualities
that define health and maturity, Winnicott offered his thoughts on what those
without these qualities move toward. Winnicott variously described maturity in
humans as: a capacity to be alone (1958a); an ability to be concerned (1963c);
integration (1960a); an ability to relax ["unintegrate"] (1967c); relative independence (1960f); and an ability to play (1955a, 1971i). Each of these makes a
contribution to one's understanding of the qualities Winnicott thought mature
humans to possess. Several of these qualities were discussed in other contexts
and there is no need to elaborate on them other than to note that development of
these characteristics is rooted in the quality of the early care-giving interactions.

However, one also notes that in his last major theoretical paper, Winnicott
(1971k) spoke of maturation as one's ability to "use" objects, a complex concept
that referred to the ability to recognize and relate to the other as a person in his
or her own right, rather than as a projection of one's own needs and wishes.

Emotional development at this level involves coming to terms with both one's aggressive and love impulses, and a recognition that those one loves (and hates) survive one's strong desires (because they are more than just one's projections of and about them). It accords to and recognizes a wholeness and subjectivity in the other. The ability to relate in this way reminds one of the earlier point that human life not only begins in but matures in a social-relational matrix. Thus, one sees that the sense of aliveness and being that makes life worth living is not achieved in isolation or through some private psychic experience for Winnicott. The health or maturation that humans aspire to and move toward occurs in relationship with others.

How Things Go Wrong

At this point two observations about Winnicott's thoughts on the quest to feel real and alive and the journey toward maturity are noteworthy. First, he realized that these are aspirations, ideal states that do not always belong to actuality. He recognized that even those who have been started off well with good enough mothering have much they can yet grow into, though relatively healthy and mature (cf. Winnicott, 1967c). However, the more important point to acknowledge is that Winnicott was very much aware that some people do not get started well (cf. Winnicott, 1959c). It was this notion of failures to start well and the residual effects of this in his patients that led Winnicott to reflect on the various types of failure that might occur in the environmental-individual set up. Much of his clinical practice and his theoretical work was directed to understanding, explaining (and rectifying) these failures.

This section takes up Winnicott's thoughts on what thwarts these aspirations. In theology these questions are addressed under the categories of "sin" and "the fall." Winnicott's thoughts on how and when things go wrong take up the issue from two sides: (1) the role of the environment and, (2) how these failures manifest in the person.

One can summarize much of Winnicott's thought in this area by noting that his central answer to this question focused on early environmental failures. Because people start life in a state of absolute dependence, Winnicott put most of the weight for things going right or wrong upon the environment (e.g., the mother). Although he recognized some contribution to potential failure from the side of the infant, he placed much more emphasis on the environment's failure to be attuned to this absolutely dependent being. It is important to remember that Winnicott (1966i) did not intend the naming of these failures to be an occasion for blame; only an occasion for explaining how things go wrong. This tendency to locate the source of failure in the environment is consistent with Winnicott's focus on an original goodness in the infant. That is, to speak theological language, the origin of sin lies more with the environment than with the person for Winnicott, at least in this early stage.[9]

Thus, Winnicott's central thrust is his understanding that a lack of health in humans (being less than humans are destined to be) is due to breakdowns in environmental provision. This breakdown might be framed as a breakdown in relational functioning; this leads in turn to breakdowns in the emergence of healthy patterns of relating in the individual (Winnicott, 1969e). Even the "fear of breakdown" that some of his patients suffered actually pointed to a breakdown that had already occurred long ago in these early environmental provisions (Winnicott, 1963e).

If the origin of sin is environmental failure, then the chief way sin manifests in the daily life of the person is through the emergence of a false self. The false self is the result of a lack of responsive attunement to the infant's gestures. In such situations, the infant's sense of self becomes "split" with a false self emerging to protect or hide the true self potential (Winnicott, 1960e, 1960h). This failure in care that contributes to the emergence of the false self produces a "fall" from one's potential. The presence of the false self stands at some level as a betrayal of the true self. The false self is thus one way to speak about the theological concepts of fall and sin in Winnicott.[10] As a way to think about these concepts, the false self is not a quality of life to be nurtured or emulated (Parker & Davis, 2009). Rather, false self living ideally gives way to true self living.

Restoration

The final aspect of Winnicott's soteriology concerns his thoughts on how things might be restored when something goes wrong. Theologically this encompasses the categories of grace and redemption.

Although he tended to see the world as generally benign, Winnicott was aware that things can and do go wrong; thus, he offered thoughts on the processes of restoration. If the early environmental care did not adequately help the emerging self in its journey from absolute dependence to relative independence; if it did not provide both illusion and disillusion at the proper times; if it did not allow and honor the infant's spontaneous gestures, then the emerging self is destined to repeated attempts to get what it missed, or to hiding, or to psychosis depending upon the level of failure. In Winnicott's (1962b) words, the infant felt as if it were "going to pieces," or was "falling forever" and becomes severely hampered in the forming of a self that is separate from its environment (p. 58).

Hope for such people lies in the possibility of experiencing what they missed in the early environment. Although it may happen in other contexts (Winnicott, 1954h, 1961f), its best chance of happening is in a therapeutic context according to Winnicott (cf. 1960h, 1961f, 1971h). The therapist becomes in many ways a substitute mother who is able to provide the patient with alternate experiences that help fill in the deficits from childhood. The "good enough therapist" provides a safe place for "regression to dependence," nurtures the spontaneous gestures of the true self, provides a temporary illusion of omnipotence, gradually disillusions the patient's projections, invites play, and offers him/herself as an object for use as the case warrants.

Summary Statement

Human destiny involves becoming one's true self for Winnicott. The brokenness found in humans is due primarily to environmental failures, not to one's lack of goodness. Thus, he puts less emphasis on humanity's "fallen" state; if things have gone well, as they do for most people, there is not some grave sinfulness from which humans need to be saved. However, since things do not go well for all, there are some who need to be saved from the effects of a poor environment. This happens through provision of an alternative environment that allows the experiencing of that which was missed in early relational interactions.

Comparison with Wesley's Soteriology

How does Winnicott's psychological soteriology compare with Wesley's theological one? This section briefly notes similarities and differences between these two visions.

Creation, Aspirations and Destiny

One sees similarity between Winnicott's and Wesley's vision of creation. For instance, one sees the common notion of a graced environment for both. The similarity between Winnicott's description of the mother's holding and Wesley's notion of prevenient grace has been noted. Through her good enough care the mother lends her ego strength to the infant and holds at bay a "reality" that the infant is not ready to handle on its own (Winnicott, 1963n). Like Wesley's idea of prevenient grace the mother's care is a gift given prior to the infant's ability to handle the demands of the world. The mother's holding provides a graced environment for the absolutely dependent infant.

Winnicott's idea that what made life worth living was a sense of aliveness or realness finds a parallel in Wesley's (1767) emphasis that God gave life through the Holy Spirit. As observed in chapter 9, Winnicott also on occasion connected God to the giving of life. Similarly, Winnicott's notion that human destiny is to be one's true self evokes Wesley's (1759) articulation of the renewal of the image of God in humans as the great purpose of life. What is different of course is the degree of emphasis on God's role in these processes. Wesley (1788b) would add to the idea of God as the giver of the aliveness that humans seek that the destiny of humans is to glorify this God who gives them life and there find that life which is eternal. Although this spiritual emphasis is much more obvious in Wesley, one concedes that Winnicott's focus on the aliveness of the true self owed something to his Wesleyan heritage.

"Fallen"

This is the aspect of Winnicott's soteriology that diverges most from a Wesleyan one. Wesley's focus on human freedom emphasized personal responsibility for the human condition in a way that Winnicott found negligible. Although Winnicott and Wesley both preserve a space for some remaining goodness in humans, humans have "fallen" further for Wesley than for Winnicott. Concurrently, Wesley is more attuned to the qualities of human brokenness and intractability than Winnicott, who is overly optimistic regarding human goodness and potential.[11]

Redemption

If one has not fallen far, then one's need for redemption is less as well. Nevertheless, despite the fact of less need for redemption, when Winnicott spoke regarding restoration of what was lost, he clearly reflected his Wesleyan background. For Winnicott, redemption occurred when some other was able to provide the missing elements from the original environment. Recall for instance, Winnicott's idea that a therapist that can be used by a client is very much a "Christ-like" therapist in that he or she can survive the patient's aggression and projections without retaliation. That such provision is not without sacrifice (and suffering) on the part of the therapist is another similarity to Christian notions of redemption.

Hoffman (2010) has written of analytically oriented therapy as recapitulating the Christian movements of "incarnation, crucifixion, and resurrection" (p. 126). By empathically entering into the other's subjectivity the therapist demonstrates a type of incarnation. Yet empathic understanding alone is not sufficient for a person in therapy to grasp his or her repeated patterns of dysfunctional relating. Hoffman appropriated Winnicott's essay on object usage and his idea that the therapist was both "destroyed" by the patient (in fantasy) yet able to "survive" this destruction as illustrative of how the further movements of crucifixion (and resurrection) were enacted in analytic therapy.[12]

One might further note that this notion of restoration via someone outside the person mirrors Wesley's notion that the ongoing work of redemption is accomplished through a synergy that involves God's grace and human response to that grace (cf. Chilcote, 2004; Maddox, 1994). So too, in therapy, growth involves a synergy between the patient and the therapist; the patient must learn to use the therapist who has made him or herself available for use. In turn, the good-enough therapist becomes an instrument of grace to the patient.

This chapter concludes by noting that Winnicott's theory of the emotional development of the infant reveals an implicit theology that mirrors many themes from his Wesleyan Methodist background. His thoughts on how one comes to know, the kind of world in which one finds oneself, the nature of human beings and how one reaches that to which one aspires, all show him to be deeply indebted to his religious heritage in articulating much of his psychoanalytic theory. This indebtedness remains dominant despite the few places where he has reacted against and diverged from it.

Notes

1. Here I treat epistemological questions as including a theological purview. Scholars often consider epistemology more philosophical than theological in nature depending on how the relationship between the two fields is construed (cf. Hebblethwaite, 1983; Tracy, 1981).

2. It may be that Winnicott's remarks about certainty recall this Wesleyan doctrine. Although Wesley's doctrine of assurance changed over the course of his life, this doctrine remained one of the hallmarks of Wesleyan Methodism (Clapper, 1989; Maddox, 1994). In Wesley's early writings, one could not even claim to be a real Christian if one did not have this assurance. "All true Christians have such a faith as implies an assurance of God's love" (Wesley, 1744, p. 276). Later in his ministry, he modified his thinking to recognize that people had varying degrees of assurance. That is, not all Christians had "full assurance" and there might even be a few Christians who did not experience assurance, though Wesley felt such experiences rare, being either the result of bodily illness or ignorance of the gospel promises (Wesley, 1760b, 1768). Wesley (1738a) also gave personal affirmation of such knowledge. It is not always easy to know what of early Wesleyan doctrine survived in the pews over a century later, but if Winnicott's comments about certainty reflected something of the early Wesleyan emphasis on assurance, it might be that in this distinction what one sees is Winnicott's resistance to one dimension of his early Wesleyan Methodist upbringing, or at least to a certain popularizing of this doctrine.

However, the Wesleyan doctrine of assurance is more complex than a reduction to certainty would suggest. Wesley's doctrine of assurance was tied closely to his understanding of "faith," a broader concept. Wesley wrote of faith in terms of its objects and outcomes (e.g., faith in Christ, justifying faith, sanctifying faith) and its connection to things "hoped for" yet "not seen" (cf. Wesley, 1755a). Thus for Wesley, faith was both gift and response; it contained both certainty and openness. In this way, Winnicott's notion of the "faith" that belonged to "science" is not so different from a Wesleyan or New Testament understanding of faith (cf. Hopkins, 1997). While the objects of faith may be different for Winnicott and Wesley, the processes by which faith operates are similar. Another similarity between Wesley's emphasis on assurance and Winnicott's epistemology was noted in linking Wesley's doctrine of assurance to his emphasis on personal experience.

3. One might recall that Winnicott's comments on the soul portrayed it as having a strong material basis including its dependence upon brain functioning (Winnicott, 1954c). Although such an understanding of the soul has affinities with both Wesleyan and certain

contemporary understandings of the soul (cf. Cousineau, 1994, Maddox, 1994; Malony, 1996; Osterhaven, 1985, Wesley, 1788b), the term soul in both Winnicott and these more contemporary understandings conveys less of the similarity as well as the contrast that Winnicott was trying to make than does the term true self.

4.   One should note here that Winnicott is not always consistent with his use of the word psyche and expressed some drawbacks to its use (Winnicott, 1969j). In one place, Winnicott (1954c) not only described the psyche as the "imaginative elaboration of physical functioning," but noted that it had "as its most important duty the binding together of past experiences, potentialities, and the present moment awareness, and expectancy for the future. Thus, the self comes into existence" (p. 19). Here the psyche is an elaboration of physical functioning and the self a further elaboration of the psyche. Abram (2007b) has summarized that although the psyche might best be thought of as an *aspect* of the "self" for Winnicott, he will occasionally use psyche as a synonym for self.

5.   Recall that for Winnicott (1958f, 1968h) the roots of aggression lay in early infant movements prior to the time that motive could be attributed to them. Even though one might be hurt by an infant's kick, there was no intent to harm and thus this was not aggression in the sense of intent to harm by one's physical movements. Later, infants learn that movements can harm and might even intend to harm, but this was not so at the beginning. Such intentions to harm from aggression arise only after a failure of the environment to respond to the infant's attempts to connect and be recognized by their environment. Even early "antisocial tendencies" were exercises in hope that the environment might yet respond to the child's needs before the child passed over to the secondary gains that characterize aggression in true anti-social disorder (Winnicott, 1956a).

This is not to say that Winnicott did not recognize that children could be aggressive in destructive ways or that children did not develop aggressive tendencies that must be managed. Yet even when he spoke of the two dimensions to aggression and destructiveness, Winnicott's emphasis was on the positive aspects. Recall that in his last major theoretical paper (on object usage) Winnicott (1971k) spoke of two kinds of destructiveness; one that is imaginative and related to health and another that is related to pathology. It is interesting to note that in a posthumously published paper Winnicott (1963d) shared that it was a dream about destructiveness following his reading of Jung's autobiography (cf. Winnicott, 1964h) that helped him formulate the ideas that made their way into the object usage paper (although precursors to these ideas had long been part of his thinking; cf. Winnicott, 1939, 1950a; Abram, 2007b). Jung (1917) of course is famous for his concept of the shadow as a way to speak of an intractable darkness in humans and for the need to integrate the shadow into the psyche or total personality. Although Winnicott (1960a, 1960e, 1967d) made a similar argument on the need to integrate one's aggression into the personality, he did not share Jung's darker view of humanity.

6.   Compare Wesley's (1782) comment: "An embodied spirit cannot form one thought but by the mediation of its bodily organs. For thinking is not, as many suppose, the act of a pure spirit, but the act of a spirit connected with a body, and playing upon a set of material keys" (pp. 405-06). As Maddox (1994) has noted, humans were "embodied" soul/spirit for him; though the material and non-material can be distinguished, the human is a unity of the two (p. 71; cf. Wesley, 1788a, 1788b).

However, in noting the similarity between Winnicott's and Wesley's ideas regarding the psychosomatic unity in humans note also that in making his point about the dependence of thought upon "material keys" Wesley is making a different point than Winnicott. Wesley's point was to counter those who saw the essence of the human as non-material being. He wished to affirm the body as also a good of God's creation; not Winnicott's point at all.

7.   For Wesley, a sense of choice is not simply a feeling one might have but a gift from a gracious God who has created humans with freedom (Wesley, 1739, 1745, 1772). This sense of agency not only allowed humans to resist God's grace should they chose, more importantly it allowed them to respond in true freedom to God's grace. Thus graced, humans could participate in the sanctification process in that they cooperated with God's indwelling grace. Wesley's focus on human agency was one of the chief ways that he differed from other Protestant expressions of Christianity and was often a reason he was considered theologically suspect by more strict Reformed traditions such as Calvinism which emphasized God's sovereignty over human agency (Maddox, 1994).

8.   One might ask at this point whether Winnicott's ideas about original goodness are too optimistic? Aside from the theological issues, one would note that Winnicott's very optimistic view of human goodness is a product of his own cultural milieu. The post-WWII boom economically with it upward social mobility and optimism about scientific progress certainly contributed to Winnicott's optimism about human goodness and unlimited human capacities (cf. Goldman, 1993). One wonders if, over half a century later, whether the clear evidence of the destructive side of progress, the exploitation and near exhaustion of some renewable resources, along with the continuing presence of human oppression would have given Winnicott pause to re-think the limits of human goodness.

9.   It is interesting to note how different Winnicott's position is from Klein's (1935) who laid much of the cause for pathology at the feet of the infant and its fantasy life. Winnicott, by contrast, makes only the briefest acknowledgment of a more personal, individual contribution to how things might go wrong. He noted this potential personal contribution in his comments about the emergence of individuality or sense of self where he spoke of the anxiety connected with this "self-assertion" (Winnicott, 1963e, p. 95). However, he quickly re-directed the focus to the need for the environment to be sufficiently attuned to the infant's anxiety so as to moderate it.

One must keep in mind that Winnicott's severe emphasis on the role of the environment was to a large extent a reaction to the work of Klein and others whom he felt neglected the role of the environment in their (over)emphasis on the role of the infant's fantasy life. It is not that Winnicott is unaware of the infant's contributions but his attempts at correcting what he saw as neglect of the environmental influence tended at times to its own neglect (cf. Jacobs, 1995). Strenger (1997) tied these differences between Klein and Winnicott to their differing visions of the world; Klein's "classic" vision saw the world as unavoidably painful whereas Winnicott's "romantic" vision saw it as potentially harmonious.

10.   One also might point out that the movement from an illusion of omnipotence to the necessary disillusioning of this illusion could be viewed as a type of fall in Winnicott. This movement is reminiscent of the creation story in Scripture. As Winnicott (1970e) described the scene, the newborn infant was creator of its world, a small god omnipotent in its domain. However, this omnipotence was an illusion and this supposed idyllic state must be abandoned (and mercifully so for those who care for the infant). Since this "fall" from omnipotence to recognition of absolute dependence is really a description of things going right rather than wrong, this movement is really not a fall in the sense intended in this section.

11.   One can see further evidence of Winnicott's divergence from this Wesleyan view of the fall in Winnicott's treatment of guilt. In the Western Christian tradition, the self-

awareness of disobedience was felt as guilt. Yet, for Winnicott guilt was not the result of a personal failure that needed atoned for; rather, guilt was part of the innate moral tendencies that belonged to the young child. These innate tendencies need not be implanted; they only needed to be nurtured by the mother's reliable care. The mother's ability to "survive" and remain a "live person in the baby's life makes it possible for the baby to find that innate sense of guilt which is the only valuable guilt feeling, and which is the main source of the urge to mend and to re-create and to give" (Winnicott, 1949j, p. 98). Although guilt has a salutatory dimension for both Winnicott and Christianity in that it points one toward the need for reparation, Winnicott sought to avoid the negative implications obvious in the Western Christian view of guilt.

It is interesting to note that Winnicott's comments on guilt mostly come from a period when Klein's influence was more clearly seen in his work. Later he preferred to speak of these feelings of guilt and desire for reparation under the more positive rubric of a "capacity for concern" (Winnicott, 1963c, p. 73). Re-framing Klein's concepts of guilt and reparation in terms of concern clearly fits with Winnicott's tendency to attribute "goodness" to the infant.

12. In Hoffman's (2011) extended version of her thesis, her structure implies that she found Winnicott's theory inadequate for the third movement she outlined, that of resurrection. In charting the steps "toward mutual recognition," she saw Winnicott as particularly helpful in outlining a psychoanalytic vision of the first two steps: recognition as incarnation/ identification (cf. Benjamin, 1988; Winnicott, 1959d) and recognition as crucifixion/ surrender, which included a recognition of difference—a negation (cf. Benjamin, 1990, 2004; Winnicott, 1971k). Hoffman articulated Winnicott's version of negation and surrender through his reflections on object usage. Although others (e.g., Hopkins, 1989) have seen object usage as pointing to themes of resurrection, Hoffman saw both the object's "destruction" as well as its "survival" as an expression of negation and subsumed both themes of object usage under the rubric of crucifixion. She turned to other theorists (especially Ricoeur [e.g., 2005]) to articulate a notion of recognition as gratitude/resurrection, a movement that included an appreciation of the other. In Ricoeur she found a deeper appreciation of human brokenness than in Winnicott, and thus a space for gratitude that she saw missing in Winnicott.

Chapter 12
Conclusion

"Integration into a unit does not mean the individual has achieved peace"

In a presentation to a group of senior psychoanalysts from the British society about four years before he died, Winnicott (1967h) confessed:

> I realized more and more as time went on what a tremendous lot I've lost from not properly correlating my work with the work of others. It's not only annoying to other people but it's also rude and it has meant that what I've said has been isolated and people have to do a lot of work to get at it. It happens to be my temperament, and it's a big fault. (p. 573)

This is a telling story in that it highlights several themes from Winnicott's life and work that bear lifting up in this conclusion. These include his recognition that a deep aspect of his temperament had not always served him or others well and that he wished to acknowledge this in the hope of doing something differently, at least in this presentation. In this presentation he made a beginning at connecting his theoretical contributions to the work of others and invited his audience to help him do this further. The story also highlights Winnicott's acknowledgement that even though he desired to do differently, actually doing so was more challenging.

The purpose of this chapter is to outline lessons that can be drawn from Winnicott's biography, especially his religious journey. It is not so much a chapter devoted to summarizing his important theoretical contributions, though those are several and include insights about religious development. Rather, it reflects on how Winnicott's journey, especially his religious journey, can illumine one's own religious biography.

The Power of the Early Environment

One of the chief things Winnicott reveals about one's religious development is the formative power of one's early environment, especially the role of the mother in attending to the needs of her infant. In the context of his own life one can see how Winnicott's (1978) disclosure that in his early life he was left too much to all his "mothers" (p. 24) played a role in his dedication of his professional life to understanding something of the role of the "ordinary devoted mother" in human development (Winnicott, 1957d). Being left to mothers also seems to have made the fewer interactions with his father very memorable as well as shaped his understanding of the role of the father (e.g., as the first whole object that the child encounters—cf. Winnicott, 1969l). The influence of these early caregiving interactions on shaping his views of things religious has been the central focus of this monograph. The benign and stable environment that characterized Winnicott's early life included a pious family deeply active in the local Wesleyan Methodist community. These experiences with his family left him predisposed to positive feelings about religion and its role in family and culture.

This early environment left its mark in other ways. Winnicott's aversion to dogmatism and his desire to make the insights of psychoanalysis more widely accessible reveal the lingering influence of his Wesleyan Methodist upbringing. The very form and content of his thought are deeply influenced by this heritage (e.g. developmental patterns to growth; belief in a benign environment; cf. Goldman, 1993). The devotion of a significant portion of Winnicott's intellectual life to articulation of a positive role for religion in life and culture also testifies to the influence of his Wesleyan Methodist background.

Thus, Winnicott, through both his theoretical work and his own life, teaches one to attend to the powerful formative role of the early environment in shaping one's religious development. These early influences linger throughout the remainder of one's life providing the foundation not only for one's engagements with others but with the Other. Although these experiences can shape one's religious development in negative ways, Winnicott's contribution to this dialogue alerts one to the potential for creative and adaptive ways such experiences shape religious development.

The Creative Role of the Imagination

A second thing learned from Winnicott's life and work that helps one understand his or her own religious journey is his insight into the creative role of the imagination. Despite the fact that Winnicott devoted most of his effort to describing the importance of the environment in development, he was aware that the individual also contributed to that development. Winnicott's focus on environmental factors derived in part from his interactions with Klein and her influence in the British Psychoanalytic Society. He thought that Klein and her followers had swung so far in arguing for the individual's contribution to emotional development that the role of the environment was neglected. He sought to remedy this oversight. In his fervor to articulate the role of the environment he tended to downplay the individual's contribution at times. However, a careful reading of Winnicott shows that he too appreciated the role of the individual in contributing to his or her development. What one sees in Winnicott is a re-casting of Klein's (1935) focus on the imaginative fantasies (phantasies) of the young child into the positive language of the "intermediate area" where play and creativity contribute to adaptive and vitalizing qualities in life (Winnicott, 1951b). Klein tended to see the child's active imagination as contributing to terrifying and stultifying engagement with life. Winnicott on the other hand re-cast the imaginative qualities of the infant in much more positive terms.

One can see this creative role of the imagination in religious contexts in several ways. In addition to what the environment contributes to one's images and understandings of God, Winnicott argued that the creative imagination of the infant also played a role in fashioning these images. "God" can become a repository into which good or bad is placed. Thus, negative images of God might arise through early imaginative terrors in the infant (e.g., *talion* fears—cf. Winnicott, 1962c). Winnicott (1963j) helped one see that such images needed tempered by the mother's survival of such (fantasized) images and further "humanized" by the images and concepts of God from culture (including theology).

However, Winnicott also helps one see that there are creative, adaptive aspects of the infant's imagination. These positive aspects are most obviously at work in the intermediate area of play and transitional phenomena (Winnicott, 1951b). Images of God also are influenced by such positive imaginings. Furthermore, it is through such personal images that God becomes real to a person (cf. Parker, 2008; Ulanov, 2001). It was noted earlier how this means that to some degree each person projects onto and fashions a God after his or her liking. Nevertheless, Winnicott's work opens up the possibility that one can relate to God in mature and adult ways, and not be restricted to Freud's (1927) notion that all interaction with one's images of God must involve infantile wishes. Recall the point that object usage can be applied to relationship with God, thus not simply restricting God to one's projections. That is, religious growth not only involves "object relating" to God but maturing to "object usage." This does not mean an exploitation of God, but rather an opposite idea. In object usage God is no longer related to as a part object or simply a projection but becomes an object accorded its own subjectivity and thus reality. Winnicott, more than anyone else before him helped open the door for envisioning the creative, adaptive and vitalizing ways in which religion can influence positive emotional development. Despite his own struggle over growing up out of religious practice, Winnicott articulated a way in which religion can partake of one's most mature ways of interacting with others.

Winnicott's work regarding how such images of God are formed has led to much fruitful work in understanding and working with these images. A number of people have built on Winnicott's work to show how these images are connected to one's early environmental exposure (Jones, 1991; Meissner, 1984;

Parker, 1996, 1999; Rizzuto, 1979); others use his work to provide insights for changing these images (Moriarty, 2006; Moriarty & Hoffman, 2007). Winnicott's work was even used reflexively in this monograph to trace something of his own images of God to his developmental history.

Before leaving this section on the creative role of the imagination one might note another lesson learned from Winnicott's life and work that has special relevance to the work of reading (and writing) biography, including religious biography. According to Winnicott, people engage in these same creative mental and emotional processes in other aspects of life, such as watching a play or listening to Bach. What must now be acknowledged is that such an understanding of human development means that one not only fashions gods to one's liking, but that to some extent everyone fashions others that one reads about (or writes about) to one's liking as well. Thus, Greenberg and Mitchell (1983) spoke of Winnicott's idiosyncratic reading of Freud as fashioning a Freud to Winnicott's own liking, as indeed one must to some extent. That means that when one reads Winnicott then to some extent one fashions a Winnicott to one's liking as well. This seems especially true for those who might attempt a biography. I have already sought in the introduction to acknowledge some of the qualities in Winnicott that drew me to him. Such attractions have no doubt guided the selection of aspects of his life story and caused the neglect of other areas. For the reader, who also is about the task of "creating" a Winnicott of his or her own in the way Winnicott envisioned, even hoped for, the view outlined in this monograph comes alongside that of others available in culture and hopefully helps make Winnicott "real" as readers modify or solidify their previous judgments about Winnicott.

The Call of the True Self

A third way Winnicott's life and work illumines religious development is in his focus on nurturing the true self. He reminds one that there is within everyone a true self that yearns for liberation and some kind of expression. Winnicott's own struggle with becoming and expressing his true self manifested in several ways. One was his continued growth via his self-analysis carried on both in his theoretical work and his work with clients (Winnicott, 1947c). The most salient aspect of his continued growth toward his true self was his lifelong struggle with his aggression and its expression (Rodman, 1987). This struggle disclosed itself in his work as an analyst and theorist in his reflections on how health included the ability to integrate one's aggression into the personality (Winnicott, 1960a, 1960e, 1967d) and how aggression manifested itself in the "hate" of patients and others (Winnicott, 1947c). Splitting off one's aggression was a manifestation of the false self (Winnicott, 1960e).

A second way Winnicott sought to express his true self was in offering his theoretical contributions as "gestures" to his colleagues. Although he wished that people like Klein would have acknowledged these gestures more, he was not content to let his gestures be muted or changed (Winnicott, 1952b). Yet another aspect of Winnicott's attempts to express his true self was his repeated penchant to re-cast other people's theory into his own language (cf. Khan, 1975; Rodman, 2003). Finally, one observes that Winnicott's struggle to express his true self manifested in his becoming religious in his own way. Though he struggled with the question of whether he was religious or not at times, he seemed most content to think of himself as religious, but not in a way that capitulated to the desires of others regarding his religiosity.

Thus, one learns from Winnicott that growth and maturity, including religious development, involves attending to and nurturing the call of the true self even though it is not always easy to hear or to heed. That is, Winnicott helps one see that true religion, religion that is "real" means finding one's own way and not merely relying on or complying with the ideas of others. He points out how religion can be an area of no compromise (Winnicott, 1964a); how it can contribute to and nurture the true self (Winnicott, 1961f). This may occur through various religious practices or through the friendships and social support that religion offers (cf. Parker & Davis, 2009). Religion can provide opportunities for the regression to dependence necessary to emotional development when certain critical early experiences were missed (cf. Ulanov, 2001). Winnicott helps one see both how emotional development influences religious development and conversely how religious development can aid emotional development.

Accepting the Paradoxical

Winnicott often spoke of the paradoxical quality of life: the capacity to be alone develops in the presence of another (Winnicott, 1954c, 1958a); the infant creates the objects it finds (Winnicott, 1963a); the environment is both a part of the infant yet not a part (Winnicott, 1967h). His most famous paradox is that of transitional phenomena which belong to both shared and personal reality (Winnicott, 1951b). He even noted that the question of whether there is a God who creates people to have projections of God is a paradox that must be accepted and not resolved (Winnicott, 1968g). This paradoxical quality of life means that the task of sorting inner and outer reality is a never-ending one from which one seeks occasional relief (Winnicott, 1951b). That is, the "integration" of one's personality does not mean the cessation of all internal conflicts. "Integration into a unit does not mean that the individual has achieved peace. What the individual has achieved is a self which can contain the conflicts of all kinds that belong to the instincts and to the subtle needs of the spirit . . ." (Winnicott, 1969b, p. 222).This then is the last thing noted in terms of how Winnicott's own journey illumines that of others. He teaches one about the necessity of accepting the unfinished—the transitional and paradoxical—qualities of human development, including those that manifest in the religious journey.

This paradoxical quality to human development manifests itself in two ways. One is the recognition that there will always be areas of life where a person's desire to have neat, rational categories and resolution of tensions will go unmet. If people are to join the ranks of the healthy and mature they must learn to tolerate a certain amount of tension and ambiguity in life and in doing so find themselves more alive and real than if they forced an artificial resolution.

Second, these paradoxical qualities in one's development also mean that one's ability to live with these tensions is often uneven. One is more successful at "relating inner and outer reality" some days than others (Winnicott, 1951b). This unevenness in accepting the paradoxical quality of life can manifest in certain inconsistencies in one's practical living.[1]

Winnicott's use of this language offers a way to acknowledge that growth is an ongoing process and that growth in one area does not mean one has grown in other areas. Winnicott helps one understand that it is not always easy to integrate one's personal life with one's own best thinking. Things may make sense in theory and yet be hard to translate into one's life. Even Winnicott (1963i) acknowledged that one cannot live out of the true self at all times; reality will not bear it. Everyone makes some compromise formations to get along in the world. One sometimes holds out for an idealistic good in things (like religion) but in practice one sees the shortcomings attendant to them. Sometimes one "knows" the good, but to "live" the good is harder to do.

One sees this paradoxical quality of growth in Winnicott's personal life in several ways. Strides forward are coupled with retrenchments and inconsistencies. For instance, he could be moralistic (even dogmatic) at times, while decrying this in others (Winnicott, 1963j). He was not above using religious language and imagery to moralize about the dangers of moralizing, especially in religion! Similarly, Mitchell (1993) argued that he could be dogmatic in his adherence to analytic theory sometimes to the detriment of his patients. Thus, even though he eschewed dogmatism and moralizing generally, and worked to rid himself of such tendencies, he was not free from an occasional relapse. Rodman's (1987, 2003) identification of Winnicott's struggle to acknowledge and express his aggression in more healthy ways confirms that his growth in this area was a lifelong quest characterized by hits as well as misses. Similarly, Phillips's (1988) discussion of Winnicott's glossing over his oedipal feelings about his father points to another area where despite his years of analysis Winnicott seems to have carried some blind spots.[2]

One sees this paradoxical quality of his growth in his religious life as well. It manifested in several ways. One was his caricaturing of religion with a concomitant failure to fully acknowledge his own preference for intuitive knowing. Moreover, he did not take into account his own work in transitional phenomena, the intermediate area, and "believing in" in formulating his ideas about the differences in scientific and religious knowing. Furthermore, despite his theoretical work that carved out a way to speak of religion as having great adaptive and creative potential, in his own religious life he struggled to find a place for religious practice. Although he persuasively argued that religion can contribute to the integration of personality and provide a venue for expression of the true self, he thought himself to have matured beyond the need for religious practice.

Thus, through his life and work Winnicott points out that religious development also is characterized by this paradoxical quality. This means that there will always be areas of religious life that elude one's desires for rational explanations. It further means that religion and religious practices can paradoxically participate in one's highest aspirations and achievements as well as in one's most dysfunctional adaptations. It means that one often inconsistently lives out one's best ideals.

Conclusion

In bringing this story of Winnicott to a close, one sees that he was a man who continued to have a deep fascination with religion and its role in life and culture. It has become obvious how much he was a product of his own Wesleyan Methodist background and how deeply this seems to have settled into the very fiber of his being. There is something about Winnicott's temperament that seems well suited to the temperament of Wesleyan Methodism so that even though he converts to Anglicanism as a young adult and eventually leaves off "church religious practice," he nevertheless continued to embrace and even embody the heart of his Wesleyan Methodist background, sometimes more deeply than he himself was aware. This is not to say that he did not struggle with certain aspects of this background because he did and consciously tried to move beyond it in certain areas.

The story told here is one of a lingering religiosity (Goldman, 1993), though clearly that is only part of the story. Similarly, Phillips (1988) claimed that Winnicott's life was defined by continuity with and reaction against his Wesleyan Methodist upbringing; that too has been part of the story told. And although Winnicott's religious development as well as the development of his thinking about religion, were explored these too are only part of the story. What has become clear is that Winnicott's religious journey is the story of someone who struggled to live out his own best thinking about religion. It is the story of one who struggled (not always successfully) to try to integrate his religious sentiments with his "scientific" bent.

It is a story of someone who knew that religion could provide a venue for expression of the true self but was never quite at peace with the place of religion in his own personal journey to express his true self. On the one hand he valued religion, could not shake it off, did not wish to shake it off, having found a deep and lasting value in the Wesleyan Methodism of his youth (Winnicott, 1967f). On the other hand his quest to make things real for himself led to struggles over various Christian doctrines and left him feeling at odds with traditional religion. Though there was something about the simple faith of his father that attracted him, it also troubled him. He spent a lifetime reflecting on its value.

Notes

1.   Similarly, in a clinical context Winnicott taught the importance of finding ways to acknowledge one's own humanity and limits. Paradoxically, without encountering such limits in the therapist, patients could never experience the disillusionment necessary to their further growth (Winnicott, 1963a).

2.   Others have called attention to areas where Winnicott's ideas were not always progressive. For instance, Gerson (2004) has argued that Winnicott's position on feminism was not especially forward looking and reflected a social-cultural context of patriarchy and hierarchy. There also may have been some latent anti-Semitism in Winnicott. Biographers of Masud Khan, Winnicott's analysand and later editor for collections of his early papers, hint at this possibility (cf. Hopkins, 2006; Willoughby, 2005). Willoughby also reported a "racialized" comment about Indians (pp. 41–42. Cf. a similar type of comment in Winnicott, 1931a, p. 72). Like everyone, Winnicott was a product of his cultural milieu and thus blind in some ways (e.g., Winnicott's downplaying the negative qualities of aggression and over-valuing of human goodness reflected the postwar optimism about social progress; although correcting Klein's emphasis on personal responsibility for one's problems, his emphasis on the environment diminished a sense of agency). What can be hoped for most people is that they become aware of how their socio-cultural environment might prejudice them in unhelpful ways and strive to overcome such biases. This one finds in Winnicott. And in Winnicott's own way of thinking, it is acknowledgment of such problematical qualities in a person that actually keeps them "real" and not simply a repository of projections about them.

References

Abram, J. (2007a). Donald Woods Winnicott (1896–1971): A brief introduction. *International Journal of Psychoanalysis, 89,* 1189–1217. Special Education Section.

Abram, J. (2007b). *The language of Winnicott* (2nd edition). London: Karnac.

Anderson, R. S. (1982). *On being human: Essays in theological anthropology.* Grand Rapids, MI: William B. Eerdmans.

Anderson, R. S. (1990). Imago Dei. In R. J. Hunter (Ed.). *Dictionary of pastoral care and counseling* (pp. 571–572). Nashville, TN: Abingdon Press.

Aquinas, T. (1981) Treatise on the angels. In *Summa theologica: Complete English edition in five volumes.* Notre Dame, IN: Ava Maria Press. Reprint by Christian Classics.

Aron, L. & Mitchell, S. A. (Eds.). (1999). *Relational psychoanalysis: The emergence of a tradition* (Vol. 1). Hillsdale, NJ: The Analytic Press.

Aten, J. D., O'Grady, K. A. & Worthington, E. L. (2011). (Eds.) *The psychology of religion and spirituality for clinicians: Using research in your practice.* New York: Routledge.

Atkins, D. C. & Kessel, D. E. (2008). Religiousness and infidelity: Attendance, but not faith and prayer, predict marital fidelity. *Journal of Marriage and Family, 70,* 407-418.

Baer, R. A. (1976). Quaker silence, Catholic liturgy, and Pentecostal glossolalia: Some functional similarities. In R. P. Spittler (Ed.), *Perspectives on the new Pentecostalism* (pp. 150–164). Grand Rapids, MI: Baker Book House.

Bagenal, H. (1949). Letter of Easter to D.W. Winnicott. Donald Woods Winnicott Papers (PP/DWW/B/A/2, Box 6). Wellcome Library, 183 Euston Road, London NW1 2BE.

Baker, D. (1975). *Partnership in excellence: A late-Victorian education adventure: The Leys School, Cambridge 1875–1975.* Cambridge: Governors of The Leys School.

Barbour, I. G. (1974). *Myths, models, and paradigms: A comparative study of science and religion.* San Francisco: Harper and Row.

Benjamin, J. (1988). *The bonds of love.* New York: Pantheon Books.

Benjamin, J. (1990). Recognition and destruction: An outline of intersubjectivity. In L. Aron & S. A. Mitchell (Eds.), *Relational psychoanalysis: The emergence of a tradition* (pp. 181–210). Hillsdale, NJ: The Analytic Press.

Benjamin, J. (2004). Escape from the hall of mirrors: Commentary on paper by Jody Messler Davies. *Psychoanalytic Dialogues, 14,* 743–753.

Bernstein, R. J. (1983). *Beyond objectivism and relativism: Science, hermeneutics, and praxis.* Philadelphia: University of Pennsylvania Press.

Boyd, J. H. (1998). A history of the concept of the soul during the 20th century. *Journal of Psychology and Theology, 26,* 66–82.

Britton, E. (1951). Letter to D.W. Winnicott, December 26. Donald Woods Winnicott Papers (PP/DWW/B/A/3, Box 6). Wellcome Library, 183 Euston Road, London NW1 2BE.

Britton, K. (1967). Letter to D.W. Winnicott, November 11. Donald W. Winnicott Personal Papers. Courtesy of Oskar Diethelm Library, DeWitt Wallace Institute for the History of Psychiatry, Weill Cornell Medical College, Archives and Manuscripts, New York, NY.

Brokaw, B. F. & Edwards, K. J. (1994). The relationship of God image to level of object relations development. *Journal of Psychology and Theology, 22,* 352–371.

Brown, R. F. (1975). On the necessary imperfection of creation: Irenaeus's *Adversus haereses* IV, 38. *Scottish Journal of Theology, 28* (1), 17–25.

Brown, T. E. (1990). Vocation. In R. J. Hunter (Ed.), *Dictionary of pastoral care and counseling* (pp. 1308–1309). Nashville, TN: Abingdon Press.

Brown, V.B. (1990). Limbo. In R. J. Hunter (Ed.). *Dictionary of pastoral care and counseling* (pp. 652–653). Nashville, TN: Abingdon Press.

Browning, D. S. (1987). *Religious thought and the modern psychologies.* Philadelphia: Fortress.

Burdette, A. M., Ellison, C. G., Sherkat, D. E., & Gore, K. A. (2007). Are there religious variations in marital infidelity. *Journal of Family Issues, 28,* 1553–1581.

Burns-Smith, C. (1999). Theology and Winnicott's object relations theory: A conversation. *Journal of Psychology and Theology, 27,* 3–19.

Butterfield, J. (1998). Determinism and indeterminism. In E. Craig (Ed.), *Routledge encyclopedia of philosophy* (Vol. 3, pp. 33–39). London: Routledge.

Chilcote, P. W. (2004). *Recapturing the Wesleys' vision: An introduction to the faith of John and Charles Wesley.* Downers Grove, IL: Intervarsity Press.

Clancier, A. & Kalmanovitch, J. (1987). *Winnicott and paradox: From birth to creation.* London: Tavistock.

Clapper, G. S. (1989). *John Wesley on religious affections: His views on experience and emotion and their role in the Christian life and theology.* Metuchen, NJ: Scarecrow Press.

Clarke, S., Hoggett, P. & Hahn, H. (Eds.). (2008). *Object relations and social relations: The implications of the relational turn in psychoanalysis.* London: Karnac Books.

Collins, K. J. (2007). *The theology of John Wesley: Holy love and the shape of grace.* Nashville, TN: Abingdon Press.

Coriden, J. A. (2007). *The rights of catholics in the church.* Mahwah, NJ: Paulist Press.

Cousineau, P. (1994). *Soul: An archaeology: Readings from Socrates to Ray Charles.* San Francisco: HarperSanFrancisco.

Davies, R. (1983). Vocation. In A. Richardson & J. Bowden (Eds.), *The Westminster dictionary of Christian theology* (pp. 601–602). Philadelphia: Westminster Press.

Dietrich, D.J. (Ed.). (2003). *Christian responses to the holocaust.* Syracuse, NY: Syracuse University Press.

Dobie, L. (1966). Letter to D.W. Winnicott. Donald W. Winnicott Personal Papers. Courtesy of Oskar Diethelm Library, DeWitt Wallace Institute for the History of Psychiatry, Weill Cornell Medical College, Archives and Manuscripts, New York, NY.

Ede, S. (Jim). (1940). Letter to D.W. Winnicott, January 8. Donald Woods Winnicott Papers (PP/DWW/B/A/8, Box 8). Wellcome Library, 183 Euston Road, London NW1 2BE.

Edles, L. D. (2002). *Cultural sociology in practice.* Malden, MA: Blackwell Publishers.

Eigen, M. (1981). The area of faith in Winnicott, Lacan and Bion. *International Journal of Psycho-Analysis, 62,* 413–433.

Eigen, M. (1998) *The psychoanalytic mystic.* London: Free Association Books.

Emmons, R. A. (2003). *The psychology of ultimate concerns.* New York: Guilford Press.

Erikson, E. H. (1968). *Identity, youth and crisis.* New York: W.W. Norton.

Flew, A. (1978). Transitional objects and transitional phenomena: Comments and interpretations. In S. A. Grolnick & L. Barkin (Eds.) in collaboration with W. Muensterberger. *Between reality and fantasy: Winnicott's concepts of transitional objects and phenomena* (pp. 483–502). Northvale, NJ: Jason Aronson, Inc.

Ford, A. (2004). Ussher, James (1581–1656). In H. C. G. Matthew and B. Harrison (Eds.), *Oxford dictionary of national biography.* Oxford: Oxford University Press.

Fowler, J. W. (1981). *Stages of faith: The psychology of human development and the quest for meaning.* San Francisco, CA: Harper and Row.

Fowler, J. W. (1996). Pluralism and oneness in religious experience: William James, faith development theory, and clinical practice. In E. P. Shafranske (Ed.), *Religion and the clinical practice of psychology* (pp. 165–186). Washington, DC: American Psychological Association.

Frame, M. W. (2002). *Integrating religion and spirituality into counseling.* Pacific Grove, CA: Brooks Cole.

Francis, L.J. & Egan, J. (1990). The Catholic school as "faith community"—An empirical inquiry. *Religious Education, 85,* 588–603.

Freud. E.L. (1970). (Ed.) *The letters of Sigmund Freud and Arnold Aweig.* Robson-Scott, E., Robson-Scott, W., translators. New York: Harcourt, Brace and World.

Freud, S. (1900). *Interpretation of dreams.* In J. Strachey (Ed. & Trans.), *The standard edition of the complete psychological works of Sigmund Freud* (Vol. 4, pp. xxiii–627). London: Hogarth, 1953.

Freud, S. (1905). Three essays on the theory of sexuality. In J. Strachey (Ed. & Trans.), *The standard edition of the complete psychological works of Sigmund Freud* (Vol. 7, pp.123–245). London: Hogarth, 1953.

Freud, S. (1907). Obsessive actions and religious practices. In J. Strachey (Ed. & Trans.), *The standard edition of the complete psychological works of Sigmund Freud* (Vol. 9, pp. 115–127). London: Hogarth, 1959.

Freud, S. (1913). *Totem and taboo.* In J. Strachey (Ed. & Trans.), *The standard edition of the complete psychological works of Sigmund Freud* (Vol. 13, pp. 1–162). London: Hogarth, 1955.

Freud, S. (1920). *Beyond the pleasure principle.* In J. Strachey (Ed. & Trans.), *The standard edition of the complete psychological works of Sigmund Freud* (Vol. 18, pp. 1–64). London: Hogarth, 1955.

Freud, S. (1927). *The future of an illusion.* In J. Strachey (Ed. and Trans.), *The standard edition of the complete psychological works of Sigmund Freud* (Vol. 21, pp. 3–56). London: Hogarth, 1961.

Freud, S. (1930). *Civilization and its discontents.* In J. Strachey (Ed. & Trans.), *The standard edition of the complete psychological works of Sigmund Freud* (Vol. 21, pp. 59–145). London: Hogarth, 1961.

Freud, S. (1939). *Moses and monotheism.* In J. Strachey (Ed. & Trans.), *The standard edition of the complete psychological works of Sigmund Freud* (Vol. 23, pp. 1–137). London: Hogarth, 1964.

Gay, V. P. (1983). Winnicott's contribution to religious studies: The resurrection of the culture hero. *Journal of American Academy of Religion, 51*(3), 371–395

Gerkin, C. V. (1984). *The living human document.* Nashville, TN: Abingdon Press.

Gerson, G. (2004). Winnicott, participation and gender. *Feminism and Psychology, 14,* 561–581.

Goldman, D. (1993). *In search of the real: The origins and originality of D.W. Winnicott.* Northvale, NJ: Aronson.

Graves, R. (1947). *King Jesus.* London: Cassell

Graves, R. & Podro, J. (1954). *The Nazarene gospel restored.* New York: Doubleday.

Green, A. (2005). Winnicott at the start of the third millennium. In L. Caldwell (Ed.), *Sex and sexuality: Winnicottian perspectives* (pp. 11–32). London: Karnac.

Greenberg, J. R. & Mitchell, S. A. (1983). *Object relations in psychoanalytic theory.* Cambridge, MA: Harvard University Press.

Grentz, S. J. (2001). *The social God and the relational self.* Louisville, KY: Westminster John Knox.

Grosskurth, P. (1986). *Melanie Klein: Her world and her work.* Northvale, NJ: Aronson.

Grudem, W. (1994). *Systematic theology.* Grand Rapids, MI: Zondervan.

Guardini, R. (1935). *The spirit of the liturgy.* London: Sheed and Ward.

Hamilton, V.P. (1995). *The book of Genesis: Chapters 18–50.* (The New International Commentary on the Old Testament). Grand Rapids, MI: William B. Eerdmans.

Hansen, D. & Drovdahl, R. (2006). The holding power of love: John Wesley and D.W. Winnicott in conversation. *Journal of Psychology and Christianity, 25,* 54–62.

Harding, J. (2006). *The chapel: A brief history.* John Harding and the Governors of The Leys School. Cambridge: Cambridge Printing.

Hardy, D. S. (2003). Implicit theologies in psychologies: Claiming experience as an authoritative source for theologizing. *Cross Currents, 53,* 368–377.

Healy, K. C. (2004). Looking on the one we have pierced: Repentance, resurrection, and Winnicott's "capacity for concern." *Pastoral Psychology, 53* (2) 53–62.

Hebblethwaite, B. (1983). Epistemology. In A. Richardson & J. Bowden (Eds.), *The Westminster dictionary of Christian theology* (pp. 182–183). Philadelphia: Westminster Press.

Heitzenrater, R. P. (1995). *The people called Methodists.* Nashville, Tenn.: Abingdon Press.

Hoffman, M. (2004). From enemy combatant to strange bedfellow: The role of religious narratives in the work of W. R. D. Fairbairn and D. W. Winnicott. *Psychoanalytic Dialogues, 14,* 769–804.

Hoffman, M. (2007). Fairbairn and Winnicott on my mind: Counterpoints, tensions, and oscillations in the clinical setting. *Contemporary Psychoanalysis, 44,* 454–475.

Hoffman, M. T. (2010). Incarnation, crucifixion and resurrection in psychoanalytic thought. *Journal of Psychology and Christianity, 29,* 121–129.

Hoffman, M. T. (2011). *Toward mutual recognition: Relational psychoanalysis and the Christian narrative.* New York: Routledge.

Hopkins, B. (1989). Jesus and object use: A Winnicottian account of the resurrection myth. *International Review of Psycho-Analysis, 16,* 93–100.

Hopkins, B. (1997) Winnicott and the capacity to believe. *The International Journal of Psychoanalysis, 78,* 485–497.

Hopkins, L. (2006). *False self: The life of Masud Khan.* NY: Other Press.

Hopkins, L. B. (2004). Red shoes, untapped madness and Winnicott on the cross: An Interview with Marion Milner. *The Annual of Psychoanalysis, 32,* 233–243.

Hughes, A. (2004). Ancestral vs. original sin: An overview with implications for psychotherapy. *Journal of Psychology and Christianity, 23,* 271–277.

Ingram, J. A. (1999). The *Imago Dei* in personality theory. In D. G. Benner & P. C. Hill (Eds.), *Baker Encyclopedia of psychology and counseling.* 2nd edition. (pp. 608–611). Grand Rapids, MI: Baker Books.

Jacobs, A. (2008). *Original sin: A cultural history.* New York: HarperCollins.

Jacobs, M. (1995). *D.W. Winnicott.* London: Sage.

James, W. (1902). *The varieties of religious experience.* New York: Longmans, Green & Co.

Jones, E. (1953). *The life and work of Sigmund Freud. Vol. 1.* New York: Basic Books.

Jones, J. W. (1991). *Contemporary psychoanalysis and religion.* New Haven: Yale University Press.

Julian, J. (1892). Rock of ages. In J. Julian (Ed.), *A dictionary of hymnody* (pp. 970–972). New York: Charles Scribner's Sons.

Jung, C. G. (1917). Two essays on analytical psychology. *The collected works of C. G. Jung* (Vol. 7, pp. 1–349). Princeton, NJ: Princeton University Press. 1953 and 1966.

Kahr, B. (1996). *D. W. Winnicott: A biographical portrait*. London: Karnac.

Kahr, B. (2011). Winnicott's "anni horribiles": The biographical roots of "Hate in the Counter-Transference." *American Imago, 68*, 173–211.

Kanter, J. S. (2004). *Face to face with children: The life and work of Clare Winnicott*. London: Karnac.

Kapitan, T. (1999). Free will problem. In R. Audi (Ed.), *The Cambridge dictionary of philosophy* (pp. 326–328). Cambridge: University Press.

Kessen, W. (1979). The American child and other cultural inventions. *American Psychologist, 34*, 815–820.

Kessen, W. (1990). *The rise and fall of development*. Worcester, MA: Clark University Press.

Khan, M. R. (1975). Introduction. In D. Winnicott, *Through paediatrics to psychoanalysis* (pp. xi–1). Reprint. New York: Basic Books.

Khan, M. R. (1986). Introduction. In D. Winnicott, *Holding and interpretation: Fragment of an analysis* (pp. 1–18). New York: Grove Press.

Kilian, M. K. & Parker, S. (2001). A Wesleyan spirituality: Implications for clinical practice. *Journal of Psychology and Theology, 29*, 72–80.

Kirschner, S. R. (1996). *The religious and romantic origins of psychoanalysis*. Cambridge: Cambridge University Press.

Klein, M. (1935). A contribution to the psychogenesis of manic-depressive states. *International Journal of Psych-Analysis, 16*, 145–174.

Klein, M. (1946). Notes on some schizoid mechanisms. In M. Klein, *Envy and gratitude and other works 1946–1963* (pp. 1–24). London: Hogarth Press, 1975.

Klein, M. (1948). On the theory of anxiety and guilt. In M. Klein, *Envy and gratitude and other works 1946–1963* (pp. 25–42). London: Hogarth Press, 1975.

Klein, M. (1957). Envy and gratitude. In M. Klein, *Envy and gratitude and other works 1946–1963* (pp. 176–235). London: Hogarth Press, 1975.

Lambert, K. (1987). Some religious implications of the work of Freud, Jung, and Winnicott. *Winnicott Studies: The Journal of the Squiggle Foundation, 2*, 49–70.

Lawrence, R. T. (1997). Measuring the image of God: The God image inventory and the God image scales. *Journal of Psychology and Theology, 25* (2), 214–226.

Lawrence, Brother (Nicholas Hermann 1605–1691). (1968). *Practicing the presence of God*. Old Tappan, NJ: Revell.

McCarthy, A.T. (2010). *Francis of Assisi as artist of the spiritual life: An object relations theory perspective*. Lanham, MD: University Press of America.

McDargh, J. (1983). *Psychoanalytic object relations theory and the study of religion*. Washington, DC: University Press of America.

McFague, S. (1982). *Metaphorical theology: Models of God in religious language*. Philadelphia: Fortress.

Maddox, R. L. (1994). *Responsible grace: John Wesley's practical theology*. Nashville, TN: Abingdon Press.

Maddox, R. L. (2004). Psychology and Wesleyan theology: Precedents and prospects for a renewed engagement. *Journal of Psychology and Christianity, 23*, 101–109.

Malony, H. N. (1996). John Wesley's *Primitive Physick*: An 18th-century health psychology. *Journal of Health Psychology, 1*, 147–159.

Malony, H. N. (1999). John Wesley and psychology. *Journal of Psychology and Christianity, 18*, 5–18.

Meadow, M. J. (1999). Mysticism. In D. G. Benner & P. C. Hill (Eds.), *Baker encyclopedia of psychology and counseling*. 2nd edition. (pp. 778–779). Grand Rapids, MI: Baker Books.

Meisel, P. & Kendrick, W. (1985). Introduction. In P. Meisel & W. Kendrick (Eds.), *Bloomsbury/Freud: The letters of James and Alix Strachey 1924–1925* (pp. 3–49). New York: Basic Books.

Meissner, W. W. (1984). *Psychoanalysis and religious experience*. New Haven: Yale University Press.

Meng, H. & Freud, E. L. (Eds.) (1963). *Psychoanalysis and faith: The letters of Sigmund Freud and Oskar Pfister*. New York: Basic Books.

Miller, G. A. (2002). *Incorporating spirituality in counseling and psychotherapy*. New York: Wiley.

Minns, D. (1994). *Irenaeus*. Washington, D.C.: Georgetown University Press.

Mitchell, S. A. (1988). *Relational concepts in psychoanalysis: An integration.* Cambridge, MA: Harvard University Press.

Mitchell, S. A. (1993). *Hope and dread in psychoanalysis*. New York: Basic Books.

Moltman, J. (1981). *The trinity and the kingdom*. San Francisco: Harper and Row.

Moon, G. W. (1999). Soul. In D. G. Benner & P. C. Hill (Eds.), *Baker encyclopedia of psychology and counseling*. 2nd edition. (pp. 1147–1148). Grand Rapids, MI: Baker Books.

Moreland, J. P. & Ciocchi, D. M. (Eds.). (1993). *Christian perspectives on being human*. Grand Rapids, MI: Baker Book House.

Moriarty, G. (2006). *Pastoral care of depression*. New York: Haworth Press.

Moriarty, G. & Hoffman, L. (2007). *God image handbook for spiritual counseling and psychotherapy: Research, theory and practice*. Binghamton, NY: Haworth Press.

Muller, R. A. (1990). Soul. In R. J. Hunter (Ed.), *Dictionary of pastoral care and counseling*. (pp. 1201–1203). Nashville, TN: Abingdon Press.

Myers, D. G. (1978). *The human puzzle: Psychological research and Christian belief*. San Francisco: Harper and Row.

Nesbitt, C.F. (1955). Review of *Nazarene Gospel Restored. Interpretation, 9*, 102–105.

Newman, A. (1995). *Non-compliance in Winnicott's words*. New York: New York University Press.

Oden, T. C. (1978). *Kerygma and counseling*. San Francisco: Harper and Row.

Osterhaven, M. E. (1984). Soul. In W. A. Elwell (Ed.), *Evangelical dictionary of theology* (pp. 1036–1037). Grand Rapids, MI: Baker Books.

Otto, R. (1923). *The idea of the holy*. London: Oxford University Press.

Outler, A. C. (1985). The Wesleyan quadrilateral in Wesley. *Wesleyan Theological Journal, 20* (1), 7–18.

Pargament, K. I. (2007). *Spiritually integrated psychotherapy: Understanding and addressing the sacred*. New York: Guilford Press.

Parker, S. E. (1996). *Led by the Spirit: Toward a practical theology of Pentecostal discernment and decision making*. Sheffield, England: Sheffield Academic Press.

Parker, S. (1999). Hearing God's Spirit: Impacts of developmental history on adult religious experience. *Journal of Psychology and Christianity, 18*, 154–164.

Parker, S. (2008). Winnicott's object relations theory and the work of the Holy Spirit. *Journal of Psychology and Theology, 36*, 285–293.

Parker, S. (2009). Scriptural allusions in the writings of D.W. Winnicott. *Psychoanalytic Review, 96*, 633–648.

Parker, S. (2011). Spirituality in counseling: A faith development perspective. *Journal of Counseling and Development, 89*, 114–121.

References   237

Parker, S. & Davis, E. (2009). The false self in Christian contexts: A Winnicottian perspective. *Journal of Psychology and Christianity, 28,* 315–325.
Pfister, O. (1917). *The psychoanalytic method.* London: Routledge & Kegan Paul.
Phillips, A. (1988). *Winnicott.* Cambridge, Mass.: Harvard University Press.
Piaget, J. (1970). Piaget's theory. In P. Mussen (Ed.), *Charmichel's manual of child psychology,* 3rd Edition., Vol. 1 (pp. 703–732). New York: John Wiley and Sons.
Pinnock, C. H. (2001). *Most moved mover: A theology of God's openness.* Grand Rapids, MI: Baker Academic.
Pontalis, J.-B. (1987). Paradoxes of the Winnicott effect: Interview with J.-B. Pontalis. In A. Clancier and J. Kalmanovitch (Eds.), *Winnicott and paradox: From birth to creation* (pp. 138–143). London: Tavistock.
Price, D. J. (2002). *Karl Barth's anthropology in light of modern thought.* Grand Rapids, MI: William B. Eerdmans.
Pritchard, F.C. (1983). Education. In R. E. Davies, A. R. George, & E. G. Rupp (Eds.), *A history of the Methodist church in Great Britain, Vol. 3* (pp. 279–308). London: Epworth.
Pruyser, P.W. (1983). *The play of the imagination: Toward a psychoanalysis of culture.* NewYork: International Universities Press.
Rack, H. (1983). Wesleyan Methodism 1849–1902. In R. E. Davies, A. R. George, & E. G. Rupp (Eds.), *A history of the Methodist church in Great Britain, Vol. 3,* (pp. 110–166). London: Epworth.
Rayner, E. (1991). *The independent mind in British psychoanalysis.* London: Free Association Press.
Reiland, H. (2004). The object beyond objects and the sacred. *The Scandinavian Psychoanalytic Review, 27,* 78–86.
Richards, P. S. & Bergin, A. E. (2005). *A spiritual strategy for counseling and psychotherapy.* (2nd Edition). Washington, DC: American Psychological Association.
Ricoeur, P. (2005). *The course of recognition.* Cambridge, MA: Harvard University Press.
Rizzuto, A.-M. (1979). *The birth of the living god.* Chicago: University Press.
Rizzuto, A.-M. (2005). Psychoanalytic considerations about spiritually oriented psychotherapy. In L. Sperry & E. P. Shafranske (Eds.), *Spiritually oriented psychotherapy* (pp. 31–50). Washington, DC: American Psychological Association.
Roazen, P. (1974). *Freud and his followers.* New York: Alfred Knopf.
Rodman, F. R. (1987). Introduction. In F. R. Rodman (Ed.) *The spontaneous gesture: Selected letters of D. W. Winnicott.* (pp. xiii–xxxiii). Cambridge, MA: Harvard University Press.
Rodman, F. R. (2003). *Winnicott: Life and work.* Cambridge, MA: Perseus Books.
Rollins, W. G. (1999). *Soul and psyche.* Minneapolis: Augsburg Fortress.
Rollins, W. G. (2007). Soul and psyche: The Bible in psychological perspective. In W. G. Rollins & D. A. Kille (Eds.), *Psychological insight into the Bible* (pp. 24–33). Grand Rapids, MI: William B. Eerdmans Publishing.
Rubenstein, R. L. (1992). *After Auschwitz: History, theology and contemporary Judaism.* 2nd edition. (1st edition 1966). Baltimore, MD: Johns Hopkins University Press.
Rudnytsky, P. L. (1991). *The psychoanalytic vocation: Rank, Winnicott and the legacy of Freud.* London: Routledge.
Runyon, T. (1998). *The new creation: John Wesley's theology today.* Nashville, TN: Abingdon Press.
St. Clair, M. (1994). *Human relationships and the experience of God.* Mahwah, NJ: Paulist Press.

St. John of the Cross. (1959). *Dark night of the soul.* E.A. Peers (Trans.). New York: Doubleday.

Schlauch, C. (2007). Introducing the concepts of "positions," "space," and "worlds": Seeing human being and becoming—and religion—in new ways. *Pastoral Psychology, 55,* 367–390.

Segel, E. (1999). *Why didn't I learn this in Hebrew school.* Northvale, NJ: Aronson.

Semmel, B. (1973). *The Methodist revolution.* New York: Basic Books.

Smith, C. (2003). *Moral, believing animals: Human personhood and culture.* Oxford: University Press.

Smith, C. (2010). *What is a person? Rethinking humanity, social life, and the moral good from the person up.* Chicago: University Press.

Smith, J.K.A. (2009). *Desiring the kingdom: Worship, worldview and cultural formation.* Grand Rapids, MI: Baker Academic.

Smith, J.K.A. (2010). The (re) turn to the person in contemporary theory. *Christian Scholars Review, xl,* 77–92.

Smith, W. C. (1963). *The meaning and end of religion.* New York: Macmillan.

Sorenson, R. L. (2004). *Minding spirituality.* Hillsdale, NJ: Analytic Press.

Sperry, L. & Shafranske, E. P. (2004). (Eds.). *Spiritually-oriented psychotherapy.* Washington, DC: American Psychological Association.

Steenberg, M. C. (2004). Children in paradise: Adam and Eve as "infants" in Irenaeus of Lyons. *Journal of Early Christian Studies, 12* (1), 1–22.

Strachey, J. (1924). Letter of November 11 to Alix Strachey. In P. Meisel & W. Kendrick (Eds.), *Bloomsbury/Freud: The letters of James and Alex Strachey 1924–1925.* (pp. 115–116). New York: Basic Books.

Strachey, J. (1925). Letter of February 11 to Alix Strachey. In P. Meisel & W. Kendrick (Eds.), *Bloomsbury/Freud: The letters of James and Alex Strachey 1924–1925.* (pp. 329–330). New York: Basic Books.

Strawn, B. & Leffel, G. (2001). John Wesley's orthokardia and Harry Guntrip's "Heart of the Personal": Convergent aims and complementary practices in psychotherapy and spiritual formation. *Journal of Psychology and Christianity, 20,* 351–359.

Strawson, G. (1998). Free will. In E. Craig (Ed.), *Routledge encyclopedia of philosophy* (Vol. 2, pp. 743–753). London: Routledge.

Strenger, C. (1997). Further remarks on the classic and romantic visions in psychoanalysis: Klein, Winnicott, and ethics. *Psychoanalysis and Contemporary Thought, 20,* 207–244.

Tatelbaum, J. (1989). *You don't have to suffer: A handbook for moving beyond life's crises.* New York: HarperCollins.

Thomas, R. & Parker, S. (2004). Toward a theological understanding of shame. *Journal of Psychology and Christianity, 23,* 176–182.

Tillich, P. (1952). *The courage to be.* New Haven, CT: Yale University Press.

Time (1954). Review of *Nazarene Gospel Restored,* July 26 issue.

Tinsley, E. J. (1983). Mysticism. In A. Richardson & J. Bowden (Eds.), *The Westminster dictionary of Christian theology* (pp. 387–389). Philadelphia: Westminster Press.

Titelman, G. (1996). *Random House dictionary of popular proverbs and sayings.* New York: Random House.

Tracy, D. (1981). *The analogical imagination.* New York: Crossroad.

Tuber, S. (2008). *Attachment, play and authenticity: A Winnicott primer.* New York: Aronson.

Turner, J. M. (1983). Methodism in England 1900–1932. In R. E. Davies, A. R. George, & E. G. Rupp (Eds.). *A history of the Methodist church in Great Britain, Vol. 3* (pp. 309–361). London: Epworth.

Turner, J. F. (2002). A brief history of illusion: Milner, Winnicott and Rycroft. *The International Journal of Psychoanalysis, 83*, 1063–1082.

Turner, V. (1969). *The ritual process.* Chicago: Aldine Publishing.

Ulanov, A. B. (2001). *Finding space: Winnicott, God, and psychic reality.* Philadelphia: Westminster/John Knox.

Underwood, R. L. (1986). The presence and absence of God in object relational and theological perspectives. *Journal of Psychology and Theology, 14*, 298–305.

Vawter, B. (1983). Original sin. In A. Richardson & J. Bowden (Eds.), *The Westminster dictionary of Christian theology* (pp. 420–421). Philadelphia: Westminster Press.

Ware, B. A. (Ed.). (2008). *Perspectives on the doctrine of God: Four views.* Nashville, TN: B & H Publishing.

Wesley, J. (1733). Sermon 144, The love of God. In A. C. Outler (Ed.), *The bicentennial edition of the works of John Wesley, Vol. 4, Sermons IV* (pp. 331–345). Nashville: Abingdon Press, 1987.

Wesley, J. (1738a). May 24, 1738. In W. R. Ward and R. P. Heitzenrater (Eds.), *The bicentennial edition of the works of John Wesley, Vol. 18, Journal and diaries I (1735–1738)* (pp. 242–250). Nashville: Abingdon Press, 1988.

Wesley, J. (1738b). Rules of the band societies. In R. E. Davies (Ed.), *The bicentennial edition of the works of John Wesley, Vol. 9, The Methodist societies* (pp. 77–78). Nashville: Abingdon Press, 1989.

Wesley, J. (1738c). Sermon 1, Salvation by faith. In A. C. Outler (Ed.), *The bicentennial edition of the works of John Wesley, Vol. 1, Sermons I* (pp. 109–130). Nashville: Abingdon Press, 1984.

Wesley, J. (1739). Sermon 110, Free grace. In A. C. Outler (Ed.) *The bicentennial edition of the works of John Wesley, Vol. 3, Sermons III* (pp. 542–563). Nashville: Abingdon Press, 1986.

Wesley, J. (1741). Sermon 2, The almost Christian. In A. C. Outler (Ed.), *The bicentennial edition of the works of John Wesley, Vol. 1, Sermons I* (pp. 131–141). Nashville: Abingdon Press, 1984.

Wesley, J. (1743a). An earnest appeal to men of reason and religion. In G. R. Cragg (Ed.), *The bicentennial edition of the works of John Wesley, Vol. 11, The appeals to men of reason and religion and certain related open letters* (pp. 37–94). Oxford: Clarendon Press, 1975.

Wesley, J. (1743b). September 22, 1743. In W. R. Ward and R. P. Heitzenrater (Eds.), *The bicentennial edition of the works of John Wesley, Vol. 19, Journal and diaries II (1738-1743)* (pp. 341–342). Nashville: Abingdon Press, 1990.

Wesley, J. (1744). Minutes of some late conversations between the Rev. Mr. Wesley and others. In T. Jackson (Ed.), *The works of John Wesley, 14 Vols., 3rd Edition* (pp. 8:275–298). London: Wesleyan Methodist Book Room, 1872.

Wesley, J. (1745). Advice to the people called Methodists. In R. E. Davies (Ed.), *The bicentennial edition of the works of John Wesley, Vol. 9, The Methodist societies* (pp. 123–131). Nashville: Abingdon Press, 1989.

Wesley, J. (1746a). Sermon 5, Justification by faith. In A. C. Outler (Ed.), *The bicentennial edition of the works of John Wesley, Vol. 1, Sermons I* (pp. 181–199). Nashville: Abingdon Press, 1984.

Wesley, J. (1746b). Preface to sermons. In A. C. Outler (Ed.), *The bicentennial edition of the works of John Wesley, Vol. 1, Sermons I* (pp. 103–107). Nashville: Abingdon Press, 1984.

Wesley, J. (1746c). Sermon 8, The first fruits of the Spirit. In A. C. Outler (Ed.), *The bicentennial edition of the works of John Wesley, Vol. 1, Sermons I* (pp. 233–247). Nashville: Abingdon Press, 1984.

Wesley, J. (1746d). Sermon 10, Witness of the Spirit I. In A. C. Outler (Ed.), *The bicentennial edition of the works of John Wesley, Vol. 1, Sermons I* (pp. 267–284). Nashville: Abingdon Press, 1984.

Wesley, J. (1746e). Sermon 12, The witness of our own spirit. In A. C. Outler (Ed.), *The bicentennial edition of the works of John Wesley, Vol. 1, Sermons I* (pp. 299–313). Nashville: Abingdon Press, 1984.

Wesley, J. (1746f). Sermon 16, The means of grace. In A. C. Outler (Ed.), *The bicentennial edition of the works of John Wesley, Vol. 1, Sermons I* (pp. 376–397). Nashville: Abingdon Press, 1984.

Wesley, J. (1747). June 4, 1747. In W. R. Ward and R. P. Heitzenrater (Eds.), *The bicentennial edition of the works of John Wesley, Vol. 20, Journal and diaries III (1743–1754)* (pp. 176–177). Nashville: Abingdon Press, 1993.

Wesley, J. (1748a). Sermon 19, The great privilege of those that are born of God. In A. C. Outler (Ed.), *The bicentennial edition of the works of John Wesley, Vol. 1, Sermons I* (pp. 431–443). Nashville: Abingdon Press, 1984.

Wesley, J. (1748b). Sermon 22, Upon our Lord's sermon on the mount, discourse 2. In A. C. Outler (Ed.), *The bicentennial edition of the works of John Wesley, Vol. 1, Sermons I* (pp. 488–509). Nashville: Abingdon Press, 1984.

Wesley, J. (1748c). Sermon 24, Upon our Lord's sermon on the mount, discourse 4. In A. C. Outler (Ed.), *The bicentennial edition of the works of John Wesley, Vol. 1, Sermons I* (pp. 531–549). Nashville: Abingdon Press, 1984.

Wesley, J. (1748d). Sermon 26, Upon our Lord's sermon on the mount, discourse 6. In A. C. Outler (Ed.), *The bicentennial edition of the works of John Wesley, Vol. 1, Sermons I* (pp. 572–591). Nashville: Abingdon Press, 1984.

Wesley, J. (1749). A letter to a Roman Catholic. In T. Jackson (Ed.), *The works of John Wesley, 14 Vols., 3rd Edition* (pp. 10:80–86). London: Wesleyan Methodist Book Room, 1872.

Wesley, J. (1750). August, 1750. In W. R. Ward and R. P. Heitzenrater (Eds.), *The bicentennial edition of the works of John Wesley, Vol. 20, Journal and diaries III (1743–1754)* (pp. 354–359). Nashville: Abingdon Press, 1993.

Wesley, J. (1755a). *Explanatory notes upon the New Testament* (2 Vols). London: Bowyer. Reprint Edition Grand Rapids, MI: Baker Book House Reprint 1981. Comment is upon Hebrews 11:1 (no pagination).

Wesley, J. (1755b). *Explanatory notes upon the New Testament* (2 Vols). London: Bowyer. Reprint Edition Grand Rapids, MI: Baker Book House Reprint 1981. Comment is upon I John 4:8 (no pagination).

Wesley, J. (1756a). Letter to William Law. In J. Telford (Ed.), *The letters of the Rev. John Wesley*, 8 volumes (pp. 3:332–370). London: Epworth Press, 1931.

Wesley, J. (1756b). The doctrine of original sin according to Scripture, reason and experience. In T. Jackson (Ed.), *The works of John Wesley, 14 Vols., 3rd Edition* (pp. 9:191–464). London: Wesleyan Methodist Book Room, 1872.

Wesley, J. (1759). Sermon 44, Original sin. In A. C. Outler (Ed.), *The bicentennial edition of the works of John Wesley, Vol. 2, Sermons II* (pp. 170–185). Nashville: Abingdon Press, 1985.

Wesley, J. (1760a). Sermon 45, The new birth. In A. C. Outler (Ed.), *The bicentennial edition of the works of John Wesley, Vol. 2, Sermons II* (pp. 186–201). Nashville: Abingdon Press, 1985.

Wesley, J. (1760b). Sermon 47, Heaviness through manifold temptations. In A. C. Outler (Ed.), *The bicentennial edition of the works of John Wesley, Vol. 2, Sermons II* (pp. 222–235). Nashville: Abingdon Press, 1985.

Wesley, J. (1763a) May 31, 1763. In N. Curnock (Ed.), *The journal of John Wesley*, 8 volumes (p. 5:15). London: The Epworth Press, 1938.

Wesley, J. (1763b). Sermon 13, On sin in believers. In A. C. Outler (Ed.), *The bicentennial edition of the works of John Wesley, Vol. 1, Sermons I* (pp. 314–334). Nashville: Abingdon Press, 1984.

Wesley, J. (1765). Sermon 20, The Lord our righteousness. In A. C. Outler (Ed.), *The bicentennial edition of the works of John Wesley, Vol. 1, Sermons I* (pp. 444–465). Nashville: Abingdon Press, 1984.

Wesley, J. (1767). Sermon 11, Witness of the Spirit II. In A. C. Outler (Ed.), *The bicentennial edition of the works of John Wesley, Vol. 1, Sermons I* (pp. 285–298). Nashville: Abingdon Press, 1984.

Wesley, J. (1768). Letter to Dr. Rutherforth. In R. E. Davies (Ed.), *The bicentennial edition of the works of John Wesley, Vol. 9, The Methodist societies* (pp. 373–388). Nashville: Abingdon Press, 1989.

Wesley, J. (1772). Thoughts upon liberty. In T. Jackson (Ed.), *The works of John Wesley, 14 Vols., 3rd Edition* (pp. 11:34-46). London: Wesleyan Methodist Book Room, 1872.

Wesley, J. (1777). A plain account of Christian perfection. In T. Jackson (Ed.), *The works of John Wesley, 14 Vols., 3rd Edition* (pp. 11:366–446). London: Wesleyan Methodist Book Room, 1872.

Wesley, J. (1780). *A collection of hymns, for the use of the people called Methodists*. In F. Hildebrandt & O. Beckerlegge (Eds.), *The bicentennial edition of the works of John Wesley, Vol. 7*. New York: Oxford University Press, 1984.

Wesley, J. (1782). Sermon 57, On the fall of man. In A. C. Outler (Ed.), *The bicentennial edition of the works of John Wesley, Vol. 2, Sermons II* (pp. 400–412). Nashville: Abingdon Press, 1985.

Wesley, J. (1783). Sermon 63, The general spread of the gospel. In A. C. Outler (Ed.), *The bicentennial edition of the works of John Wesley, Vol. 2, Sermons II* (pp. 267–284). Nashville: Abingdon Press, 1985.

Wesley, J. (1785). Sermon 85, On working out our own salvation. In A. C. Outler (Ed.) *The bicentennial edition of the works of John Wesley, Vol. 3, Sermons III* (pp. 199–209). Nashville: Abingdon Press, 1986.

Wesley, J. (1786). Sermon 67, On divine providence. In A. C. Outler (Ed.), *The bicentennial edition of the works of John Wesley, Vol. 2, Sermons II* (pp. 267–284). Nashville: Abingdon Press, 1985.

Wesley, J. (1788a). Sermon 103, What is man. In A. C. Outler (Ed.) *The bicentennial edition of the works of John Wesley, Vol. 3, Sermons III* (pp. 267–284). Nashville: Abingdon Press, 1986.

Wesley, J. (1788b). Sermon 116, What is man. In A. C. Outler (Ed.), *The bicentennial edition of the works of John Wesley, Vol. 4, Sermons IV* (pp. 20–27). Nashville: Abingdon Press, 1987.

Wesley, J. (1790a). March 14, 1790. In N. Curnock (Ed.), *The journal of John Wesley*, 8 volumes (p. 8:49). London: The Epworth Press, 1938.

Wesley, J. (1790b). Sermon 120, The unity of the divine being. In A. C. Outler (Ed.), *The bicentennial edition of the works of John Wesley, Vol. 4, Sermons IV* (pp. 60–74). Nashville: Abingdon Press, 1987.

Wesley, J. (1791). Sermon 127, On the wedding garment. In A. C. Outler (Ed.), *The bicentennial edition of the works of John Wesley, Vol. 4, Sermons IV* (pp. 139–148). Nashville: Abingdon Press, 1987.

Wesley, J. (1792). Sermon 130, On living without God. In A. C. Outler (Ed.), *The bicentennial edition of the works of John Wesley, Vol. 4, Sermons IV* (pp. 168–176). Nashville: Abingdon Press, 1987.

Williams, C. W. (1960). *John Wesley's theology today.* Nashville, TN: Abingdon Press.

Willoughby, R. (2005). *Masud Khan: The myth and the reality.* London: Free Association Press.

Winnicott, C. (ca. 1941-45). Letter to D. W. Winnicott, April 2. Donald Woods Winnicott Papers (PP/DWW/B/D/14, Box 28). Wellcome Library, 183 Euston Road, London NW1 2BE.

Winnicott, C. (1978). D.W.W.: A reflection. In S. A. Grolnick & L. Barkin (Eds.) in collaboration with W. Muensterberger, *Between reality and fantasy: Winnicott's concepts of transitional objects and phenomena* (pp. 15-34). Northvale, NJ: Jason Aronson, Inc.

Winnicott, C. (1983). Interview with Dr. Michael Neve, June, 1983. Courtesy of Oskar Diethelm Library, DeWitt Wallace Institute for the History of Psychiatry, Weill Cornell Medical College, Archives and Manuscripts, New York, NY. Transcribed and printed as Appendix B in P. L. Rudnytsky, *The psychoanalytic vocation: Rank, Winnicott and the legacy of Freud.* London: Routledge, 1991.

Winnicott, C. (1984). Introduction. In C. Winnicott, R. Shepherd, & M. Davis (Eds.), *Deprivation and delinquency* (pp. 1-5). London: Routledge, 1990.

Winnicott, D. W. (1913). Smith. *The Leys Fortnightly,* V. 38, #665, October 17. Published by The Leys School, Cambridge.

Winnicott, D. W. (1914). The best remedy. *The Leys Fortnightly,* V. 38, #677, June 12. Published by The Leys School, Cambridge.

Winnicott, D. W. (1916). Letter to Elizabeth Winnicott. In F. R. Rodman, *Winnicott: Life and work.* Cambridge, Mass.: Perseus Books.

Winnicott, D. W. (1919). Letter to Violet Winnicott. In F. R. Rodman, (Ed.), *The spontaneous gesture: Selected letters of D. W. Winnicott* (pp. 1–4). Cambridge, MA: Harvard University Press, 1987.

Winnicott, D. W. (1931a). *Clinical notes on disorders of childhood.* London: William Heinemann.

Winnicott, D. W. (1931b). A note on normality and anxiety. In *Collected papers: Through paediatrics to psycho-analysis* (pp. 3–21). New York: Basic Books, 1958.

Winnicott, D. W. (1934). Papular urticaria and the dynamics of skin sensation. In R. Shepherd, J. Johns, & H. T. Robinson (Eds.), *Thinking about children* (pp. 157–169). Reading, MA: Addison-Wesley Publishing, 1996. Reprinted by Perseus, 1998.

Winnicott, D. W. (1935). The manic defense. In *Collected papers: Through paediatrics to psycho-analysis* (pp. 129–144). New York: Basic Books, 1958.

Winnicott, D. W. (1936a). Mental hygiene in the pre-school child. In R. Shepherd, J. Johns, & H. T. Robinson (Eds.), *Thinking about children* (pp. 59–76). Reading, MA: Addison-Wesley Publishing, 1996. Reprinted by Perseus, 1998.

Winnicott, D. W. (1936b). The teacher, the parent, and the doctor. In R. Shepherd, J. Johns, & H. T. Robinson (Eds.), *Thinking about children* (pp. 79–93). Reading, MA: Addison-Wesley Publishing, 1996. Reprinted by Perseus, 1998.

Winnicott, D. W. (1938). Shyness and nervous disorders in children. In *The child and the outside world* (pp. 35–39). London: Tavistock, 1957. Reprinted by Routledge, 2001.

Winnicott, D. W. (1939). Aggression. In *The child and the outside world* (pp. 167–175). London: Tavistock, 1957. Reprinted by Routledge, 2001.

Winnicott, D. W. (1940). Letter to Kate Friedlander. In F. R. Rodman (Ed.), *The spontaneous gesture: Selected letters of D. W. Winnicott* (pp. 5–6). Cambridge, MA: Harvard University Press, 1987.

Winnicott, D. W. (1941a). Observation of infants in a set situation. In *Collected papers: Through paediatrics to psycho-analysis* (pp. 52–69). New York: Basic Books, 1958.

Winnicott, D. W. (1941b). On influencing and being influenced. In *The child and the outside world* (pp. 24–28). London: Tavistock, 1957. Reprinted by Routledge, 2001.

Winnicott, D. W. (1942). Why children play. In *The child and the outside world* (pp. 149–152). London: Tavistock, 1957. Reprinted by Routledge, 2001.

Winnicott, D. W. (1943). Prefrontal leucotomy. In C. Winnicott, R. Shepherd, & M. Davis (Eds.), *Psychoanalytic explorations* (pp.542–543). Cambridge, MA: Harvard University Press, 1989.

Winnicott, D. W. (1943). Shock treatment of mental disorder. In C. Winnicott, R. Shepherd, & M. Davis (Eds.), *Psychoanalytic explorations* (pp. 522–523). Cambridge, MA: Harvard University Press, 1989.

Winnicott, D. W. (1944). Their standards and yours. In *The child and the family* (pp. 87–91). London: Tavistock, 1957. Reprinted by Routledge, 2001.

Winnicott, D. W. (1945a). Infant feeding. In *The child and the family* (pp. 18–22). London: Tavistock, 1957. Reprinted by Routledge, 2001.

Winnicott, D. W. (1945b). Letter to Editor of British Medical Journal. In F. R. Rodman (Ed.), *The spontaneous gesture: Selected letters of D. W. Winnicott* (pp. 192–194). Cambridge, MA: Harvard University Press, 1987.

Winnicott, D. W. (1945c). Primitive emotional development. In *Collected papers: Through paediatrics to psycho-analysis* (pp. 145–156). New York: Basic Books, 1958.

Winnicott, D. W. (1945d). Thinking and the unconscious. In C. Winnicott, R. Shepherd, & M. Davis (Eds.), *Home is where we start from: Essays by a psychoanalyst* (pp. 169–171). New York: W. W. Norton, 1986.

Winnicott, D. W. (1945e). Towards and objective study of human nature. In *The child and the outside world* (pp. 125–133). London: Tavistock, 1957. Reprinted by Routledge, 2001.

Winnicott, D. W. (1946a). Educational diagnosis. In *The child and the outside world* (pp. 29–34). London: Tavistock, 1957. Reprinted by Routledge, 2001.

Winnicott, D. W. (1946b). What do we mean by a normal child. In *The child and the family* (pp. 100–106). London: Tavistock, 1957. Reprinted by Routledge, 2001.

Winnicott, D. W. (1947a). Further thoughts on babies as persons. In *The child and the outside world* (pp. 134–140). London: Tavistock, 1957. Reprinted by Routledge, 2001.

Winnicott, D. W. (1947b). Child and sex. In *The child and the outside world* (pp. 153–166). London: Tavistock, 1957. Reprinted by Routledge, 2001.

Winnicott, D. W. (1947c). Hate in the countertransference. In *Collected papers: Through paediatrics to psycho-analysis* (pp. 194–203). New York: Basic Books, 1958.

Winnicott, D. W. (1947d). Physical therapy of mental disorder. In C. Winnicott, R. Shepherd, & M. Davis (Eds.), *Psychoanalytic explorations* (pp. 534–541). Cambridge, MA: Harvard University Press, 1989.

Winnicott, D. W. (1948a). Pediatrics and psychiatry. In *Collected papers: Through paediatrics to psycho-analysis* (pp. 157–173). New York: Basic Books, 1958.

Winnicott, D. W. (1948b). Reparation in respect of Mother's organized defence against depression. In *Collected papers: Through paediatrics to psycho-analysis* (pp. 91–96). New York: Basic Books, 1958.

Winnicott, D. W. (1949a). Birth memories, birth trauma, and anxiety. In *Collected papers: Through paediatrics to psycho-analysis* (pp. 174–193). New York: Basic Books, 1958.

Winnicott, D. W. (1949b). Innate morality of the baby. In *The child and the family* (pp. 59–63). London: Tavistock, 1957. Reprinted by Routledge, 2001.

Winnicott, D. W. (1949c). Leucotomy. In C. Winnicott, R. Shepherd, & M. Davis (Eds.), *Psychoanalytic explorations* (pp. 543–547). Cambridge, MA: Harvard University Press, 1989. Originally published in *British Medical Students' Journal, 3*(2), 35–38.

Winnicott, D. W. (1949d). Letter to L. Livingstone, February 18. Donald Woods Winnicott Papers (PP/DWW/B/A/19, Box 10). Wellcome Library, 183 Euston Road, London NW1 2BE.

Winnicott, D. W. (1949e). Letter to S.H. Hodge. In F. R. Rodman (Ed.), *The spontaneous gesture: Selected letters of D. W. Winnicott* (pp. 192–194). Cambridge, MA: Harvard University Press, 1987.

Winnicott, D. W. (1949f). Man looks at motherhood. In *The child and the family* (pp. 3–6). London: Tavistock, 1957. Reprinted by Routledge, 2001.

Winnicott, D. W. (1949g). Mind and its relation to the psyche-soma. In *Collected papers: Through paediatrics to psycho-analysis* (pp. 243–254). New York: Basic Books, 1958.

Winnicott, D. W. (1949h). Sex education in schools. In *The child and the outside world* (pp. 40–49). London: Tavistock, 1957. Reprinted by Routledge, 2001.

Winnicott, D. W. (1949i). World in small doses. In *The child and the family* (pp. 53–58). London: Tavistock, 1957. Reprinted by Routledge, 2001.

Winnicott, D. W. (1949j). Young children and other people. In *The child and the family* (pp. 92–99). London: Tavistock, 1957. Reprinted by Routledge, 2001.

Winnicott, D. W. (1950a). Aggression in relation to emotional development. In *Collected papers: Through paediatrics to psycho-analysis* (pp. 204–218). New York: Basic Books, 1958.

Winnicott, D. W. (1950b). Deprived child and how he can be compensated for loss of family life. In *The family and individual development* (pp. 132–150). London: Tavistock, 1965. Reprinted by Routledge, 1990.

Winnicott, D. W. (1950c). Growth and development in immaturity. In *The family and individual development* (pp. 21–29). London: Tavistock, 1965. Reprinted by Routledge, 1990.

Winnicott, D. W. (1950d). Letter to George and Sylvia, December 6. Donald Woods Winnicott Papers (PP/DWW/B/A/10, Box 8). Wellcome Library, 183 Euston Road, London NW1 2BE.

Winnicott, D. W. (1950e). Some thoughts on the meaning of the word "democracy." In C. Winnicott, R. Shepherd, & M. Davis (Eds.), *Home is where we start from: Essays by a psychoanalyst* (pp. 239–259). New York: W. W. Norton, 1986.

Winnicott, D. W. (1951a). Notes on the general implications of leucotomy. In C. Winnicott, R. Shepherd, & M. Davis (Eds.), *Psychoanalytic explorations* (pp.548–552). Cambridge, MA: Harvard University Press, 1989.

Winnicott, D. W. (1951b). Transitional objects and transitional phenomena. In *Collected papers: Through paediatrics to psycho-analysis* (pp. 229–242). New York: Basic Books, 1958.

Winnicott, D. W. (1952a). Anxiety associated with insecurity. In *Collected papers: Through paediatrics to psycho-analysis* (pp. 97–100). New York: Basic Books, 1958.

Winnicott, D. W. (1952b). Letter to Melanie Klein. In F. R. Rodman (Ed.), *The spontaneous gesture: Selected letters of D. W. Winnicott* (pp. 33–38). Cambridge, MA: Harvard University Press, 1987.

Winnicott, D. W. (1952c). Letter to Roger Money-Kyrle. In F. R. Rodman (Ed.), *The spontaneous gesture: Selected letters of D. W. Winnicott* (pp. 38–43). Cambridge, MA: Harvard University Press, 1987.

Winnicott, D. W. (1952d). Psychoses and child care. In *Collected papers: Through paediatrics to psycho-analysis* (pp. 219–228). New York: Basic Books, 1958.

Winnicott, D. W. (1953a). Letter to David Rapaport. In F. R. Rodman (Ed.), *The spontaneous gesture: Selected letters of D. W. Winnicott* (pp. 53–54). Cambridge, MA: Harvard University Press, 1987.

Winnicott, D. W. (1953b). Review of "Psychoanalytic studies of the personality" (written with M. Khan). In C. Winnicott, R. Shepherd, & M. Davis (Eds.), *Psychoanalytic explorations* (pp. 413–422). Cambridge, MA: Harvard University Press, 1989. Originally published in *International Journal of Psycho-Analysis, 34*, 329–333.

Winnicott, D. W. (1954a). Breast feeding. In *The child and the outside world* (pp. 141–148). London: Tavistock, 1957. Reprinted by Routledge, 2001.

Winnicott, D. W. (1954b). Depressive position in normal emotional development. In *Collected papers: Through paediatrics to psycho-analysis* (pp. 262–277). New York: Basic Books, 1958.

Winnicott, D. W. (1954c). *Human nature*. C. Bollas, M. Davis, & R. Shepherd (Eds.). New York: Schocken, 1984.

Winnicott, D. W. (1954d). Letter to Anna Freud and Melanie Klein. In F. R. Rodman (Ed.), *The spontaneous gesture: Selected letters of D. W. Winnicott* (pp. 71–74). Cambridge, MA: Harvard University Press, 1987.

Winnicott, D. W. (1954e). Letter to E. Stengal, Feburary 5. Donald Woods Winnicott Papers (PP/DWW/B/A/28, Box 11). Wellcome Library, 183 Euston Road, London NW1 2BE.

Winnicott, D. W. (1954f). Letter to Harry Guntrip. In F. R. Rodman (Ed.), *The spontaneous gesture: Selected letters of D. W. Winnicott* (pp. 75–76). Cambridge, MA: Harvard University Press, 1987.

Winnicott, D. W. (1954g). Letter to Michael Fordham. In F. R. Rodman (Ed.), *The spontaneous gesture: Selected letters of D. W. Winnicott* (pp. 192–194). Cambridge, MA: Harvard University Press, 1987.

Winnicott, D. W. (1954h). Metapsychological and clinical aspects of regression within the psycho-analytical set-up. In *Collected papers: Through paediatrics to psychoanalysis* (pp. 278–294). New York: Basic Books, 1958.

Winnicott, D. W. (1954i). Michael Balint: Character types: The foolhardy and the cautious. In C. Winnicott, R. Shepherd, & M. Davis (Eds.), *Psychoanalytic explorations* (pp. 433–437). Cambridge, MA: Harvard University Press, 1989.

Winnicott, D. W. (1954j). Needs of the under-fives in a changing society. In *The child and the outside world* (pp. 3–13). London: Tavistock, 1957. Reprinted by Routledge, 2001.

Winnicott, D. W. (1955a). First experiments in independence. In *The child and the family* (pp. 131–136). London: Tavistock, 1957. Reprinted by Routledge, 2001.

Winnicott, D. W. (1955b). Group influences and the maladjusted child: The school aspect. In *The family and individual development* (pp. 146–154). London: Tavistock, 1965. Reprinted by Routledge, 1990.

Winnicott, D. W. (1956a). Antisocial tendency. In *Collected papers: Through paediatrics to psycho-analysis* (pp. 306–315). New York: Basic Books, 1958.

Winnicott, D. W. (1956b). Letter to Barbara Lantos. In F. R. Rodman (Ed.), *The spontaneous gesture: Selected letters of D. W. Winnicott* (pp. 107–110). Cambridge, MA: Harvard University Press, 1987.

Winnicott, D. W. (1956c). Letter to Gabriel Casuso. In F. R. Rodman (Ed.), *The spontaneous gesture: Selected letters of D. W. Winnicott* (pp. 192–194). Cambridge, MA: Harvard University Press, 1987.

Winnicott, D. W. (1956d). Paediatrics and childhood neurosis. In *Collected papers: Through paediatrics to psycho-analysis* (pp. 316–321). New York: Basic Books, 1958.

Winnicott, D. W. (1956e). Prefrontal leucotomy. In C. Winnicott, R. Shepherd, & M. Davis (Eds.), *Psychoanalytic explorations* (pp.553–554). Cambridge, MA: Harvard University Press, 1989.

Winnicott, D. W. (1956f). Primary maternal preoccupation. In *Collected papers: Through paediatrics to psycho-analysis* (pp. 300–305). New York: Basic Books, 1958.

Winnicott, D. W. (1956g). What do we know about babies as cloth suckers? In C. Winnicott, C. Bollas, M. Davis, & R. Shepherd (Eds.), *Talking to parents* (pp. 15–20). Cambridge, MA: Perseus Publishing, 1993. Reprinted by Perseus, 1994.

Winnicott, D. W. (1957a). Contribution of psycho-analysis to midwifery. In *The family and individual development* (pp. 106–113). London: Tavistock, 1965. Reprinted by Routledge, 1990.

Winnicott, D. W. (1957b). Contribution of psychoanalysis to midwifery. In C. Winnicott, R. Shepherd, & M. Davis (Eds.), *Babies and their mothers* (pp. 69–81). Reading, MA: Addison-Wesley, 1987. Reprinted by Perseus, 1992.

Winnicott, D. W. (1957c). Letter to Michael Balint. In F. R. Rodman (Ed.), *Winnicott: Life and work* (p. 239). Cambridge, MA: Perseus Books, 2003.

Winnicott, D. W. (1957d). Mother's contribution to society. In *The child and the family* (pp. 141–144). London: Tavistock, 1957. Reprinted by Routledge, 2001.

Winnicott, D. W. (1957e). On the contribution of direct child observation to psycho-analysis. In *The maturational processes and the facilitating environment* (pp. 109–114). Madison, CT: International Universities Press, 1965.

Winnicott, D. W. (1958a). Capacity to be alone. In *The maturational processes and the facilitating environment* (pp. 29–36). Madison, CT: International Universities Press, 1965.

Winnicott, D. W. (1958b). Child analysis in the latency period. In *The maturational processes and the facilitating environment* (pp. 115–123). Madison, CT: International Universities Press, 1965.

Winnicott, D. W. (1958c). Ernest Jones funeral address. In C. Winnicott, R. Shepherd, & M. Davis (Eds.), *Psychoanalytic explorations* (pp. 405–407). Cambridge, MA: Harvard University Press, 1989.

Winnicott, D. W. (1958d). Ernest Jones obituary. In C. Winnicott, R. Shepherd, & M. Davis (Eds.), *Psychoanalytic explorations* (pp. 393–404). Cambridge, MA: Harvard University Press, 1989.

Winnicott, D. W. (1958e). Family affected by depressive illness in one or both of parents. In *The family and individual development* (pp. 50–60). London: Tavistock, 1965. Reprinted by Routledge, 1990.

Winnicott, D. W. (1958f). First year of life. In *The family and individual development* (pp. 3–14). London: Tavistock, 1965. Reprinted by Routledge, 1990.

Winnicott, D. W. (1958g). Psycho-analysis and the sense of guilt. In *The maturational processes and the facilitating environment* (pp. 15–28). Madison, CT: International Universities Press, 1965.

Winnicott, D. W. (1958h). Theoretical statement of the field of child psychiatry. In *The family and individual development* (pp. 97–105). London: Tavistock, 1965. Reprinted by Routledge, 1990.

Winnicott, D. W. (1959a). Casework with mentally ill children. In *The family and individual development* (pp. 121-131). London: Tavistock, 1965. Reprinted by Routledge, 1990.

Winnicott, D. W. (1959b). Clinical approach to family problems: The family. In R. Shepherd, J. Johns, & H. T. Robinson (Eds.), *Thinking about children* (pp. 54–56). Reading, MA: Addison-Wesley Publishing, 1996. Reprinted by Perseus, 1998.

Winnicott, D. W. (1959c). Effect of psychotic parents on the emotional development of the child. In *The family and individual development* (pp. 69–78). London: Tavistock, 1965. Reprinted by Routledge, 1990.

Winnicott, D. W. (1959d). Fate of transitional object. In C. Winnicott, R. Shepherd, & M. Davis (Eds.), *Psychoanalytic explorations* (pp. 53–58). Cambridge, MA: Harvard University Press, 1989.

Winnicott, D. W. (1959e). Partially filled out questionnaire. Donald W. Winnicott Personal Papers. Courtesy of Oskar Diethelm Library, DeWitt Wallace Institute for the History of Psychiatry, Weill Cornell Medical College, Archives and Manuscripts, New York, NY.

Winnicott, D. W. (1959-1964). Classification: Is there a psychoanalytic contribution to psychiatric classification. In *The maturational processes and the facilitating environment* (pp. 124–139). Madison, CT: International Universities Press, 1965.

Winnicott, D. W. (1960a). Aggression, guilt and reparation. In C. Winnicott, R. Shepherd, & M. Davis (Eds.), *Deprivation and delinquency* (pp. 136–144). London: Routledge, 1990.

Winnicott, D. W. (1960b). Comments on "On the concept of the superego." In C. Winnicott, R. Shepherd, & M. Davis (Eds.), *Psychoanalytic explorations* (pp. 465–473). Cambridge, MA: Harvard University Press, 1989.

Winnicott, D. W. (1960c). Counter-transference. In *The maturational processes and the facilitating environment* (pp. 158–165). Madison, CT: International Universities Press, 1965.

Winnicott, D. W. (1960d). Effects of psychosis on family life. In *The family and individual development* (pp. 61–68). London: Tavistock, 1965. Reprinted by Routledge, 1990.

Winnicott, D. W. (1960e). Ego distortions in terms of true and false self. In *The maturational processes and the facilitating environment* (pp. 140–152). Madison, CT: International Universities Press, 1965.

Winnicott, D. W. (1960f). Family and emotional maturity. In *The family and individual development* (pp. 88–94). London: Tavistock, 1965. Reprinted by Routledge, 1990.

Winnicott, D. W. (1960g). Letter to Michael Balint. In F. R. Rodman (Ed.), *The spontaneous gesture: Selected letters of D. W. Winnicott* (pp. 126–127). Cambridge, MA: Harvard University Press, 1987.

Winnicott, D. W. (1960h). Relationship of a mother to her baby at the beginning. In *The family and individual development* (pp. 15–20). London: Tavistock, 1965. Reprinted by Routledge, 1990.

Winnicott, D. W. (1960i). Theory of the parent-infant relationship. In *The maturational processes and the facilitating environment* (pp. 37–55). Madison, CT: International Universities Press, 1965.

Winnicott, D. W. (1961a). Adolescence: Struggling through the doldrums. In *The family and individual development* (pp. 79–86). London: Tavistock, 1965. Reprinted by Routledge, 1990.

Winnicott, D. W. (1961b). Letter to Arthur Guinness Son & Co., October 31. Donald W. Winnicott Personal Papers. Courtesy of Oskar Diethelm Library, DeWitt Wallace Institute for the History of Psychiatry, Weill Cornell Medical College, Archives and Manuscripts, New York, NY.

Winnicott, D. W. (1961c). Personal view. *St. Mary's Hospital Gazette* July/August V. LXVII # 5, pp. 137–138.

Winnicott, D. W. (1961d). Psychoanalysis and science: Friends or relations? In C. Winnicott, R. Shepherd, & M. Davis (Eds.), *Home is where we start from: Essays by a psychoanalyst* (pp. 13–18). New York: W. W. Norton, 1986.

Winnicott, D. W. (1961e). Training for child psychiatry: The paediatric department of psychology. In R. Shepherd, J. Johns, & H. T. Robinson (Eds.), *Thinking about children* (pp. 227–230). Reading, MA: Addison-Wesley Publishing, 1996. Reprinted by Perseus, 1998.

Winnicott, D. W. (1961f). Varieties of psychotherapy. In C. Winnicott, R. Shepherd, & M. Davis (Eds.), *Home is where we start from: Essays by a psychoanalyst* (pp. 101–111). New York: W. W. Norton, 1986.

Winnicott, D. W. (1962a). Development of a child's sense of right and wrong. In C. Winnicott, C. Bollas, M. Davis, & R. Shepherd (Eds.), *Talking to parents* (pp. 105–110). Cambridge, MA: Perseus Publishing, 1993. Reprinted by Perseus, 1994.

Winnicott, D. W. (1962b). Ego integration in child development. In *The maturational processes and the facilitating environment* (pp. 56–63). Madison, CT: International Universities Press, 1965.

Winnicott, D. W. (1962c). Personal view of the Kleinian contribution. In *The maturational processes and the facilitating environment* (pp. 171–178). Madison, CT: International Universities Press, 1965.

Winnicott, D. W. (1962d). Providing for the child in health and in crisis. In *The maturational processes and the facilitating environment* (pp. 64–72). Madison, CT: International Universities Press, 1965.

Winnicott, D. W. (1963a). Communicating and not communicating leading to a study of certain opposites. In The *maturational processes and the facilitating environment* (pp. 179–192). Madison, CT: International Universities Press, 1965.

Winnicott, D. W. (1963b). Dependence in infant care, in child care, and in the psychoanalytic setting. In *The maturational processes and the facilitating environment* (pp. 249–260). Madison, CT: International Universities Press, 1965.

Winnicott, D. W. (1963c). Development of the capacity for concern. In *The maturational processes and the facilitating environment* (pp. 73–82). Madison, CT: International Universities Press, 1965.

Winnicott, D. W. (1963d). DWW's dream related to reviewing Jung. In C. Winnicott, R. Shepherd, & M. Davis (Eds.), *Psychoanalytic explorations* (pp.228–230). Cambridge, MA: Harvard University Press, 1989.

Winnicott, D. W. (1963e). Fear of breakdown. In C. Winnicott, R. Shepherd, & M. Davis (Eds.), *Psychoanalytic explorations* (pp. 87–95). Cambridge, MA: Harvard University Press, 1989.

Winnicott, D. W. (1963f). From dependence towards independence in the development of the individual. In *The maturational processes and the facilitating environment* (pp. 83–92). Madison, CT: International Universities Press, 1965.

Winnicott, D. W. (1963g). Harold F. Searles. Review of "The non-human environment in normal development and in schizophrenia." In C. Winnicott, R. Shepherd, & M. Davis (Eds.), *Psychoanalytic explorations* (pp.478–481). Cambridge, MA: Harvard University Press, 1989. Originally published in *International Journal of Psycho-Analysis, 43*, 237–238.

Winnicott, D. W. (1963h). Letter to Timothy Raison. In F. R. Rodman (Ed.), *The spontaneous gesture: Selected letters of D. W. Winnicott* (pp. 139–140). Cambridge, MA: Harvard University Press, 1987.

Winnicott, D. W. (1963i). Mentally ill in your caseload. In *The maturational processes and the facilitating environment* (pp. 217–229). Madison, CT: International Universities Press, 1965.

Winnicott, D. W. (1963j). Morals and education. In *The maturational processes and the facilitating environment* (pp. 93–105). Madison, CT: International Universities Press, 1965.

Winnicott, D. W. (1963k). Psychiatric disorder in terms of infantile maturational processes. In *The maturational processes and the facilitating environment* (pp. 230–241). Madison, CT: International Universities Press, 1965.

Winnicott, D. W. (1963l). Psychotherapy of character disorders. In *The maturational processes and the facilitating environment* (pp. 203–216). Madison, CT: International Universities Press, 1965.

Winnicott, D. W. (1963m). Two notes on the use of silence. In C. Winnicott, R. Shepherd, & M. Davis (Eds.), *Psychoanalytic explorations* (pp. 81–86). Cambridge, MA: Harvard University Press, 1989.

Winnicott, D. W. (1963n). Value of depression. In C. Winnicott, R. Shepherd, & M. Davis (Eds.), *Home is where we start from: Essays by a psychoanalyst* (pp. 71–79). New York: W. W. Norton, 1986.

Winnicott, D. W. (1964a). Concept of the false self. In C. Winnicott, R. Shepherd, & M. Davis (Eds.), *Home is where we start from: Essays by a psychoanalyst* (pp. 65–70). New York: W. W. Norton, 1986.

Winnicott, D. W. (1964b). Handwritten notes on typescript of "This Feminism." Donald W. Winnicott Personal Papers. Courtesy of Oskar Diethelm Library, DeWitt Wallace Institute for the History of Psychiatry, Weill Cornell Medical College, Archives and Manuscripts, New York, NY.

Winnicott, D. W. (1964c). Innate morality of the child. In *The child, the family and the outside world* (pp. 93–97). Middlesex, England: Penguin Books, 1964.

Winnicott, D. W. (1964d). Letter to the London Times (unpublished), April 19. Donald W. Winnicott Personal Papers. Courtesy of Oskar Diethelm Library, DeWitt Wallace Institute for the History of Psychiatry, Weill Cornell Medical College, Archives and Manuscripts, New York, NY.

Winnicott, D. W. (1964e). Letter to John O. Wisdom. In F. R. Rodman (Ed.), *The spontaneous gesture: Selected letters of D. W. Winnicott* (pp. 192–194). Cambridge, MA: Harvard University Press, 1987.

References

Winnicott, D. W. (1964f). Newborn and his mother. In C. Winnicott, R. Shepherd, & M. Davis (Eds.), *Babies and their mothers* (pp. 35–49). Reading, MA: Addison-Wesley, 1987. Reprinted by Perseus, 1992.

Winnicott, D. W. (1964g). Psychosomatic illness in its positive and negative aspects. In C. Winnicott, R. Shepherd, & M. Davis (Eds.), *Psychoanalytic explorations* (pp.103–114). Cambridge, MA: Harvard University Press, 1989.

Winnicott, D. W. (1964h). Review of memories, dreams, reflections. In C. Winnicott, R. Shepherd, & M. Davis (Eds.), *Psychoanalytic explorations* (pp. 482–492). Cambridge, MA: Harvard University Press, 1989.

Winnicott, D. W. (1964i). Roots of aggression. In C. Winnicott, R. Shepherd, & M. Davis (Eds.), *Deprivation and delinquency* (pp. 92–99). London: Routledge, 1990.

Winnicott, D. W. (1964j). Stealing and telling lies. In *The child, the family and the outside world* (pp. 161–166). Middlesex, England: Penguin Books, 1964.

Winnicott, D. W. (1964k). This feminism. In C. Winnicott, R. Shepherd, & M. Davis (Eds.), *Home is where we start from: Essays by a psychoanalyst* (pp. 183–194). New York: W. W. Norton, 1986.

Winnicott, D. W. (1964-1968). Squiggle game. In C. Winnicott, R. Shepherd, & M. Davis (Eds.), *Psychoanalytic explorations* (pp.299–317). Cambridge, MA: Harvard University Press, 1989.

Winnicott, D. W. (1965a). Child psychiatry case illustrating delayed reaction to loss. In C. Winnicott, R. Shepherd, & M. Davis (Eds.), *Psychoanalytic explorations* (pp. 341–368). Cambridge, MA: Harvard University Press, 1989.

Winnicott, D. W. (1965b). Letter to Joyce and Arthur Coles, August 23. Donald Woods Winnicott Papers (PP/DWW/B/C/1, Box 13). Wellcome Library, 183 Euston Road, London NW1 2BE.

Winnicott, D. W. (1965c). New light on children's thinking. In C. Winnicott, R. Shepherd, & M. Davis (Eds.), *Psychoanalytic explorations* (pp. 152–157). Cambridge, MA: Harvard University Press, 1989.

Winnicott, D. W. (1965d). Price of disregarding psychoanalytic research. In C. Winnicott, R. Shepherd, & M. Davis (Eds.), *Home is where we start from: Essays by a psychoanalyst* (pp. 172–182). New York: W. W. Norton, 1986.

Winnicott, D. W. (1965e). Psychology of madness: A contribution to psychoanalysis. In C. Winnicott, R. Shepherd, & M. Davis (Eds.), *Psychoanalytic explorations* (pp.119–129). Cambridge, MA: Harvard University Press, 1989.

Winnicott, D. W. (1965f). Value of the therapeutic consultation. In C. Winnicott, R. Shepherd, & M. Davis (Eds.), *Psychoanalytic explorations* (pp. 318–324). Cambridge, MA: Harvard University Press, 1989.

Winnicott, D. W. (1965g). Virginia Axline: Commentary on play therapy. In C. Winnicott, R. Shepherd, & M. Davis (Eds.), *Psychoanalytic explorations* (pp.495–498). Cambridge, MA: Harvard University Press, 1989.

Winnicott, D. W. (1966a). Absence and presence of a sense of guilt illustrated in two patients. In C. Winnicott, R. Shepherd, & M. Davis (Eds.), *Psychoanalytic explorations* (pp. 163–167). Cambridge, MA: Harvard University Press, 1989.

Winnicott, D. W. (1966b). An allotted spanner in the works. Unpublished note. Donald Woods Winnicott Papers (PP/DWW/G/4, Box 28). Wellcome Library, 183 Euston Road, London NW1 2BE.

Winnicott, D. W. (1966c). Absence of a sense of guilt. In C. Winnicott, R. Shepherd, & M. Davis (Eds.), *Deprivation and delinquency* (pp. 106–112). London: Routledge, 1990.

Winnicott, D. W. (1966d). Autism. In R. Shepherd, J. Johns, & H. Robinson (Eds.), *Thinking about children* (pp. 197–217). Reading, MA: Addison-Wesley Publishing, 1996. Reprinted by Perseus, 1998.

Winnicott, D. W. (1966e). Beginning of the individual. In C. Winnicott, R. Shepherd, & M. Davis (Eds.), *Babies and their mothers* (pp. 51–58). Reading, MA: Addison-Wesley, 1987. Reprinted by Perseus, 1992.

Winnicott, D. W. (1966f). Child in the family group. In C. Winnicott, R. Shepherd, & M. Davis (Eds.), *Home is where we start from: Essays by a psychoanalyst* (pp. 128–141). New York: W. W. Norton, 1986.

Winnicott, D. W. (1966g). Letter to L. Dobie. March 21. Donald W. Winnicott Personal Papers. Courtesy of Oskar Diethelm Library, DeWitt Wallace Institute for the History of Psychiatry, Weill Cornell Medical College, Archives and Manuscripts, New York, NY.

Winnicott, D. W. (1966h). Letter to K. Whitehorn, September 23. In D. Goldman, *In search of the real: The origins and originality of D.W. Winnicott* (p. 42). Northvale, NJ: Aronson.

Winnicott, D. W. (1966i). Ordinary devoted mother. In C. Winnicott, R. Shepherd, & M. Davis (Eds.), *Babies and their mothers* (pp. 3–14). Reading, MA: Addison-Wesley, 1987. Reprinted by Perseus, 1992.

Winnicott, D. W. (1967a). Association for Child Psychology and Psychiatry observed as a group phenomenon. In R. Shepherd, J. Johns, & H. T. Robinson (Eds.), *Thinking about children* (pp. 235–254). Reading, MA: Addison-Wesley Publishing, 1996. Reprinted by Perseus, 1998.

Winnicott, D. W. (1967b). Concept of clinical regression compared with that of defense organization. In C. Winnicott, R. Shepherd, & M. Davis (Eds.), *Psychoanalytic explorations* (pp.193–199). Cambridge, MA: Harvard University Press, 1989.

Winnicott, D. W. (1967c). Concept of a healthy individual. In C. Winnicott, R. Shepherd, & M. Davis (Eds.), *Home is where we start from: Essays by a psychoanalyst* (pp. 21–38). New York: W. W. Norton, 1986.

Winnicott, D. W. (1967d). Delinquency as a sign of hope. In C. Winnicott, R. Shepherd, & M. Davis (Eds.), *Home is where we start from: Essays by a psychoanalyst* (pp. 90–100). New York: W. W. Norton, 1986.

Winnicott, D. W. (1967e). Letter to Margaret Torrie. In F. R. Rodman (Ed.), *The spontaneous gesture: Selected letters of D. W. Winnicott* (pp. 192–194). Cambridge, MA: Harvard University Press, 1987.

Winnicott, D. W. (1967f). Letter to Wilford Bion. In F. R. Rodman (Ed.), *The spontaneous gesture: Selected letters of D. W. Winnicott* (pp. 192–194). Cambridge, MA: Harvard University Press, 1987.

Winnicott, D. W. (1967g). Mirror role of mother and family in child development. In *Playing and reality* (pp. 111–118). New York: Routledge, 1989.

Winnicott, D. W. (1967h). Postscript: D.W.W. on D.W.W. In C. Winnicott, R. Shepherd, & M. Davis (Eds.), *Psychoanalytic explorations* (pp.569–582). Cambridge, MA: Harvard University Press, 1989.

Winnicott, D. W. (1968a). Case IX 'Ashton' aet 12 years. In *Therapeutic consultations in child psychiatry (*pp. 147–160). New York, NY: Basic Books, 1971.

Winnicott, D. W. (1968b). Children learning. In C. Winnicott, R. Shepherd, & M. Davis (Eds.), *Home is where we start from: Essays by a psychoanalyst* (pp. 142–149). New York: W. W. Norton, 1986.

Winnicott, D. W. (1968c). Clinical illustration of the "use of an object." In C. Winnicott, R. Shepherd, & M. Davis (Eds.), *Psychoanalytic explorations* (pp. 235–238). Cambridge, MA: Harvard University Press, 1989.

Winnicott, D. W. (1968d). Communication between infant and mother, and mother and infant, compared and contrasted. In C. Winnicott, R. Shepherd, & M. Davis (Eds.), *Babies and their mothers* (pp. 89–103). Reading, MA: Addison-Wesley, 1987. Reprinted by Perseus, 1992.

Winnicott, D. W. (1968e). Letter to D. Holbrook, January 15. Donald W. Winnicott Personal Papers. Courtesy of Oskar Diethelm Library, DeWitt Wallace Institute for the History of Psychiatry, Weill Cornell Medical College, Archives and Manuscripts, New York, NY.

Winnicott, D. W. (1968f). Letter to Donald Gough. In F. R. Rodman (Ed.), *The spontaneous gesture: Selected letters of D. W. Winnicott* (pp. 176–177). Cambridge, MA: Harvard University Press, 1987.

Winnicott, D. W. (1968g). Playing and culture. In C. Winnicott, R. Shepherd, & M. Davis (Eds.), *Psychoanalytic explorations* (pp. 203–206). Cambridge, MA: Harvard University Press, 1989.

Winnicott, D. W. (1968h). Roots of aggression. In C. Winnicott, R. Shepherd, & M. Davis (Eds.), *Psychoanalytic explorations* (pp. 458–461). Cambridge, MA: Harvard University Press, 1989.

Winnicott, D. W/ (1968i). Sum, I am. In C. Winnicott, R. Shepherd, & M. Davis (Eds.), *Home is where we start from: Essays by a psychoanalyst* (pp. 55–64). New York: W. W. Norton, 1986.

Winnicott, D. W. (1968j). Use of the word "use". In C. Winnicott, R. Shepherd, & M. Davis (Eds.), *Psychoanalytic explorations* (pp. 233–235). Cambridge, MA: Harvard University Press, 1989.

Winnicott, D. W. (1969a). Behaviour therapy. In C. Winnicott, R. Shepherd, & M. Davis (Eds.), *Psychoanalytic explorations* (pp. 558–560). Cambridge, MA: Harvard University Press, 1989.

Winnicott, D. W. (1969b). Berlin walls. In C. Winnicott, R. Shepherd, & M. Davis (Eds.), *Home is where we start from: Essays by a psychoanalyst* (pp. 221–227). New York: W. W. Norton, 1986.

Winnicott, D. W. (1969c). Freedom. In C. Winnicott, R. Shepherd, & M. Davis (Eds.), *Home is where we start from: Essays by a psychoanalyst* (pp. 228–238). New York: W. W. Norton, 1986.

Winnicott, D. W. (1969d). James Strachey obituary. In C. Winnicott, R. Shepherd, & M. Davis (Eds.), *Psychoanalytic explorations* (pp. 506–510). Cambridge, MA: Harvard University Press, 1989. Originally published in *International Journal of Psycho-Analysis, 50*, 129-132.

Winnicott, D. W. (1969e). Letter to M. B. Conran. In F. R. Rodman (Ed.), *The spontaneous gesture: Selected letters of D. W. Winnicott,* (pp. 188–191). Cambridge, MA: Harvard University Press, 1987.

Winnicott, D. W. (1969f) Letter to the *London Times* (unpublished), December 22. Donald W. Winnicott Personal Papers.Courtesy of Oskar Diethelm Library, DeWitt Wallace Institute for the History of Psychiatry, Weill Cornell Medical College, Archives and Manuscripts, New York, NY.

Winnicott, D. W. (1969g). Letter to I. Rodger, June 3. Donald W. Winnicott Personal Papers. Courtesy of Oskar Diethelm Library, DeWitt Wallace Institute for the History of Psychiatry, Weill Cornell Medical College, Archives and Manuscripts, New York, NY.

Winnicott, D. W. (1969h). Letter to William Sargant. In F. R. Rodman (Ed.), *The sponta-neous gesture: Selected letters of D. W. Winnicott* (pp. 192–194). Cambridge, MA: Harvard University Press, 1987.

Winnicott, D. W. (1969i). Mother-infant experience of mutuality. In C. Winnicott, R. Shepherd, & M. Davis (Eds.), *Psychoanalytic explorations* (pp. 251–260). Cambridge, MA: Harvard University Press, 1989.

Winnicott, D. W. (1969j). Physiotherapy and human relations. In C. Winnicott, R. Shepherd, & M. Davis (Eds.), *Psychoanalytic explorations* (pp. 561–568). Cambridge, MA: Harvard University Press, 1989.

Winnicott, D. W. (1969k). Pill and the moon. In C. Winnicott, R. Shepherd, & M. Davis (Eds.), *Home is where we start from: Essays by a psychoanalyst* (pp. 195–209). New York: W. W. Norton, 1986.

Winnicott, D. W. (1969l). Use of an object in the context of *Moses and Monotheism*. In C. Winnicott, R. Shepherd, & M. Davis (Eds.), *Psychoanalytic explorations* (pp. 240–246). Cambridge, MA: Harvard University Press, 1989.

Winnicott, D. W. (1970a). Basis for self in body. In C. Winnicott, R. Shepherd, & M. Davis (Eds.), *Psychoanalytic explorations* (pp. 261–271). Cambridge, MA: Harvard University Press, 1989.

Winnicott, D. W. (1970b). Case XII 'Milton' aet 8 years. In *Therapeutic consultations in child psychiatry* (pp. 194–219). New York, NY: Basic Books, 1971.

Winnicott, D. W. (1970c). Child psychiatry, social work, and alternative care. In R. Shepherd, J. Johns, & H. T. Robinson (Eds.), *Thinking about children* (pp. 277–281). Reading, MA: Addison-Wesley Publishing, 1996. Reprinted by Perseus, 1998.

Winnicott, D. W. (1970d). Cure. In C. Winnicott, R. Shepherd, & M. Davis (Eds.), *Home is where we start from: Essays by a psychoanalyst* (pp. 112–120). New York: W. W. Norton, 1986.

Winnicott, D. W. (1970e). Living creatively. In C. Winnicott, R. Shepherd, & M. Davis (Eds.), *Home is where we start from: Essays by a psychoanalyst* (pp. 39–54). New York: W. W. Norton, 1986.

Winnicott, D. W. (1970f). Place of the monarchy. In C. Winnicott, R. Shepherd, & M. Davis (Eds.), *Home is where we start from: Essays by a psychoanalyst* (pp. 260–268). New York: W. W. Norton, 1986.

Winnicott, D. W. (1970g). Residential care as therapy. In C. Winnicott, R. Shepherd, & M. Davis (Eds.), *Deprivation and delinquency* (pp. 220–228). London: Routledge, 1990.

Winnicott, D. W. (1970h). Two further clinical examples. In C. Winnicott, R. Shepherd, & M. Davis (Eds.), *Psychoanalytic explorations* (pp. 272–283). Cambridge, MA: Harvard University Press, 1989.

Winnicott, D. W. (1970i). Unpublished notes marked: Newcastle ACPP 1970 (A Personal Statement about Dynamic Psychology). Donald Woods Winnicott Papers (PP/DWW/A/M/1, Box 38). Wellcome Library, 183 Euston Road, London NW1 2BE.

Winnicott, D. W. (1971a). Case XVIII 'Mrs. X' aet 30 years. In *Therapeutic consultations in child psychiatry* (pp. 331–341). New York, NY: Basic Books, 1971.

Winnicott, D. W. (1971b). Creativity and its origins. In *Playing and reality* (pp. 65-85). New York: Routledge, 1989.

Winnicott, D. W. (1971c). Dreaming, fantasying, and living: A case-history describing a primary dissociation. In *Playing and reality* (pp. 26–37). New York: Routledge, 1989.

Winnicott, D. W. (1971d). Interrelating apart from instinctual drive and in terms of cross-identifications. In *Playing and reality* (pp. 119–137). New York: Routledge, 1989.

Winnicott, D. W. (1971e). Location of cultural experience. In *Playing and reality* (pp. 95–103). New York: Routledge, 1989.

Winnicott, D. W. (1971f). Part I Introduction. In *Therapeutic consultations in child psychiatry* (pp.1–11). New York: Basic Books, 1971.

Winnicott, D. W. (1971g). Part II Introduction. In *Therapeutic consultations in child psychiatry* (pp.127–128). New York: Basic Books, 1971.

Winnicott, D. W. (1971h). Place where we live. In *Playing and reality* (pp. 104–110). New York: Routledge, 1989.

Winnicott, D. W. (1971i). Playing: A theoretical statement. In *Playing and reality* (pp. 38–52). New York: Routledge, 1989.

Winnicott, D. W. (1971j). Playing: Creative activity and the search for the self. In *Playing and reality* (pp. 53–64). New York: Routledge, 1989.

Winnicott, D. W. (1971k). Use of an object and relating through identifications. In *Playing and reality* (pp. 86–94). New York: Routledge, 1989.

Winnicott, D. W. (1971l). Transitional objects and transitional phenomena. In *Playing and reality* (pp. 1–25). New York: Routledge, 1989.

Winnicott, D. W. (1977). *The piggle: An account of the psychoanalytic treatment of a little girl*. I. Ramzy (Ed.). New York: International Universities Press.

Winnicott, D. W. (n.d.1). Letter to J. Coles, August 4, no year. Donald Woods Winnicott Papers (PP/DWW/B/C/2, Box 13). Wellcome Library, 183 Euston Road, London NW1 2BE.

Winnicott, D. W. (n.d.2). Letter to H. Loewald. Donald Woods Winnicott Papers (PP/DWW/B/A/19, Box 10). Wellcome Library, 183 Euston Road, London NW1 2BE.

Winnicott, D. W. (n.d.3). "My object this evening is to plead for a Christianity which is more nearly related to Christ..." Unpublished handwritten manuscript for presentation to Christian Union St. Bart's. Donald Woods Winnicott Papers (PP/DWW/A/M/3, Box 38). Wellcome Library, 183 Euston Road, London NW1 2BE.

Winnicott, D. W. (n.d.4). Niffle. In R. Shepherd, J. Johns, & H. T. Robinson (Eds.), *Thinking about children* (pp. 104–109). Reading, MA: Addison-Wesley Publishing, 1996. Reprinted by Perseus, 1998.

Winnicott, D. W. (n.d.5). Notes on play. In C. Winnicott, R. Shepherd, & M. Davis (Eds.), *Psychoanalytic explorations* (pp.59–63). Cambridge, MA: Harvard University Press, 1989.

Winnicott, D. W. (n.d.6). Rabbi Ben Ezra. Unpublished handwritten manuscript, Donald Woods Winnicott Papers (PP/DWW/A/M/1, Box 38). Wellcome Library, 183 Euston Road, London NW1 2BE.

Winnicott, J. F. (1934). Letter to D.W. Winnicott, January 21. Donald Woods Winnicott Papers (PP/DWW/B/D/1, Box 27). Wellcome Library, 183 Euston Road, London NW1 2BE.

Winnicott, J. F. (1940). Letter to D.W. Winnicott, July 14. Donald Woods Winnicott Papers (PP/DWW/B/D/1, Box 27). Wellcome Library, 183 Euston Road, London NW1 2BE.

Winnicott, J. F. (ca. 1941, n.d.). Letter to D.W. Winnicott. Donald Woods Winnicott Papers (PP/DWW/B/D/1, Box 27). Wellcome Library, 183 Euston Road, London NW1 2BE.

Winnicott, J. F. (1942a). Letter to D.W. Winnicott, January 15. Donald Woods Winnicott Papers (PP/DWW/B/D/1, Box 27). Wellcome Library, 183 Euston Road, London NW1 2BE.

Winnicott, J. F. (1942b). Letter to D.W. Winnicott, March 14. Donald Woods Winnicott Papers (PP/DWW/B/D/1, Box 27). Wellcome Library, 183 Euston Road, London NW1 2BE.

Winnicott, J. F. (1943). Letter to D.W. Winnicott, April 4. Donald Woods Winnicott Papers (PP/DWW/B/D/1, Box 27). Wellcome Library, 183 Euston Road, London NW1 2BE.

Winnicott, J. F. (1947). Letter to D.W. Winnicott, January 19. Donald Woods Winnicott Papers (PP/DWW/B/D/1, Box 27). Wellcome Library, 183 Euston Road, London NW1 2BE.

Winnicott, K. (1966). Letter to D.W. Winnicott, October 11. Donald W. Winnicott Personal Papers. Courtesy of Oskar Diethelm Library, DeWitt Wallace Institute for the History of Psychiatry, Weill Cornell Medical College, Archives and Manuscripts, New York, NY.

Winnicott, V. (ca. 1941-44). Letter to D.W. Winnicott. Donald Woods Winnicott Papers (PP/DWW/B/D/3, Box 27). Wellcome Library, 183 Euston Road, London NW1 2BE.

Winnicott, V. (1942). Letter to D.W. Winnicott, March 9. Donald Woods Winnicott Papers (PP/DWW/B/D/3, Box 27). Wellcome Library, 183 Euston Road, London NW1 2BE.

Winnicott, V. (n.d.). Letter to D.W. Winnicott. Donald Woods Winnicott Papers (PP/DWW/B/D/3, Box 27). Wellcome Library, 183 Euston Road, London NW1 2BE.

Wynkoop, M. B. (1967). *Foundations of Wesleyan-Arminian theology.* Kansas City, MO: Beacon Hill Press.

Appendix A

This is a transcript of a handwritten, unpublished manuscript from the Donald Woods Winnicott Papers at the Wellcome Library, 183 Euston Road, London NW1 2BE (PP/DWW/A/M/3, Box 38). Square brackets [ ] indicate Winnicott's original spelling and punctuation; capitalization is as it appears in the manuscript. Other brackets { } indicate words inserted for readability. Dashes are in the original. Reproduced by permission of The Winnicott Trust.

My object this evening is to plead for a Christianity which is more nearly related to Christ than the Christianity which is represented by the Bart's Christian Union, indeed for a Christianity which is—as it should be—the working out of the Christ ideals in life. You will wonder why I presume to pose as a preacher, who am so deficient in the Christ-ideals in my daily life. I own that I do fail in this, the great test. But I offer no apology to you; for [altho'] I fall short of what I would be I have the cause of Christ very much at heart.

I would pray you not to mistake me when I am dogmatic, assuming that I have a conceit about my own opinions all out of proportion to the size of my skull. If I am dogmatic it is to be concise, and also in order to give you definite handles by which you may grasp me at the end, and tear me to bits.

In this hospital the name of "Christian" is monopolized by a handful of men who may be termed the orthodox. These orthodox Christians—who if they are broad are so only in so far that they claim to be able to see that when others do not agree with them it is due to unfortunate environment and not to their own dare devilment. They consider that they belong to the chosen few who shall inherit the eternal life, and heaven, and all that they consider counts. They have been brought up on orthodox teaching, all spontaneity in them has been subordinated to the orthodox conception of the Word, and the reaction has not yet come.

As an example of their methods, if they think that the Old Testament says that Adam was created in the year 4000 or so B.C. in such and such a manner they accept it. However much Science asserts that this is not according to fact, they heed not, but nobly set aside thought—exclaim Science lies. Indeed some do not get so far as this, but simply shrink from the sunlight with the feeling that it is not right even to entertain a doubt as to the accuracy of the orthodox conception of the meaning of the Bible. They say—this is not our idea of the meaning, it *is* the meaning.

There are three courses open for these persons. Several of them remain curled up in their orthodox shells and think that the pearl will grow whilst they sleep. The majority react and give up all religion, which they had come to believe to be based on these so called facts. A few—alas only a few—count thought to be as sacred a gift as the [bible], and allow themselves honestly to re-examine the text of the Bible for themselves, thus breaking away from the Curse of Orthodoxy.

The Curse of Orthodoxy! Nay the Insult to God of Orthodoxy. What is this "saved" man's code of ethics or his conception of God? Is either above that of the ordinary man who is honest and sincere and who thinks?

Is there some subtle theological difference between the selfishness of a man or woman who works for the cause of Right in order that he or she may gain Eternal life and the so called pleasures of this literal and prosaic Heaven, and that of a drunkard who works for his beer instead of for his wife and children? What is the cunning distinction between the attributing to God of vengeance and the will eternally to torment, and the vulgar anthropomorphism of the heathen worshipper of wooden gods and gods of stone?

Orthodoxy brings up our children to a view of life which is false and insipid, which blights them and the world which they adorn. Orthodoxy cuts off the youth and maiden from free thought and individual development at the very time of life when personality must grow or die. Orthodoxy hides the weak in the mist of tradition and drives the man of feeling to a violent unlovely reaction. "Thus ye have made the commandment of God of no effect by your tradition."[1]

Now, every man has a right to a development of himself in the direction of his own temperament and talent; indeed it is his duty to his Creator to use all his powers to develop all his parts—bodily, mental and spiritual—in a beautiful proportion. We have been shown the example of a child, who has a perfect symmetry of parts. But we must remember that a child is always growing, and if we are to be as children we cannot accept dogmas and traditions because we are so taught, and then remain like a Cretin. We must be growing. We must set aside what we have been taught and each of us examine Christ for himself. A boy or girl should do this early, before the fruits of prejudice have set in, and yet not before that actual contact with life itself which alone makes Christianity intelligible. The reason why so many can retain the old views about Christ for so long is that the present system of education lacks any introduction of the child to the problems of life itself.

Christianity is essentially a method of life—living in the crudest most integral elements. Religion, on the other hand is the attitude of mind, the psychological pose which men and women assume to serve the place of habits in the preserving continuously of an adopted direction which points towards the ideals (be they Christian or otherwise) which that man or woman has chosen. You may relieve the mental distress of a sinner and give him warmth for his conscience by supplying him with the cloak of religion. You may give him confidence and a sense of security by telling that his soul is saved. But only in so far as the resulting life is altered, only in so far as the old ideals and ambitions have changed is that man [become] a better man. If the new ideals are those of Christ and the man's life becomes imbued with the virtues which some see in Christ—then it may be said—as a matter of terminology, that that man has been converted to Christianity. But he may not believe any of the orthodox views about the Resurrection, the Virgin birth and other very interesting problems. The question is— Does his future life and thought become active and turned to the activity of

Christ? If he merely now works to go to heaven, he is no better, but only more selfish.

Imagine, then, a man of deep thought and unselfish motives face to face with Christianity as it is advertised at this hospital. He may or may not own that his ideals are derived from Christ. He may believe or not that Christ is divine—whatever exactly divine does mean. But he is not keen on theological quibbles over the meanings of certain phrases in the Bible: he is not fond of working up his emotions and feeling religious. Perhaps, like me, he does not see the connection between the life and teaching of Christ and the doctrine of saving souls forever by a trick of conversion or the eternal damnation of the honest unbeliever. Perhaps he would even care to argue with Paul about the aims of Christ. [And] he does not care to go to a prayer meeting to expose his sensitive soul to the gaze of all and sundry. Moreover—alas—he believes in the Darwinian Theory!

Anyway, he needn't worry. He is without the chosen fold—so he is told; Christians deny him the right to enter unless he violates the sacred shrine of his temperament, gives up the precious gift of free thought, and settles down to lukewarm late-middle-life philosophy. This he is too much of a man to do. Therefore he is damned.

[Of course—]The disciples once were getting too keen about the details of acknowledgement of Christ and forbad a man for doing good as a [christian] when he wasn't amongst the chosen few—as they began to think they were.—Our Lord was only too eager to reprove them and hastened, with the words, "He that is not against us is on our side"[2] to place that man on an equal footing with the disciples. But orthodox Christianity respects tradition more than Christ, and so looks for other explanations of the words which fit in more nearly with preconceived notions.

The advertisement of Christianity in this hospital is contained in the words which [strain?] at modesty and shout "There will be a prayer meeting...."

Now—I am one of the first {to} acknowledge the potency of prayer which I have tested all my life. Answer to prayer is a psychological fact. On the one hand there is the act of concentration: that in itself accounts for much of the good of prayer. On the other hand there is the putting of the mind in an attitude or orientation which will direct the stream of thought, action and reaction as the little gully which the child hollows out with a tiny twig directs the small ocean from a mud puddle to a neighbouring cart rut.

Answer to prayer is also a psychic fact—in that one personality by an act of concentration has an influence over another by the unexplained and ill-defined laws of telepathy.

Prayer also provides the required periods of meditation which the mystic needs to get into touch with his maker, or reality—or whatever term you prefer.

These properties of prayer require faith, be it in the god to whom the [prayer's] offered or in the laws of nature—which after all are also God—which promise a fruitful issue to your meditation. It is according to what you consider is the name of the factor behind all these laws. In other words the answer to prayer is the same to a true believer, be he an atheist—a worshipper of idols, a Christian mystic or a fun scientist. The only essential factor is belief.

Now faith without works is dead.

This ancient discovery lessens the value of prayer only in the eyes of the orthodox who are on the verge of reaction. Indeed, in the eyes of those who realize what prayer now becomes the discovery raises our conception of prayer. Prayer now becomes a {here the manuscript ends}

Notes

1. Compare Matthew 15:6, *King James Version*
2. Compare Mark 9:40, *New English Bible,* New Testament © 1961 Oxford University Press and Cambridge University Press.

Index

About the Author

Stephen E. Parker (Ph.D. Theology and Personality Studies, Emory University) is Professor in the School of Psychology and Counseling, Regent University, Virginia Beach, VA. He teaches courses in counseling and personality theories and is a Licensed Professional Counselor in the Commonwealth of Virginia. He has published several articles on the interface of personality theory and theology as well as on spiritual and religious development, including articles on the implications of Winnicott's developmental theory for these areas. He is the author of *Led by the Spirit: Toward a Practical Theology of Pentecostal Discernment and Decision-making* (Sheffield Academic Press, an Imprint of Continuum), a psychological and theological examination of people's claims to divine guidance.

CPSIA information can be obtained at www.ICGtesting.com
Printed in the USA
BVOW041902210512

290612BV00003B/2/P